LIBYA ARCHAEOL

CYRENAICA

by
Philip Kenrick

with a contribution by
Ahmed Buzaian

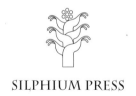

SILPHIUM PRESS

Libya Archaeological Guides
CYRENAICA
by Philip Kenrick, with a contribution by Ahmed Buzaian

Produced by Silphium Books, an imprint of
The Society for Libyan Studies
c/o The Institute of Archaeology
31–34 Gordon Square
London WC1H 0PY

www.societyforlibyanstudies.org

Cover design: cbdesign and Philip Kenrick

ISBN 978-1-900971-14-0

Designed by Chris Bell, cbdesign

Printed in India by Imprint Digital

Published with support from the A. G. Leventis Foundation and the Global Heritage Fund

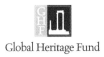

CONTENTS

SOURCES OF ILLUSTRATIONS

The maps and drawings in this volume have been prepared by Philip Kenrick. Those which are traceable more or less directly to previous publications have been drawn from the sources listed below. Note the following conventions:

'Reproduced from ...' = reproduced directly without alteration

'Redrawn from ...' = as the source, with changes only of style or use of colour

'Based on ...' = derived principally from the cited source, but with additions or modifications

'Compiled from ...' = redrawn from more than one source.

The following abbreviations have been used for convenience:

Chr. Mon.: J. B. Ward-Perkins & R. G. Goodchild, *Christian Monuments of Cyrenaica*, edited by Joyce Reynolds (London 2003).

Goodchild, LS: R. G. Goodchild, *Libyan Studies: selected papers of the late R. G. Goodchild*, edited by Joyce Reynolds (London 1976)

Kraeling: C. Kraeling, *Ptolemais: City of the Libyan Pentapolis* (Chicago 1962)

Quad. Libia: Quaderni di archeologia della Libia (Rome)

Stucchi: S. Stucchi, *Architettura cirenaica* (Rome 1975)

Fig. 7: redrawn from *The Society for Libyan Studies Annual Report* 3 (1971–72) 19 fig. 6.

Fig. 9: redrawn from *The Society for Libyan Studies Annual Report* 3 (1971–72) 18 fig. 4.

Fig. 13: redrawn from Goodchild, *LS*, 190 fig. 58.

Fig. 17: based on Goodchild, *LS*, 176–7, figs. 51 and 53.

Fig. 19: redrawn from *The Society for Libyan Studies Annual Report* 3 (1971–72) 14 fig. 2.

Fig. 25: based on J. A. Lloyd et al., *Excavations at Sidi Khrebish, Benghazi (Berenice)*I (Tripoli 1977: Department of Antiquities) figs. 52–55.

Fig. 30: based on *Libyan Studies* 29 (1998) plan facing p. 82 and other sources.

Fig. 32: redrawn from *Chr. Mon.* 204, illus. 156.

Fig. 34: redrawn from *Libyan Studies* 30 (1999) 18 fig. 1.

Fig. 36: redrawn from *Libyan Studies* 15 (1984) 109 fig. 2.

Fig. 37: redrawn from *Libyan Studies* 14 (1983) 117 fig. 9.

Fig. 38: redrawn from *Chr. Mon.* 215, illus. 168.

Fig. 39: redrawn from *Libyan Studies* 24 (1993) 108 fig. 31.

Fig. 42: based on Kraeling plan xxii and on T. Mikocki, *Ptolemais: Archaeological Tourist Guide* (Warsaw 2006), plan inside rear cover.

Fig. 43: based on Kraeling 76 fig. 15 and on Stucchi 340 fig. 348.

Fig. 45: based on Kraeling 161 fig. 56 and on Stucchi 349 fig. 359 and 467 fig. 481.

Fig. 47: based on *Libyan Studies* 17 (1986) 115 fig. 5 and 119 fig. 7.

Fig. 48: based on *Libyan Studies* 17 (1986) 129 fig. 12 and 135 fig. 15.

Fig. 52: redrawn from Kraeling 101 fig. 27.

Fig. 53: redrawn from G. Pesce, *Il palazzo delle colonne in Tolemaide* (Rome 1950) pls. xi, xii.

Fig. 55: redrawn from Stucchi 130 fig. 111 and 459 fig. 467.

Fig. 60: redrawn from Kraeling 121 fig. 43.

Fig. 64: redrawn from *Chr. Mon.* 182 illus. 133.

Fig. 67: redrawn from Kraeling 111 fig. 38.

Fig. 69: based on Kraeling 112 fig. 39 and *Quad. Libia* 12 (1987) 290 fig. 77.

Fig. 79: reproduced from Goodchild, *LS*, 197 fig. 60.

Fig. 80: redrawn from *Libyan Studies* 39 (2008) 118 fig. 2.

Fig. 82: redrawn from Stucchi 264 fig. 259.

Fig. 84: redrawn from E. Catani & S. M. Marengo (a cura di), *La Cirenaica in età antica* (Macerata 1998) 117 fig. 2.

Fig. 90: based on Goodchild, *LS*, 202 fig. 63.

Fig. 92: redrawn from Goodchild, *LS*, 202 fig. 64.

Fig. 95: redrawn from *Chr. Mon.* 274 illus. 218.

Fig. 96: redrawn from *Chr. Mon.* 266 illus. 211.

Fig. 97: reproduced from E. Alföldi-Rosenbaum & J. B. Ward-Perkins, *Justinianic Mosaic Pavements in Cyrenaican Churches* (Rome 1980) 122 fig. 10.

Fig. 102: reproduced from *Quad. Libia* 12 (1987) 435 fig. 27.

Fig. 104: redrawn from *Libya Antiqua* 11–12 (1974–75) 267 fig. 1.

Fig. 107: redrawn from *Chr. Mon.* 374 illus. 316.

Fig. 109: redrawn from *Arch. Cir.* pl. I.

Fig. 111: redrawn from *Papers of the British School at Rome* 26 (1958) pl. xxvi b.

Fig. 116: redrawn from R. G. Goodchild, *Kyrene und Apollonia* (Zurich 1971) 81 fig. 6.

Fig. 121: redrawn from S. Stucchi & I. Bacchielli, *L'Agorà di Cirene* II.4 (Rome 1983) 116 fig. 80.

Fig. 122: based on *Rendiconti della reale accademia dei Lincei* (1925) 414 fig. 4, Stucchi 235 fig. 216, Fig. 282 fig. 284 and 343 fig. 351.

Fig. 123: based on Stucchi 50 fig. 37 and 242 fig. 230.

Fig. 126: reproduced from S. Stucchi, *L'Agorà di Cirene* I (Rome 1965) drawing facing p. 216.

Fig. 129: redrawn from *Quad. Libia* 8 (1976) 194 fig. 1.

Fig. 130: based on R. G. Goodchild, Kyrene und Apollonia (Zurich 1971) 106 fig. 11.

Fig. 131: redrawn from *Arch. Cir.* pl. I.

Fig. 133: based on *Libyan Studies* 18 (1987) 45 fig. 2.

Fig. 134: reproduced from *Libyan Studies* 18 (1987) 56 fig. 11.

Sources of illustrations

Fig. 136: redrawn from *Arch. Cir.* pl. I.

Fig. 139: Compiled from Stucchi 212 fig. 201, 283 fig. 286, 349 fig. 358 and 469 fig. 483.

Fig. 141: Compiled from Stucchi 16 fig. 8, 92 fig. 82, 198 fig. 186 and 237 fig. 219.

Fig. 143: reproduced from N. Bonacasa, S. Ensoli, *Cirene* (Milan 2000) 112.

Fig. 145: Compiled from Stucchi 35 fig. 24, 68 fig. 54, 136 fig. 115, 209 fig. 198, 287 fig. 291 and 288 fig. 292.

Fig. 148: redrawn from *Journal of Hellenic Studies* 77 (1957) 306 fig. 5.

Fig. 151: based on Stucchi 24 fig. 13.

Fig. 153: based on *Chr. Mon.* 135 illus. 89 and E. Fabricotti & O. Menozzi, *Cirenaica: studi, scavi e scoperte. Parte i: nuovi dati da città e territorio* (Oxford 2006) colour plate viii.

Fig. 155: redrawn from M. Luni (a cura di), *Cirene "Atene d'Africa" ii* (Rome 2010) 35 fig. 20.

Fig. 157: Compiled from *American Journal of Archaeology* 85 (1981) 13–30, ills. 2–6.

Fig. 158: reproduced from D. White, The Extramural Sanctuary of Demeter and Persephone at Cyrene, Libya, Final Reports VIII (Philadelphia 2012) 174 fig. 67.

Fig. 159: based on *Papers of the British School at Rome* 23 (1955) 24–5 figs. 3 and 4.

Fig. 173: based on *Libya Antiqua* New Series 2 (1996) 183.

Fig. 174: based on *Chr. Mon.* 78 illus. 46, 86 illus. 53 and 104 illus. 68.

Fig. 176: redrawn from *Chr. Mon.* 58 illus. 26.

Fig. 179: based on R. G. Goodchild et al., *Apollonia, the Port of Cyrene: Excavations by the University of Michigan 1965–1967* (Tripoli 1976) 178 fig. 2 and *Libya Antiqua* 15–16 (1978–79) 266–7 figs. 2 and 3.

Fig. 180: redrawn from R. G. Goodchild et al., *Apollonia, the Port of Cyrene: Excavations by the University of Michigan 1965–1967* (Tripoli 1976) 246 fig. 1.

Fig. 182: redrawn from *Chr. Mon.* 38 illus. 3.

Fig. 190: based on *Chr. Mon.* 244 illus. 184 and A. Laronde, v. Michel, *La basilique occidental d'Erythron (Latrun)* (Libya 2004) plan on p. 4.

Fig. 192: based on *Chr. Mon.* 234 illus. 174 and *Les Nouvelles de l'archéologie* 123 (March 2011) 32 fig. 6.

Fig. 199: redrawn from *Quad. Libia* 12 (1987) 339 fig. 150 and 374 fig. 208.

Fig. 211: reproduced from *Libyan Studies* 25 (1994) 121 fig. 1.

The outlines and contours upon which the maps in figs. 4, 5, 22, 76 and 187 have been drawn are © 2011, Ancient World Mapping Center (www.unc.edu/awmc). Terrain depiction calculated from Environmental Systems Research Institute. SRTM Shaded Relief, on ESRI Data & Maps 2008 [DVD-ROM]. Redlands, CA. Available: UNC-CH Library Controlled Access. I am grateful to the Acting Director Brian Turner for his assistance in making the contour base available to me.

Any maps and plans which are not acknowledged above have been drawn by Philip Kenrick, making extensive use of that remarkable public resource *Google Earth*.

Sources of illustrations

The photographs are by Philip Kenrick apart from the following:

Figs. 31, 65: Miron Bogacki, Polish Archaeological Mission in Ptolemais
(http://www.mironbogacki.pl/)
Figs. 41, 59, 115, 167: by kind permission of Steven Sklifas
(http://www.stevensklifas.com/)
Figs. 1, 113: the Trustees of the British Museum
Fig. 2: Wikimedia Commons. Photo by 'Tigerente'.

PREFACE

This guidebook is a sequel to the *Libya Archaeological Guide: Tripolitania* (London 2009: Society for Libyan Studies), the favourable reception of which has been a definite encouragement. *Cyrenaica* was always going to be a bigger task, both because of the richness of the visible antiquities and because of the lack of any prior model on a comparable scale. Indeed, the only previous guide in the English language which made any attempt to cover the same ground was *Cyrene and Ancient Cyrenaica: a Guide Book* by C. G. C. Hyslop and S. Applebaum, published in some haste by the British Military Administration in Cyrenaica in 1945 'while it can still be of use to the Allied Forces.' When one contemplates the nature of military forces, of any place or time, the exhortation in the foreword has a timeless relevance: 'Please assist the work of conservation by not damaging or defacing the monuments, which are the heritage of the civilized world.'

During the compilation of this work, Libya has passed through another upheaval and, at the time of writing, the future is still far from clear. It is greatly to be hoped, however, that a new stability will lend itself to a return of tourism and to greater opportunities for both Libyans and foreign visitors to appreciate the cultural heritage which belongs to everyone.

The chronological scope of this volume is intended to be somewhat broader than that of its predecessor. For *Tripolitania* I chose the invasion of the Bani Hilal and the Bani Sulaym in AD 1051 as my lower cut-off point, partly because I did not feel confident with the more recent material and partly because I felt that (so far as I could tell) it was treated more competently by those new-generation guidebooks that were already available. I was criticised for that by some, and I have therefore tried in this volume to extend my coverage to everything prior to the Italian invasion in 1911. It is still a very preliminary sketch, but I have done what I can. There is a difficulty in dealing with mosques, not just because of the variability of access, but because there still prevails in many quarters an insensitivity to the interest of the past for its own sake: this manifests itself in the wholesale restoration or remodelling of historic mosques in order to make them more modern and more beautiful. It has not been kind to their historic features. A further, very worrying, development of the period immediately following the fall of Muammar Qadhafi has been the determination of adherents of the Salafist strain of Islam. These puritans abominate the veneration of saints as a deviation from worship of the One and Only God, and have damaged or demolished a large number of tombs of holy men. Since these modest domed and whitewashed monuments have for centuries served as navigational features in the landscape, they are not infrequently mentioned in this guide. It has not been possible to verify how many of them still exist.

Finding one's way around

The visitor to Libya who wishes to do more than to see the principal attractions along the main coast road will be faced with substantial obstacles with regard to navigation. The road maps of the country which are publicly available are much more detailed than they were a generation ago, but they still incorporate many inaccuracies, both in terms of new road-building which has not yet found its way onto the maps, and in terms of roads which were once intended to be built but which have never actually existed. There is also a serious dearth of signposts (whether in Arabic or any other script). It was therefore apparent to me that it would be indispensable to provide geographical co-ordinates wherever possible, and to commend to the traveller the use of a GPS (Geographical Positioning System) device. This further circumvents a problem which I have myself experienced, where either the locals express no knowledge of what you are looking for or – and this is typical of an environment where place-names are not codified by maps or signboards – a name is found to have transferred itself from one building or location to another! Formerly, of course, many of the monuments described were accessible only with the aid of local knowledge and of a 4-wheel-drive vehicle. Now, some of them are within easy walking-distance of an asphalted road and may be visited by saloon car. Where this is NOT the case, I hope that I have made it sufficiently clear.

Spelling of names

This is another problem which teases the visitor. Even where names are well established, their transliteration from Arabic has produced very variable results. On the whole, there is a choice of at least three different forms: an Italian phonetic transliteration, which imitates well the local pronunciation of the name; an 'old' English transliteration, which works in the same way, but less reliably, owing to the inherent uncertainties in how unfamiliar names written in English should be pronounced; and a transliteration according to formal, internationally agreed rules, which typically results in something which one simply would not associate with the sound of the spoken name! I have mostly opted, with some reluctance, for the third and least satisfactory solution, on the basis that that is what the traveller will find written on maps. This will inevitably conflict with what one will see in other books or on labels in museums; but in an area where no consistency exists, none can be imposed. I have given alternative spellings, both in the text and in the index, where this seemed likely to be helpful.

Acknowledgements

The fieldwork for the guidebook was carried out on two occasions, in November 2010 and in April 2012. On the first occasion I was able to base myself in a rest-house at Cyrene belonging to the Department of Antiquities. I was accompanied for part of the time by Paul Bennett and was driven around the countryside by Ahmed Buzaian. I am grateful to both of these for their company and for the useful observations that they contributed. It will be apparent from the title of the work that the participation of Ahmed Buzaian went far beyond this, however. He made fully available to me his extensive knowledge of the countryside, together with many useful social contacts. He has written the section on Tukrah, where he himself has been involved in excavations for a number of years, and he has been throughout a tremendous source of support. I am grateful also to Ahmad Sabr (Controller of Antiquities at Cyrene in 2010) and to Abdelkarim Gazala and Ahmed Abdulkariem (Department of Antiquities staff) for their support and assistance on this occasion, also to Muhammad Tuwati (al-Bayda) and Abdussalam Bazama (Ptolemais). The latter's knowledge of Ptolemais, where he has worked since he was recruited by Richard Goodchild in the 1950s, has significantly enriched my account of that site.

In 2012 my field trip took place in the very different environment of a post-revolutionary Libya lacking in the essentials of central government. On this occasion, my decision to entrust myself to the capable hands of Yasser Mohammed Ali, who had accompanied my forays in Tripolitania, proved to be well-founded. Between them, he and the driver whom he procured, Abdelaziz Aguri, contrived a reconnaissance in very uncertain circumstances which far exceeded my expectations in terms of covering the ground and locating sites which have not been visited or described by archaeologists for many years. I am deeply grateful to them, as to Salah Alhasi, Director-General of Antiquities for Libya both before and after the revolution of 2011, who offered the official support of the Department to both of my explorations. On my second trip, I am happy to record also the assistance of Sanusi Abdallah (Awjilah), Faraj Khalifa and Idris Abdelgader (Tubruq) and particularly of my long-standing friend Abdussalam al-Kawash, who introduced me to his native town of Darnah.

I have been assisted also by various friends and colleagues who have offered advice or who have kindly responded to queries; these include Catherine Dobias-Lalou, Serenella Ensoli, Susan Kane, Mario Luni, Oliva Menozzi, Charlotte Roueché and Donald White. The photographer Steven Sklifas contacted me at an early stage and kindly offered me free use of his images of Libya. A greater debt of gratitude is due to Andrew Wilson, who kindly read and commented in detail on the first draft of the text. As usual, my written work has also been minutely examined by my wife Sue, who might have pursued the career of copy-editor very effectively. She has undoubtedly enhanced its intelligibility, and most remaining (technical) blemishes have been seized upon and queried by Victoria Leitch, the Publications Manager of the Society for Libyan Studies, whom it has also been a pleasure to work with.

I am grateful to the Officers and Council of the Society for Libyan Studies for their continued and unhesitating support for this guidebook, and to the A. G. Leventis Foundation and the Global Heritage Fund for their contributions towards the production costs.

Philip Kenrick
Abingdon, Oxfordshire
January 2013

HISTORICAL INTRODUCTION

The geography of Cyrenaica

The settled region of Cyrenaica is characterized largely by the upland plateau of the Jabal Akhdar (the Green Mountain) which projects northwards into the Mediterranean between the Gulf of Sidra (the Greater Syrtis) to the W and the low, arid coastlands of the Marmaric region towards Alexandria. The plateau rises in two steps, and while on the W there is a wide coastal strip between the foot of the jabal and Benghazi, this narrows progressively as one travels north-eastward; disappearing almost completely beyond Ptolemais. Towards the E, the land drops more gradually and as it becomes drier, so settlement is more sparse towards Tubruq. On the southern side, the high ground drops slowly away to the S without any defining limit, merging eventually into the vast wastes of the Calanshu Sand Sea. In the sands of the desert lie important but isolated oases, at Awjilah and Jaghbub. The latter is not very far (in desert terms) from the great oasis of Siwa in Egypt, home of the ancient oracle of Zeus Ammon.

The Jabal Akhdar, composed mainly of limestones, rises to over 800 m above sea level and enjoys higher rainfall than any other part of Libya (up to 500 mm per year). Frost and snow are not uncommon in winter. The vegetation and the general character of the terrain are more reminiscent of Greece and Asia Minor than of Tripolitania or other parts of North Africa. (Tripolitanians who visit the Jabal Akhdar for the first time often express amazement that this is part of 'their' country!) During Classical antiquity this upland zone was densely settled, and while for much of the time it was known as the Libyan Pentapolis (federation of five cities), these cities did not dominate their hinterland in the way that those of Punic Tripolitania came to do. In Tripolitania there is little sign of villages or small towns; in Cyrenaica, by contrast, there are many of which extensive remains are still visible.

Prehistory

For the tourist, prehistory usually means stone tools in museums or figures of men and animals carved on rock faces. Neither are prominent in the area covered by this guide, though there are traces of prehistoric rock-art in a few places. There are, on the other hand, caves and rock-shelters which have been used as habitations, and which are sometimes prominent features in the landscape. Listed here are the caves known as Haqfat at-Tayrah to the E of Benghazi; Haqfat ad-Dabba, one of many caves in the gorge of the Wadi Kuf; and Hawa Ftiyah, a huge rock-shelter close to Apollonia. Their interest for scholars lies more in what has been found within them by excavation than in anything which is visible to the passer-by. The Hawa Ftiyah in particular is of great importance with regard to the history of human occupation in north Africa.

Greek colonization (seventh century BC)

During the Bronze Age, there were certainly contacts between Cyrenaica and the seafarers of the Aegean and Crete (Mycenaeans, Minoans). These have mostly been attested only by sporadic discoveries of potsherds, though the recent discovery at Cyrene of a Minoan altar is highly significant (p. 200, Baths of Trajan). The first settlers of whom we have clear evidence in the historic period are Greeks from the Aegean island of Thera. The traditional account of how this came about is related by the historian Herodotus of Halicarnassus (now Bodrum in Turkey), writing in the fifth century BC. His account is largely corroborated by an inscription of the fourth century found in the excavations of Cyrene.

In the latter part of the eighth century BC, many Greek cities were beginning to suffer from over-population and consequent famine. The solution which was often adopted was to send part of the population away to look for a new home. This not only relieved the immediate stress, but also had the potential that, in favourable circumstances, the new settlement might generate an economic surplus which would help the mother city. Herodotus relates how such problems on the island of Thera (or Santorini, in the Cyclades) led to the despatch of an expedition in 631 BC. The Theraeans had gone to Delphi to consult the famous Oracle of Apollo about their distress. The Oracle (famously mischievous in its advice, or so it seems to the modern reader) told the Theraeans to found a colony in Libya, under the leadership of a certain Aristoteles who was one of the party and who had come to ask advice about a stammer! He didn't think much of this idea, and neither did his companions, for they had no idea where Libya might be. They returned home and did nothing, but their situation did not improve. A second embassy to the Oracle was reminded of the earlier instruction, and this time they sent out a scouting party, which found in Crete a merchant named Corobios who claimed to know the way at least to the island of *Platea* off the Libyan coast (in the Gulf of Bumba) and took them there. A settlement expedition then made its way there, but did not thrive. After two years, a third embassy went to Delphi to complain about the previous advice, but was sent away with a flea in its ear: 'If you know Libya, which gives good pasture to sheep, better than I (though I have been there and you have not), you must be mighty smart!' (The text of Herodotus conveys the sarcasm.) The Greeks then moved to the nearby site of *Aziris* on the mainland and dwelt there for a further six years, after which time friendly Libyans offered to show them a better site on the plateau to the west. The guides apparently led the Greeks through the finest part of the country by night, so that they should not see it, and then presented them with the site of Cyrene, advocating it as a good place to settle, 'For here the sky is perforated!' (This does not sound so poetic as 'Here there is a hole in the heavens,' but it conveys more effectively the language of Herodotus which clearly alludes to abundant rainfall.)

The site of Aziris has been identified near the mouth of the Wadi Khalij. Traces of walling have been reported which are probably related to Hellenistic pottery found on the surface; there was, however, also pottery which has been attributed to the second quarter of the seventh century BC.

The Battiad monarchy (631–c. 440 BC)

Aristoteles took the name Battos, and there followed at Cyrene a succession of eight kings, alternately named Battos and Arkesilaos. Under the third of these (Battos II) there was a substantial further influx of Greek settlers, which upset the Libyans who were driven off their lands in order to make room. Their king Adikran appealed for help to the Egyptian pharaoh Apries (Wahibre or Hophra), but his forces were routed by the Greeks at Irasa in about 570. Political relations within Cyrene itself deteriorated under

Arkesilaos II 'the Cruel' (560–550). His brothers left the city and founded a new settlement at Barka (al-Marj); it is now clear from the archaeology that Greeks, whether from Cyrene or from other parts of the Greek world, were already spreading out from Cyrene and founding other settlements before the end of the seventh century. Conflict between Barka and Cyrene resulted in huge loss of life and this was followed by constitutional reform brokered (through the agency once again of the Delphic Oracle) by Demonax of Mantinea. These reforms, accepted by Battos III (550–530), were repudiated by Arkesilaos III (530–515), who was then ousted along with his mother Pheretima and driven into exile. The king succeeded, with Samian military help, in returning briefly to Cyrene, but was then obliged to retire to the ostensibly safer refuge of Barka – where however he was assassinated. Pheretima fled to Egypt, and sought the help of the Persian governor, Aryandes, on the basis that Arkesilaos had promised that Cyrene would pay tribute to Persia. This kind of appeal is usually a mistake: the Persians came willingly enough, and with a large force, but probably with the intention of conquering Cyrenaica for themselves. In the event, Barka was besieged unsuccessfully for many months before the Persians tricked the besieged into a false treaty which caused them to open their gates; at this point, the Persians rushed in and Pheretima took bloody revenge for the death of her son.

In the course of the return of the Persian forces to Egypt, a curious incident took place at Cyrene. The Persians were allowed to pass through the city on their way; they did so without molesting it, but then halted on the 'Hill of Lykaean Zeus' beyond and immediately regretted their missed opportunity. In the mean time, the Cyreneans had hastily closed their gates and now refused them entrance. Herodotus reports that there was no fighting; the Persians retreated some seven miles in panic before making camp. They then received orders to return forthwith to Egypt, which they did while being harried all the way by the Libyans of the countryside. There are elements in the archaeology of Cyrene which may be related to this episode (p. 242).

After this point, Herodotus has no more to tell us of Cyrene or Cyrenaica, and its history is less detailed, and certainly less colourful, as a result. Two more kings, Battos IV and Arkesilaos IV, were to follow. The latter won a victory in the chariot race at the Pythian Games, held at Delphi in 462, celebrated in odes by the contemporary poet Pindar which have come down to us. He also promoted the western city of Euesperides by encouraging new immigrants from Greece to settle there, perhaps in the hope of securing their loyalty. Once again, the selected safe haven was illusory, and he was assassinated there in about 440.

Republican government (c. 440–322 BC)
The death of Arkesilaos IV signalled the end of the monarchy at Cyrene, and this was succeeded by constant shifts of power within individual cities between aristocratic and popular parties. There were corresponding alliances of very uncertain duration between different cities, and the displaced Libyans on the margins took advantage of any weakness to intensify their raids on the lands of the immigrants. In 414 BC Euesperides was under siege by Libyans and was saved only by the providential arrival of a Spartan force which had been blown off course when it was on its way to intervene in quite another conflict, the Athenian siege of Syracuse in Sicily. The westward expansion of Greek settlement in Cyrenaica had in due course brought

them into contact with the Phoenicians in Tripolitania. It was in the later sixth century that a Spartan expedition, led by Dorieus, had attempted to found a settlement at the mouth of the River *Cinyps* (Wadi Caam, to the E of Lepcis Magna); after three years they were expelled by the 'Carthaginians' (probably the people of Lepcis). The legend of the Philaeni, concerning the establishment of an agreed frontier between the Phoenician and Greek zones of influence, is thought to relate to the early Republican period. This was at Ras al-Aali, about half-way between al-Uqaylah and Ras Lanuf. (For details of the legend and of the place, see *Libya Archaeological Guides: Tripolitania*, p. 155.)

Monarchy again, under Egyptian control
(322–96 BC, the 'Ptolemaic' period)

The Persian domination of Egypt was brought to an end by the conquests of Alexander the Great of Macedon. This was marked by the foundation in 331 BC of Alexandria. Alexander marched westwards towards Cyrenaica, but his goal was the desert oasis of Siwa and the famed Oracle of Zeus Ammon (which sensibly greeted him as the 'son of Zeus'). The Cyreneans (also sensibly) sent a delegation to meet him with appropriate gifts, including 300 war-horses (Cyrene had long been famous for its horses) and five four-horse chariots. This gesture freed them from direct intervention at the time, but in the confusion that followed the death of Alexander in 323, the region fell prey to the ambitions of a Spartan adventurer named Thibron. This man, with a substantial army, managed to obtain and hold Apollonia and Taucheira, and to exact tribute from Cyrene. However, the resistance against him increased under the leadership of Mnasicles, one of his officers who defected to the opposition, and he was driven out. When he returned with reinforcements and laid siege to Cyrene, a faction within the city sought help from Egypt, now ruled by Ptolemy I Soter. Ptolemy sent an army under his general Ophellas, who defeated, captured and executed Thibron. The Cyreneans did not, however, regain their liberty, and could hardly have expected to do so. Ophellas was installed as governor on Ptolemy's behalf and ruled the region until he was succeeded in 300 by Magas, a stepson of Ptolemy. Ptolemaic interest in the region was probably emphasized by the refoundation and fortification of the port of Barka as *Ptolemais* at this time.

Magas remained loyal to Ptolemy I until the latter's death in 283, but repudiated any allegiance to Ptolemy II Philadelphus (his half-brother) and styled himself king. Indeed, in 274 he set about an invasion of Egypt, but was frustrated by the necessity to deal with a revolt of the Marmaridae in his rear. In 260 he was reconciled to Ptolemy, and by a promise that his daughter Berenice would marry Ptolemy's son (Ptolemy III Euergetes), Cyrenaica could expect to be reunited with Egypt. On the death of Magas (in 258 or 250: our information is ambiguous), his widow Apama had other ideas which led to further strife; but in 246, when Ptolemy III ascended to the throne, the marriage and the reunification took place. The relocation of Euesperides to the new site of Berenice (named after the bride, and fortified) marked this event. It is also at this time that coins of Magas are overstruck on behalf of the KOINON, a federation of five cities which came to be known as the Libyan *pentapolis*. The first literary reference to this federation is in the first century AD (in the works of Pliny), when the component cities were Cyrene, Apollonia, Ptolemais, Taucheira/Arsinoë and Berenice.

An important native of Cyrene who lived in the first half of the third century was the poet Callimachus (c. 305–240), a noted scholar in the famous Library of Alexandria. In his *Hymn to Demeter* he describes a procession in honour of the goddess, and while he never states where this took place, it is usually assumed that he is referring to the topography of Cyrene.

In the succeeding years, there were further dynastic squabbles in the Egyptian royal household, only two elements of which need concern us here. In 155, Ptolemy Physcon, at the time ruling Cyrenaica while his brother Ptolemy Philometor was in control of Egypt, felt sufficiently threatened that he made a will under which, should he leave no heir, his domain was to be bequeathed to the Senate and People of Rome. The text of the will is known from a marble tablet which was set up at Cyrene and which was found in the excavations (p. 243); by this device he hoped to secure the protection of Rome. This eventuality did not come about; Physcon succeeded his brother in Egypt in 145 and ruled until his death in 116. After this, he was succeeded in Egypt by one of his legitimate sons, while a bastard son by a Cyrenean woman, Ptolemy Apion, was given authority over Cyrenaica. Apion died in 96, having made the same provision in his will as his father, and on this occasion the region did pass into the possession of the Roman state.

Roman rule (96 BC–AD 645)

The Senate did not immediately take an interest in its new possession, and Cyrenaica suffered an extended period of instability, with squabbles within the cities, between the cities and between the Greeks and the Libyans of the interior. (It is inconceivable that after so many hundred years there was not extensive intermarriage between the immigrant Greeks and the native Libyan population; but there would always have been tension between the settled urban and agricultural communities and the nomadic pastoralists on the margins of the desert.) It was only in 74 that a Roman magistrate, Publius Cornelius Lentulus Marcellinus, was sent out as *quaestor* (essentially a financial officer) to establish the proper administration of a Roman province. This improved internal stability, and a few years later, in 67, the successful campaign of Pompey the Great against pirates in the eastern Mediterranean further improved the security of the coastal cities. During this campaign, Crete was conquered, and either now or following the Battle of Actium in 31 BC, Crete and Cyrene were conjoined for administrative purposes into a single senatorial (therefore, non-militarized) province. (The fact that Cyrenaican monuments of the Roman period often bear dates counted from the Battle of Actium perhaps favours the latter.)

Cyrenaica figures momentarily in the history of the Roman civil wars of the first century BC. Following the defeat of Pompey by Caesar at Pharsalus in 48 and the murder of Pompey when he fled to Egypt, an army of his supporters led by the younger Cato sailed to Cyrenaica and was denied a landing at Phykous. After landing further west, however, and setting off again for Carthage, they were driven back by a storm and then made an epic march around the Syrtic Gulf by land. This was commemorated in bombastic verse in Book ix of the *Pharsalia* of Lucan.

With the reign of Augustus (27 BC–AD 14), Cyrenaica appears to embark upon a period of relative stability and security, and much public building is attributable to the time of Augustus and of his successor Tiberius (AD 14–37). Under the emperors

Claudius to Vespasian, Roman officials set about 'normalizing' the state of the former Ptolemaic royal lands, which had passed into its possession under the will of Ptolemy Apion but which had evidently been neglected to the extent that their tenants had ceased to pay rent or to acknowledge public ownership. These lands were now surveyed, recovered to the State and sometimes leased out again on new terms. A number of the boundary markers set up to record this activity have been found, and may be seen at Cyrene or in the museum at Apollonia (pp. 233, 285).

This era of growth and prosperity was interrupted abruptly in 115 by the **Jewish Revolt**. There was a substantial Jewish community in Cyrenaica (note the presence of a Simon of Cyrene in Jerusalem at the time of the crucifixion) and tension with the Roman authorities had run high, particularly after the destruction of the temple in Jerusalem in 70. In 115 a revolt broke out in Cyrene, whence it spread to Alexandria, Antioch and many other cities of the eastern Mediterranean. It was characterized by extreme violence and bloodshed, and took three years to bring under control. Archaeological evidence for this event in other parts of Cyrenaica is limited and circumstantial, but in Cyrene itself it is well documented inasmuch as almost all of the public buildings were severely damaged. Subsequent restoration, recorded by inscriptions, took more than two generations to complete. Much of the initial work was done under Hadrian, who brought in new settlers to Cyrene and indeed founded an entire new city between Berenice and Taucheira, named Hadrianopolis (not, however, a huge success: see p. 47).

In the later second and early third centuries, Cyrenaica seems certainly to have returned to prosperity: in the cities we find buildings, both public and private, increasingly embellished with coloured marbles and mosaic floors. But by the middle of the third century a decline had certainly set in: Berenice received a new defensive circuit which enclosed probably only a small proportion of the earlier city (p. 42) and at Cyrene also there are signs of a substantial reduction in the earlier circuit (p. 189). As in other parts of the Roman Empire, peoples beyond the frontiers took advantage of the administrative turmoil to attack; an inscription in the Cyrene museum (p. 243) records the defeat in 268–9 of the Marmaridae by the Prefect of Egypt, Tenegino Probus, and the refounding of Cyrene as *Claudiopolis* in honour of the emperor (Claudius Gothicus). Archaeological evidence has also shown that Cyrene was severely damaged by earthquake c. 262.

The decline of Cyrene was emphasized by the empire-wide administrative reforms of Diocletian at the end of the third century. The old province of Crete and Cyrene was dissolved, and Cyrenaica itself was divided in two. The main part became known as *Libya Superior* or *Pentapolis*, with its capital at Ptolemais, while the eastern stretch, from Darnis (Darnah) to Alexandria, became *Libya Inferior* or *Sicca* (dry), ruled initially from Paraetonium (Marsa Matruh) and subsequently from Darnis.

The Byzantine period (from AD 395)

Diocletian's reforms began the process by which the entire Roman Empire was divided in two. After the death of Theodosius the Great in 395 there ceased to be any pretence of a single empire. Cyrenaica fell within the eastern half, ruled from Constantinople, the former Greek city of Byzantium which had been renamed by the emperor Constantine in 324. It is an entirely modern scholarly device that the eastern empire (which survived, at least vestigially, until the capture of Constantinople by the Turks in 1453) is described as 'Byzantine': the term would simply not have been understood by its inhabitants at the time; though they spoke Greek, they referred to themselves as Romans.

There was therefore no historic event in the history of Cyrenaica itself on the basis of which we might say that before this it was 'Roman' and afterwards it was 'Byzantine'; 395 is used in this guide purely for convenience. In terms of cultural change, there is also a natural tendency to associate the 'Roman' period with traditional paganism and the 'Byzantine' period with Christianity, since this was adopted progressively between the Edict of Toleration in 311 (which first made it permissible to be both a Roman and a Christian) and the time of Theodosius, who promulgated a series of decrees aimed at the suppression of pagan practices. Christianity had, of course, been spreading long before either of these dates. The first known Cyrenaican bishop was Ammonas of Berenice in 260. Many Christian churches have been located in Cyrenaica, but few have been scientifically excavated; their chronology is therefore mostly uncertain. It is fairly unlikely, however, that any of those which are visible are earlier than the fifth century, and much scholarly debate still rages about which of them were built (or refurbished) in the time of Justinian (527–65), an emperor noted for his building activity and promotion of churches throughout the empire.

With regard to historical events of this period, a great earthquake recorded on 21 July 365 must be mentioned. This event was recorded by several ancient writers and a likely epicentre has been identified beneath the sea to the south-west of Crete. More than a hundred towns were reported to have been destroyed in that island, together with 'all and every one of the cities in Libya'. It also generated a tsunami which had devastating effects in Alexandria (still commemorated annually in the sixth century as the Day of Horror), on the west coast of the Peloponnese (where the historian Ammianus Marcellinus saw some years later a ship which had been carried far inland) and on the east coast of Sicily. Both ancient writers and modern archaeologists have readily associated destruction over a huge radius with this event, but archaeological dating is insufficiently precise for us to be sure that we are not looking at a chain of related (but not simultaneous) occurrences. The same may be true of some of the ancient writers. Destruction levels attributed to 262 and to 365 have been widely identified at Cyrene itself, and the city was described by Ammianus in the aftermath as *urbs antiqua sed deserta* (an ancient but deserted city). A painted inscription once visible in a tomb in the North Necropolis (no. N83, p. 239) recorded the burial of a certain Demetria and her son who had been killed in an earthquake, which may have been at this time. Skeletons crushed beneath fallen masonry represent quite convincing evidence of earthquake, and such have been found. The discovery of associated hoards of coins (a purse carried on the person, or a reserve tucked away in a pot or box: p. 118) might be regarded as particularly fortunate for the archaeologist, when the latest coins are dated to 364. But even here, the evidence must be treated with great care: a recent study has indicated that many of the coins had been altered to conform to a later weight-standard which was introduced only in 375!

Synesius of Cyrene, Bishop of Ptolemais (c. 370–413)

Synesius of Cyrene is a man who briefly, through his surviving correspondence, shines an intense light on what it was like to be a member of the landed gentry in Cyrenaica at the end of the fourth century. Synesius was born and grew up on a landed estate somewhere near Cyrene (probably between Balagrae and Phykous). He studied in Alexandria under the Neo-Platonist philosopher Hypatia, who became a close friend. In 397 he led an embassy from the province to the emperor Arcadius at Constantinople: his speech to the emperor pleaded for tax concessions in view of the region's recent misfortunes (plagues of locusts, incursions by the Austuriani, inefficient or corrupt military governors). Around 406 (the date is not entirely certain), despite the fact that he was not a Christian (though married to a Christian wife), he was asked to become bishop of Ptolemais. According to his letters, he agonized over this for some six months, but eventually reached agreement with Theophilus, Bishop of Alexandria, that he would undertake the duties and preach what the church required, provided that he could in private adhere to his own beliefs and that he should not have to put away his wife. His correspondence shows him (through his own words, of course) to have been an aristocrat with a strong sense of patriotism and public duty; it is telling that at this period such service was most readily expressed through office in the church, rather than in civil magistracies. Synesius attended to disputes between communities (see Ain Marah, p. 287), wrote regularly to his brother Euoptius near Phykous (p. 147) and, when occasion demanded, organized local resistance to Libyan raiders. He complained about the ineffectiveness of the military authorities, inasmuch as those military forces which existed were kept shut up in the towns and did nothing to protect the countryside. They were also affected by defence cuts, which were met with predictable criticism: 'I have with me some of the corps of the Balagritae. Before Cerialis had taken over the command of the province, these men were mounted bowmen; but when he entered upon his functions, their horses were sold and they became only archers'. A letter written by Synesius to his brother gives a graphic illustration of self-defence in the countryside.

> May all good things befall the priests of Axomis! While the soldiers were hiding themselves in the gorges of the mountains to take care of their precious lives, these priests called the peasants about them, and led them straight from the very church door against the enemy, and then they called upon God, and erected a trophy in the Myrtle Valley!
>
> This is a long ravine, deep and covered with forests. The barbarians, when they found no resistance in their way, rashly entered this dangerous defile, but they had to meet the valiant Faustus, the deacon of the church. This man, unarmed, when marching at the head of his troops, was himself the first to encounter an infantryman. He snatches up a stone, not to hurl it, but, holding it in his hand and leaping upon him as with a clenched fist he strikes the other violently on the temple. He knocks him down, strips him of his armour, and heaps many of the barbarians upon him. If any other man gave proof of courage in that battle, it is to Faustus that credit is due, both on account of his personal bravery, and for the orders which he gave at the critical moment …

If only we are men in such a crisis as this, even the second prize will be honourable. Fate perchance might accord us even the first, if instead of being fifteen irregulars, hiking in a valley to forage, we were able to give battle in the open, in regular warfare, mass against mass.

(Letter 122: the writings of Synesius are of easy public access at www.livius.org)

In the *Catastasis*, either a letter or a speech written perhaps in 412, Synesius lamented the coming extinction of the Pentapolis and foresaw his own death at the altar. We do not know the actual circumstances of his death.

The Pentapolis did not die with Synesius. At some point around the middle of the fifth century, the seat of the provincial administration was transferred from Ptolemais to Apollonia/Sozousa and in the time of Anastasius (491–518) new regulations concerning military dispositions were promulgated and displayed in public: texts have been found at Apollonia, Ptolemais and Taucheira. The reign of Justinian (527–565) was marked in Cyrenaica, as elsewhere, by renewed building activity, with the restoration of defences, of aqueducts and of churches. It may however be doubted how far the Byzantine administration controlled the interior of the country; certainly, there are ruins of substantial villages which were occupied in this period, but they may well have been autonomous by now, a mixed Greek/Roman/Libyan population known as the Berber Luwatah.

In 608 the Prefect of Africa, Heraclius, recruited military forces in the Pentapolis to support his revolt against the emperor Phocas. He stormed Alexandria and in 610 was crowned emperor in Constantinople. Only six years later, however, Egypt was captured by the Sasanians (Persians) under King Khosrau II. Heraclius did not succeed in dislodging them until Khosrau had been defeated at Nineveh in 628. There is no evidence of Sasanian moves against Cyrenaica, but it is possible that some hasty Byzantine military construction was occasioned by nervousness at events in Egypt (pp. 51, 61).

The Islamic conquest (642–5)

Heraclius did not long enjoy his victory over the Sasanians. The prophet Muhammad died in 632 and within four years the Arab armies, inspired by the new faith that he had given them, had overrun the eastern shores of the Mediterranean. Heraclius was soundly defeated at the Battle of Yarmouk in 636 and Alexandria fell to the Arabs in November 641. In the following year, under Amr ibn al-Aasi, they swept westwards through Cyrenaica and then southwards as far as Zuwaylah in Fazzan. These forces moved across the Jabal Akhdar, largely ignoring the coastal cities, but laid siege to Barka, which capitulated and agreed to an annual tribute of 13,000 dinars. It was apparently a condition of the treaty that the Barkaeans might sell their children to pay the tax! It was later reported that the Barkaeans were so peaceable and punctilious in paying their tax that tax-collectors never had to be sent to them! The rapidity of the advance may suggest that the villages of the interior (which certainly still flourished at this time) were beyond the effective control of the Byzantine administration and felt no inclination to defend it. In the following year, Amr pressed on to Tripolitania and took Tripoli and Sabratha.

In 644 or 645 a second expedition was sent along the coast, in ships commanded by a Duke Sanutius (from his name, a Copt). This presumably mopped up the remainder of the coastal cities. We are told that on the previous occasion, the Byzantine governor Apollonius had retreated to Taucheira and remained there within the walls; now he was either driven out or found to have fled.

With the advent of the Arabs, maritime links were broken. As a result, the coastal cities generally went into decline whereas Barka, on the edge of its fertile plain, became the seat of administration. It is surely a reflection of this shift of focus that Ptolemais, the port of Barka, alone of the coastal sites enjoyed some continuing prosperity (p. 69). One of the early governors of the region, which we should now call Barqa, was Ruwayfi bin Thabit, a companion of the prophet who died in 663 and whose tomb (on the western edge of al-Bayda, p. 121) is still venerated today. In the mid-ninth century, Barqa was provided with new city-walls, and was at this time supplying Cairo with cattle, wool, honey and oil. There was, however, another important East-West overland route which ran south of the Jabal Akhdar, through Makhayli and Zawiyat Masus, approaching the coast of the Gulf of Sidra through the settlement known in the Roman period as Corniclanum, now Ajdabiya. Ajdabiya flourished in the early Islamic period; in the early tenth century it was sacked by the first Fatimid caliph, Ubayd'allah for its allegiance to the Abbasids in Baghdad, but later in the same century it received a new mosque and a fortress-palace. In the early eleventh century it was described as having a mosque, baths and bazaars; but after that it seems to have gone into decline.

The Bani Hilal

Barqa had in the early Islamic period been subject to the Ummayads in Damascus and then the Abbasids in Baghdad. When the independent Fatimid dynasty of Mahdia in Tunisia made its successful bid for Egypt in 969, Egypt and the Maghrib were reunited. Within less than a hundred years, however, the Zirid governors in the West had shaken off their allegiance to Cairo. The caliph al-Mustansir in Cairo decided to resolve two problems at the same time. There was then in Egypt a large body of semi-nomadic Arabs, known as the Bani Hilal (Children of the Moon). They were becoming increasingly difficult to control and the caliph encouraged them to undertake a campaign against his rebellious subjects in the Maghrib in return for promises of land. The device worked: they set off westwards in 1051, and while they showed no more allegiance to Cairo than the Zirids had done, they were off his hands and had taught the Zirids a lesson! Barqa had not been in revolt, but was overrun nonetheless, and those of the migrants who chose to remain there became known as the Bani Sulaym. The remainder progressively fought their way westwards, returning the entire littoral of present-day Libya to a state of nomadic pastoralism and finally extinguishing the urban civilisation which had been built up in the Greek and Roman periods. (This, at any rate, is the picture painted by the 14th-century historian Ibn Khaldun: scholars now tend to take a more nuanced view, and suspect that the decline was well advanced before the arrival of the new settlers.) In the later medieval period we know very little of Cyrenaica. Al-Idrisi, a geographer at the court of Roger II in Sicily in the mid-twelfth century said of Barqa that few people lived there and that its markets were little frequented;

Ajdabiya he described as two castles in the sand. In 1216 the Republic of Genoa made a treaty with the Emir of Berenice, obtaining thereby exclusive access to the port, and 'Bernik' appears on navigational charts from about 1250. But these are fragmentary glimpses of history and they are not today matched by any visible structures.

The Ottoman period

The Ottoman Turks were called to the defence of the Maghrib in the sixteenth century when European (mainly Spanish) expansion towards the southern shores of the Mediterranean followed the expulsion of the Moors from Spain. They took Tripoli from the Knights of Malta, who were established there, in 1551. This brought Cyrenaica notionally within their power, but this had little practical effect until 1638, when a military expedition was sent from Tripoli to occupy the province. A castle was built at Benghazi, a governor (bey) was installed there with a garrison and tax was collected. Control remained, however, very limited, particularly with regard to the difficult terrain of the Jabal Akhdar, and further sporadic military expeditions were made to reassert the authority of Tripoli. We have some account of such expeditions from the writings of Agostino Cervelli who travelled as a medical officer with Yusuf Pasha Karamanli in 1811–12 and Paolo della Cella who performed the same service for a similar expedition in 1817.

Cyrenaica remained an economic backwater until towards the end of the nineteenth century, when a more energetic Turkish administration (under Rashid Pasha and Tahir Pasha) began to develop the ports of Benghazi and Darnah while the religious brotherhood of the Sanussi, established at al-Bayda in 1843, brought new order and agricultural prosperity to the hinterland. In 1908 the Jabal Akhdar was visited by a commission of the Jewish Territorial Organization of London which was looking for a potential new home for the Jews. The commission concluded that the water supply was inadequate, but three years later Cyrenaica was a target of Italian colonization, a brutal process which took some twenty years to complete. The scope of this guide comes to an end with their arrival.

Silphium

Cyrene (often representing the entire region of Cyrenaica) was recorded in antiquity to have generated a variety of agricultural produce, such as olives, dates, apples, grapes and cereals, but it was particularly renowned for its horses and for the medicinal plant *silphium*. Horses figured in the victory at Delphi in 462 BC of Arkesilaos IV (p. 3), and in the gifts offered by the Cyreneans to Alexander the Great in 331 BC (p. 4). Silphium was of sufficient importance to the economy that it was frequently represented on the coins of Cyrene (fig. 1). We know from these representations and from ancient descriptions that it was a plant resembling fennel, with use being made of the flowers (for perfume), the stalk and the long, thick root. It was used as a seasoning in food, and had an implausibly wide range of medical uses: these included relief of indigestion, fevers, aches and pains; removal of warts; restoration of hair; neutralisation of poisons etc. – but it does not seem to have been used, despite the fantasies of several scholars, as either an aphrodisiac or to provoke abortion! It was said by some writers to grow only in the wild and to be

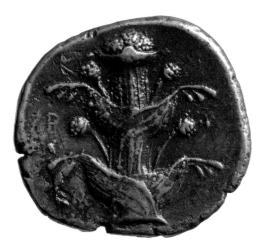

Fig. 1. A coin of Cyrene of 435–375 BC, showing a silphium plant.
(© The Trustees of the British Museum.)

incapable of cultivation, for which reason it was virtually extinct in the first century AD, when a stalk was presented to the emperor Nero as a curiosity. Its demise was attributed variously to over-harvesting or over-grazing by animals. However, in the early fifth century AD, Synesius (see above) wrote to his brother, who lived near Phykous (Zawiyat al-Hamamah), thanking him for a fine specimen of silphium which he had grown in his garden.

We can never be certain that all of the ancient writers were referring to the same plant, since they had no suitable botanic catalogues to consult, and for the same reason it is impossible to arrive at a precise identification. A recent identification with *Cachrys ferulacea*, an umbellifer currently found in southern Italy, northern Sicily and in the Jabal Akhdar, has been contested as not proven to the exclusion of other possibilities; it seems the best we can say is that it was a plant related to *ferula communis*, the giant fennel (fig. 2), and that it may indeed have become extinct in the first century AD.

Church architecture

This is not the place for an extended essay on church architecture, but a few points which may puzzle the non-specialist visitor are worthy of brief note. The dating of the buildings is still very controversial and often founded on very weak evidence. Christianity was well established in Cyrenaica already in the third century AD, but it is unlikely that any of the church buildings which have been discovered are earlier than the fifth century. The question which has preoccupied many scholars is how many of them were built or rebuilt in the time of the emperor Justinian (527–565). It has been argued that the most characteristic ground plan – nave, aisles, semi-circular apse with side-chapels, all contained within a rectangular outer perimeter (e.g. the Central Church at Apollonia, p. 263) – is Justinianic and that plans which depart substantially from this (e.g. the East Church at Apollonia, p. 274) may be earlier.

It must be admitted at present that in many cases the dating of the buildings cannot convincingly be narrowed down.

It is notable that not all of the churches face the East. There are no examples which do not face approximately either east or west; but quite a number do face west and these are often built in close proximity to others which face in the opposite direction (e.g. at Qasr Libya, p. 129, and at al-Athrun, p. 289). In the case of the East Church at Cyrene (p. 225), the orientation was actually changed from east to west. It is difficult at present to see any particular rationale behind the choice and it is, perhaps, surprising that where the chronology offers any clues at all, the westerly apses are later than those which face east. While Cyrenaica was not affected by the Donatist Schism which rent much of Christian Africa in two, there certainly was dissension between adherents of the orthodox church and those of various heretical groups. However, we cannot see these different strands of belief in the physical attributes of the churches.

Another issue which has been widely debated is whether some of the churches were initially built, or later modified, with defensive functions in mind. In practical terms, in many of the smaller villages, the church was probably the most robust building in the community, which might therefore have served as a temporary refuge. Some of them have had their walls partially strengthened by sloping revetments on the outside, some also have (partial) rock-cut ditches or moats around them; but these features are not exclusive to churches and must be considered in the broader context discussed below.

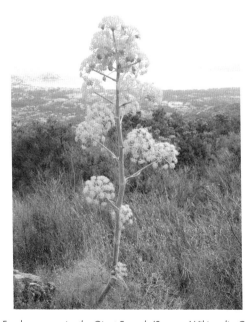

Fig. 2. Ferula communis, *the Giant Fennel. (Source: Wikimedia Commons.)*

Defensive structures in the countryside

Much ancient building work which is still visible in the countryside of Cyrenaica consists of very high-quality ashlar masonry work, sometimes characterized further by slightly projecting horizontal string-courses and by narrow external slit-windows. (See Qasr al-Wushish, p. 125 and fig. 89.) Richard Goodchild, who was Controller of Antiquities for Cyrenaica in 1953–66 and who explored the countryside probably to a greater extent than anyone before or since, considered that these structures must be military, or at least 'official', buildings. However, in the light of evolving perceptions of settlement in the pre-desert zone of Tripolitania, it seems to the present writer that this is not sustainable. It seems more likely that this handsome building-style was the 'norm' in a region where relatively easily-worked limestone was plentiful and there were presumably stonemasons in the community to match. This style of architecture certainly was used in substantial late Roman military buildings, of which the most prominent is the 'Fortress of the Dux' at Ptolemais (p. 80). It is also found in non-military contexts such as the 'monastery' at Sirat al-Jamil (p. 120). At Qasr Migdim (p. 136) and Qasr ash-Shahdiyn (p. 126), the nature and scale of the buildings strongly suggest a military purpose (at least for the latter), but Qasr az-Zaarura (p. 123) is surely no more than a fortified farm.

The last-mentioned has a sloping revetment which has been added all around the perimeter, and this characteristic is found also in several churches. It has been suggested both that this represents a strengthening for military defence and that it is an attempt to stabilize a collapsing structure. The former argument seems to me particularly weak and misplaced. Such a feature might be useful as a defence against heavy artillery, but in the face of infantry attack or marauding bands, it provides a ready means of climbing the wall which was not available when it had a vertical face! The latter interpretation is supported in certain instances by evidence of construction against a wall which was demonstrably bowing outwards or which (in the case of Qasr az-Zaarura) was fractured by vertical cracks. The reinforcement surely follows earthquake damage. We cannot, without firmer evidence, associate the practice with specific earthquakes, since the region suffered several of which we are aware in the Classical period, and possibly others of which we are not.

Another feature of many major buildings in the countryside is a rock-cut moat or ditch around the outside. This has been variously interpreted as a defensive device, as an uncovered reservoir for rainwater, or simply as a convenient source of stone from which the structure was built. Where such cuttings occur, they mostly do not encompass the entire perimeter and their defensive value is limited. Equally, large unprotected reservoirs are much less effective for water storage in the climate of Cyrenaica than covered cisterns. These cuttings surely did constitute quarries, but to what extent they were designed to serve other purposes we cannot be sure. In some instances their vertical faces provided a suitable location for the excavation of chamber-tombs.

A final curiosity to be mentioned here is the use of 'curtain brackets.' These are stone blocks, set transversely through the thickness of a wall on either side of an arched doorway and at the level of the springers of the arch. On the 'outer' face they terminate in decorative corbels, while on the 'inside' they are cut into two projecting hooks, presumably intended to carry a substantial pole or beam. From this must have been hung a closure of some kind; one might imagine a curtain, were it not for the fact that the blocks seem massively over-engineered for such a modest task and that they sometimes flank the only external entrance into a building (as at Qasr ash-Shahdiyn, p. 127). (A top-hung wooden door would be inconvenient for daily use, but would pack a hefty punch if dropped in a hurry in the face of an unwelcome visitor!)

The rediscovery of ancient Cyrenaica

In modern times, European travellers and classical scholars began to visit Cyrenaica in the 18th and 19th centuries, making notes and drawings of the antiquities. In 1821–22 the brothers Frederick and Henry Beechey led an expedition sponsored by the British Admiralty which made the first accurate chart of the Libyan coastline from Tripoli eastwards. They visited the major ancient sites in Cyrenaica and made impressive site plans of them. Just a couple of years later, a French artist, Jean-Raimond Pacho, covered much of the same ground in Cyrenaica, whence he travelled south to Awjilah, then eastward to Siwa and so to the Nile. In the middle years of the century the French consul at Benghazi, J. Vattier de Bourville, dug for antiquities in the ancient cemeteries around Benghazi, but also further afield. At Ptolemais he cut away from the 'Fortress of the Dux' the important decree of Anastasius which is now in the Louvre in Paris; and at Cyrene he similarly sawed off the painted decoration of a tomb in the West Necropolis (likewise now in the Louvre).

The first 'scientific' expedition to excavate at Cyrene was that led by Captain R. Murdoch Smith and Commander E. A. Porcher in 1860–61. They worked initially at their own expense, but they did obtain a permit to excavate from the Turkish government. Once it was clear that they were making interesting discoveries and that there were potential dividends for the British Museum, the British government (and the museum) took a greater interest and were rewarded with a rich haul of sculpture and other artefacts, now in London.

In 1910–11 the next authorised (and more scientific) expedition to Cyrene was an American one under the direction of Richard Norton. Its activities were curtailed by the Italian invasion of Libya in 1911, but by then it had already suffered the discomfort of its epigrapher, Herbert de Cou, being shot dead on the excavation. The reason for this remains unclear to the present day, but the grave of De Cou may still be seen at Cyrene (p. 237). With the advent of the Italians there came a more determined effort to investigate the classical antiquities of Cyrenaica. This was certainly scholarly in intent, though technically primitive by today's standards in terms of execution and record. However, archaeology also became increasingly a tool of propaganda for the colonial regime, which was anxious to demonstrate its previous beneficial presence in the land. In Cyrenaica, the major effort was always focussed on Cyrene itself, though minor excavations were also carried out at Ptolemais and Apollonia; in the early years there was also considerable interest in visiting and identifying the rural sites.

After the expulsion of the Italians in 1943, a British Military Administration was responsible for the region until the sovereign state of Libya was established by the United Nations at the end of 1951. The structure of the antiquities service created by the Italians was retained, and from 1953–66 the Controller of Antiquities for Cyrenaica was an Englishman, Richard Goodchild. The country was poor and he had few resources. However, he carried out excavations at Taucheira, Ptolemais and Cyrene and made extensive topographic explorations, recording the existence of many rural sites. He also encouraged the return of the Italian Mission to Cyrene (not least to begin the necessary process of publishing the work that they had carried out in the colonial period) and he invited other foreign expeditions to work in the region (Americans at Ptolemais, the French at Apollonia). Most importantly, he took into the service and trained up native Libyan archaeologists, many of whom have subsequently played a loyal and significant role in the investigation and protection of the antiquities of Libya. Goodchild left Libya in 1966 but died tragically young, two years later. (It has been an enduring puzzle since then that none of the basic records of his excavations have been found – adding considerably to the difficulty of publishing these projects.) The head of the Italian Mission during these years was Professor Sandro Stucchi, responsible for major restoration work in Cyrene (particularly the Stoa of Hermes and Herakles and the Temple of Zeus). Stucchi also explored widely in the countryside and published in 1975 a huge volume on Cyrenaican architecture. This has been a crucial source for this guidebook, for he described in it, from direct inspection, more monuments than anyone else; it has, however, to be used with great caution, for he put forward with great confidence many interpretations which have not been accepted by other members of the scientific community.

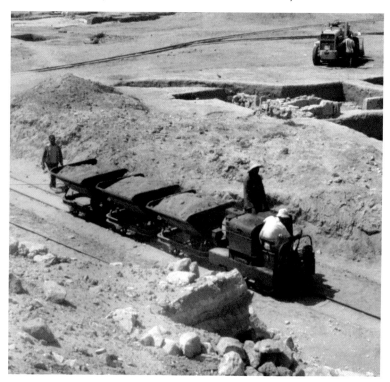

Fig. 3. Decauville railway in use in Benghazi, 1973.

Since the advent to power of Muammar Qadhafi in 1969, the Department of Antiquities has continued to function and to do its work. Many foreign missions have worked in Cyrenaica to great scholarly profit, though the Department itself has been kept so short of funds by the Libyan government that it has had little opportunity to embark on initiatives of its own, as it did in Goodchild's time. At the time of writing, Libya is facing an era of unparalleled change. It is greatly to be hoped that this will bring new benefits both to archaeology and to tourism, and that it will result in a level of public understanding of history and archaeology amongst the Libyans themselves which they have never previously been invited to participate in. The reader will find in the following pages many apparent criticisms of neglect or poor management of the ancient monuments. These are intended merely as factual observations: as explained above, the Department of Antiquities has simply not had the means to pursue an active policy of any kind. I hope that this will soon change.

Decauville railways

The present-day visitor to major archaeological sites in Libya is often intrigued and puzzled by the presence of rusting sections of light-weight railway track. These are remnants of the portable Decauville Railway system. This was invented by the French sugar-beet farmer and railway pioneer Paul Decauville in 1875 and widely used thereafter in mining and military operations (for instance in the trenches in the First World War). The Italian excavators in Libya used the system extensively: in the 1970s there was still a working layout at Cyrene which encompassed all the principal areas in the upper part of the site. Track and a locomotive were brought to Benghazi for the excavations at Sidi Khrebish at that time (fig. 3). The system was well-suited to the large-scale excavations of the Italian colonial period, in which large quantities of soil needed to be moved considerable distances. In subsequent smaller operations, the investment of time required to lay and re-lay the track outweighed the benefits and the light railway has itself become a historic relic!

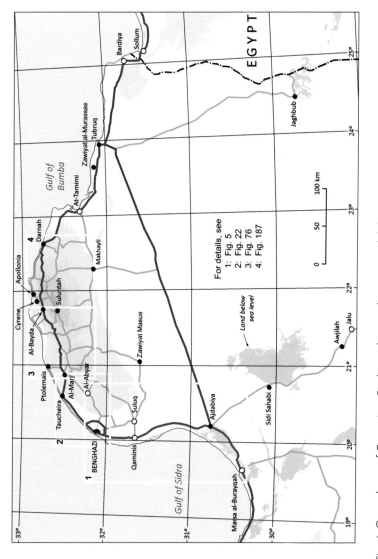

Fig. 4. General map of Cyrenaica. On this and succeeding maps, solid dots represent locations mentioned in the gazetteer.

GAZETTEER

The gazetteer is arranged in nine sections, proceeding broadly from west to east. Three of these are devoted to the individual sites of Ptolemais, Cyrene and Apollonia. The remaining sections represent geographical areas which have some unity of terrain and which are more or less conveniently united by modern roads. Within these areas, the sites are listed alphabetically; I have made no attempt to compose them into itineraries, and the maps and navigational instructions should be sufficient for the reader to devise his or her own programme of visits. I have used the time-honoured device of star-ratings to indicate approximate grades of importance for those who are pressed for time, or who have no desire to examine every detail. All of the locations mentioned are marked on at least one of the five maps in figures 4, 5, 22, 76 and 187. For all of those which are not easily identifiable on commercial maps, I have given geographical coordinates (based on the WGS 84 datum) and navigational instructions.

Very few of the sites described in this guide are guarded and charge a modest fee for entry (Taucheira, Ptolemais, Qasr Libya, Cyrene, Apollonia); where a museum stands within a site, it may be charged for separately. At the time of writing, Libya is still in a state of flux following the fall of the Qadhafi regime, but immediately prior to this it was permissible to use cameras both on sites and within museums (except where specifically forbidden) freely and without charge.

Many of the rural sites are on agricultural land which is actively farmed. In such cases it is important to respect the rights of the landowner and not to enter upon private land without permission, where the means can be seen of asking for it. In the writer's experience, those living on the land are generally conscious of their link with antiquity and are sympathetic to an interest in 'their' heritage.

1 SITES TO THE SOUTH OF BENGHAZI

If one is arriving in Cyrenaica by road from the W, the transition from the barren Syrtic desert to more fertile lands is a very gradual one. It is marked first by Ajdabiya, not on the coast but an important source of fresh water. There was a small settlement here in Classical times, but it acquired much greater importance during the medieval period as a stopping-point on the pilgrimage route from the Maghrib, which at this point passed to the S of the Jabal Akhdar by means of the oases of Awjilah/Jalu, Jaghbub and Siwa to the Nile. (A second, more northerly, route passed through Zawiyat Masus and Makhayli, rejoining the coast at the Gulf of Bumba.)

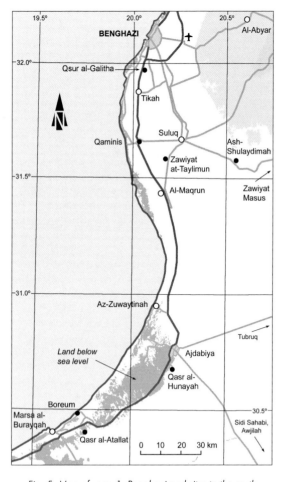

Fig. 5. Map of zone 1, Benghazi and sites to the south.

1 Sites to the south of Benghazi

There continues to be little vegetation on the flat plain to the N of Ajdabiya until one approaches the vicinity of Qaminis. From here on, there are scattered modern farms, becoming gradually more dense towards Benghazi. The appearance of this landscape will not have been greatly different in ancient times, with very scattered settlement to the S, probably more military in purpose than agricultural, and an increasing density further N, where it was conversely more agricultural than military. This terrain is easily traversed in most places on a camel or a horse, and it will always have been difficult to control the movements of the semi-nomadic native peoples, the *Nasamones*, and to prevent them from raiding the settled zone of the Jabal Akhdar. For this reason there was certainly a line of military posts in Roman times extending eastwards from the coast to the S of Qaminis (e.g. Zawiyat at-Taylimun, Ash-Shulaydimah, Zawiyat Masus). Only the most basic archaeological field survey has been done in this region (in the 1950s) and practically no excavation. There remains therefore much to be discovered, both in terms of settlement sites and of their relative chronology.

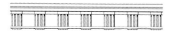

AJDABIYA اجدابيا

Coordinates: N 30° 45.68', E 20° 13.17'
Directions: The coordinates given are those of the roundabout in the centre of the town (see fig. 6). The road which leads to the desert oases of Awjilah, Jalu and Kufrah leads out of town from this point in a south-easterly direction, and it is off the same road that the two major Fatimid monuments described below may be found.

Ajdabiya, 150 km to the S of Benghazi, has always been important to communications over the vast desert regions. There are good sources of water here, to sustain both those travelling along the coast of the Greater Syrtis and caravans crossing the desert from here to Awjilah, Kufra, and so to Chad and the Sudan. Roman soldiers, some of them from Apamea in Syria, cut their names on the rock by the wells at dates between AD 39 and 51. (As far as I can tell, these wells were roughly half-way between the qasr and the mosque, in an area which has been built over since the 1970s.) There was therefore at that time a settlement with a military garrison; we know

from the Peutinger Table (based on information from the second century AD) that its name was *Corniclanum*. Fragments of masonry re-used in the mosque bear names of Roman soldiers, sometimes describing themselves as 'soldier' or 'centurion': similar inscriptions are still

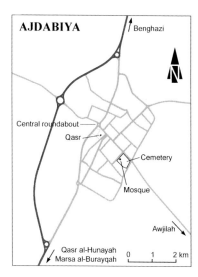

Fig. 6. Location of ancient monuments in Ajdabiya.

visible on the Roman outpost at Zawiyat Masus (p. 36). No actual structures dating from Classical antiquity have hitherto been found, but the Roman military strongpoint at Qasr al-Hunayah 5 km to the SW is still identifiable (p. 31).

It is clear from literary sources that the settlement continued to exist, and indeed to flourish, under the Arabs. In the early 10th century it was sacked by the first Fatimid caliph, Ubayd'allah (based at Mahdiya in Tunisia), for its allegiance to the Abbasids in Baghdad. Later in his reign, his son Abu'l Qasim built a new mosque there, the ruins of which can still be seen. The other monument which survives in part from this period was a fortress-palace, probably constructed c. 970. The town was still prosperous in the early 11th century, when it was described as possessing a mosque, baths and bazaars. Thereafter it fell into decline and abandonment, probably as a result of the upheaval caused by the invasion in 1051 of the Bani Hilal and the Bani Sulaym. It was only resettled under Turkish rule towards the end of the 19th century. This is one of the very few places in Libya where upstanding monuments of the medieval period can be seen; it is very sad that in recent years they do not seem to have been valued.

Qasr ★

Nineteenth-century travellers visiting Ajdabiya saw a substantial building which they were inclined to interpret as the remains of a church. However, clearance and excavations in the 1950s and 1970s showed conclusively that it had been a fortress-palace of the Islamic period. The ruins now stand within their own enclosure in an open space in the centre of the modern town. To find them, leave the central roundabout in the direction of Awjilah (fig. 6) and turn R into a side-street after

400 m; after a further 150 m you will find a large open space to your R, across which you will see the gate leading into the archaeological enclosure.

The fortress or *qasr* (figs. 7, 8) was a rectangular structure built entirely of carefully dressed stone. It was provided with circular towers at the corners and square towers mid-way along each of the longer sides. It was entered through a monumental porch, flanked internally by semicircular niches, on the NE side. The porch led into a vestibule, from which it was originally necessary to turn to the left and then to the right in order to enter the central courtyard and the other rooms opening off it. This type of 'bent entrance', of defensive value and also preventing someone at the door from looking directly into the courtyard, is typical of early Islamic buildings in the Maghrib. There is, in fact, now an axial doorway leading into the courtyard, but close examination shows that it is secondary, having been roughly hacked

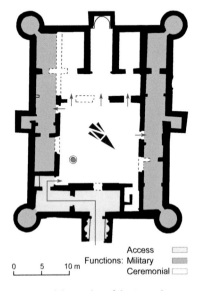

Fig. 7. Ajdabiya: plan of the Fatimid qasr.

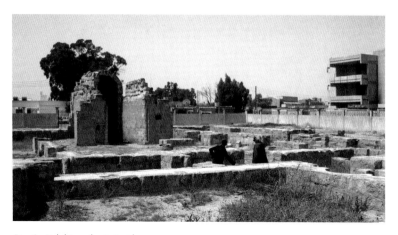

Fig. 8. Ajdabiya: the Fatimid qasr.

through the blank wall; its sill is also not placed squarely over the footings.

Once in the courtyard (where there is a well or cistern head), the visitor has access to suites of rooms on each of the long sides, and to something much grander on the opposite side to the entrance, which may fairly be described as a T-shaped audience-hall with side-chambers. The central part is still well-preserved, with part of its vault intact; the architecture is enlivened by the use of engaged columns and the apse at the far end is covered by a semi-dome, supported in the corners by shell-head squinches. Fragments of stucco show that there was also a frieze with a vegetal scroll.

The building was clearly a fortress and the lateral rooms in the long sides, with access to the towers, must have provided accommodation for troops. However, the grand entrance and the audience hall bespeak ceremonial, rather than military, concerns – so it was surely a place in which a governor or some other dignitary might hold court. On the other hand, the suite of 'palatial' rooms is far too mean for such a person to occupy in comfort. The building was not, therefore,

the permanent residence of the governor. Its architectural style clearly identifies it as a product of the Fatimid period (909–1051 in Cyrenaica), but there is no direct evidence which enables us to pin down its date more closely than that. The 14th-century writer al-Tijani tells us that the caliph al-Mu'izz ordered a series of rest-houses to be built along the route of his triumphal progress (in 969–972) from Tunisia to his new capital at Cairo. It has been plausibly suggested that the Ajdabiya fortress-palace was one of these rest-houses; this implies, of course, that other such buildings remain to be found.

Jami' Sahnun

The Jami' Sahnun is a mosque named after a great religious judge who practised under the Aghlabids of Qayrawan in the ninth century AD. The minaret and parts of the sanctuary were still standing when sketched by the traveller J.-R. Pacho in 1824. Despite its ruinous condition, the site continued to be venerated, and indeed the surrounding cemetery was still in use in 1970 (though it is now closed up and unkempt). Archaeological excavations were begun in 1954, and further

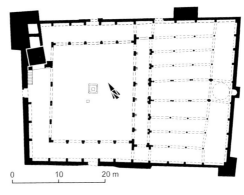

Fig. 9. Ajdabiya: plan of the Jami' Sahnun.

work was carried out in the 1970s, which established the details of the plan. The entire cemetery, on the right-hand side of the road to Awjilah (fig. 6), is walled and in 2012 access was possible only through an iron gate on the NW side, some 70 m from the junction with the main road. Once inside the gate, turn R and follow the path which remains close to the perimeter wall. The ruins of the mosque will be easily recognized at a distance of about 200 m from the gate.

The mosque (fig. 9) had maximum dimensions of 47 × 31 m; it was built using a combination of stone for the weight-bearing elements and mud-brick for the walls, and the architect paid little regard to right angles or exact symmetry. Entrances on three sides led into a courtyard with a single arcade around its perimeter. Just inside the main entrance (close to the cemetery wall) are the first few steps of the staircase which led up into the minaret; of this only the square foundation, in neatly coursed stonework, remains. (Photographs taken in about 1934 show the top of the square base and the first two courses of an octagonal shaft.) The sanctuary, on the far side of the courtyard from the main entrance, was four bays deep and nine bays wide;

it is likely that there was a dome covering the intersection in front of the mihrab. Two of the outer corners of the entire structure were enclosed by massive sloping buttresses, and there are irregular traces of others.

The mosque shows striking similarities of design to that built by the first Fatimid caliph Ubayd'allah at Mahdiya in Tunisia in 912 and an inscription recovered from the Ajdabiya mosque bears the date 922 or 932. The 11th-century geographer Al-Bakri wrote that a beautiful mosque with an octagonal minaret was built there by Abu'l Qasim (son of Ubayd'allah and caliph 934–946). It is possible therefore that the Ajdabiya mosque was built by Abu'l Qasim during the lifetime of his father.

Small excavations beneath the floor of the mosque have shown that it succeeded an earlier mosque on the same site, and that this too was preceded by occupation in the Roman period.

The N corner of the present cemetery is crossed obliquely by the footings of a massive wall of mud-brick, 1.7 m thick (just detectable now as a discolouration in the soil); this has been plausibly interpreted as part of the northern defensive wall of the Fatimid town. Humps and masses of rubble in other parts of the cemetery are likely to be remains of the houses of this period.

ASH-SHULAYDIMAH (ESC-SCELEIDIMA) الشليظيمه

Coordinates: N 31° 34.43′, E 20° 32.39′
Directions: The fort stands prominently above the road from Suluq to Zawiyat Masus, on the left-hand side. In order to approach it, turn L at N 32° 34.52′ E 20° 31.34′ onto an asphalted road which leads to a dispersed modern settlement. After 700 m, turn R off the asphalt and follow a very rough track which climbs up to the fort. (The distance from the asphalt is about 1.2 km: if you don't have a four-wheel-drive vehicle, it is best to walk.)

Multi-period fort

This is a strategic position, with wide views over the coastal plain and commanding a valley which offers access to the higher ground of the Jabal Akhdar from the SW. It therefore appealed to the Italians in the early 20th century just as it had to the Romans at a much earlier period. The Italian fort was for many years abandoned, but then refurbished in recent years and again abandoned. A substantial length of large coursed blockwork in the lower part of its outer wall shows that the Italians built directly on the remains of a Roman redoubt. The Roman defences probably included an outer ditch, but this too has been substantially modified in the 20th century.

AWJILAH (AUGILA) أوجلة

Coordinates: N 29° 7.65′, E 21° 17.46′
Directions: The centre of this desert oasis is about 220 km SE of Ajdabiya. The road which leads to it is asphalted all the way and is mostly of good quality, though in need of maintenance in some stretches. After the environs of Ajdabiya, where there is light scrub, the vegetation gives way rapidly to bare rock and sand. The site of Sidi Sahabi (p. 34) offers a reason for a brief stretch of the legs along the way. The coordinates given are those of the Jami' al-Kibir. On the approach to the oasis, the main road divides at N29° 8.19′ E 21° 17.61′; keep to the R. About 800 m beyond this fork the road swings round to the left, and the oldest part of the settlement is immediately below the road to the R.

Ancient oasis village ★ ★

This oasis, together with that of Jaghbub (p. 329), constituted throughout pre-modern history an important

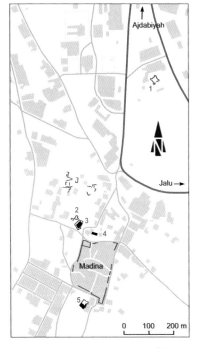

Fig. 10. Awjilah: the central part of the oasis. 1, 2, Turkish forts; 3, Jami' al-Kibir; 4, Mosque of Sidi Ahmad Zarruq; 5, Mosque and tomb of Sidi Abdallah.

25

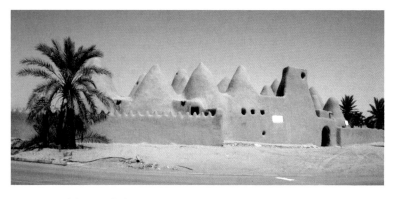

Fig. 11. Awjilah: Jami al-Kibir.

watering-point for caravans taking the inland route westwards from the Nile Valley to the Syrtic Gulf. It was mentioned in the fifth century BC by the Greek historian Herodotus as an important source of dates. Procopius reported that, in the sixth century AD, the emperor Justinian converted the Augilites to Christianity (suppressing cults of Ammon and of Alexander), and built a church for them, but of this no trace has yet been found. (It is significant that Justinian considered his empire to extend thus far inland.) It was later said that Augila at its zenith (before the Turkish conquest) had a population of some 15,000 inhabitants; again, the quality of its dates is mentioned.

The directions given above will bring you to the edge of the oldest part of the settlement (fig. 10). Both around it and amongst its decaying ruins there are scattered modern houses, but in recent years the local community has made a determined effort to restore and preserve some of the old mud-brick architecture before it disappears completely.

Jami' al-Kibir ★

The position of the Jami' al-Kibir or Jami' al-Atiq (Great Mosque or Old Mosque:

fig. 11) is that of the coordinates given above for the oasis. It is at a distance of about 300 m to the SW of the point where the main road curves to the left (see fig. 10:3). The mosque is claimed to have been built originally in AD 666; it was extensively restored in 1984 and in 2006, but using traditional materials and surely in accordance with its original form. The building is constructed from limestone slabs plastered over with mud, and takes the approximate internal form of five aisles (parallel to the qibla wall), each divided into nine bays. Each bay is joined to its neighbours by semi-circular arches and the first three rows are roofed with individual beehive domes. The fourth and fifth aisles, which are probably a secondary addition, have flat roofs. Light is provided principally by lateral doorways opening into a courtyard which runs round three sides of the building. Immediately on the R inside the main entrance from the street, are the steps of the minbar, and beyond that the mihrab. Round to the L are steps leading up to the open-topped minaret: this has a taller wall on the front of the building, with a circular window through which the call to prayer was issued.

The style of construction seen in the Jami' al-Kibir is typical of the pre-modern mosques in the Awjilah oasis. However, only one other, the mosque of Sidi Abdallah ibn Abi Sarh (see below) is of great antiquity. When the traveller Gerhart Rohlfs visited the oasis in 1869, he saw only three mosques; returning ten years later he found many more.

Behind the mosque (i.e. to the N and W of it) is an area of abandoned buildings of mud-brick, including remains of a 'Turkish castle' which was still used in the Italian colonial period (fig. 10:2). A large arch marks the original entrance to this building. Just 50 m to the E of the Jami' al-Kibir is the little **Masjid Sidi Ahmad Zarruq** (fig. 10:4). Six bays of the old mosque, with beehive domes, survive alongside its modern replacement, which has a prominent octagonal minaret. The supposed founder, a Moroccan scholar, passed through Awjilah several times on pilgrimages to Mecca, and lived there from 1474 to 1493.

Madina

Immediately to the S of the Masjid Sidi Ahmad Zarruq is the restored gateway to the Madina of Awjilah. Within, on the right, has been recreated a typical oasis farm with various enclosures for animals, and a well-head lined with palm-trunks. Some of the old houses in this area have also been restored and furnished in traditional fashion. There is a photographic display of martyrs of the resistance to the Italian occupation, including Fadil Bu Omar, a companion of Omar Mukhtar who came from Awjilah and was killed at al-Athrun. Another display in another house shows the progressive restoration of the madina.

Mosque of Sidi Abdallah ★

Outside the madina on the S side (fig. 10:5) may be found the mosque and tomb of Sidi Abdallah ibn Sa'ad ibn Abi-Sarh, who was a scribe of the Prophet and subsequently governor of Upper Egypt; he died in AD 656. The mosque should therefore go back to a similar foundation date

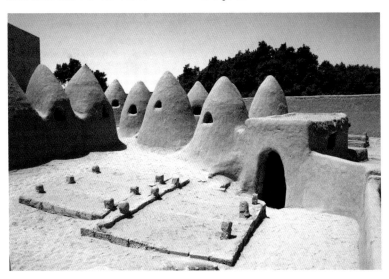

Fig. 12. Awjilah: the mosque of Sidi Abdallah.

to that of the Jami' al-Kibir (above). What is visible now is part only of an originally larger complex which included a zawiya and a madrasa; these were swept away in the 1960s in order to make way for the modern buildings which now occupy much of the site. The surviving old parts were restored in 1993–94.

The main mosque (fig. 12) is now below the surrounding ground-level, suggesting the accumulation of debris and the possible continued existence of other early structures which are now buried. It is surrounded by graves at a high level, which are recent. Steps lead down into a prayer hall composed of four by two bays, each roofed by a beehive dome with an opening for light. In the SE corner, a blocked arch formerly led to the tomb of the saint: the tomb is now enclosed within a new two-storey building with a green dome. A grave at the lower level, next to this space, is not old.

On higher ground to the N of the madina and between the two branches of the main road may be seen the walls of a small rectangular **military post** with projecting round towers (fig. 10:1); this is of Turkish or Italian date.

BOREUM/BU GRADA   بوقراده

Coordinates: N 30° 28.52', E 19° 42.10'
Directions: Going from Ajdabiya towards Marsa al-Burayqah, fork obliquely R at N 30° 25.82' E 19° 48.13', follow this road for 6.8 km and then turn R again towards the coast. This will take you round the R side of the modern village of New Brega (a settlement for oil workers) and along the sea-front. Where the road begins to curve inland again, turn to the R in order to remain close to the coast, and the site will be found on a small promontory to the R of the road, 1.7 km beyond the last turning.

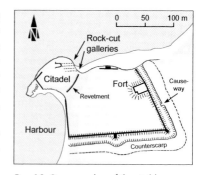

Fig. 13. Boreum: plan of the visible remains. (Contours are schematic.)

Fortified ancient village

The site is recorded in the *Stadiasmus Maris Magni*, a mariner's manual (probably) of around AD 200, as an anchorage protected from the S, together with a village with water and a ruined castle. A bishop Sentianus was based here in the fourth century AD and in the sixth century the emperor Justinian enclosed the settlement with 'very strong defences' as the last outpost towards the west of Byzantine rule in Cyrenaica. The settlement apparently had a large Jewish community at the time, which Justinian converted to Christianity (transforming their synagogue into a church – this has not been located).

On a small headland (fig. 13), it is possible to make out the remains of a fortification, presumably that referred to in the Stadiasmus; there are extensive rock-cut galleries beneath, facing, and now eroded by, the sea. The whole is separated from the village behind by a silted-up ditch. The village is protected by the massive rampart of the Justinianic period, which runs across the high ground to the E of the promontory, and down to the sea on the S side. The defence consisted of a wall of the very friable local sandstone, fronted by a broad ditch on the landward sides with a counterscarp in front. In the NE quarter, the outlines of a fort adjoin the inner face of the wall; on the S side may be traced two bastions and on the N side a further bastion can be made out on the edge of the cliff. The entrance seems to have been on the E side: there are traces here of a causeway, in the form of a shelf of natural rock projecting into the ditch from its outer edge. Internally, there is a jumble of fallen blocks and a dense scatter of late Roman pottery, but little detail can be made out.

Military frontier posts

About 8 km directly inland from Boreum may be found two rectangular moated structures of Roman date, which are probably military outposts guarding the approaches to the Pentapolis. Their locations are shown in figure 14. In order to reach them, a 4-wheel-drive vehicle is desirable but not essential. Heading towards Marsa al-Burayqah from Ajdabiya, pass by the fork which leads to New Brega (forgive the inconsistency of spelling!) and Boreum. Four km beyond this point, the main road curves to the L around the head of a salt-marsh; just after the marsh, fork L onto an unmade track at N 30° 26.54′ E 19° 45.21′. Follow this track in a more-or-less straight line for 3.6 km (do not curve L round the edge of the marsh) until you reach a pumping-station

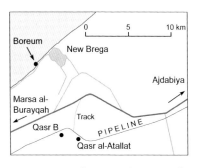

Fig. 14. Ancient features in the vicinity of New Brega.

on a pipeline. Cross the pipeline and then travel SE, between the pipeline and a line of electricity pylons, for a distance of about 900 m, which will bring you to **Qasr al-Atallat** at N 30° 24.27′ E 19° 45.02′. This is a rectangular castle built of carefully coursed blocks of local shelly limestone: eight or more courses are still visible in places. There is a doorway into the interior on the long NE side, but otherwise little detail can be made out. The castle was surrounded by a ditch, but in 2012 this was almost entirely obscured by blown sand.

If you follow the pipeline as it curves westward, you will come within 2 km of Qasr al-Atallat to a very similar moated site. I have not discovered any specific name for it, so it is indicated (very prosaically) in figure 14 as **Qasr B**. Its location is N 30° 24.48′ E 19° 43.77′. Here the superstructure has dissolved entirely into a shapeless mass, but the surrounding ditch, partly cut into the native rock with vertical sides, is very apparent. There seems to be an open forecourt within the ditch on the W side. A cistern nearby, which is in current use, is very likely to have an ancient origin associated with this building. According to various writers, there are several other similar castles in the vicinity. The terrain is desert and it is difficult to believe that they were there for agricultural purposes. In so far as any detail is visible, they resemble the undoubted military posts at Qasr al-Hunayah and Qasr ar-Rimthayat (pp. 31, 312). They are certainly Roman or Byzantine in date.

QAMINIS   قمينس
Coordinates: N 31° 40.25′, E 20° 1.25′
Directions: The village is skirted by the main road from Benghazi to Ajdabiya, at a distance of some 50 km from the former.

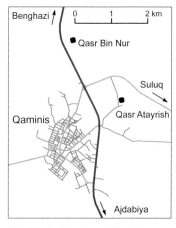

Fig. 15. Ancient sites at Qaminis.

The coordinates given are those of the northerly road junction where lesser roads lead W into the village and E towards Suluq.

Ancient forts – or farms?

Around the village of Qaminis on the coastal plain have been identified a number of ancient rectangular structures, formerly described as forts. They are characterized by sloping walls of large, roughly-shaped blocks and by rounded corners. It has been inferred that, while they look 'un-Roman', they are likely to belong to the Roman or Byzantine periods and to have played a rôle in the defence of western Cyrenaica. Three of these are listed here, as selective examples of the type which are readily accessible. The locations of the first two are shown in figure 15; the third lies a few kilometres to the N.

Qasr Atayrish ★ (Castle of the Deaf) is the largest and best preserved example (fig. 16). It lies on the edge of the modern village and to the E of the main road, at N 32° 40.05' E 20° 1.85'. Its massive outer walls stand some 3 m high, enclosing a core approximately 38 × 36 m which is now solid but probably filled by the collapse of the superstructure. During the Italian occupation it was incorporated into a modern fort and an observation tower was built on top; this has since been entirely removed. On the upper surface there is now a large circular foundation of double-faced masonry; this looks like ancient, rather than Italian, work. At the SE corner, the foundation seems to be interrupted by several drum-like blocks which perhaps framed a portal of some kind. On the E side of the main revetment wall are traces

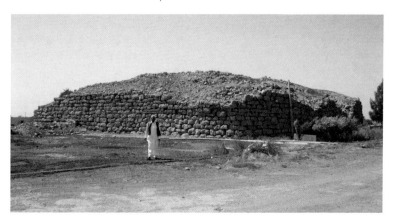

Fig. 16. Qaminis: Qasr Atayrish.

of an arched doorway at ground-level. Unlike many buildings in the Jabal Akhdar with sloping revetments (e.g. Qasr al-Maraghah, Qasr Bu Hassan, Qasr Wurtij, pp. 310, 315, 318), there is no trace here of an inner structure of good ashlar masonry to which the revetment has been added. The encroachment of modern buildings around Qasr Atayrish has obscured the nature of any ancillary structures which may originally have been associated with it.

Qasr Bin Nur (Castle of the son of light) lies close to the E side of the main road, about a kilometre to the N of the road junction for the village, at N 32° 40.89′ E 20° 1.06′. This is a similar structure to Qasr Atayrish but less well preserved. The outline is a very rounded rectangle. Roman pottery of the fifth or sixth century AD has been found in the vicinity.

Qasr al-Khayl (Castle of the horses) lies approximately 6 km (by road) N of the road junction and some 900 m E of the main road. It is visible from the road, beneath the nearby power lines. A track which leaves the road at N 32° 43.41′ E 20° 1.47′ leads towards a modern farm. Passing to the N of this, another track leads to the site at N 31° 43.21′ E 20° 2.01′. The principal building here is enclosed by moderately well coursed ashlar masonry, but still with rounded corners; it is about 25 m square and the surviving perimeter wall is about 2 m high. No interior detail is visible. This building stands in an area of flat cultivable land; there are stony patches in which may be seen the outlines of both irregular and neatly rectangular stone buildings. There must have been an extensive agricultural settlement here in the Roman period, of which the qasr was the focus and strongpoint.

This area of marginal fertility, between the desert of the Syrtic region and the fertile uplands of the Jabal Akhdar, is probably very comparable, in terms of the settlement pattern in the late Roman and Byzantine periods, to the pre-desert zone in Tripolitania. The inhabitants of these settlements and their strongpoints are probably to be thought of as the local population of farmers rather than as an imposed military presence. It seems that they did not have skilled stonemasons like those who built such elegant farm buildings in the jabal (e.g. Qasr az-Zaarura, p. 123).

QASR AL-HUNAYAH   قصر لحَنِية

Coordinates: N 30° 40.69′, E 20° 12.08′
Directions: Head S from Ajdabiya along the main road towards Marsa al-Burayqah for 1.25 km from the southern end of the Ajdabiya bypass. Turn L at N 30° 42.34′ E 20° 11.39′: this will lead you, after 3 km in a straight line, to the entrance of a large military base. The site is in the centre of the base!

Roman castle

This fascinating castle now stands in the centre of a huge munitions depot, and unfortunately has been much damaged in recent years by the military. However, it is worth describing because it is probably just one of a series of similar castles which have yet to be more closely investigated. In April 2012 the military base was completely abandoned and it was possible to walk in and to visit the Roman monument; this may not continue to be the case!

The site, on a slight rise in a desolate plain, was noted by various travellers in the 19th and 20th centuries, and was surveyed in 1950 by Richard Goodchild, upon whose drawings the plan in figure 17 is based. The structure may appropriately be described as a castle, since it stands on a platform 23 m square defined by a rock-cut ditch with vertical sides, which is 4 m wide and was probably about 5 m deep. There was access to the castle by means of a bridge on the S side. (Cuttings at either side for voussoir blocks could be made out.) Part of the internal superstructure, in ashlar masonry, still survives, but the real interest of the monument lies in the extensive rooms cut out of the living rock below ground-level. These were sufficiently accessible in 1950 to be surveyed in some detail. Unfortunately, at some time during the recent life of the military base, these underground rooms seem to have been regarded as a security risk (in case there was a tunnel leading into the base from outside?) and all voids were closed by bulldozing the upstanding masonry into the openings. While all of the ditch and part of the superstructure are still apparent, much damage has certainly

been caused. The description is therefore based on Goodchild's observations.

In the centre of the castle was a light-well and a staircase leading to the floor below. Here, cut out of the rock, were various vaulted chambers, lit by small windows cut through the inner face of the ditch; there were also numerous niches for lamps. The basement rooms included a two-seater latrine. There were not only window openings into the ditch (some of which may be seen in fig. 18), but also store-rooms (simple rectangular chambers) and stables. There was external access to the ditch by means of a ramp on the N side which is now buried, though there is a slight hollow in the ground. This led down through an underground chamber and a barred doorway flanked by guardrooms to a stable and thence to the ditch. The stable was identified as such because of the presence of tethering-rings cut in the stone ceiling. On the inner side of the ditch, a doorway led to a second stable, beneath the

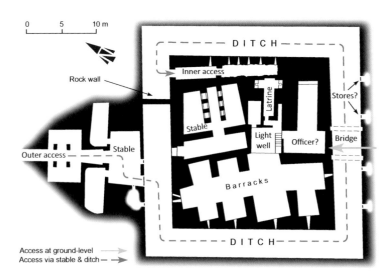

Fig. 17. Qasr al-Hunayah, plan of rock-cut features below ground-level.

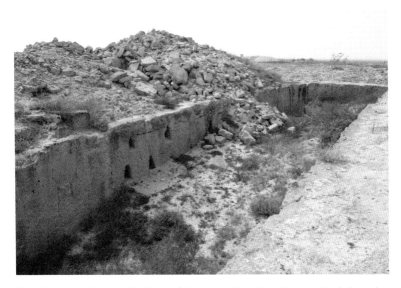

Fig. 18. Qasr al-Hunayah: the E side of the surrounding ditch. The triangular holes in the wall are windows into the rock-cut chambers behind.

castle but not communicating with it. This was provided with rock-cut mangers for six horses. (Similar features may be seen at Qasr ash-Shahdiyn, p. 128.) Another doorway, close to the NE corner, seems to have provided internal access to the ditch from the castle. The effectiveness of the ditch as a means of defence, while also serving as a means of communication, was ensured by the retention of a narrow wall of rock between the outer and inner entrances; this forced anyone seeking to enter the castle through the ditch to make a circuit of all four sides in order to do so!

There is no direct dating-evidence for this intriguing structure; there can, however, be no doubt that it is Roman, and probably early rather than late Roman or Byzantine. It is clearly of essentially similar design to the castle of Qasr ar-Rimthayat (p. 312) and Goodchild placed the fort at Ain Marah (p. 287), now barely detectable, in the same category. These

are both certainly pre-Byzantine, and there can be no doubt from the very specialized design that these structures are military posts, not farms.

QSUR AL-GALITHA   قصور الغليثه

Coordinates: N 31° 57.98', E 20° 1.94'
Directions: This site is immediately on the E side of the main road from Benghazi to Ajdabiya, at a distance of 16 km from the centre of Benghazi or 10 km from the entrance to the university.

Fortified farm

This is a small ditched, Roman farm, next to the main road and easy of access. It has been partly excavated. An arched entrance on the W side leads into a vestibule with a staircase to the R and two other doorways leading to a lateral room and to a central courtyard. The construction is in ashlar masonry, but of poor quality, with joints infilled with smaller stones.

Where the doorways are sufficiently well preserved, they may be seen to be flanked by 'curtain brackets' (see p. 14). There appears also to be an added revetment around the exterior; this is mostly in the form of an earth or rubble bank, but with a stone facing on part of the W side. The constructional characteristics suggest a late Roman/Byzantine date, and two carved crosses have been observed on a jamb of the entrance.

SIDI SAHABI   سيدي الصحابي

Coordinates: N 30° 0.43′, E 20° 47.79′

Directions: This site makes a convenient break on the way from Ajdabiya to Awjilah, at a distance of almost exactly 100 km from the former. The road is initially straight and fast, with light scrub soon giving way to bare rock and sand. The terrain then becomes more broken, with confusing natural outcrops of rock. However, the site is readily identifiable from the road and lies 1.0 km to the W of it. There is no track leading to it. The surface is sandy but reasonably firm; a 4-wheel-drive vehicle is advisable unless you walk across.

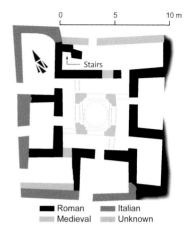

■ Roman ■ Italian
■ Medieval ■ Unknown

Fig. 19. Qasr as-Sahabi, plan.

Qasr as-Sahabi, Roman farm

Here, at an isolated point on the long road from Ajdabiya to Awjilah, is a ruined building of many periods (figs. 19, 20). As in so many places, its last incarnation was as an Italian military post, of curiously rhomboid shape but with typical round corner-towers. Roughly in the centre of this, and standing rather higher than the remains of the 20th century, may be discerned the core of a typical late

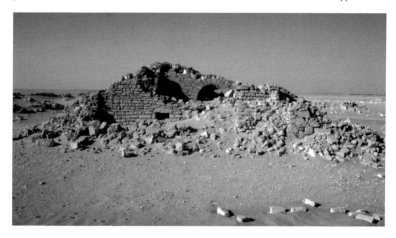

Fig. 20. Qasr as-Sahabi, NE side.

Roman farm. It is in the form of a compact rectangular building with seven rooms around a central courtyard; a flight of steps (seen in 1972 but not evident now) provided access to either an upper storey or the roof. The walls are of coursed mortared stone, with occasional courses laid diagonally on edge – a feature found in Tripolitania in the late Roman period (for instance at Bir Shedewa) and in Cyrenaica at Madinat Bu Hindi (p. 301). The roofs took the form of barrel-vaults and the doors had massive semi-circular lintels above. In the central courtyard, a feature with substantial horseshoe arches and traces of a central dome suggests refurbishment in the medieval period, perhaps as the tomb of Sidi Sahabi, who was reputedly a clerk to the Prophet.

It would seem always to have been a fairly thankless task to farm in this area, and while the design of the Roman building is no different from other farms of the period, one must presume that the raison d'être of this post in ancient times, as more recently, was military.

ZAWIYAT AT-TAYLIMUN زاوية الطيلمون

Coordinates: N 31° 35.32′, E 20° 10.41′
Directions: From Suluq, two parallel roads run SW towards al-Maqrun; the easterly one is the service road for the Great Man-Made River (of which there is a reservoir just N of Suluq) and the westerly one runs close by the hamlet of Zawiyat at-Taylimun. Where this road divides, 8.5 km from Suluq, take the right fork. This will curve sharply to the L and bring you to the zawiya at just over 11 km from Suluq.

Roman fort

This is a rectangular Roman fort with angle-towers, of which two courses at most of good ashlar masonry may be

seen in places. The ruins are immediately to the W of, and partly overlain by, the Sanusi zawiya; when visited in 2012 the area was in use as an animal pen and permission should be sought before entering the area. Parts of only three outer walls, and of two angle-towers, remain above the ground. The fort appears to have measured 38 × 44 m, and to have been divided internally by two walled streets or intersecting corridors meeting at right-angles. An arched doorway gave access to the NW angle-tower from the inside of the fort. There are no definite traces of a surrounding ditch.

The projecting rectangular angle-towers identify this as a military structure. Together with the forts at ash-Shulaydimah (p. 25) and Zawiyat Masus (below) it must have composed an inner line of defence at the western extremity of Cyrenaica. It has not been excavated or dated.

ZAWIYAT MASUS زاوية مسوس

Coordinates: N 31° 34.97′, E 21° 0.51′
Directions: It is likely that you will approach this site by means of the road which runs eastwards from Suluq and past ash-Shulaydimah (p. 25). Immediately beyond ash-Shulaydimah, the road climbs up to a broad featureless plateau with little vegetation. The hamlet around Zawiyat Masus is small, and the main road makes a right-angled turn to the R. Ignore this and continue straight on, passing the zawiya on your R; the Roman building will be directly in front of you, approximately 300 m from the main road.

Roman military post ★

The Roman outpost here, like that at ash-Shulaydimah (p. 25), became incorporated in an Italian military structure in the 20th century. This in its turn is in decay,

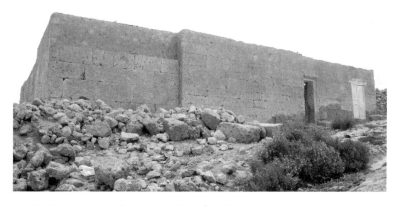

Fig. 21. Zawiyat Masus: the Roman building from the W.

but the (more solid) Roman building is once again inhabited and is private property – therefore to be approached with due courtesy. At the NW extremity of the Italian fort is an enclosure about 19.5 m square (fig. 21) with an external facing of carefully drafted limestone masonry, certainly of Roman date. The inner facing is of rubble masonry, which is less readily dated but by no means inconsistent with Roman practice. This enclosure was entered through the present smaller doorway with a carved lintel on the W side; the larger doorway to the R of this is new, having been cut through the wall since 1950. To the L of both doors, the wall projects forward slightly: this is an independently constructed watch-tower, entered from within the enclosure.

Both the door-lintel and other parts of the Roman walls are inscribed with names written in Greek. The writing on the door-lintel reads 'Alexander, son of Pantaleon, soldier'; other names are accompanied by dates (unfortunately ambiguous) and by descriptions such as 'cavalryman' and *tesserarius* (Commander of the Watch): these are clearly members of the unit stationed here. The style of the lettering and of the masonry have been judged to indicate a date in the first century AD. Upwards of sixty such texts have been recorded, and their occurrence on the actual fabric of a military building is most unusual. It has been suggested that there was perhaps a shrine within the tower which caused these men to commemorate their presence in this way. Something similar has been found at Dura-Europos in Syria, and we do know that Syrians formed part of the garrison of Ajdabiya in the first century AD (p. 21). The names recorded at Zawiyat Masus show an interesting mixture of Greek (Alexander, Aristoteles), Latin (C. Iulius Capito) and Libyan characteristics (Mallulas, Itthannuras).

2 BENGHAZI TO TAUCHEIRA

The visitor to Cyrenaica is likely to start here, on arriving at Benghazi. Approaching by air, one flies in from the coast, low over the barely fertile coastal plain, dotted with the curious 'sunken gardens' which characterise the immediate vicinity of Benghazi (see p. 45), to land at Baninah, just below the first gentle stirring of the Jabal Akhdar escarpment. The coastal plain is about 25 km wide at this point, and as one travels NE from Benghazi it becomes progressively narrower, until at Tukrah/Taucheira it is barely more than 5 km wide. At the same time the edge of the jabal escarpment becomes steeper, higher and more dramatic. At Tukrah there is a choice, either to remain with the coastal strip, which continues to dwindle away towards Tulmaythah (Ptolemais), or to climb the scarp (now cut by two successive modern roads) onto the plain of al-Marj. The higher ground of the jabal, about 300 m above sea level at this point, enjoys a better rainfall and has deeper and more fertile soils than the coastal strip.

When one drives along the main road between Benghazi and Tukrah (the ancient Pentapolis cities of Euesperides/Berenice and Taucheira/Arsinoë) one is aware not only of the jabal marching ever closer on the landward side, but of coastal salt-pans and marshes between the road and the sea. This is an inhospitable coast, and even today ships are wrecked upon its shelving reefs. The modest natural harbour at Benghazi (now difficult to visualize amidst modern artificial development) will always have been an important haven for shipping, and undoubtedly justified its early choice for a Greek settlement. Likewise, Taucheira was blessed with plentiful water. There are other signs of occupation in ancient times, but they

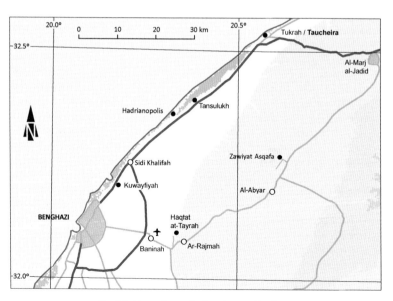

Fig. 22. Map of zone 2, Benghazi to Taucheira.

are extremely modest and are almost all under threat from modern development, whether agricultural or urban. Apart from the two major sites, which are treated in detail, I have selected just a few others which are historically significant or reasonably easy of access.

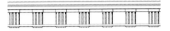

AR-RAJMAH (ER-REGIMA) الرجمة

Coordinates: N 32° 5.32', E 20° 19.58'

Directions: From Benghazi, take the road to the airport at Baninah. Immediately before arriving at the airport, at N 32° 5.51' E 20° 14.81', turn R onto the road which skirts the airport and village on the way to al-Abyar. Where the road curves round to the L, just at the foot of the escarpment, fork L (at N 32° 3.65' E 20° 19.06'); this will take you past a military base and the asphalt road comes to an end 2.7 km from the fork. Beyond this the ground is rough: the cave described below is slightly less than 1 km from here, so walkable, though you may be able to get closer by vehicle, depending on its robustness! At the end of the asphalt road, various tracks diverge: turn 90° to your right into a quarry area. You want to climb gradually to your L, and you should be able to pick up the track-bed of the old railway line in a shallow cutting. If you follow this, you will soon see the cave on the hillside above you, and a large natural sink-hole below. The latter is now being used as a rubbish tip.

Haqfat at-Tayrah prehistoric cave

An Italian fort on the ridge above Baninah once protected the airfield. Immediately beneath the fort is a huge cave, where white flint chippings from prehistoric occupation are evident on the scree running down from the cave mouth. Internally, it extends for some 70 m, with side-galleries and occasional stalactites and stalagmites, though it is silted up to the extent that the headroom is rarely more than 1.5 m. Excavations within the cave in the 1930s and in 1948 yielded animal bones and flint tools of the Upper Palaeolithic period. Niches, both natural and man-made, in the rock face near the entrance suggest a primitive shrine or funerary practice. Some of these look very Roman in character. There are also rock-cut shelves, cisterns and an area of Roman waterproof plaster; at the bottom of the slope are squared blocks and the outline of a (Roman?) building. Pottery of the Hellenistic and Roman periods is scattered about.

BENGHAZI بنغازي

The sprawling modern city of Benghazi (the heart of which alone is shown in fig. 23) has grown up very largely since the Second World War. Prior to that, a small town had developed since the fifteenth century in the immediate vicinity of the harbour, and it was backed on the landward side by a string of saline coastal lagoons. Benghazi changed hands five times during the North African campaign in 1941–43 and suffered accordingly. The little Ottoman castle, built in 1638, had already been demolished by the Italians in 1914, but much of the historic centre was destroyed by bombing during those events. As a result, the core of the city does not have the historical character which still survives in the madina of Tripoli, though there are a few buildings of interest from the Ottoman period which are accessible.

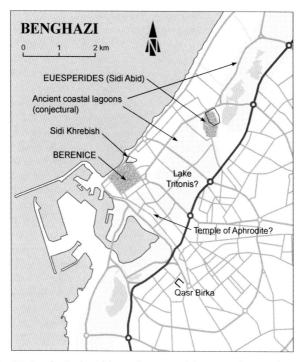

Fig. 23. Benghazi: plan of the modern city with locations of ancient features.

The modern city is the ultimate successor to two settlements of the Classical period, both of which now lie beneath and have been engulfed by it. (Paolo della Cella, passing through Benghazi in 1817, noted that 'The whole city is littered with beautifully-cut stones and other remains of ancient buildings. The people of Benghazi reduce these fine stones to rubble to build up their wretched hovels.') The first of these ancient cities was *Euesperides*, a Greek settlement established by migrants from Cyrene. Our first knowledge of this settlement in the literary record relates to 515 BC, when a Persian military expedition sent from Egypt against Barka, at the request of Queen Pheretima (p. 3) travelled as far west as Euesperides; recent excavations have shown, however, that the settlement

goes back to the late seventh century BC, and was first fortified by about 580. The settlement received a further organized influx of settlers from various parts of Greece in 462 BC, on the initiative of King Arkesilaos IV of Cyrene, but was evidently still vulnerable to attacks by the Libyan tribes of the Syrtic region. In 414 BC the city was besieged by Libyans, and was saved only by the fortuitous arrival of a Spartan fleet under the command of Gylippus, which had been sailing westwards to the relief of Syracuse (under siege by an Athenian expedition) but had been blown off course.

The site of Euesperides was identified only as recently as 1946, in the area of the cemetery of Sidi Abid, to the N of the later city centre and on a small hill projecting into the Sabkha as-Salmani (see fig. 23). Here Greek pottery was picked up, and subsequent examination of aerial photographs revealed that a considerable part of the street-plan of the ancient city could be made out! Excavations were carried out in 1952–53, 1969 and in 1995–2006 (see below).

The city of Euesperides was superseded by the foundation of *Berenice* on another site around 250 BC. It was for long thought that the move was occasioned by the silting up of the lagoon, such that the old settlement was no longer accessible by sea whereas the new site was still close to sufficiently deep water. However, an alternative hypothesis, more recently proposed, is that Euesperides had chosen the losing side in the civil conflict which followed the death of Magas in 258 or 250 BC (the relevant source, Eusebius, is ambiguous on the date) and that the population had been forcibly relocated in the aftermath. The new city was named after the wife of Ptolemy III Euergetes (and daughter of Magas: she whose hair became a constellation in the night sky!). The recent excavations at Euesperides have shown, not only that houses were refurbished very shortly before the final abandonment (implying no progressive decline), but that the wells so far discovered were all deliberately filled in at that time. This seems clear evidence of a forced resettlement, with the blocking of the wells being carried out in order to prevent any return to the old site.

Berenice occupied most of the area close to the present harbour and beneath the later Ottoman settlement. The development of modern Benghazi in the 1930s by the Italians brought to light several coin hoards, numerous pieces of sculpture and occasional mosaics in the course of building works, but no systematic archaeological investigations took place before 1971. At this time, a decision was made to clear and build upon the Turkish cemetery of Sidi Khrebish, beneath the old lighthouse. Here bulldozers soon exposed more ancient structures and Roman mosaics, and the Department of Antiquities succeeded in obtaining a stay of execution while emergency excavations were carried out. These took place between 1971 and 1975, and provided the first detailed information about Hellenistic and Roman Berenice (described below). As elsewhere, it was found that the ancient settlement persisted for a while after the Arab conquest in the seventh century AD, but gradually dwindled away. It may have disappeared before the invasion of the Bani Hilal in the 11th century, but it certainly lasted no later than that. There is mention of a commercial treaty in 1216 between the Republic of Genoa and the emir of Bernik, so there was evidently some kind of conurbation at that time, but it is impossible to demonstrate any physical continuity between classical Berenice and the settlement which, in the 15th century, took its new name from Sidi Ibn Ghazi.

Euesperides

Euesperides is visually (and aromatically) unrewarding to visit at the time of writing. The centre of the settlement was around a very low eminence on the seaward side of the coastal salt-pan, occupied in recent history by the cemetery of Sidi Abid (at N 32° 8.05' E 20° 5.27'). As it grew, the settlement expanded southwards onto lower ground; the street layout of this part of the town was revealed by aerial photography and verified by excavation, including parts of a presumed defensive wall (fig. 24). The ancient levels are severely pock-marked by 20th-century burials (now removed),

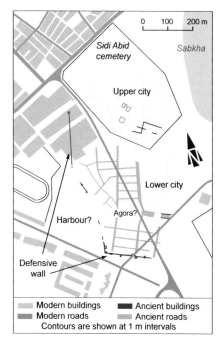

Fig. 24. Benghazi: plan of identified remains of Euesperides.

and striking outcome of the study of the pottery found at the site is the extent of its long-distance trade, including well-established contacts with regions under Punic (rather than Greek) domination. Though fragments of mosaic flooring remain in place, little remains of the superstructure of the buildings, for the stone was removed both at the time when the city was relocated to Berenice and on more recent occasions. In the southern (lower) part of the settlement, to the S of the road which bisects the site, traces of streets may still be made out amid the encroaching and omnipresent rubbish; selective excavations have shown that the occupied area extended substantially further E than the recorded street-plan suggests. On the W side of the site, the curving line of the defences probably marks the ancient waterfront and the location of the harbour.

but the archaeological importance of the site lies in the fact that they were not overlaid by occupation of the Roman and Byzantine periods. There is therefore a recoverable sequence which is limited to the span between the seventh and the mid third centuries BC.

The excavations have shown that in the latest period of occupation (first half of the third century BC), houses were being paved in mosaic composed partly of pebbles and partly of cut tesserae – important evidence for the evolution of mosaic decoration. Finds have also shown a wide variety of imported pottery, demonstrating wide trading connections, perhaps supported by the export (amongst other things) of dyed cloth; considerable quantities were found of murex shells, from which purple dye was extracted. A novel

Berenice ★

There is rather more to see of ancient Berenice than there is of Euesperides. Excavations carried out in the 1970s in the cemetery of Sidi Khrebish are still in part exposed and retained as a protected archaeological zone. The site, next to the water-front Shari' Ahmad Rafiq al-Mahdawi, is the easiest location to find in the entire city, for in the centre of it stands the old lighthouse. (See figure 26. A first lighthouse was built at Benghazi in 1880 by a French company, under the auspices of the governor Ali Kamal Pasha. It was replaced by the present building in 1935.) The plan in figure 25 shows the excavated features, not all of which are now visible. The lettering on the plan corresponds to area designations

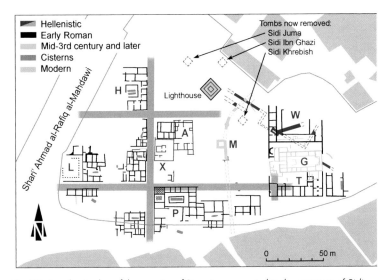

Fig. 25. Benghazi: plan of the remains of Berenice excavated in the cemetery of Sidi Khrebish.

devised at the time, and the entrance to the site is on the S side, close to Area P. The excavation revealed a regular grid-plan of streets aligned to the cardinal points of the compass and laid out in the early part of the second century BC at the latest. The subsequent sequence of structures did not depart significantly from this alignment. The area was mainly residential, but the buildings on the western part of the site were abandoned and systematically demolished around the middle of the third century AD. This seems to have been connected with the construction of a new defensive wall, running N–S across the centre of the site and enclosing only the ground to the E of it. It appears that the population of Berenice was shrinking and that new defences were required, probably in the face of the widely attested unrest which followed the fall of the Severan dynasty in 235. (Note the virtual sack of Cyrene in 268: p. 149).

In subsequent centuries, there was some evidence for re-occupation of small areas of the S and W part of the site, but this seems mostly to have been connected with craft activities (i.e. with vats, kilns and ovens). The only substantial later building was a church built on the eastern part of the site. Later artefacts, and a small circular bastion added to the mid-Roman defensive wall (no longer apparent) are indicative of continued occupation following the Arab conquest, but the latest coins from the site belong to the 10th century.

During the excavations, a considerable number of Roman mosaic floors were discovered. These have all been subjected to more or less disastrous attempts at conservation; apart from one which is reasonably well preserved beneath a cover building (in Area H), the remainder have now been reduced, almost without exception, to depressing heaps of loose tesserae mixed with rusty reinforcing bars. When visiting the site now, it is also necessary to distinguish carefully between ancient walling and modern restoration and enclosure walls, which may otherwise confuse the eye!

In the adjoining **Areas A and X**, on the western part of the site, may be seen a courtyard house and a modest shrine within an enclosed precinct, both of Hellenistic date. Of similar date was a substantial defensive wall in Area W, running from NW to SE (thus cutting off the promontory on which the new city was located more or less at right-angles), but this was dismantled by the early Roman period, when it was overlaid by other structures.

During the course of the first century AD, most of the buildings in the area were replaced at a higher level. A public water supply (the destination of which was not discovered) ran from N to S beneath the street in front of Area X, and the channel in which the terracotta pipe was laid is visible in several places. In **Area H**, a little further on and on the opposite side of the street, much of a typical courtyard house of the early Roman period is still preserved. This house was large enough to have had a peristyle around the courtyard, and some of its internal walls were decorated with painted representations of the Muses. At a later date, it presumably changed its use, going down in the social scale, for the fallen fragments of the wall-plaster were found to have been defaced by

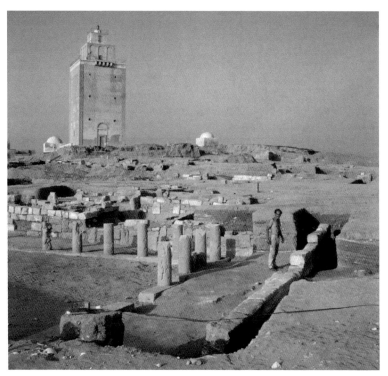

Fig. 26. Benghazi: Area L at Sidi Khrebish (Berenice) at the time of excavation. Behind the lighthouse may be seen the tombs of Sidi Ibn Ghazi and Sidi Khrebish (since removed).

graffiti of all kinds. These are typical of what one might expect in a hostelry in a seaport. Yet more intriguing was the discovery in the cistern beneath the courtyard of a bone assemblage which included three adult humans, a child of about five years old, forty babies, four cats and twenty dogs! Was this a 'house of ill repute'? This is perhaps unlikely, for the bones were disarticulated (i.e. they were thrown in as loose rubbish, not deposited as intact bodies); a more likely, but equally gruesome, explanation is that decomposed bodies were thrown into the cistern following an outbreak of plague. A modern cover building has been erected over a room in the SW corner of this house, preserving a mosaic with an attractive circular geometric design around a central disc of grey slate. The corners of the design are filled by cups (*kantharoi*) surrounded by tendrils. The house was abandoned in the early third century AD.

Returning southwards, In **Area L** on the western edge of the site, a much larger peristyle is visible (fig. 26). This was constructed in the early second century AD and appears to belong to a (public?) complex, perhaps baths which lay to the W and beneath the modern road. In the southern part of the site, several long cisterns originally lay beneath courtyards, whence they collected rainwater; crumbling mosaics also reflect the prosperity of this quarter of the town in the second and early third centuries AD. Moving now towards the E, one passes an array of buried vats (probably for the fermentation of wine) in two rooms of a peristyle house in **Area P**. These also pre-date the demolitions of the mid third century.

On the rising ground to the E at **Area M** may be seen part of the mid-Roman defensive wall, built of re-used material and provided here with a small square bastion. To the E of this, the complex occupying **Areas T and W** seems to have been public in character, perhaps facing an open piazza to the S. This was built in the early third century AD and was richly decorated with floors of marble and mosaic. The complex is not now easy to make out, since the same spot was chosen in the late fifth century for the construction of a church (**Area G**). This is almost the only church in Cyrenaica for which there is direct dating evidence, and it was certainly built before the time of Justinian (527–565), to whose interest so many churches have been attributed. The building (the remains of which were very ruinous as a result of stone-robbing) was solid and plain, with an apse at the E end set within the rectangular perimeter of the whole, and a tripartite narthex at the W end. There were separate rooms or chapels at each of the four corners and a projecting tower at the NW corner. A baptismal tank towards the E end of the N aisle was later converted into a vat for secular purposes. The whole was built of re-used materials, and two inscriptions carrying dedications to Apollo suggest that at an earlier period there had been a temple of Apollo not very far away.

Post-classical monuments

Despite the terrible bombardments which Benghazi suffered during the Second World War (when it changed hands five times) there are still monuments of historic interest in the centre of the city. The locations of the most notable of these are marked in fig. 27.

Close to the old (Italian) municipality building and closing the eastern end of Shari' Omar al-Mukhtar, is the **Jami' al-Kibir** (Grand Mosque, also known as the Old Mosque, Jami' al-Atiq). This was built by Abdalsalam al-Qadi at the beginning of the 16th century and restored on numerous occasions, most extensively by Tahir Pasha, governor of Benghazi 1893–1904). Its minaret, described in the mid 19th century as one of the very rare standing monuments in the city, was destroyed at the beginning of the Italian occupation and subsequently replaced. More recently, both the minaret and the adjoining forehall on the NW side (towards the sea) have been completely replaced. The core of the building is square, with a central dome supported on four piers; there are four smaller hemispherical domes over the corners and elongated domes in between them on each of the four sides. This is a typical Ottoman design feature.

Just 50 m to the N of the Jami' al-Kibir, on the far side of an open square, is the **Jami' Osman** or Ottoman Mosque, built by Rashid Pasha II (governor 1882–93) on the ruins of the earlier Abu Galaz mosque. The layout is similar to that of the Jami' al-Kibir, but the fluted minaret is original. Within (not accessible at the time of writing) is the tomb of Rashid Pasha.

On the E side of the main post office, Shari' al-Agib runs southwards past the former Italian meat market (on the left-hand side). Note the capitals of the columns flanking the entrance, which are decorated with the tree which bore the golden apples in the Garden of the Hesperides, guarded by the serpent Ladon (see below). On either side are the letters A VIII, for Year 8 of the Fascist era – 1930. A little further on, on the right-hand side, a fine portal gives access to the **Bayt al-Madina al-Thaqafi ★**. This is the 200-year-old town house of Omar Pasha Mansur al-Kikhia, an Ottoman pasha from a prominent Benghazi family; it is now a cultural centre and

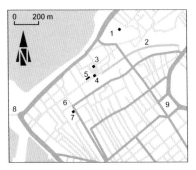

Fig. 27. Benghazi: plan of the town centre. 1, Lighthouse and Sidi Khrebish excavation; 2, Covered souk; 3, Jami' Osman; 4, Jami' al-Kibir; 5, Italian town hall; 6, Post Office; 7, Bayt Madina al-Thaqafi; 8, Entrance to port; 9, Omar Mukhtar Square.

museum. There are rooms on two floors around a courtyard with a central fountain, and it may be presumed that there are still at least a few similar houses still in existence in the old city.

Finally, mention should be made of the very fine late Ottoman barrack-building of **Qasr Birka ★** in the southern part of the city (the coordinates are N 32° 5.75' E 20° 4.62'). The front elevation of this huge building (fig. 28) was completed by Rashid Pasha II in 1895 and the wings were added by the Italians. (The date 1911 on the keystone of the portal relates to Italian work.) After many years of neglect, its restoration was begun before the revolution of 2011 (in which it suffered further damage due to its proximity to the current military barracks); it is to be hoped that it will be resumed.

The Gardens of the Hesperides and Lake Tritonis

By the Hellenistic period, if not earlier, the vicinity of Benghazi had come to be associated with an ancient Greek myth concerning the Hesperides ('Daughters

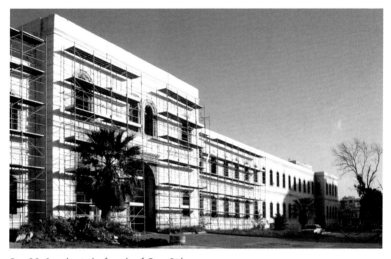

Fig. 28. Benghazi: the façade of Qasr Birka.

of the Evening') who tended a garden in which grew a magical tree bearing golden apples. The tree was guarded by a dragon, and one of the twelve labours which the demi-god Herakles was challenged to undertake by King Eurystheus was to steal the apples. The original tradition clearly located the garden somewhere in the extreme west (towards the sunset), but it was later associated with the neighbourhood of Euesperides and with the curious phenomenon of sinkholes in the limestone crust which characterise the terrain around Benghazi. There are many of these, where the dissolution of the crust by water has resulted in sunken areas, some tens of metres deep and sometimes over a hundred metres across, either water-filled in the bottom or with a well-watered soil which is home to a luxuriance of vegetation, fruit trees and palms. The crowns of the palm trees are often level with the surrounding terrain. One can easily understand how these sunken gardens came to be associated with the legend of the Garden of the Hesperides.

The largest of the depressions is situated at the village of **Kuwayfiyah** and is known as al-Tara ('the wonder'). Many years ago this was a quiet and beautiful place, full of birdsong. Latterly, it has shared the fate of most depressions in the landscape in urban areas of Libya, in becoming a refuse tip; but it is to be hoped that it may be rescued from this condition before it is lost completely. To find it, leave Benghazi on the coast road to Tukrah; after passing the power-station on the coast to your L, you will come to Ain Zayana, a beautiful blue lake which is open to the sea. Directly opposite this lake at N32° 12.79′ E20° 9.88′ is a road heading inland; follow this in a straight line for slightly less than a kilometre, and it will bring you to the rim of the depression.

A second depression associated with the ancient legends is currently inaccessible within the military academy to the N of the Baninah (airport) road. Here, at N 32° 6.97′ E20° 9.42′, the **Jokh al-Kibir** is a deep depression entered by a flight of (modern) steps, which leads down to a lake in a cavern. This was identified by ancient writers with Lethe, the River of Forgetfulness of which all souls were required to drink when entering the Underworld (a less than promising asset for a military academy!).

A final feature of the ancient landscape which is worthy of comment is **Lake Tritonis**. According to the geographer Strabo, writing in the first century AD, there was close to Berenice a lake of this name with an island in the middle, upon which stood a temple of Aphrodite. One suggestion for its identification is the small lake of Bukhayrat Bu Dzirah, on the right-hand side of the main road to Tukrah, approximately 8.5 km from the centre of Benghazi. This lake, fed from an underground source (and apparently the largest fresh-water lake between Tunis and Alexandria!) is now a leisure park equipped with water-slides. It has an island in the centre, upon which are masonry foundations 'of uncertain antiquity'. This might have been Lake Tritonis, but it has also been proposed that the lake was the lagoon whose water lapped both Berenice and Euesperides; in this case the island might have been the high ground at Sidi Husayn (close to the Tibesti Hotel). I have followed this hypothesis in figure 23, showing this area as an island at the mouth of the ancient lagoon.

HADRIANOPOLIS   دريانه

Coordinates: N 32° 21.56', E 20° 18.91'
Directions: The coordinates are those of the mosque mentioned below. To reach this, if approaching from Benghazi, fork left (keeping to the 'old' road where the main road now by-passes Daryanah) at N 32° 19.57' E 20° 17.18'; if approaching from the opposite direction, fork R onto the 'old' road at N 32° 21.96' E 20° 20.97'.

From either direction, you need to turn off towards the sea at the extreme northern end of the current settlement of Daryanah, at N 32° 21.49' E 20° 19.59'. At a T-junction after 400 m, turn L and after a further 400 m, follow the asphalt road, which turns 90° to the right. The mosque is a further 450 m towards the sea, and a track on the L, shortly after the turn, leads towards it.

Failed Roman town

The name of Hadrianopolis, a city founded by Hadrian after the Jewish Revolt in the second century AD, is perpetuated in the modern place-name Daryanah, on the coast slightly more than half-way from Benghazi to Tukrah. Traces of the ancient settlement were recorded in 1969, including elements of a street grid, but very little now remains. The most extensive ancient masonry was found in the immediate vicinity of the mosque of Sidi Ibrahim al-Ghamari. Between the mosque and its cemetery were said to be lines of masonry indicating a street running parallel to the coast. Gravediggers in the cemetery have apparently, in the past, fallen through into ancient cisterns beneath! However, recent activity by a bulldozer on the seaward side of the mosque has all but obliterated anything that was here. A quarry is located about 800 m to the S: to reach it, return to the main road through the village and head towards Benghazi for a distance of 1.6 km. Turn towards the sea again along the right-hand side of a school; the quarry will be found behind the houses and round to the R, at N 32° 21.06' E 20° 18.83'. It has recently become a rubbish tip, and this may already have been the fate of a smaller quarry nearby, which incorporated rock-cut tombs with Greek inscriptions at their entrances, naming their occupants: of this, no trace could be identified in 2010.

Finds at the site have shown that there was some occupation here before the time of Hadrian, but it was probably never a very prosperous settlement, as it had no useful anchorage on the coast and only a meagre water supply, brought from the edge of the jabal 17 km to the SE by means of an aqueduct. This was partially traceable in 1969, but has now virtually disappeared. No evidence has been found of occupation in the Byzantine period.

TANSULUKH   تنسلوخ

Coordinates: N 32° 23.05′, E 20° 22.29′
Directions: The structures described below lie about 150 m to seaward of the main road between Benghazi and Tukrah, 2.9 km NE of the point at which the old road through the village of Daryanah merges with the main road. The ruins lie on open ground, just behind some recently abandoned buildings facing the main road.

Roman settlement

This is the site of an ancient settlement whose name is unknown. Two buildings immediately stand out. The first is a square watch-tower of some sort in finely-cut large ashlar masonry (fig. 29); it has an arched entrance on the W side, and the crown of a second arch (with distinctive projecting keystone) is visible in the interior. This building is most readily understood as having some military significance. Some 70 m to the W of that is a fully ditched rectangular qasr faced with medium-sized ashlar blocks. Similar masonry has been used to face part of the outer edge of the ditch. Very little can be made out of the internal arrangement of this building: there are traces of walls in crude rubble masonry, but no visible arches. It has been inferred that the building was a church, but this cannot be stated with confidence.

In the flat, stony terrain round about, scattered orthostats suggest the doorways of several other buildings, also elements of olive-presses. Close to two rows of blocks which seem to have been arranged in recent times as a vehicle service-ramp, the base of a Roman milestone pokes out of the bushes. The visible remains appear to be late Roman in character.

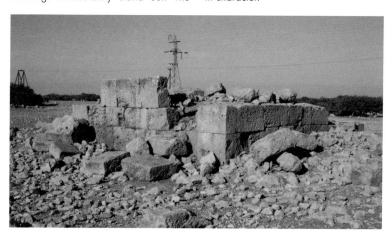

Fig. 29. Tansulukh: the base of a (military?) watch-tower.

TAUCHEIRA
(TOCRA, TUKRAH) ★ ★ توكرة
by Ahmad Buzaian
Coordinates: N 32° 32.39′, E 20° 34.15′
Directions: The coordinates refer to the entrance to the ancient site. In order to reach it when coming along the coast road from Benghazi, it is necessary first of all to leave the main (by-pass) road at N 32° 30.77′ E 20° 32.53′ where it curves away to the R. Continue straight on for 3.5 km into the centre of the modern settlement of Tukrah and then turn L (crossing straight over a roundabout) onto the road to Dirsiya/Ptolemais. After the roundabout, take the first L, which brings you rapidly into the centre of the (now decaying) 20th-century colonial-period village. Continue straight on, and the road terminates at the entrance to the Turco-Italian fort. On your return, you may leave the old village square to the R of where you entered it: this will bring you back to the centre of the modern town without difficulty.

The site of ancient Taucheira (or Teucheira) lies on the Mediterranean coast 69 km NE of Euesperides/Berenice (modern Benghazi), where the coastal plain starts to open out to the W between the plateau of the Jabal Akhdar and the sea. The plain, which is here about 6 km wide, is a semi-arid zone with an average annual rainfall today of 160 mm, although the higher ground to the S receives up to 500 mm around al-Marj on the Lower Plateau, and over 500 mm on the Upper Plateau. The rainfall average allows the cultivation of wheat and barley and the raising of livestock. The city has not been extensively excavated, although it has now become the site of annual training excavations by Benghazi University.

Taucheira, like Apollonia, was said to have been founded from Cyrene. Excavations by the British School at Athens of deposits associated with a sanctuary of Demeter and Kore (on the foreshore) produced material from the late seventh century BC onwards, suggesting that the city was founded shortly after the traditional date for the foundation of Cyrene, 631 BC. Herodotus seems to imply that in the fifth century BC Taucheira came under the control of Barka; in the late fourth century it was besieged by Thibron (p. 4), and it came under Ptolemaic rule in 322 BC with the rest of Cyrenaica. The city received the name *Arsinoë* during the Hellenistic period; it has been widely assumed until recently that the granting of this name, together with the 'foundation' of *Ptolemais* to the E (p. 68) and the resiting of Euesperides as *Berenice* to the W (p. 40), relates to the re-assertion of Alexandrian control over Cyrenaica by Ptolemy III Euergetes in 246 BC. However, it has been pointed out that in the case of Taucheira there is no independent evidence in support of this specific date. The mother of Ptolemy I was called Arsinoë, as was the wife of Ptolemy II (who was the mother of Ptolemy III); Ptolemy IV also married an Arsinoë – so there are many different dates between 322 and 220 BC when this name might have been bestowed on the city! At a later period it became a Roman colony, and it seems to have reverted to being Taucheira in Roman times.

Taucheira/Arsinoë was one of the five cities of the Cyrenaican Pentapolis. Little is known in detail of the city's history: it will have participated in the experiences of the region as a whole. At the time of the Arab invasion, Taucheira had been chosen by the Byzantine administration as a last stronghold, probably because it had a natural supply of abundant groundwater within the wall circuit and was not therefore dependent on an aqueduct like the other cities of the Pentapolis. It was by-passed in the light-

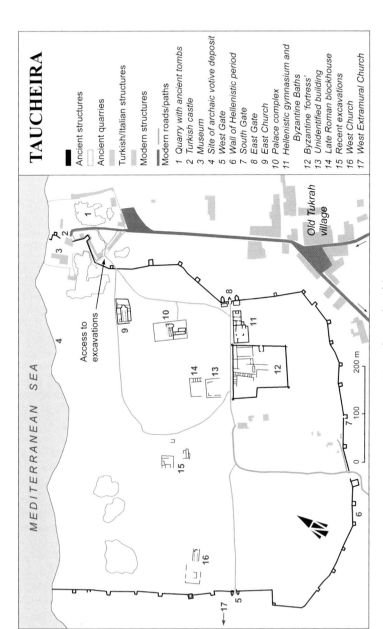

TAUCHEIRA

■ Ancient structures

☐ Ancient quarries

Turkish/Italian structures

Modern structures

Modern roads/paths

1 Quarry with ancient tombs
2 Turkish castle
3 Museum
4 Site of archaic votive deposit
5 West Gate
6 Wall of Hellenistic period
7 South Gate
8 East Gate
9 East Church
10 Palace complex
11 Hellenistic gymnasium and
   Byzantine Baths
12 Byzantine 'fortress'
13 Unidentified building
14 Late Roman blockhouse
15 Recent excavations
16 West Church
17 West Extramural Church

MEDITERRANEAN SEA

Access to
excavations

Old Tukrah
village

0   100   200 m

Fig. 30. Taucheira: plan of the site.

ning dash of 642, but the governor and the last of his garrison must have been expelled by the second Arab expedition of 644–5. Occupation of the site seems, however, to have continued possibly until the 10th century AD.

The general layout of the archaeological site is shown in figure 30; numbers relating to features refer to this drawing. The original settlement of the Archaic period seems to have lain between the quarries by the Turkish fort to the E, and quarries later incorporated within the Hellenistic wall circuit to the W. In the Hellenistic period the city expanded and received an enlarged wall circuit, apparently rebuilt on much the same lines in the early Roman period, and restored in the Byzantine era.

The later city was laid out on a grid plan dominated by a thoroughfare running between the E and W gates (conventionally termed the *Decumanus Maximus*); two further E–W streets are traceable to the north of this, crossed by N–S streets running at a slightly skewed angle. The *insula* blocks do not lie in regular, straight rows, but are somewhat staggered, an arrangement that would have provided some shelter from the strong north-westerly and north-easterly winds. A mound of rubble at the intersection of the main E–W and N–S streets may have been a triumphal arch.

Underwater exploration has shown that Taucheira had an artificial harbour with two quays and a mole 220 m long. The city's cemeteries were located within former quarries, with rock-cut chambers bearing Greek inscriptions: a mixed population is suggested by some with Jewish names, and also Egyptian names for the months. A large inhumation cemetery lay just outside the east wall.

Most of the standing remains on land date from the Roman to early Islamic peri-

ods, but they are not well understood. A building (10) to the south of the East Church has a Christian mosaic, but may originally have served as a set of baths or have had some other function. The East and West Churches (9, 16) are both thought to belong to the sixth-century; a third church (17), outside the walls some 200 m W of the Berenice gate, is probably also of the sixth century. Another extramural church, to the S, is now partly covered by a mosque. Inside the walls, a Hellenistic gymnasium (11) lay immediately inside the East Gate, later partly succeeded by a Roman bath-house which was modified during the Byzantine period and which may have continued in use yet later. To the S of the *decumanus* and W of the baths, a large Byzantine fortress (12) was constructed hastily, and without foundations, over previous buildings. This used stone taken from other monuments, especially the nearby baths, which were partly demolished to provide a clear field of fire. Barracks and a small bath-house, possibly for senior officers, have been identified within the fortress. The fortress was probably constructed in the face of the Arab advance after the Byzantine commander Apollonius withdrew from Apollonia to Arsinoë, and has therefore been identified as the last stronghold of Byzantine rule in Cyrenaica. It might on the other hand have been built in 618, on the occasion of the Sasanid invasion of Egypt (p. 9). Secondary structures built against the outside of this fortress on the NW side must post-date any defensive function and are therefore likely to be of Islamic date.

The entrance to the site is, imposingly, the entrance to the Turco-Italian fort, built in and around the ancient quarries on the NE side of the city.

Quarries ★ (1)

The quarries of Taucheira were cut in consolidated dune deposits that are generally frequent along the coastline of the Benghazi plain. These low rounded fossil dunes are datable to the Pleistocene age and they are composed of minute shell fragments cemented with calcite (= calcarenite); they often have the appearance of sandstone. The fossil dunes have played an important role as a source of building stone since classical times. The use of abandoned quarries as locations for rock-cut tombs was a common practice in the coastal cities of Cyrenaica.

At Taucheira, there are over 30 quarries extending alongside the coast on the E and W sides of the city; some are located inside the city and many of these housed rock-cut tomb-chambers. These, as was the case at other Cyrenaican sites, attracted the attention of the 19th-century explorers and European consuls based in Benghazi and became subject to extensive looting.

Hundreds of funerary inscriptions were carved either on the façades of the quarries or inside the chambers or on loose gravestones. The Beechey brothers in 1822 are considered the first foreign travellers to have copied many of them. They were followed by J.-R. Pacho in 1825 who copied over 120 different inscriptions. Almost all of them were written in the Greek language because of the prevailing Greek culture even when the province passed under Roman rule. Often the inscriptions show the date of death (day-month-year), the name of the deceased and the name of his father, and age at death. Ancient Egyptian months were used in some of the inscriptions, such as Mesore (May 15–June 15), Thoth (June 15–July 15) and Mekhir (November 15–December 15). Personal names are often indicative of the origin of those who passed away and of their religion: most of them were Roman, Libyan or Jewish and their religions varied from paganism to Judaism and Christianity.

After passing through the modern gate of the fort there are, on the R of the path, Roman tombs cut in previous quarries (1). The first one is composed of a stepped *dromos* leading to a sunken court with 17 openings leading to small chambers with burial recesses. On its eastern side, and opposite the entrance, are chambers of less systematic organisation with few recesses and a couple of rough cists dug in the floor. The chamber on the L of the *dromos* shows more organized recesses and a much better planning of space.

Turco-Italian fort (2)

Situated at the NE corner of the city on relatively high ground which overlooks the coast, the little Turkish castle enjoys a strategic location within the expanded circuit of Italian date. Federico Halbherr, during his visit to the city in 1910, was the first traveller to mention the castle: he believed that it was built on the ancient acropolis of the city. Remains of Tower 31 were in fact incorporated in the S wall of the building (detectable by virtue of its larger blocks and the vertical straight joints next to it). Halbherr reported that a small garrison was resident at the castle and that there was a telegraph station.

The Turkish building witnessed episodes of later modification and alteration that hinder the identification of its original plan. Only the outer wall can be assigned to the first phase building: this was built of ashlar stone extracted from the nearby city wall. In 1913 Italian troops occupied Tukrah. On the western side of the castle, they added a stairway of seven steps leading to a small entrance. They established an upper storey and added a watchtower, a kitchen and two other rooms. The outer wall-circuit is also of Italian date.

The fort witnessed the execution of two Libyans during the Italian occupation of the country. During the Second World War the town was briefly occupied by Australian forces, who were then expelled by German and Italian forces until it was seized definitively by the Allies in 1943. Thereafter the fort was occupied by the British military administration. In the late 1960s it passed into the hands of the Department of Antiquities. Within the enclosure there are now workshops, storerooms, a small rest house (below the path on the L) and a museum (behind the Turkish castle).

The area of the ancient city is reached through a gate in the Italian wall-circuit on the left-hand side, beyond the first range of buildings next to the main gate (fig. 30).

Museum (3)

The first museum at Taucheira was opened for a temporary period during the year 1945 to exhibit the grave goods found in a small excavation of tombs conducted by RAF officers. In 1972 a larger museum was opened to the W of the Turkish fort. The major part of the collection on display consisted of painted Greek pottery from an emergency excavation carried out on the foreshore (at 4 in fig. 30) in 1963–5. Here, coastal erosion had exposed part of a votive deposit belonging to a sanctuary dedicated to Demeter and Kore. The finds ranged in date between the last quarter of the seventh century BC and the third quarter of the sixth; the pottery included Athenian, Corinthian, Laconian, Cycladic and Rhodian products.

Unfortunately, at the time of writing, this interesting museum is closed and awaiting renovation.

Defences ★

The city wall is undoubtedly the most striking monument at Taucheira and it impressed many European travellers during their visits to the region. The defences are over 2 km long with a curtain wall up to 2m wide, flanked by 31 rectangular towers, excluding those flanking the East and West Gates. Three sides of the circuit are preserved with little interruption, while little survives of the seafront wall as a direct consequence of wave action and erosion. The defences were first built in the Hellenistic period and rebuilt in late Hellenistic or early Roman times; they were reinforced under Justinian and finally witnessed some modifications to gates and towers when the city was selected by the Byzantines for their last stand in Cyrenaica against Islamic troops in AD 642–5.

Generally, the wall was constructed with local sandstone ashlar laid in alternate courses of headers and stretchers with very few parts built with only large stretchers. Three different styles of ashlar blocks were used in the construction. The masonry of the first period took the form of isodomic blocks with hammered faces and drafted margins: this technique can be seen immediately N of the West Gate (5). The masonry of the first reconstruction (period II) was also isodomic but with light diagonal cut marks and bevelled edges: this survives in the curtain between Towers 13 and 14 (6) and on both sides of the portal of the East Gate (8), in the lower courses of its flanking towers. The rest of the curtain was generally of plain ashlar blocks as visible in the surviving towers: this is Justinianic work.

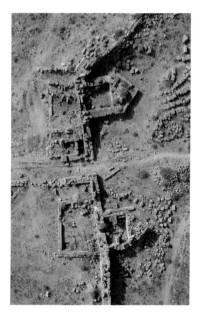

Fig. 31. Taucheira: aerial view of the East Gate. Photo by Miron Bogacki.

At the seaward end of the E side, the curtain wall kinked outwards to make use of a free standing rock-wall which had been left between two earlier quarries. After that, the course of the wall headed towards the Turco-Italian fort and passed under its south wall (at Tower 31, already mentioned). The circuit was completed by a wall running along the coast itself: this has largely been destroyed by erosion, but a few traces still remain.

The West Gate (5)

This has been cleared down to the road surface of the *Decumanus Maximus* and has an opening 3.45 m wide. In the second period the gateway was protected on either side by two projecting rectangular towers in bevelled ashlar masonry. These were initially quite asymmetrical: the one at the N was set off 2.40 m from the portal and was about 5.50 m

wide with a forward projection of 3.55 m, while that on the S was set off 1.40 m from the gateway and was c. 6.0 m wide, projecting 4.38 m. In the Byzantine period both towers were modified to have almost the same width but with triangular fronts projecting considerably further.

The South Gate (7)

Close examination of Tower 17 shows a large opening (3.34 m wide) in the N wall of the tower with the remains of a semi-circular arch above. This opening indicates that this was originally a gateway on the south side of the city and seems possibly to mark the south end of the *cardo maximus*. The gateway was (subsequently?) enclosed within the tower, which is of Byzantine construction with a guard-chamber and a small postern in the W face.

The East Gate ★ (8)

This was located at the opposite end of the *Decumanus Maximus* to the West Gate (fig. 31). The dimensions of this gate give the impression that it functioned as the principal access to the walled city and, although less prominent, may even have been considered to match the so-called Taucheira Gate at Ptolemais (p. 94). The portal was rebuilt in the late Roman period with an opening 3.10 m wide and with provision for both hinged portals and a portcullis. The present N and S flanking towers with triangular fronts (as those of the West Gate) are of Byzantine date but conform to foundations of the early Roman period. The towers are set well apart and project over 12 m forward of the curtain. Only 1.55 m outside the portal of the East Gate are remains of an unusual V-shaped structure. This late feature effectively prevented frontal access to the gate and must have been erected hastily as a defence against bombardment or ramming. (It has no foundations.) It could be circumvented by wheeled traffic in peaceful times, but only with difficulty.

The Proteichisma

An extra-mural or outer defence (known as a *proteichisma*) appears to belong to the early Byzantine period. It runs parallel to the line of the city wall and a short distance from it; it is some 2 m wide and composed of disturbed building stones. This feature is evident in three sections: a line of stone-works at the point where the western wall meets the sea, another in a tract to the S of the West Gate and the third outside the E wall to the S of the East Gate.

East Church ★ (9)

This is the first building that one encounters when entering the site from the direction of the Turkish fort. It was partially excavated before the Second World War and has been further explored since. The excavated complex (figs. 32, 33) is composed of a three-aisled columnar basilica with a range of rooms, including what appears to be some kind of ceremonial hall, along the south side; a narrow western narthex; and a further northern range, with a possible small atrium. It should be noted that part of the enclosing wall is modern.

The nave colonnades, which had Attic bases and Doric capitals, stood on plinths. Slots cut in the tops of these plinths and in the column-bases indicate the former position of screen-slabs, which separated the nave from the aisles and enclosed the eastern half of the nave as a chancel. Parts of a re-used Inscription can be seen in the plinths of the nave colonnade: this records Hadrian's gift of a basilica to the city, suggesting that the church was built out of the ruins of a former civil basilica. The flooring of the nave and aisles is of calcarenite (sandy limestone) flags; in the S aisle, however, there are fragments of a mosaic floor which was mostly removed,

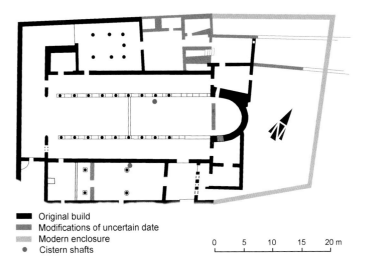

■ Original build
▨ Modifications of uncertain date
▨ Modern enclosure
● Cistern shafts

0   5   10   15   20 m

Fig. 32. Taucheira: plan of the East Church.

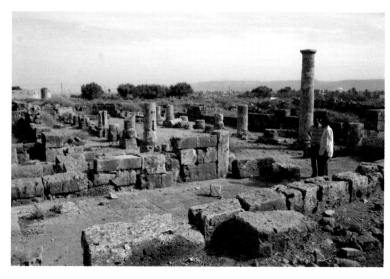

Fig. 33. Taucheira: the East Church from the W.

but preserved here after being covered by a bench. Beneath the nave is a large rock-cut cistern, probably pre-dating the church but retained for its needs.

The apse was constructed independently of the adjoining rooms: there are angle-chapels and vestibules on either side, added rather irregularly. The vestibule on the N appears to have provided access from a street to the E. A doorway cut through the apse masonry on the S side, but later blocked, gave access to a chapel with a small adjoining room. These two rooms are paved with a distinctive white limestone, and were presumably linked in function.

The E end of the S aisle was connected by an archway with a square vestibule, which seems to have been a principal entrance on this side. A similar arched doorway led from this vestibule westwards into a large hall, divided into three roughly equal bays by two pairs of columns. (A dividing-wall in the western part of the hall is secondary.) A shaft into a cistern was cut through the floor of the

hall against the south wall of the nave. This cistern was lined with waterproof mortar and was probably connected to the other cistern located in the nave. The hall was paved with calcarenite slabs and two steps towards the W end led up to a raised area with a marble pavement. In the centre of the W wall is a projecting rectangular slab which is raised even higher, suggesting the presence of a throne. A doorway placed in the north wall of this room gave direct access to the south aisle. These features suggest an audience hall for the use of the presiding bishop.

At the western end and running right across the building was a narrow corridor-like narthex, of which the central part was open to its full width into the nave and flanked by half-columnar pilasters set on the line of the nave colonnades.

The north wing, alongside the street, has been partially robbed and the chronology and purpose of its various components is not clear. Towards the W is a small atrium with six different re-used columns: two are of local stone, monolithic but grooved as if composed of separate drums; others are of grey marble. The room has been interpreted as a baptistery or as a *martyrion*, but there is no evidence for either interpretation. Amongst the rooms to the E of this is the base of a stairway. On the vertical face of the lowest step is carved a plain cross, while the fourth step carries another fragment of the Hadrianic inscription previously mentioned.

The extensive use of spolia to construct the church, and the total absence (apart perhaps from the surviving mosaic in the S aisle) of any identifiable sixth-century fittings, have led to the conclusion that the church was built in the fifth century AD.

Palace complex ★ (10)

Some 100 m to the S of the East Church lies a complex which was partly excavated in 1972 by the Archaeological Department of Benghazi University. The building occupies a whole *insula* of about 38.50 × 72 m (fig. 34). The northern part of the structure (built around a peristyle) was not fully investigated. The elements of this building which have been revealed so far are as follows: a long corridor flanking the SE side of the peristyle; a wide hall with an apse towards the SE and associated lateral rooms; a longer apsed hall, entered via two antechambers; a large rectangular tank located immediately along the NE side of this, two other tanks and a vaulted underground chamber.

The corridor occupies most of the NW end of the excavated area. It is evident that the corridor originally bordered a peristyle. Remains of the stylobate and the bases of some columns of the peristyle are preserved *in situ*. A principal

access to the corridor at the SW end was framed by monolithic piers carrying a finely decorated semi-circular arch, the blocks of which now lie on the ground nearby; towards the opposite end, a wide entrance led southwards into a large hall with an inscribed apse at the far end. The apse was flanked by semi-circular niches on both sides. A small marble column was found in the centre of the apse. The communication between this large room and those on either side of it was probably through triple archways (partially blocked at a later date). The voussoirs of a triple arcade now laid out in the corridor probably belong to one of these openings. To the west of the principal hall there was a succession of rooms, some of which were furnished with benches.

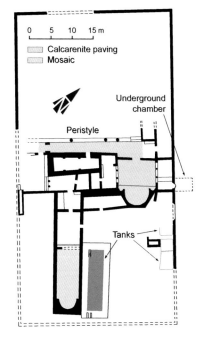

Fig. 34. Taucheira: plan of the 'palace' complex.

The walls of the corridor and the hall were built of carefully worked ashlar masonry and both had a perfectly laid out pavement of regular calcarenite slabs.

An underground vaulted chamber of uncertain purpose was found to the NE of the hall. (The absence of any water-proof lining precludes the possibility that it was a cistern.) To the SE of this were two tanks lined with waterproof mortar. They were rectangular in shape and one was bounded on its NW side by a gen-tly sloping mortared ramp (as if draining water away from a working surface).

In the southern part of the complex there was a second, more elongated, rectangular hall with an apse towards the SE. Four floor levels have been reported: two successive polychrome mosaic floors and above them one of mortar and one of plaster. The latest of these is typical of refurbishment after the Arab conquest. The later mosaic floor which had been partially destroyed (now lifted but not on display) presented in each of the four corners one of the rivers of Paradise. (Parts of Euphrates and Phison survive, represented as pagan gods like those shown on the mosaic floor of the East Church at Qasr Libya, p. 134.) In front of the apse were three figures stand-ing side by side, each displayed under one of the arches of a triple arcade and representing personifications of *Ktisis* (Foundation), *Kosmesis* (Adornment) and *Ananeosis* (Renewal). Below them was a Nilotic scene bordered by representa-tions of rural life. This mosaic was laid in the sixth century, probably by the same mosaicists who worked at Qasr Libya in 538/9.

The earlier floor, which has been dated to the fourth or fifth century AD and is still *in situ*, is composed of 55 panels representing birds, animals, fish, flowers and baskets of fruit; below the

design, across the threshold, is a long rectangular panel containing a Greek inscription between crosses which is an Old-Testament salutation: 'Your entry (arrival?) is peace, high priest, the seer'.

A large rectangular tank (14 × 3.70 m) is located immediately to the NE of the apsed hall with steps for access to the water at the W corner. Water flowed into the tank through a channel with sluice-gate in the S corner. The tank has been interpreted as a baptismal basin and the adjacent hall as a *consignatorium*, or chapel where the newly baptised were confirmed into the Church. However, while the Christian significance of the inscription in the mosaic is clear from the crosses at either end, the hall has quite the wrong orientation for a chapel and the tank has none of the characteristics of a baptistery. It is more likely, in view of the proximity of the East Church, that this is part of the bishop's palace. The combination of rooms which has been exposed is remarkably similar to that found in the House of the Triapsidal Hall at Ptolemais (p. 77). Both have two con-temporary apsidal halls, one wide (a dining room?) and one narrow (an audi-ence hall?) and both have fish-tanks or pools in the courtyard or garden.

Gymnasium ★ (11)

The site of the Hellenistic gymnasium lies on the S of the *Decumanus Maximus* and just inside the East Gate. It is iden-tifiable from a series of ephebic inscrip-tions (relating to the athletes) both along the outer wall flanking the road and on the inner face of the defensive wall nearby (which in this section is Hellenis-tic in date: fig. 35). In certain places, this front wall is well preserved to a height of six courses of the original construc-tion. The overall length of the remaining front wall of the gymnasium is 38.25 m.

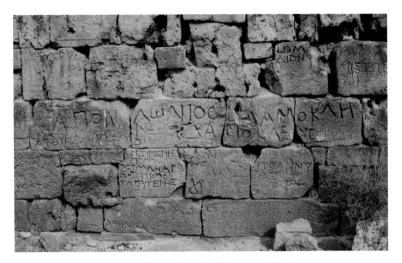

Fig. 35. Taucheira: ephebic graffiti on the inside of the city wall by the East Gate.

From the evidence, it seems possible that the gymnasium was first founded in the Hellenistic period and the texts, as they survive, run from approximately the second century BC to some time around the middle of the second century AD. It was perhaps abandoned as a result of the Jewish Revolt of AD 115–7 or it may have continued well into the third century AD, though there were no later inscriptions similar to those previously cut on the front wall. During the Byzantine period the outer wall of the gymnasium was retained and the interior modified to house a bath-house (see below).

The gymnasium was more than just a gym in the modern sense of the word. Sport was recognized as a very Greek custom; visiting the gymnasium was stressing one's 'Greekness'. The ephebic inscriptions cut on the wall can be divided into two main groups. The first consists of unframed graffiti on blocks found on the inner face of the city wall immediately south of the East Gate (which must here have formed part of the gymnasium enclosure), and on the

inside of the gymnasium wall. These consist mostly of personal names, often in pairs and with an indication that these pairs were friends or lovers. They are thought to be Hellenistic. The second series, which probably all belong to the Roman imperial period, consists of dates with Latin names rendered in the Greek alphabet; the letters are neatly cut and normally framed by a representation of a wreath, a *tabula ansata* or a palm branch. These may be seen on the N face of the gymnasium wall, facing the street. Names presented in wreaths are a common occurrence throughout the Greek world and represent victors in an athletic competition. A few of the graffiti show dates in the Actian era, others seem to be regnal years of Roman emperors. These carved names constitute an important source of information on the population of Taucheira. Many favoured Cyrenaican Greek names were exhibited in these texts such as Arimmas, Barkaios, Jason, Karnedas. Some less familiar ones, such as Aeropos and Telephos, may have been specifically local.

Byzantine bath-house

Within the ruins of the Hellenistic gymnasium and against its N wall was built a bath-house in the Byzantine period (fig. 36). The entrance to the baths appears to have made use of the original gymnasium entrance, and to have comprised a triple opening, subsequently much altered. This led into an *atrium* with an asymmetrical portico; from the N corner of the portico,

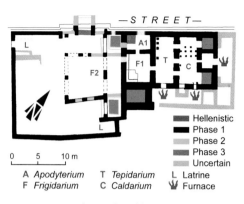

Hellenistic	
Phase 1	
Phase 2	
Phase 3	
Uncertain	

A Apodyterium	T Tepidarium	L Latrine
F Frigidarium	C Caldarium	🜏 Furnace

Fig. 36. Taucheira: plan of the Byzantine Baths.

a door led through a vestibule (the *apodyterium*) into a *frigidarium* with a bench along two sides. (But was it a *frigidarium*? The reported presence of *pilae* indicates that the floor was heated.) On the S side of this was a high-level cistern. On the NE side of the *frigidarium* were two heated rooms, with hot plunge-baths in the further one. The furnaces were serviced from the NE and SE sides.

In a second phase, two cold plunge-baths were installed in the *atrium*, converting this (in part at least) into a *frigidarium*. The northerly plunge-bath obstructed the previous entrance to the heated rooms, and a new one was broken through the intervening wall a little further to the S. (It may have been at this time, if not before, that the former 'frigidarium' became a heated room.) The *atrium* colonnade was also partly walled up in this phase, and the entrance from the street was remodelled, with the retention of only a single opening which was extended forward into the street. Of uncertain date is a latrine in the W corner of the *atrium* — though since another latrine in the E corner seems to have been eclipsed by the second plunge-bath, its insertion may have been part of the same reorganization of the *atrium* area.

Phase 3 involved further substantial modifications. The original street entrance was now completely closed, and two new openings were cut through the surviving wall of the Hellenistic gymnasium. One of these was opposite one of the cold plunge-baths, which must have been suppressed, and the second led into the Phase 1 *apodyterium*. Within the former *apodyterium* a tiny cold plunge-bath was now installed, and a bench or platform in one corner of the Phase 1 *frigidarium* has also been attributed to this phase.

The complex as a whole is undoubtedly Byzantine, but cannot be closely dated. The discovery of an Arabic inscription in praise of Allah has been cited as evidence of continued use following the Arab conquest, but the inscription cannot now be found and its reported position makes little sense. None the less, the alterations of Phase 3 may belong to the Islamic period.

Byzantine 'fortress' ★ (12)

On the south side of the *Decumanus Maximus*, immediately to the west of the Byzantine baths, is a vast complex of late date and evidently hasty construction (fig. 37). The complex is L-shaped, measuring 119 × 112 m. The exterior walls are thick and have a defensive character. The four outer corners were reinforced by circular and rectangular towers. The circular towers are located at both ends of the NW wall while the rectangular ones are on the SE side. There was a single entrance almost in the middle of the NE wall.

It seems that the complex was constructed in great haste. Its walls were built of re-used stones and rested directly on earlier walls and compacted earth, resulting in uneven subsidence. The names of the emperors Valentinian and Valens (AD 363–7) appear on an inscription re-used within the E end of the N wall, providing a *terminus post quem* for the structure. It is likely that it was built either in 618, when Cyrenaica would have felt threatened by the Sasanid occupation of Egypt, or in the face of the Arab invasion of 642–5. If it was built at the earlier date, the corner-towers (which are secondary) may have been added on the latter occasion. It has been questioned by some whether the complex was sufficiently defensible to be described as a fortress, and whether it should not be thought of more as a military barrack. Walls of later structures, which adjoin the NW wall of the complex and extend across the line of the former *decumanus*, must be of Islamic date.

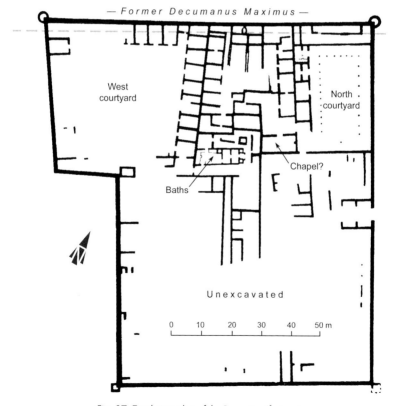

Fig. 37. Taucheira: plan of the Byzantine 'fortress'.

The interior was occupied by roughly constructed buildings clustered around two main courtyards located in the N and W corners. The first has a relatively comfortable residential aspect while the latter appears to have had a peristyle of wooden uprights and the rooms lining the courtyard were almost certainly intended for the accommodation of the soldiers. The W peristyle received a second phase of modification, probably on the eve of the Islamic conquest by Amr Ibn al-Aasi. A small bath suite is sited near the centre of the fortress. It consisted of a furnace flanked by two small hot plunge-baths; the floors of the *caldarium* and the *tepidarium* were supported on stone uprights. Further W, the *frigidarium* and the *apodyterium*, with benches set around its walls, were also identifiable. The layout is essentially similar to that of the larger baths immediately to the E. The small size of this bath suggests that it was specially reserved for superior authority, the commander of the garrison. It has also been suggested that there may be a palace chapel with an access from the S corner of the N courtyard. (This seems to be based solely on the presence of a curious round-headed stele with a cross carved on it, now lying loose in the room.)

The interior of the southern part of the complex has not been excavated.

Immediately across the *decumanus* from the fortress is an **area of ruins** (13) which was initially investigated by Italian soldiers in 1914, and then partly excavated by G. Pesce in 1940. There seems to be a large peristyle here which was once adorned with Corinthian capitals in local calcarenite; the capitals are 'inhabited' by human figures. Within the peristyle are signs of later industrial activity (vats and a furnace). To the NW of this is a **blockhouse** (14) in ashlar masonry with projecting string-courses; this is a style of construction which is found in the Fortress of the Dux at Ptolemais (p. 80) and which is characteristic of many late Roman buildings in the countryside.

Recent excavations (15)

During recent years, the Department of Archaeology of Benghazi University has been conducting training excavations in the central part of the ancient site. The structures exposed are confusing to the eye, and are not grandiose public buildings. Rather, they demonstrate a long and important sequence of occupation, extending from the Hellenistic period until early Islamic times. The buildings are modest, and show various signs of 'non-residential' use, such as a pottery kiln in the Hellenistic period and storage/fermentation vats in the Roman period. The absence of structures earlier than the Hellenistic period (together with the discovery of a Hellenistic kiln, which is not to be expected in a residential area) suggest that the nucleus of the earlier settlement did not extend this far inland. On the other hand, the early Islamic material confirms the persistence of a settlement at Taucheira for a considerable while following the Islamic conquest and the departure of the Byzantine administration.

West Church (16)

This lies near the west edge of the city about 80 m N of the West Gate. The church is a complicated structure, incorporating work of many different periods. The whole complex is largely masked by rubble and the internal arrangement is largely unclear. Although in its present state only the main lines of the building and other annexes can be made out, a great deal of it must in fact be preserved, awaiting excavation. It is, however, possible to make out the layout of a three-aisled arcaded basilica with an eastern apse. The nave was divided from the aisles by two rows of nine piers capped by single horizontal slabs with several springer blocks. The most distinctive feature is the horseshoe-shaped apse with an outer face of regular squared blocks. A curious feature here is a small semicircular stone-lined recess placed not concentric with the curve of the apse but on the centre-line of the opening. This could possibly be the remains of a *synthronon*, but the shape would be unique. A narthex-like transverse feature at the west end perhaps leads to an extensive forecomplex, like that associated with the West Church at Apollonia (p. 260).

The Church is very close to Tower 6 of the defences. The solid construction of this tower and of the adjoining curtain wall to the N, together with the presence, around the tower and fallen from it, of several carved window-mullions bearing crosses, suggests that this part of the Byzantine defences may have formed a part of the ecclesiastical complex of the West Church. The church authorities were perhaps involved in some way in the construction and defence of this sector.

West Extramural Church (17)

Outside the city walls and the fence enclosing the archaeological zone, about 220 m SW of the West Gate on bare ground and adjacent to a small, shallow quarry is the outline of another (unexcavated) church (fig. 38: the location is N 32° 32.02′ E 20° 33.69′). The plan is rectangular with walls constructed mainly of squared stones, carefully dressed and laid. The outer S wall has been doubled with faced rubble masonry that may suggest external strengthening of a pre-existing structure.

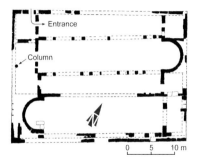

Fig. 38. Taucheira: plan of the W Extramural Church.

Two distinct architectural units are still detectable: a basilical church with an eastern apse, and a narrow hall running the full length of the south side of the building with a small anteroom at the E end and a semicircular apse towards the W. Access between the two parts was probably gained through a doorway between the south-east angle-chapel of the church and the antechamber. An arched doorway at the W end of the outer N wall led into three rooms that run the full width of the nave and aisles. Another arched doorway in the E wall of the first room gave access to the N aisle of the church. The central room was open to its full width on to the nave, through a wide archway. A re-used spirally fluted column of dark Rhodian marble was set against the W wall of the central room, perhaps as the focal point of a small shrine.

A number of rifled individual cist-graves was trenched into the rocky slope about 60 m NW of the church, close to the edge of a small quarry.

An excavation carried out on a low mound about 130 m NE of the church in 1974 revealed a pottery kiln with associated waste dumps. The kiln appeared to have been used for the manufacture of coarse pottery and lamps dated to the late second and early third centuries AD.

ZAWIYAT ASQAFAH   زاوية أسقفه

Coordinates: N 32° 15.77', E 20° 36.61'
Directions: This lies near the inland road
from Benghazi to al-Marj via Baninah and
al-Abyar. At N 32° 15.23' E 20° 37.95',
6.2 km from the northern edge of al-Abyar,
turn NW towards the zawiya, which is visible on the horizon. After 1.2 km, this road
swings round to the L: take the fork to the R
here which continues in the previous direction. After a further kilometre, the asphalt
road comes to an end at the zawiya. The
coordinates relate to the qasr, which lies
immediately to the SW of it.

Ancient settlement

Close to Zawiyat Asqafah (the stress
is on the first syllable) is the outline of
a large, approximately square building faced with large ashlar blocks. Little is preserved in elevation or by way
of internal detail, but round about are
the upstanding door-jambs and scattered stones of many more modest
buildings. Coins and pottery found on
the site extend at least from the fourth
century BC until the Arab conquest.
The ancient name of the settlement was
possibly *Chairekla*. The principal interest of this ancient village, however, lies
in a painted tomb of the fourth century
AD which was discovered in 1939.
This tomb lies 350 m almost due N of
the zawiya, at N 32° 15.96' E 20°
36.58'. It is entirely subterranean, but
may be identified from a distance by the
(decayed) fenced enclosure around it.

Tomb of Odysseus and
the Sirens ★

The painted tomb is cut into the rock of
the hillside, and is approached through
a vestibule which is also cut in the rock
but framed by ashlar masonry. Stone
steps lead down from the exterior,
through this vestibule, into an irregular,

but approximately square, chamber
(fig. 39). The walls of the chamber are
pierced by five *arcosolium* recesses for
burials and the internal surfaces are
plastered and painted throughout. On
the ceiling are representations of coffer-
ing, and on the walls is a combination
of 'carpet-style' trelliswork and a free
but lavish scattering of floral motifs.
There are also figural scenes.

Proceeding in a clockwise direction,
the first recess (a) has largely lost its plaster coating apart from a floral border; on
the wall between the first two *arcosolia*
is an indistinct figure which might be the
Sphinx, perched on her rock. The first
arcosolium on the far wall of the chamber (b) has a representation of a young
man at table, attended by a servant. On
the wall to the R of this is a naked female
figure, gesturing with the L hand (Aphrodite?). The next *arcosolium* (c) shows a
scene from the Trojan War, the death of
Troilus at the fountain (fig. 40): the youth
is attempting to escape on horseback,
but is seized by the hair by Achilles,
who has his sword ready to despatch
him. The female figure behind Achilles,
who witnesses the attack, should be Troilus' sister Polyxena. On the wall to the
R we find three sirens with female bodies terminating in birds' legs; they hold
musical instruments in their hands. To
their R, across the corner, is Odysseus
in his ship: he is tied to the mast and
several sailors are on deck around him.
Above, compressing two scenes from the
wanderings of Odysseus into one, is the
monster Scylla, in the form of a woman's
body with the foreparts of three snarling
dogs. She is brandishing an oar, and the
dogs are attempting to grasp the sailors
with their claws.

Within the first *arcosolium* on the
right-hand wall (d) is a picture of a ban-
quet, presided over by a wealthy land-

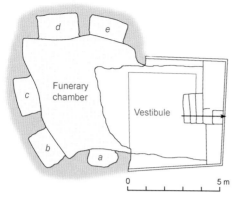

Fig. 39. Zawiyat Asqafah: plan of the Tomb of Odysseus and the Sirens.

the tomb of Achilles by his son Pyrrhus/Neoptolemus, in order to secure the favour of the gods for the homecoming of the Greek fleet.) Polyxena (identified by name) kneels, while she is seized by the hair by Pyrrhus (also named), who is standing and brandishing his sword. The decoration of the fifth recess (e) appears to be solely floral in character.

Scenes from Greek myth, and the Trojan cycle in particular, are not uncommon in tombs of the Classical period (compare the Tomb of Oedipus at Bayt Thamir, p. 296). There is an obvious preoccupation with death (usually violent), but the specific interpretations which have been put forward concerning the trials or conquests of the soul sometimes seem a little contrived. In this instance, the style of architecture and decoration are claimed to be characteristic of the latter part of the fourth century AD.

owner and his wife: they are attended by their servants, who bring them the fruits – and the wine – of their estate. (Perhaps it is their teenage son who is dining on his own in *arcosolium* b!) Between this and the next recess, we see another scene from the Trojan cycle: the sacrifice of Polyxena. (This Trojan girl, who earlier witnessed the death of her brother Troilus, was sacrificed at

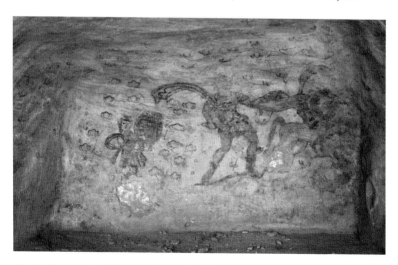

Fig. 40. Zawiyat Asqafah: painted scene of Achilles dragging Troilus from his horse.

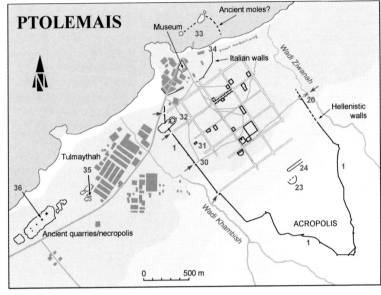

Fig. 41. Ptolemais: over-all plan of the site.

Key to numbered entries in the text and to figures 41 and 42

1	Defensive walls	20	Aqueduct and bridge
2	Arch of Constantine	21	Byzantine Theatre
3	Street of the Monuments	22	Doric Temple
4	House of Paulus	23	Upper Theatre
5	Late Baths	24	Stadium
6	Doric aula	25	'Odeon'
7	Fountain of the Maenads	26	Agora/Forum
8	Tetrastylon	27	Villa of the Four Seasons
9	NE quadrant	28	West Central Church
10	'House G'	29	West Fort
11	House of the Triapsidal Hall	30	Taucheira Gate
12	Fortress of the Dux	31	West Church
13	East Fort	32	Amphitheatre
14	House of the Twin Cisterns	33	Harbour
15	Colonnaded Palace	34	Villa of Orpheus
16	Villa with a View	35	Tomb of the Cartilii
17	Square of the Cisterns	36	Royal Tomb
18, 19	Reservoirs		

3   PTOLEMAIS ★ ★

This location, 40 km to the NE of Taucheira along the coast, is plagued by a multiplicity of names. The Greek settlement was founded in the seventh century BC and was initially referred to only as the port of Barka (al-Marj). It was named *Ptolemais* during the Hellenistic period, and retained this name until the end of antiquity. In the early 20th century the Italians created a new village on the long-abandoned site, at the water's edge, and this became known as Tulmaytha (طلميثة), an Arabized form of the ancient name (while the Italians referred to the site as Tolemaide). Now that village in turn has been largely abandoned and moved 1 km to the SW. Under Colonal Qadhafi the modern settlement was renamed ad-Dirsiyah (الدرسية), but this name has now been abandoned.

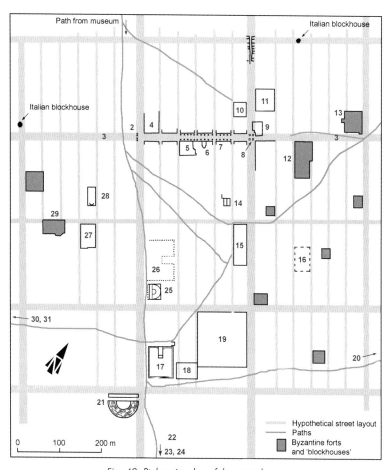

Fig. 42. Ptolemais: plan of the central area.

The ancient site was known to the 18th- and 19th-century explorers of the region, but systematic excavations were initiated only in the 20th century, during the Italian colonial period. Subsequent to that, further work was done by the Department of Antiquities, with interventions by British and American teams between the 1950s and the 1980s. Since 2000 a Polish team has been at work here, carrying out both surface survey work and limited excavations. However, it will be evident from the plan (figs. 41, 42) that it is a very large city site, and that still only a tiny fraction of it has been uncovered.

The plain of Barka (al-Marj), on the first step of the Jabal Akhdar and a few kilometres inland, offers extensive arable soils, but their successful exploitation by Greeks would have necessitated access to the sea – always their primary means of communication. This, combined with the presence of a moderately sheltered anchorage, would have been sufficient justification for an early Greek settlement on the coast at this point. We do not know a name for this early settlement, which is first mentioned simply as the port of Barka. This implies that it should be later in date than Barka itself which, according to tradition, was founded by citizens of Cyrene who found the rule of Arkesilaos II (560–550 BC) intolerable. The earliest settlement must have been close to the shore and therefore beneath the village of the Italian period. No archaeological excavations have taken place in this zone, but the earliest pottery recorded from the site goes back to the seventh century BC. As on other sites of the Pentapolis, therefore, archaeology now offers good evidence for earlier settlement than is implied by the historical sources.

It was almost universally held until recently that the settlement must have received the name *Ptolemais* in the time of Ptolemy III Euergetes, who succeeded to the throne of Egypt in 246 BC and brought Cyrenaica back under his direct control (see p. 4). However, there is now incontrovertible evidence from a papyrus document written in 252 that there were individuals in Alexandria who described themselves as from 'Ptolemais near Barka' already at that date; it has been argued cogently that we should now consider the new foundation to have been brought about by Ptolemy I in the late fourth century BC. Whatever the truth of this, it is clear that hugely expensive and ambitious works were undertaken at this time. A circuit of walls was constructed enclosing a vast area of 295 ha (which was never entirely filled by buildings, and was probably always impractical to defend), extending from the shoreline to the crown of the jabal escarpment. Within this, an entire new street-grid was laid out on the generous lines which were fashionable at the period. This was based on blocks or *insulae* of 100 × 500 Ptolemaic feet (36.5 × 182.5 m), separated by broad boulevards (*plateiai*) or narrower streets (*stenopoi*) (fig. 42). The highest part of the enclosure, at 280 m above sea-level, would have constituted an acropolis: there are up here signs of walls and rock-cut cisterns for water, but no systematic investigations have been carried out.

The city flourished in the early Roman period, but enjoyed a particularly intense period of embellishment at the beginning of the fourth century AD when, under the reforms of Diocletian, it became the capital of the new province of *Libya Superior* or *Pentapolis*. For the early fifth century, we get a brief but illuminating glimpse of life here when the aristocrat Synesius became Bishop of Ptolemais in c. 406 (p. 8). In his correspondence, he wrote passionately of a country in decline, constantly threatened by lawless raiding-parties from the interior. But the situation was not as terminal as he made out, and later buildings show that the city continued to flourish at least until the mid or later fifth century; at that point Ptolemais lost its status as provincial capital and this was transferred to Apollonia/Sozousa. Procopius, in his work on the buildings of Justinian, described the city as a shadow of its former self, depopulated largely as a result of water-shortage. Justinian provided for the restoration of the aqueduct (pp. 88–9).

In the late Roman period the indefensible circuit of Hellenistic walls was almost entirely dismantled, and was replaced by a number of separate forts or blockhouses, built of re-used material, within the city. The so-called Taucheira Gate on the western periphery was the sole survivor of the original fortifications: it was itself converted into a free-standing blockhouse and look-out point. There is no record of the city having been fought over when the Arabs came, and there is extensive evidence of later occupation. This was apparent from later alterations to buildings along the street to the NW of the tetrastylon (p. 75) together with a radiocarbon date from that excavation of AD 680–780. A surface collection of potsherds in the vicinity included pieces which can be attributed (very approximately) to between the late tenth and the early 13th centuries; and indeed, continued occupation is implied by Arab writers who refer to it as an anchorage and trading-post in the 9th, 12th and 14th centuries. At some time subsequent to this it was abandoned, for the ancient site is described as uninhabited by the 18th- and 19th-century European explorers.

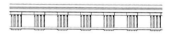

The road through the village leads to the museum, which stands in a pleasant shady garden. Here tickets are bought for the site and for the museum; there is also a restaurant and toilets. The ancient city stretched from the sea shore to the jabal escarpment, but most of the visible monuments lie some ten minutes' walk inland from the museum. (The site is deceptively large!) Leave the garden by the gateway to the L of the museum and follow the track directly uphill and through a dilapidated gateway in a fence, which signifies the boundary of the 'protected' archaeological zone. Numbered monuments or features refer to the plans in figures 41 and 42.

Defensive walls (1)

The walls of Ptolemais must, at the time, have represented the most impressive aspect of the Hellenistic 'foundation'.

They are less so now, since they seem to have been systematically dismantled in late antiquity; however, long tracts of their foundations can still be traced. The thickness of the wall is around 2.60 m, with fine drafted ashlar masonry on either face (well seen on the surviving Taucheira Gate, fig. 62) and a filling of rubble. The core was divided into compartments by headers which ran through the thickness at regular intervals. The thickness at the base implies an original height of not more than 5–7 m. The defensive value of the walls was, however, enhanced on both sides of the city by placing them close to the edge of the Wadis Khambish (on the W) and Ziwanah (on the E), which in effect provided defensive ditches in front of the walls. The walls were provided with projecting square towers at intervals, probably greater in number than those hitherto identified. The positions of four known gates are marked on figure 41 by red arrows; there must certainly have been others.

We cannot tell whether the defences were carried across the sea-front or not. It is likely that they were, but both natural erosion and the defensive works of the medieval and modern periods have combined to obscure any remaining traces. The Italians quarried ancient structures in order to build a defence around their tiny beachhead in 1911, and the defences of the medieval period described by Arab writers are likely to have enclosed a similarly modest area. The Italian defences have partly disappeared now, but the two cruciform blockhouses which constituted their forward positions are still prominent on the site (fig. 42). On the inland side, the entire circuit has been traced up onto the overlooking heights. Here the character of the masonry changed to something rougher and less showy, but serviceable none the less. This created a triangular acropolis, separated from yet higher ground beyond by a narrow spine. At the apex of the triangle the spine has been cut through to form a ditch, and there appears to be a triangular strong-point with an internal cistern. Once again, occasional towers have been identified, but the interior of the acropolis is essentially unexplored beneath the covering scrub.

The subsequent history of the defences is puzzling. Evidence in the vicinity of the Taucheira Gate (30) shows repair and re-modelling at some time in the Roman period. There is no direct evidence for the date of this, but the late third or early fourth century AD, when Ptolemais was advanced in rank (p. 68) is the most likely time for such work. Later again, it is clear that the outer defences

were both abandoned and dismantled, and that at this time the system of defence was reduced to a number of separate strong-points within the city. (See further, under the Fortress of the Dux, 12.) The late Roman baths in the centre (5) made use of masonry which appears to have been taken from the walls, but such activity still seems unlikely to account for the disappearance of all the stonework, assuming that the defences were built of limestone throughout. It has therefore been suggested that this was only partly the case, and that the upper courses may have been of mud-brick. Such a practice is well attested in Greek and Hellenistic city walls elsewhere.

Arch of Constantine ★ (2)

The track which leads inland from the museum follows the line of one of the major arteries of the ancient city, linking the harbour area with the civic centre. Purely for convenience of description, the major streets which run inland are here termed *cardines* (singular: *cardo*) and those which run at right angles to them are termed *decumani*, in conformity with

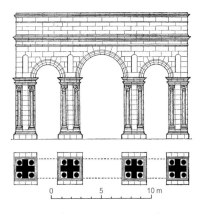

Fig. 43. Ptolemais: reconstruction drawing of the Arch of Constantine (based on drawings by L. Turba and S. Stucchi).

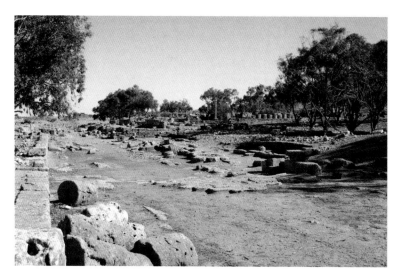

Fig. 44. Ptolemais: the 'Street of the Monuments' from the W.

Roman technical usage. The first area of excavations which you reach extends to your left along a major *decumanus*; its importance is signalled at the intersection which you have just reached by the partly restored Arch of Constantine. (It should be noted, however, that the present pathway is displaced to the W of the ancient intersection: the arch therefore framed not the length of *decumanus* to the E, but that to the W, which is unexcavated.)

The arch consisted of a thin screen with three arched openings. The bases of the piers were square, but in plan the piers themselves were cruciform, each having four columns inset on the corners. These highly decorative columns were of spirally-fluted blue-grey marble, with whitish Proconnesian marble capitals and bases. The arch was dismantled, and its materials partly re-used, in the Byzantine period, but figure 43 reproduces a plausible reconstruction of the elements. A fragmentary inscription from this arch (on marble panels, now items 29 and 35 in the museum) indicates that

it was erected in honour of Constantine and Licinius between AD 311 and 313. The inscribed sandstone blocks lying nearby are part of a text of the later fourth century which must have been placed on the monument to commemorate some refurbishment of the arch, or of the street.

Street of the Monuments ★ (3)

This *decumanus* (fig. 44) caught the eyes of early travellers by reason of the masses of masonry and architectural elements visible on the surface, and for this reason it was chosen by the Italian excavators in the 1930s for investigation. It was indeed treated in a monumental fashion, but in view of the very limited extent of excavation within the city generally, we are not in a position to say that it was exceptional. It was a very generous boulevard, composed of a paved carriageway 4.00 m wide, flanked by slightly raised pavements 2.40 m wide; and beyond those by colonnaded porticoes which varied in width between

3.00 m and 5.90 m. Thus, at its widest, it amounted to 20.60 m between opposing buildings.

The porticoes were raised substantially above the level of the pavements, to the extent that short flights of steps were necessary to access them. Their colonnades were of grey granite towards the Arch of Constantine, and of green cipollino marble further towards the E. Fallen architrave-blocks show that parts of the colonnade bore inscriptions. One such was dedicated to Valentinian and his colleagues (AD 367–75) and another to Arcadius and Honorius (395–408). The grandeur of the street was further enhanced by honorific statues: a number of bases can still be seen.

House of Paulus (4)

This building complex, found immediately on one's L after entering the Street of the Monuments through the Arch of Constantine, clearly occupied a position of some importance in the city. It was explored in the 1950s, but remains difficult to interpret. The excavators considered that the plot had been occupied by a large peristyle house in the early Roman period and that, having fallen into decay in the third century, it was renovated and reorganized in the fifth century or later. In the early period the house had incorporated a small bath-suite on the NE side, and in the Byzantine renovation this became a public facility, open to the street and provided with a latrine at the E corner. The SW part of the complex, on the other hand, was refurbished as a long hall or audience-chamber leading to a residence behind. On a paving-slab in the very centre of this hall, and integral to its refurbishment, was an inscription in Greek and in neat, small lettering, recording the execution of the work by one Paulus, who describes himself as *megaloprepestatos* (most magnificent) and *hypatikos* (of consular rank).

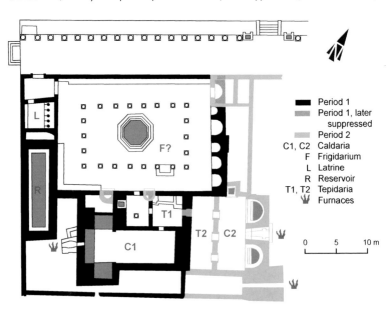

Fig. 45. Ptolemais: plan of the late Roman baths on the Street of the Monuments.

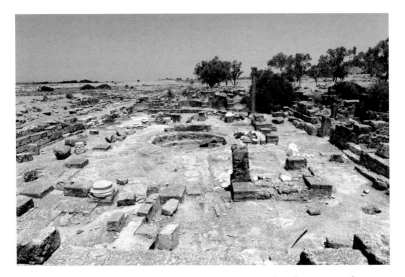

Fig. 46. Ptolemais: the frigidarium *of the late Roman Baths. (Photo by courtesy of Steven Sklifas.)*

These are titles appropriate to the civil governor of the province, but unfortunately only at a time when the seat of the governor had already been transferred from Ptolemais to Apollonia/Sozousa. While it is tempting, therefore, to see this part of the building as the official residence of the provincial governor in the late Roman or Byzantine period, the argument is not quite satisfying.

Late Baths ★ ★ (5)

This bath complex in the heart of the city (fig. 45) belongs entirely to the late Roman and Byzantine periods. There must certainly have been significant structures in this area from the Hellenistic period on, but of its antecedents nothing is known. The baths are difficult to interpret and there remain a number of issues which are disputed. The following is (hoped to be) a reasonably plausible description!

The complex is fronted on the Street of the Monuments by a raised colonnaded portico, accessed by means of steps at the street-corner towards the W, and by a flight of steps between small fountains at the N corner. In the first phase of the baths, there was a single entrance at the W corner, which led into a latrine and into a generous colonnaded court (fig. 46), of which the NE side was occupied by six semicircular niches for statues. The columns of the court were of grey marble, spirally fluted, with bases and Corinthian capitals of white marble; traces remain of the marble veneer which once adorned the walls. (Note that the plinths of the columns in the court vary greatly in height, suggesting the use of a job-lot of non-matching re-used columns!) The presence of columns of two sizes suggests that there were two storeys and the absence of any sort of gutter in the (rather irregular) marble paving suggests that the whole space was roofed. It has been suggested that the octagonal pool in the centre is secondary, but I can see no good reason for this and the lead piping which fed it from the reservoir looks original, not inserted.)

The court presumably functioned as an *apodyterium* or *frigidarium*. Off the SE side of it lay what seems to have been a rather mean suite of bathing rooms: a small vestibule with a tiny plunge-bath, a slightly larger *tepidarium*(?) and a large *caldarium* with either two or three hot plunge-baths. The range was heated by a furnace at the SW end of the *caldarium*, and there was also a large reservoir or cistern incorporated into this end of the complex. Dating-evidence for this phase of the baths is provided by the similarity of the fluted columns to those on the nearby Arch of Constantine (2); the two structures must be more or less contemporary and the baths are therefore of the early fourth century AD, following soon after the elevation of Ptolemais to the status of provincial capital.

It is possible that the second phase of the baths is contemporary with the renovation or enhancement of the street portico in the time of Arcadius and Honorius (395–408). A second entrance vestibule, providing access from the street, was provided at the N corner, at the expense of one of the niches on that side of the court. To the previous suite of hot rooms were now added a further *tepidarium* and *caldarium*, with two hot plunge-baths and a furnace sited between them. An additional furnace in the E corner was dedicated solely to heating water. At a yet later period, the new additions appear to have been blocked off again; the last activity on the site is represented by two lime-kilns, in which the former marble adornments were doubtless converted into lime for mortar. The coins found in the excavation extend only to the early seventh century, so the baths had probably gone out of use some time before the Islamic conquest.

Doric *Aula* (6)

A little further along the Street of the Monuments, and on the same side as the baths, is the so-called Doric *Aula*, which has the appearance of a public building for formal occasions of some sort. It consists of a rectangular hall with an apse, decorated with spirally-fluted grey marble columns like those on the Arch of Constantine. Its position in the street is nearly central and it has its own approach-steps from the pavement in front of it. The building has been attributed to the third century AD, with embellishments (apse and columns) in the fourth. Its name derives from the Doric frieze which formed part of its internal decoration; holes in the inner faces of the walls indicate the former presence of panels of marble veneer, held in place by metal clamps.

At the next street-intersection beyond it is the square foundation (effectively blocking the side-street) upon which once stood the Fountain of the Maenads.

Fountain of the Maenads (7)

Now in the museum (p. 106, item 57) is a reconstructed hollow drum of Pentelic marble (from near Athens) on which are carved figures of dancing maenads (the female followers of Dionysos). These beautiful reliefs were found in fragments in the Street of the Monuments in 1935, and a further head was found in the blocking of a doorway in the Late Baths (5) when they were excavated in 1956–58. On the S side of the street and close to the area in which the reliefs were found, an intersection with a minor side-street is blocked by a rectangular foundation. The foundation incorporates water-channels and undoubtedly supported a fountain of some kind, probably installed here when for the last time (under Arcadius and Honorius) the Street of the Monuments was being embellished. The date of the sculptures is disputed, with opinions ranging from Hellenistic to Antonine, though they represent a later copy of a work probably of the fifth century BC. The installation of the fountain in the position of its discovery is certainly not original: it must belong to an earlier period in the history of the city, and must have been moved here from some other public place in the late fourth century AD.

From this point eastwards, towards the *tetrastylon*, can be seen the lip of an aqueduct channel which ran beneath the street paving.

Tetrastylon (8)

At the next major intersection, the street-paving shows the presence of four approximately square foundations, now stripped down to the surrounding street-level. Found in the vicinity were parts of four monolithic columns of Proconnesian marble with Corinthian capitals, and it seems that in the Byzantine period the intersection was marked by a *tetrastylon*, a monument composed of four free-standing columns on massive, tapering plinths, presumably with statues on top (of the four evangelists?). The style of the capitals and accompanying bases is said to belong either to the fifth century or to the first half of the sixth. It has also been suggested that at an earlier period the monument had taken the quite different form of a *tetrapylon* or four-way arch, with a surmounting cupola. The only evidence for this is the size of the foundations in the street paving.

NE quadrant (9)

On the street corner to the N (or conventionally, NE) of the *tetrastylon*, Richard Goodchild partially excavated a sequence of structures. These do not now merit close examination but they serve to illustrate a point which recurs repeatedly in the excavations along the street which leads from here towards the harbour. The deepest structure, represented by fragments of ashlar walling and of four monochrome mosaics, was a wealthy peristyle house of the Hellenistic or early Roman period, built in conformity with the Ptolemaic street grid. This is overlaid by a rectangular building whose walls are made of small blocks with a rubble infill, and which encroaches onto the previous street-line by some 8 m. Later in turn is a small church-like building with a *triconchos* at its NE end. Whether or not it was built for a Christian purpose (and there is no specific evidence either way), a stone paving-block within has a name in Kufic script carved on one edge. (If you stand immediately in front of the *triconchos*, the inscription is on your L, on the long edge of the paving-block just inside the doorway.) The paving may not be original to the building, but the presence of the inscription provides clear evidence that the building was renovated, if not constructed, in the Islamic period.

This sequence therefore shows that occupation of this part of Ptolemais continued into the Islamic period and that, in its latest phase, the former boulevards had diminished to very much narrower tracks, hemmed in on either side by crowded buildings of no architectural pretension.

'House G' (10)

This designation was used for a peristyle house excavated in the 1960s by Richard Goodchild (fig. 47). The excavation was still incomplete at the time of his premature death in 1968 and the excavation records were lost; the interpretation

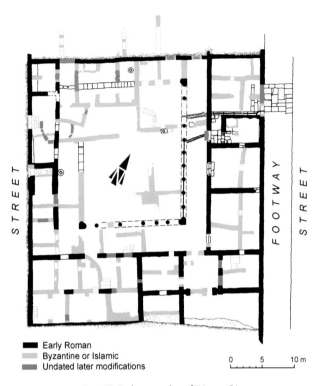

Fig. 47. Ptolemais: plan of 'House G'.

of the building is therefore subject to considerable uncertainties, particularly in regard to chronology.

The earliest identified phase of the complex was a house (probably) of the first century AD, composed in typical Cyrenaican manner of rooms opening off a peristyle court. The peristyle was composed of Ionic columns carrying a Doric frieze of metopes and triglyphs; part at least was two storeys high and slots in the surviving column-bases suggest the presence of screen-panels at ground-level. The full extent of the complex towards the SE and the NW has not been excavated; on the other two sides it has been uncovered as far as the bounding streets. The entrance was on the NE side; it led obliquely through an entrance-hall with a doorkeeper's lodge into the peristyle. Adjacent to this on the NE side were two large reception rooms, and beyond them in the E corner was a self-contained suite, perhaps for guests. The original arrangement of the remaining part of the SE range is unclear because of later alterations. Along the SW side were service rooms and perhaps a staircase; the rooms on the NW side of the peristyle have not been excavated. Partly beneath the SW side of the peristyle and partly beneath the central open space was a large rock-cut cistern, accessed by three shafts. This is largely blocked by debris, but those parts which were found to be accessible suggested a capacity of at least 160,000 litres (35,000 gallons) of water.

A second phase of occupation is marked by extensive alteration and rebuilding, using many architectural elements from the first phase. The property was subdivided into a number of smaller, semi-independent, units. Several of these included features which may be remains of oil-pressing installations (though reused architrave-blocks with beam-sockets cut in them do not necessarily represent press-uprights). These very substantial changes suggest that the masonry which was re-used had already fallen from its original position, but had remained on site. An obvious reason for this would have been collapse in an earthquake. For lack of close dating-evidence, it is impossible to link this event definitively to the earthquakes of 262 or 365. It has been suggested that the late occupation followed after a considerable interval: the refurbishment and subdivision of earlier peristyle houses into clusters of poor dwellings is a widely attested characteristic of urban housing in the Byzantine period. This occupation may even belong to the period after the Arab conquest.

A theme which runs through much of the interpretation of the residential architecture at Ptolemais (here, in the House of Paulus, the House of the Triapsidal Hall, the Villa of the Four Seasons etc.) is the likelihood that upper parts of the building were constructed, not in ashlar masonry, but in mud-brick. This would have had two consequences in the face of seismic shock: in the first place, the upper parts would have been more likely to collapse; and in the second, having done so, it would have been less laborious to remove the debris and refurbish (and the damage to floors beneath would have been less) than if the fallen material had been composed of stone blocks.

House of the Triapsidal Hall ★ (11)

This is a large residential complex of some importance (fig. 48). The *insula* in which it was situated lay in one of two strips which were 50 m wide, as opposed to the norm of 36 m for Ptolemais. (See fig. 42; the other strip is that immediately to the SW of the Arch of Constantine.) Like 'House G' on the opposite side of the street, it was excavated by Richard Goodchild, but the work was uncompleted at the time of his death and the excavation records were not subsequently found. However, even in the circumstances it demonstrates a very long sequence of occupation, which probably extends into the early medieval period.

As with the other houses which have been excavated at Ptolemais, it is difficult to demonstrate that this complex goes back to the Hellenistic period, but logic and its siting suggest that it must do so. The over-all boundaries of the property probably remained the same throughout its history, and are shown in figure 48 as belonging to the earliest period, despite later rebuilding. Within this can be made out a peristyle court, which also persisted throughout its history. The columns of the peristyle had Ionic capitals, but (as in House G) carried a Doric frieze on the architrave. Note that the columns were constructed from tall plain drums, which were scored horizontally to give the impression that they were made from smaller blocks. Some walls between the peristyle and the street on the SW side are also original, and the main entrance to the property was probably on this side, where it is still marked by two *cippi*. This entrance, which must have led into a vestibule, was subsequently blocked when a bath-building was inserted in the same area. A probable addition to the original design is the South Hall, a long apsidal hall on the

SE side of the peristyle, elaborated with 'Syrian' arches at several points.

The complex was substantially remodelled in late antiquity, the extent of the modifications suggesting that the previous building was largely ruinous, and had been so for some time. The reason for this may have been destruction in the earthquake of 262 or that of 365, but this cannot be demonstrated conclusively. The original peristyle continued to form the basis of the layout, but with a large fish-tank inserted in the E corner. (There are recesses for the fish to spawn in on the side towards the centre of the peristyle.) On the NE side was built a pair of ceremonial halls, the Triapsidal Hall (fig. 49) and, to the S of it, a hall with a single apse, paved in *opus sectile*. The building work was of very high quality (though reliance on re-used columns meant that they did not always match), and these were clearly reception rooms of some kind, intended to impress. Part of the peristyle in front of the Triapsidal Hall was enclosed in order to create a forehall to it. On the SE side of the peristyle, the South Hall was retained and modified, while other rooms in this area were laid out completely afresh around a stone-paved courtyard. The Syrian arch at the SW end of the South Hall was blocked in order, at this point, to create a vestibule to a small bath-building between it and the original main entrance to the property. The bath would have had a single cold room and a single hot one, each with a plunge-bath; but it was probably never completed and the hypocaust was certainly never fired.

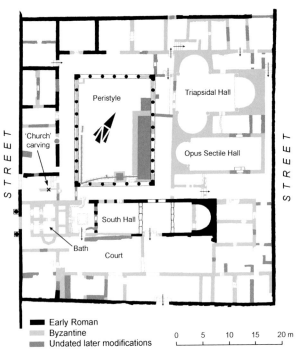

Early Roman
Byzantine
Undated later modifications

0   5   10   15   20 m

Fig. 48. Ptolemais: plan of the House of the Triapsidal Hall.

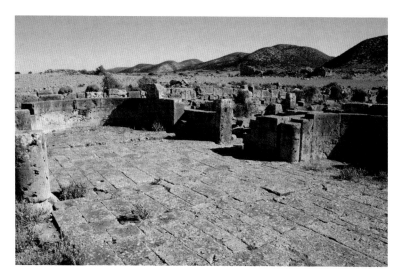

Fig. 49. Ptolemais: late reception room in the House of the Triapsidal Hall.

Further modifications to the complex involved the narrowing or blocking of doorways, creating the impression that, as in House G, the latest phase in the life of the House of the Triapsidal Hall involved its subdivision into smaller tenements. Sequences of superposed mosaic and earth floors in several rooms indicate the length and complexity of the history of the entire area.

The question of major interest, with regard to this building, is for whom the major late-antique building-works were carried out. Goodchild suggested that the scale of the formal reception rooms suited the residence of the *Dux* at the time when he was based at Ptolemais, but since then it has become apparent that building on this scale in the late antique period is not all that unusual. Indeed, there is a marked polarisation in this period between those earlier houses which went down in the social scale and became properties in multiple occupation (such as House G above) and those of the very rich. The latter

were typified by apsed audience chambers for receiving clients without letting them too far into the house and by grand, multi-apsed dining halls. (Compare the 'Palace of the Dux' at Apollonia, p. 271.) The contrast between the high quality of the reception rooms and the much poorer, almost makeshift, work carried out in other parts of the house does not sit well with the idea of an official residence. Finds from the excavation include a stone with a carving in low relief that may represent the façade of a church (fig. 50: now to be seen close to the late baths at the point marked x in fig. 48), and several other architectural blocks on which crosses are carved. This has led to the hypothesis that this could have been the residence of the Bishop of Ptolemais – but this too remains entirely speculative. It seems rather more likely that the works were carried out by some wealthy notable of the city, who found that his ambitions had outrun his means, resulting in his inability to complete the baths or to bring the domestic quarters up to the standard of his lavish banqueting suite!

Once again, questions of detailed chronology are not easily answered, but there is a strong suspicion that occupation of the complex extended well into the Islamic period.

The line of the street on which 'House G' and the House of the Triapsidal Hall were located has been cleared for a distance of some 150 m NW of the intersection with the Street of the Monuments. Beyond these two houses, no more than the width of the street itself has been exposed, but here too there is evidence of encroachment onto the line of the Ptolemaic boulevard by extensive late structures. Doorways in these structures on the side away from the street suggest that, as in the case of the two excavated houses, ruined earlier buildings were refurbished and brought back into use, in either the Byzantine or the early Islamic period.

Fortress of the Dux ★ (12)

This massive castle, measuring 75 × 45 m (figs. 51, 52), clearly proclaims its importance. The style of its masonry, of heavy but carefully cut ashlar blocks with projecting string-courses, is precisely that of the late Roman strongholds of Qasr Migdim and Qasr Shahdiyn in the Wadi Kuf area (pp. 136, 126). Its position, opening off the Street of the Monuments, is close to both the former public heart of the city and to the harbour. Upon the NW wall, facing the street, was once inscribed an edict of the Emperor Anastasius (491–518), regulating the conduct of military affairs in the province. This was removed in 1852 by the French consul, J. Vattier de Bourville, and is now in the Louvre in Paris; fragments of two other copies of the edict have been found at Taucheira and Apollonia. From this, it has been rightly argued that this building was the military headquarters of the city and a residence of the military governor, the *Dux Pentapoleos*. It was not, however, the primary residence of the Dux at

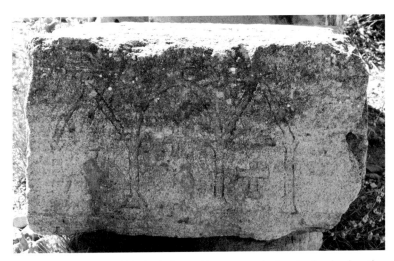

Fig. 50. Ptolemais: carved block which possibly represents the façade of a church, with crosses between the columns.

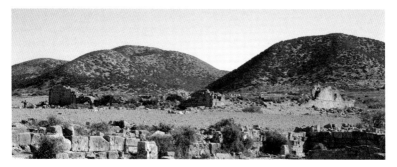

Fig. 51. Ptolemais: the Fortress of the Dux from the W.

the time when the inscription was carved: there are good reasons for supposing that he was then based in Apollonia/Sozousa. The inscription also represents only the latest date by which the building must have been built; it could have been built considerably earlier.

The construction of this fortress, and of at least two other defensive structures whose size suggests official investment (nos. 13 and 29 on fig. 42), is likely to be closely bound up with the abandonment and dismantling of the Hellenistic wall-circuit, which we know to have been restored – and therefore presumably still in service – in the first or second century AD. There is hitherto no archaeological evidence by means of which we can narrow down the major change in defensive policy. However, it has been pointed out by Richard Goodchild that Synesius (bishop in c. 406–13: p. 8) railed against the civil governor Andronicus. Amongst his other misdeeds, Synesius complained that he 'invested the city with the semblance of one taken by storm' and that he 'cut off the fairest part of it' (by reducing the wall-circuit?). He also kept his opponents 'in an impregnable fortress in the like of which the children of the poets represent that the Titans are enchained'. It is not implausible, therefore, that he was

describing precisely this event, and that the 'impregnable fortress' is the building with which we are concerned. In that case, the change must have taken place at the beginning of the fifth century.

Neither the Fortress of the Dux, nor any of the other Byzantine 'blockhouses' on the site of Ptolemais has been

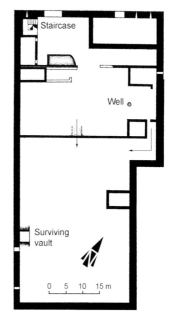

Fig. 52. Ptolemais: plan of the Fortress of the Dux.

excavated. (Apart from the East and West Forts, there are six other such structures on the plan in fig. 42.) The fortress was entered by means of two arched doorways facing the Street of the Monuments and an arched postern in the long SW wall. Internally, it seems to have been divided into two areas in which rooms opened off separate courtyards. Traces of vaulting indicate how an upper floor was supported and in the W corner there is probably a staircase-tower. A deep hollow amongst the rubble may indicate the position of a well.

The **East and West Forts (13, 29)** are of less-well-dressed masonry, but of even heavier blocks. Both have entrances on the NW side and show traces of subdivisions and vaults within. The remaining buildings share the same general character as these and as countless other Byzantine buildings in Cyrenaica. The monastery and farm now in the centre of al-Bayda (Sirat al-Jamil, p. 118) are good examples of the variety of uses to which such buildings might be put. While they are clearly intended to be defensive in character and are suited to troubled times, there is no necessary implication that they are other than private properties.

House of the Twin Cisterns (14)

The two prominent barrel-vaults here catch the eye. They form part of a complex which has not been excavated, and they are regarded as cisterns for water rather than as storerooms: they are plastered internally and have draw-holes in the crowns of their vaults. The slightly pointed profile of the vaults contrasts with the familiar semi-circular arches of typical Roman construction, and for that reason they have been attributed to the latest period in the city's history. At the present time, however, that remains an assumption. Several late houses at Ptolemais share the characteristic of having large reservoirs at ground-level, with living quarters above.

Colonnaded Palace ★ ★ (15)

This magnificent complex (fig. 53: lettering refers to this plan) was excavated in the 1930s. Its architecture is grandiose and it also yielded a surprising quantity of Egyptian antiquities, presumably the antiquarian collection of one of its residents. It was inferred at the time that this must have been the residence of the provincial governor – despite the fact that when it was supposed to have been built, in the second century BC, and in the early Roman period, there was no reason for any sort of 'governor' to be resident in Ptolemais. Now it is considered simply to have been the lavish residence of a very wealthy family, and not necessarily the only one of its kind in the city. As in the case of most of the excavated buildings at Ptolemais, stratified dating-evidence was not collected at the time of discovery; its date therefore depends on stylistic arguments and the interpretation of its architecture. There is disagreement over the date of origin (ranging from the second century BC to the later first century AD: somewhere in the middle seems plausible) and over the number of alterations, expansions and refurbishments which contributed to its final form. Human bones and a pair of gold earrings found beneath fallen blocks in the ornamental pool suggest a catastrophic end (in AD 365?) to the dignity, if not the occupation, of the great house.

The palace occupies the northern half of an *insula*, and is built on rising ground such that the *piano nobile*, or part comprising the main reception rooms, is towards the S and on the upper level,

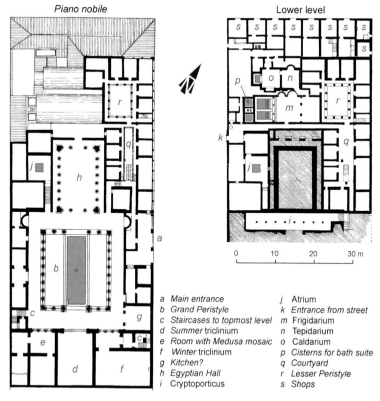

Fig. 53. Ptolemais: plan of the Colonnaded Palace.

a Main entrance
b Grand Peristyle
c Staircases to topmost level
d Summer triclinium
e Room with Medusa mosaic
f Winter triclinium
g Kitchen?
h Egyptian Hall
i Cryptoporticus
j Atrium
k Entrance from street
m Frigidarium
n Tepidarium
o Caldarium
p Cisterns for bath suite
q Courtyard
r Lesser Peristyle
s Shops

while the lower part to the N includes a bath suite and a row of lock-up shops facing the street to the NW. The main entrance (a) is on the NE side, which was embellished with engaged Ionic columns carrying a Doric frieze and framing blind rectangular windows. The entrance leads indirectly into the mosaic-paved Grand Peristyle (b). The peristyle enclosed a large ornamental pond with a fountain in the centre, flanked on either side by flower-beds; the channel from which the pond was filled is visible in the E corner. The colonnades of the peristyle were two storeys high: the presence of a further storey above is indicated by two staircases at the SE end of the building

(c, c). The columns were of local sandstone and were coated with painted stucco. Those at the corners were heart-shaped, i.e. engaged half-columns attached to square corner-piers: this is a very typical feature of Cyrenaican architecture. On the walls surrounding the peristyle, as in other parts of the mansion, can be seen traces of marble veneer, or of the bronze clamps which held the veneer panels in place.

The central room on the SE side of the peristyle (d) was a summer *triclinium*. To the SW of this was another reception room (e) with a fine mosaic with a central emblem of a Medusa head (now in the museum: p. 103, item 24), while on the opposite side a similar room served as a vestibule to a (more enclosed) winter *triclinium* (f). This fine room was paved with a combination of *opus sectile* and mosaic (a *triclinium* is almost always identifiable by the more 'economical' paving of that part which was largely covered by couches). The columns in the entrances to the two rooms flanking the summer *triclinium* had Corinthian capitals of the highest quality, decorated with figures of gods (Serapis and possibly Apollo) and wild beasts. These may be seen in the museum (p. 102, item 9).

The longer sides of the Grand Peristyle were flanked by various service rooms, possibly including a kitchen (g). On the short NW side, however, was the grandest reception room of all, a basilical hall known as an *oecus aegyptius* or Egyptian Hall (h). This had two tiers of columns and an upper gallery; through the outer walls of the latter, windows provided light to the interior. The bases of the columns in this room were adorned with a ring of acanthus leaves and the intervals between them were paved with geometric mosaics (fig. 54).

The Egyptian Hall concludes the *piano nobile* of the palace towards the N, and stairways on either side of it led down to the lower ground level. At this level there was a *cryptoporticus* (i) beneath the NW side of the Grand Peristyle. On the SW side of the Egyptian Hall, a number of rooms were grouped around an *atrium* (j) with a central *impluvium* in coloured marble. Beyond these, an entrance from the street on the SW side of the property (k) led, through a long corridor, to a small suite of baths (m–o: an insertion, certainly not pre-Roman). The water supply for the baths was provided by a well between two raised cisterns (p).

On the opposite side of the Egyptian Hall and apparently on two levels, various rooms opened off a long, narrow courtyard (q). This led in turn to a Lesser Peristyle (r) at the centre of quite a substantial self-contained apartment. Finally, at the lower level only, a row of

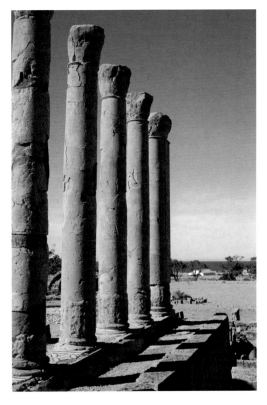

Fig. 54. Ptolemais: the re-erected columns of the Egyptian Hall in the Colonnaded Palace.

lock-up shops (s, s) with internal store-rooms faced the street on the narrow end of the *insula*.

There are many elements in the architecture of the complex (such as the figured capitals on either side of the summer *triclinium* and the grand *oecus aegyptius*) which recall Hellenistic Alexandria. A collection of some thirty Egyptian statues, found in the upper fill of the pool, remain a puzzling discovery. Most of these are small and of late date (700 BC–AD 100), but they include a statue of Amenmose, of the time of Ramesses II (1294–1224 BC). One of the owners of the property, presumably in the early Roman period, must have been a refined collector of Egyptian *objets d'art*. They were presumably arranged around the pool, but how did they survive until the collapse of the building?

Villa with a View (16)

Three blocks to the E of the Colonnaded Palace, the Polish team, which has been working on the site in recent years, is in course of excavating another very wealthy residential property, which they have named the 'Villa with a View'. Around a small peristyle of four columns open a number of rooms with lavish mosaics and painted wall-plaster; the latter is preserved to a height of 2 m in places. In at least one room was found a figured mosaic which had fallen from an upper floor; this comprised a large mythological scene from the legend of Achilles, with numerous named figures. According to information hitherto made available, the earliest occupation of the site goes back to the second century BC and the mosaic embellishments generally belong to the second or third centuries AD. The property suffered catastrophic collapse (due to earthquake?), perhaps in 262, perhaps in

365, after which, in the later fourth century, a lamp-maker's workshop existed on the site. There may have been an interval of abandonment before the major collapse, since the floors were largely undamaged, having been protected from falling masonry by a layer of sand. The latest occupation consisted of some sort of 'refuge' built amongst the ruins in the seventh century AD.

The proprietor of the villa at the time when the mosaics were laid is twice named in Greek within the decoration, as *Leukaktios*, possibly for the Latin name Lucius Actius.

The excavations are not generally accessible when the team is not at work, though it is to be hoped that in due course the site will be protected by a cover-building and opened to the public.

Square of the Cisterns ★ ★ (17)

This structure has been described as the agora of the city and as a gymnasium. Above ground, it comprises a huge open square paved with coarse mosaic, surrounded by a Doric portico on three sides, of which a few columns have been re-erected at the E corner (figs. 55, 56). It was approached on the NW (seaward) side by two flights of steps. Also on this side is a podium with an Ionic colonnade which looks at first sight like the front of a temple, until one realizes that there is not enough mass behind it. There is also a water-basin in front of it rather than a flight of steps. It has been interpreted as *rostra* (a platform for public speaking), but its function must be interpreted in the light of the complex as a whole. The complex was certainly not an agora or forum, for it is wholly lacking in the temples or basilica which would be associated with it. It may, however, have been a gymnasium, like that at Cyrene (p. 154). There are traces of walls for surrounding rooms (now quite disappeared) on the NW, NE and SE sides. Its original construction must belong to the Hellenistic period: this is shown by the drafted masonry of its outer wall, most readily visible on the NE side, where it became incorporated into a later cistern.

The real significance of this building, however, for the inhabitants of the city, is that below ground it concealed a vast reservoir made up of 17 interconnected barrel-vaulted chambers, capable of storing approximately 5 million litres of water or rather more than a million gallons (fig. 57). Today the surface of the piazza above is perforated at more or less regular intervals by unguarded openings into the voids beneath (visitors beware!). The restorer, Giacomo Caputo, recorded that he had provided new concrete lips to these openings, with reinforced glass cover-plates in order to make them safe, but these have long since disappeared and the hazard of

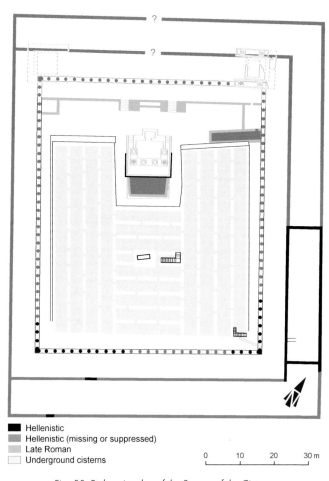

Hellenistic
Hellenistic (missing or suppressed)
Late Roman
Underground cisterns

0   10   20   30 m

Fig. 55. Ptolemais: plan of the Square of the Cisterns.

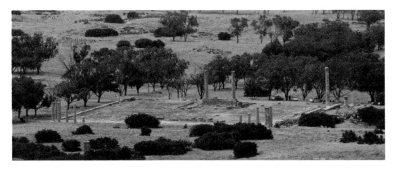

Fig. 56. Ptolemais: the Square of the Cisterns, seen from the Upper Theatre.

falling is very real. Caputo suggested that the openings belonged only to a 'late' (undated) period when the cisterns probably no longer served their original purpose and light was required within. The cisterns are virtually intact and may be entered (with care – and remember that these cisterns still collect rainwater!) by means of two stairways: one in the centre of the square and one at the E corner. Next to the former is a rectangular well enclosed in brickwork, which presumably predates the surrounding structure, since it is not aligned with it. Next to the latter may be seen remains of a late (Justinianic?) conduit from which water was fed into the system. (At an earlier date, the inlet was in the S corner.) Down below, the ground surface is uneven and is mainly composed of silt; in places, however, it has been excavated down to the original floor of waterproof cement, which also covers the walls. The original height of the chambers, from the floor to the crown of the vault, was around 4.5 m. The vaults are constructed of concrete rubble, in contrast to the walls of the chambers, which are of blockwork. This has given rise to the suggestion that the cisterns originally had a flat covering supported by timber joists at the level of the corbels which now project from the walls beneath the springing of the vaults.

However, when one considers both the absence of any seatings for such joists and the substantially lower level implied for the original floor above, this seems improbable. (The corbels would have served usefully to support timber framing beneath the vaults during construction.)

In the late Roman period, presumably after the earthquake of 365, the monument or statue-base which had stood near the middle of the piazza was replaced by the monumental *rostra* which we see now, and two of whose columns have remained standing since antiquity. (The basal moulding of the podium is Hellenistic.) By the time that was done, the NW range of rooms, on a raised terrace, had collapsed. That side of the terrace was therefore cut back in order to make a piazza on the downhill side, and this was further embellished by two colonnaded *aediculae*, facing one another in front of the *rostra*. A high-level tank at the N corner was presumably part of the distribution system.

Immediately to the NE of the Square of the Cisterns are two other rectangular features, which have been interpreted as open **reservoirs** of later date. The smaller one (18) is said to have made use of part of the original boundary wall on the NE side of the complex already described. The larger (19) is a huge

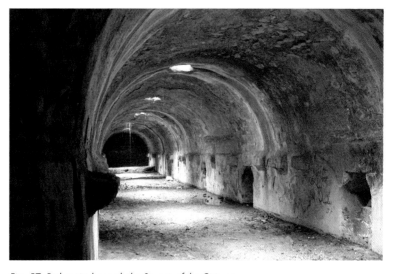

Fig. 57. Ptolemais: beneath the Square of the Cisterns.

enclosure (much larger than the Square of the Cisterns) bounded by walls of Hellenistic drafted masonry. On the NW and SW sides there are fallen column-drums and on the NW side there was once a central entrance. (Was this a gymnasium?) In a secondary phase, the whole area was given a thick lining of rubble concrete faced with water-proof cement, and this lining was carried across the former entrance. All of the features in this part of the city were well-placed to supply water to the areas closer to the sea, and they are also at a height where they could have been supplied by the aqueduct which enters the city on the E and which crossed the Wadi Ziwanah on a bridge (see below).

Aqueduct and bridge (20)

If you follow the track which runs eastward from the uphill side of the Square of the Cisterns, this will bring you past traces of a gate in the city wall (with a semi-circular enclosure on the inner side) to an ancient bridge over the Wadi Ziwanah (fig. 58). (The distance is about 900 m, and may involve climbing one or two fences on the way, but keep going in the same direction! The bridge is at N 32° 42.62′ E 21° 57.69′.) This carried both the road leading eastward to Cyrene and an incoming aqueduct over the wadi. The water ran in a cement-lined channel about 30 cm wide and 40 cm deep. It has been traced upstream (eastwards) for a distance of 24 km, as far as Wadi Habbun where it tapped its source, though all trace of the original catchment has long since been eroded away. A great deal of its course can, however, still be made out. The channel was either cut in the native rock or built up in mortared rubble; it mostly followed the contours of the land, crossing the various intervening wadis on bridges where necessary.

After crossing the Wadi Ziwanah on the downstream side of the road bridge, the channel turns northward along the W bank of the wadi and then disappears. If it led to the Square of

88

the Cisterns, it must at some point have doubled back towards the S, but the fall between the wadi crossing and the cisterns is sufficient for this to be plausible, and the channel which can be seen entering the cisterns at the E corner is similar in character to that which runs across the countryside.

With regard to date, the arched road-bridge over the Wadi Ziwanah is probably early Roman and the aqueduct might be contemporary with it. At the very latest, it may represent the refurbishment of the city's water supply which we know to have been undertaken by the emperor Justinian in the sixth century.

To the S of the Square of the Cisterns is a small unexcavated theatre, known only from a scatter of masonry on the surface; all conjecture about it is therefore based on the most slender of evidence. It has been designated the **Byzantine Theatre (21)** because (in the account by Karl Kraeling in 1962) 'its ruins lie exposed on the surface instead of being deeply buried and its stonework is coarse, with only the simplest dressing'. It is implied that it succeeded the upper theatre (23), being in a safer location, closer to what still survived of the earlier city. But if that were the case, it would seem logical that the seats robbed out from its predecessor should have been re-used in the new structure, and that they would therefore have been 'coarse' in their previous incarnation too!

The path which leads uphill past the Square of the Cisterns and the Byzantine Theatre also passes, shortly on the L, scattered elements of very large Doric columns. Their size suggests the presence of a **Doric Temple (22)**. It may be noted that, so far, no temples have been identified in the ancient city, and that such a building in this position would have been very prominent, and was therefore undoubtedly important. However, no excavations have yet been carried out at this location.

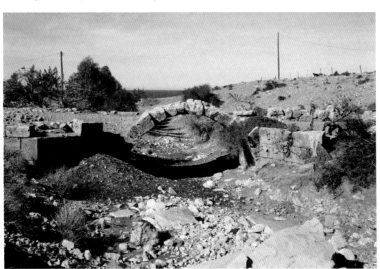

Fig. 58. Ptolemais: the Roman bridge which carried both the road and an aqueduct across the Wadi Ziwanah.

Upper Theatre ★ (23)

The path uphill comes to a fence with an abandoned custodian's hut next to it. Go through the fence and then obliquely towards the left at an angle of about 45° across open ground (no path). If you then climb up the escarpment in front of you, you will find at a distance of about 400 m the hollow in which the upper theatre was situated, at N32° 42.14' E20° 57.60'. This has barely been explored. It is a typical 'Greek' theatre, inasmuch as it makes use of the natural lie of the land, where the first steps of the jabal rises up behind the city. Limited clearance of scrub has shown cuttings in the rock of the hillside on which the blocks of the seating would have been placed; there may have been about fifty tiers of seats. Fragmentary foundations of the stage building have been identified, but it is clear that almost all of the masonry was removed for other purposes, presumably in the Byzantine period when the outer defences had been abandoned and this position would have been too remote for safe use. A few squared blocks lying about will confirm that you have found the right spot. The view over the city as a whole justifies the climb, and immediately below it is possible to make out the strip of level ground which once constituted the stadium.

Stadium (24)

The long level space and rounded end of a race-track are still visible as a piece of arable land immediately beneath and to the N of the Upper Theatre. It is bounded on the long sides by jumbled masonry where the seating used to be. This has been described as a hippodrome (for chariot races); but its length (185–210 m, approximately one stade), its total width of 25–26 m and the absence of any trace of starting gates or a central barrier clearly indicate that this was in fact a stadium for athletics.

'Odeon' ★ (25)

This small theatral building (fig. 59) faces W onto one of the principal *cardines* of the city, from which it was separated by a portico. To the NW, it lay

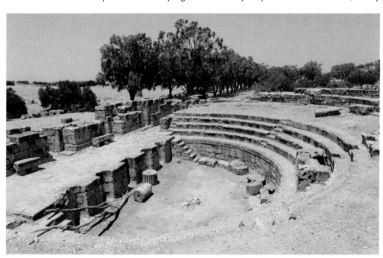

Fig. 59. Ptolemais: the 'Odeon'. Photo by courtesy of Steven Sklifas.

adjacent to an open space which may have been the agora/forum of the city; on the SE side are the stripped foundations of a pre-existing temple. The space to the NE remains unexplored. The building itself is small enough to have been roofed, and it may have started life as the *bouleuterion* or council chamber of the city. (Its position next to the presumed agora strengthens the interpretation of both structures.) The earliest phase of the design had semicircular tiers of seating, as now, but they did not extend forward to the edge of the stage; rather, they stopped about 2.5 m further to the E, and the side-entrances (*parodoi*) led down to the *orchestra* below. The character of the stage-building in this phase is unknown.

The original design was modified after an interval which cannot be determined: it may even represent a change of intent during the construction. The seating was extended forwards and the *parodoi* were made to lead onto the stage. The stage-building (*scaenafrons*) appears to have been very simple, with three unadorned doorways in it, and lateral staircases providing access to galleries above. There is no evidence of columns or other architectural embellishment, apart from cramp-holes which show that the wall was once faced with marble. The front of the stage (*pulpitum*) was as it now appears, but the floor was of timber: the sockets for the ends of the supporting joists can still be made out. The *orchestra* was separated from the seating of the *cavea* by a parapet, and was accessible in this phase only by steps leading down from the stage at either side. The *cavea* rose very much higher than it appears to do now, and probably had fifteen tiers of seats. The upper tiers were reached by means of staircases at the rear of the building.

The third phase is represented by the conversion of the *orchestra* into a water-tank by plastering it over with water-proof cement. The tank was supplied with water by means of a channel which runs into the building at the corner nearest to the Square of the Cisterns. Parts of the building appear to have been unsafe at this stage (as a result of earthquake damage?): the portico along the street-frontage was entirely walled up and pierced only by two central doorways, and the vaulted corridor beneath the upper tiers of seats (*ambulacrum*) was buttressed with inserted piers and possibly even filled in with soil. Other, lesser, modifications included the encircling of the water-tank with a railing (the sockets for which can be seen), the filling-in and solid paving of the stage and the insertion of a box-like feature (with enclosing columns?) in the centre of the *cavea*. The fact that the railing-sockets extend down the steps into the *orchestra* (indicating that the water might be entered this way) offers clear support to the inference that the building was now used for aquatic displays. The Church Father St. John Chrysostom, writing in the second half of the fourth century, fulminated against those who flocked to the theatre to see naked women swimming, and we cannot doubt that what we see here was intended for such degenerate entertainment, perhaps graced even by the *praeses* of the province in the ceremonial box!

Dates for the history of the building are difficult to establish. Neither of the excavators who have busied themselves with it (Giacomo Caputo in the 1930s, Richard Goodchild in the 1950s) paid any attention to stratified pottery, which might have helped. The arguments hitherto advanced suggest that the initial phases may belong to the first or second century AD; the conversion into a venue for swimming displays is more likely to belong to the fourth century (after the earthquake of 365) and (perhaps a tenuous argument, this) the building is likely to have ceased this function by the early fifth century, because otherwise Bishop Synesius would surely have expressed his displeasure! A statue of Athena found within the building, and the base of another, perhaps representing Dionysos and a satyr, were dedicated probably in the second century AD by a certain M. Ulpius Cominius. (Both are on display in the museum: p. 101, item 3, p. 106, item 64.)

Agora/Forum (26)

A fragmentary inscription found in front of the 'odeon' carries part of a Latin text which was to be set up 'in clear letters … in the forum' of the city. The forum is likely, therefore, to have been nearby and traces of substantial colonnades have been found immediately to the N of the 'odeon', enclosing a large area on the E side of the street, where masses of rubble may also suggest the podium of a temple. This remains to be explored.

Villa of the Four Seasons ★ (27)

This is a substantial town house of the Roman period (fig. 60). It occupied about one third of an *insula* and was therefore bounded by streets on three sides. On the NW side was a row of four shops, which opened only onto the street; there was also one indirect entrance here to the service area of the house. A second entrance led from the street on the SW side, through a corridor to the kitchen and to the internal peristyle. The principal entrance (a), however, was from the NE and was marked by two flanking circular *cippi* (fig. 61). This led into a vestibule and thence into the peristyle (b); the latter was not central to the plan

but was set closer to the NE side, with rooms around the other three sides only. It was of the type called Rhodian by the Roman architect Vitruvius, in which one side has taller (and thicker) columns than the other three; in this instance the difference was accentuated by laying out the taller SE colonnade on a curve. The centre of the peristyle was probably planted as a garden; there are foundations of an architectural feature – perhaps a fountain – which added to its adornment.

Centrally opposite the curved SE colonnade was a suite of three rooms (c) thought to be of 'public' character, perhaps offices. The private residential

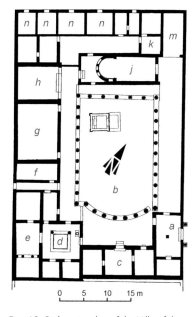

Fig. 60. Ptolemais: plan of the Villa of the Four Seasons.

a	Main entrance	f Kitchen
b	Peristyle	g, h Dining rooms
c	Offices?	j Heated room
d	Inner court	k Furnace
	of private	m Frigidarium?
	residence	n Shops
e	Oikos	

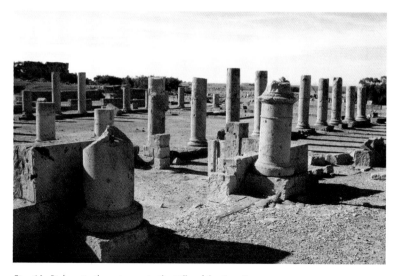

Fig. 61. Ptolemais: the entrance to the Villa of the Four Seasons.

quarter (d) was in the S corner, with rooms opening off three sides of a square inner court. The roof surrounding this court drained into a central basin, and thence into a cistern below ground (now collapsed); water could be drawn from the cistern through a cylindrical stone well-head on one side of the court. This suite of rooms included an *oikos* (e) or reception/dining room and bedrooms.

On the SW side of the peristyle, to the N of an entrance-corridor leading in from the street, was a kitchen (f) with emplacements for a fire and for a work-bench; beyond this were the two finest rooms of the house, both dining rooms. The larger (g) was enclosed and entered by two doors; the smaller (h) was entered through wide folding doors and was per-haps a summer *triclinium*.

The room on the NW side of the peristyle (j) possesses features which are particularly enigmatic. Its floor was raised on supports and possibly heated by means of a furnace in the adjoin-ing room to the N (k). The smoke from the furnace, after passing beneath the floor, was drawn up the walls through flues on the inside of the room next to the entrance and presumably also at other points. The apse at the W end of the room is a structural addition to the original building, but apparently contem-porary with the heating system, since its foundations are uniform with it. Behind the apse are a number of *dolia* sunk in the ground, typical of the type used for fermenting wine. One of these is cut by the apse, implying that they belong to the earlier history of the building. The impression now given that the apse had windows in it is false: the spaces between the piers of solid masonry were formerly filled with concrete rubble in the style of *opus africanum*.

Was this a bath? The heated floor was paved with mosaic, in the centre of which an area of pink plaster suggests the base of a basin or tank. But there is no obvious cold room (*frigidarium*) associated with it, unless the room at the N corner of the house (m) fulfilled this function. There is, however, no trace of the cold plunge-bath which might have been expected. The remaining rooms on the NW side of the property were either shops facing the street (n) or service rooms for storage or for servants.

The building represented a comfortably wealthy establishment, and was extensively provided with mosaic flooring, mostly still *in situ* but covered in order to protect it from frost. A fine mosaic which includes heads of the Four Seasons and after which the house has been named, was found in the summer *triclinium* (h). This is now on display in the museum (p. 103, item 28.) The adjoining room (g) still has traces of mosaic around the edges and of *opus sectile* paving in the centre. (Compare the House of Jason Magnus at Cyrene, p. 164.) The excavation also showed that many of the walls had been plastered and painted. Various strands of evidence suggest that the house was built in the first century AD and was well-maintained until the middle of the third. Subsequently, it suffered various degradations, though the shops on the NW side seem still to have flourished, and indeed to have expanded into the residential parts of the complex. Pottery of the Byzantine period was found on the site, so some kind of occupation took place then, though it was certainly opportunistic rather than comfortable.

West Central Church (28)
Besides the well-preserved West Church (31), two others within the city have been identified but not studied. The West Central Church is the most visible of these, in the *insula* immediately to the NW of the Villa of the Four Seasons. It is a normal basilical building, aligned with the street-grid and with its apse facing towards the SE (i.e. at right-angles to the West Church). The church is inscribed within a rectangle and the semi-dome of the apse survives almost intact; traces of the nave arcades also project from the high mound of fallen rubble, beneath which the body of the church is probably very well preserved.

West fort (29)
See p. 82.

Taucheira Gate ★ ★ (30)
The foundations and rutted paving of both the Barka Gate and the Quarry Gate have been found on the W side of the city, but the Taucheira Gate alone stands to much of its original height, an impressive monument in the landscape (fig. 62; the names of the gates are conventional, and the last-named more probably opened onto the Barka road). Here two massive rectangular towers project forwards from the line of the city wall, creating a forecourt 9.5 m wide in between them. In the rear of the forecourt is a single portal 3.8 m wide, on the line of the wall. The masonry is composed of limestone blocks, beautifully smoothed and fitted; the edges of each block are 'drafted' or recessed slightly from the level of the face, creating a most handsome effect. This is very characteristic of fine Hellenistic work, and is widely repeated in 17th- and 18th-century classicizing architecture in Europe. Close examination will show that most of the blocks are carved with complex monograms, which must be quarry marks of some sort. Many of them are also covered in graffiti, which extend from ancient (the earliest being dated to 30 BC) to modern (Italian troops in 1911 or thereabouts). The Greek texts, which have been interpreted as the doodling of soldiers on duty at the gate, are in fact identical in character to those found

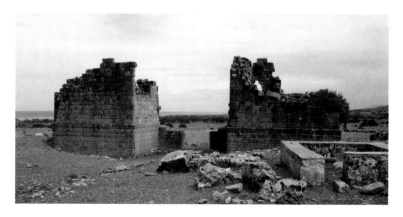

Fig. 62. Ptolemais: the outer aspect of the Taucheira Gate.

on an almost completely buried wall between the gate and the West Church (31), and in the gymnasium at Taucheira (p. 58). These are 'ephebic' inscriptions (relating to an ancient equivalent of the Boy Scouts) recording the successes of young men in the Hellenistic and early Roman periods, and do not necessarily have any military associations.

The rear faces of the towers are not so stylish. Various peculiarities suggest, in fact, that these were originally internal walls and that the flanking towers were perhaps twice the depth, allowing for guardhouses and double sets of gates. Doorways high in the rear faces of the towers suggest the level of the rampart walk; beam slots surviving in the topmost blocks of the towers indicate a roof at this level, and the previous presence of a crown of several further course of blocks above.

The curtain wall survives in the position of the gate alone, butting against the rear faces of the towers as they now stand. On the N side can be seen the slot into which the locking-beam behind the gate was withdrawn in order for the gate to be opened; on the opposite side is a blind socket into which the beam

was slid when the gate was closed. The issues of what happened to the walls of Ptolemais and when is discussed above (p. 81). In the vicinity of the Taucheira Gate two things are clear. The gate itself was modified and its towers reduced in size at some time subsequent to its original construction. Immediately adjoining segments of the wall contain re-used blocks, formerly including a monumental Latin inscription (T. FLAVIVS AV..., a little to the N of the gate) which is unlikely to pre-date the first century AD: this too signifies a rebuilding of the defences. Additionally, the rest of the wall in this sector has been dismantled down to its foundations: there are not even displaced or fallen blocks in the vicinity.

On the high ground immediately outside the gate may be observed elliptical arrangements of stones representing a 19th-century burial ground. There is also a mortared rectangular enclosure around the grave of a holy man.

West Church ★ (31)

This now isolated building on the western part of the site (figs. 63, 64) is of immense solidity; much of it has stood since antiquity, though extensive

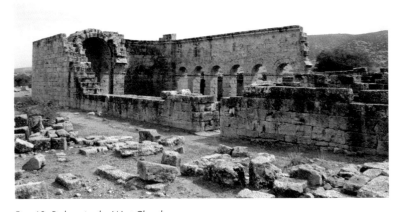

Fig. 63. Ptolemais: the West Church.

restoration was also carried out in the 1930s (involving the dome of the NE angle-chapel and the partial re-erection of the nave arcades). The form is that of a basilical church with an eastern apse between angle-chapels, all inscribed within a rectangular exterior. There are only two modest entrances: one at the W end of the N aisle, and the other in the SW corner, giving access to the narthex, to the S aisle and, via a stair-case and ramp, to upper galleries above the narthex and possibly the roof. The nave was separated from the aisles by seven rectangular piers on either side, carrying arcades; it was linked by three similar openings to the narthex. At the E end it terminates in an apse; sockets,

high in its inner face, may be all that remains of a wooden *synthronon*. The angle-chapels at either side have pilas-ters at the corners supporting arches, and that on the N side has additionally three apses in the thickness of its walls. (There is no sign of the baptistery that might have been expected here; another possible justification for its elaboration might have been that it was a *martyrion*, housing a venerated tomb.) Both of the angle-chapels were roofed with domes; the principal apse was roofed with a semi-dome and the aisles with ribbed barrel-vaults, all in solid masonry. The body of the nave was presumably roofed with timber. (If that span had also been vaulted in stone, it would hardly have left no trace!)

Of the floor of the church, nothing appears to have been detected during the course of the excavation, which has been carried to a considerably lower level. The foundations now visible in the nave belong to a pre-Christian build-ing on the same site, and the floor of the church must have been at least as high as the stylobate beneath the nave arcades.

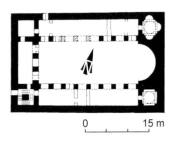

0   15 m

Fig. 64. Ptolemais: plan of the West Church.

The date and structural character of the church have been subject to fierce and unresolved debate. It is immediately apparent when looking at the building that it is unusually solid, and that its masonry, heavy ashlar work virtually without the use of rubble infill, is both fine and spare of ornament. For this reason, it has been described by some as a fortress-church, inferring that in the Byzantine period sensible economies of effort were made by combining the needs of defence (or at least of places of refuge) with the demands of religious worship. Others have rejected this concept. Many of the blocks of which the church is built bear monograms or masons' marks, and some have Greek graffiti of the kind seen on the Taucheira Gate and on an unexcavated wall nearby (pp. 94–5). This suggests that the church may have been built from materials which were readily available in a ruin close by. Majority opinion now favours a date in the sixth century for its construction (Justinianic or maybe considerably later). Some early

Arabic graffiti indicate continued use of some kind after the Islamic conquest.

Amphitheatre ★ (32)

The amphitheatre (fig. 65) is set within a quarry which, being closest to the harbour, was probably the first in the vicinity to be exploited. It may also have been one of the last, for at a date when the Hellenistic city wall had been abandoned, its course was cut through by a further extension of the quarry. The seating of the amphitheatre has gone, but the bedding for it remains, and the passageway which enclosed the arena beneath the lowest seats is still visible. On one side of this passageway was found a painted figure of a *venator* (huntsman). On the E side of the arena, towards the city, an axial entrance-passage is clear, but the arrangement on the opposite side has not been determined. The capacity of the seating has been estimated at around 7,000 persons; the entertainment presumably included *venationes*, staged animal hunts, and certainly also

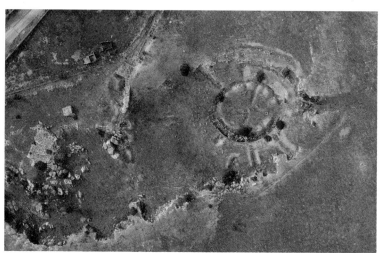

Fig. 65. Ptolemais: the amphitheatre from the air, with the former line of the city wall to the W of it. Photo by Miron Bogacki.

gladiatorial combat, which is attested by the tombstones found nearby and now in the museum (p. 104).

Harbour (33)

The coastline below the city is divided into two sectors by a projecting rocky headland; to the E of this are two small bays protected by a couple of offshore islands and a modern jetty constituting the harbour of today. Summary investigations of the coastline have shown that the two islands were probably connected in antiquity by a mole, and that there may also have been one joining the eastern island to the shore. The topography has been altered not only by erosion but by a rise in sea-level since antiquity of about a metre. Foundations and cuttings in the rock on the E side of the headland can still be made out, presumably representing dockside structures.

The larger, and less well-protected, bay on the W side of the headland was certainly also used, despite the fact that it is mostly outside the defended area. Further cuttings are visible on the W side of the headland, two of which were very probably slipways or ship-sheds. (Recesses in the vertical sides suggest the springing of a covering vault.)

Villa of Orpheus (34)

A small excavation carried out close to the shore in 1960 by the Department of Antiquities was intended to uncover the continuation of the major street leading to the ancient harbour and to demonstrate the presence even in this area of antiquities. In the event, the street was not found, but in the expected spot were found two mosaics (now in the museum: p. 105, items 53 and 55) belonging to a house whose walls had been almost

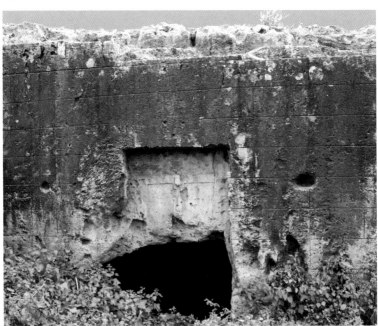

Fig. 66. Ptolemais: the Tomb of the Cartilii.

3 Ptolemais

entirely robbed out. One mosaic, possibly the central feature of a *triclinium*, shows Orpheus charming the animals; the other, one of several panels paving a corridor, depicts a winged Season, Autumn, holding apples, grapes, pomegranates and a pear. They have been attributed to the late fourth or early fifth century AD.

The large open space (partly a football ground) beside the museum, and which one passes when leaving for the site, covers another vast **underground cistern**, like the Square of the Cisterns (17) but considerably larger and with a roof supported on square piers. This has not yet been fully explored.

Tomb of the Cartilii (35)

Ptolemais, like Cyrene, was certainly surrounded by cemeteries. However, the tombs here are not nearly so prominent; cuttings in the bare rock here and there suggest that those which were built up have been almost entirely quarried away for re-use of the stone. There were also rock-cut tombs and, as at Taucheira, many households took advantage of rock-faces, created artificially by the excavation of quarries, as suitable sites for tombs. Many of these are apparent in the quarries which stretch along the coastal ridge between the abandoned military camp and the modern village of Tulmaythah. An accessible and well-preserved example of this type of tomb is the Tomb of the Cartilii.

This is a rock-tomb, cut into the vertical W face of a small quarry which currently delimits the modern settlement of Tulmaytha on the W side (see fig. 41). This quarry, like others nearby, has been adapted to contain animal pens, but is approached by a ramp at the end of the street which leads towards it. The

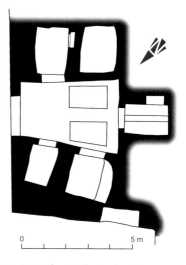

Fig. 67. Ptolemais: the Tomb of the Cartilii, plan.

precise location is N 32° 42.04′ E 20° 56.15′ and, as you descend the ramp, the tomb in question will be directly in front of you. The face of the rock is finely dressed and carved with grooves which suggest the joints of ashlar masonry (fig. 66). The upper part of the double door is likewise carved in the immovable face of the rock. The lower part has been broken away by tomb-robbers: there was probably a low opening here which was concealed by being walled up and plastered over. The name of the original owner of the tomb is carved above the doorway in Greek characters: *Aulus Cartilius Capito*. Names of other family members are carved on either side of the doorway: Cartilia Myrto, aged 14, and Sara, daughter of Cartilius, aged 10, on the left; Cartilia Petronia, aged 70+ on the right. The family was Jewish. The style of lettering has been ascribed tentatively to the first century AD. Inside the rock was a trapezoidal chamber (fig. 67), wider at the rear, with two rectangular *loculi* set into either side and one on the end. There were two further *loculi* cut into the floor of the main chamber, and all of these were large enough to accommodate extended bodies. Some of the *loculi* had rectangular niches carved into their walls, probably to receive lamps or offerings.

Royal tomb ★ (36)

The longest quarry on the seaward side of the road as one approaches Ptolemais contains the unmissable bulk of a huge tower-tomb (fig. 68). The structure is 12 m square at the base and still stands about 15 m high. The lower storey is a massive cube of finely-dressed ashlar masonry, framed by projecting pilasters at the corners with a Doric frieze of metopes and triglyphs around the top. The design is in the tradition of the grandiose Tomb of Mausollus at Halicarnassus (Bodrum in Turkey, though the best parts are in the British Museum!); from this we may infer that there were perhaps two further

storeys above, surrounded by engaged, and then free-standing, columns, terminating in a squat pyramidal roof. The whole might have been 32 m high, as shown in figure 69.

There was a funerary chamber on the ground floor, approached by a doorway nearly 4 m high on the landward side. (The interior is accessible by a rickety ladder, but does not on the whole repay the effort!) Within are eight *loculi* for extended burials on either side and others in the floor, and a staircase which, on the analogy of the tower-tombs at Palmyra in Syria, would have led to upper floors with further capacity for burials. The monument is certainly Hellenistic in date. It pre-dates the stone-quarry, which has been excavated around it, further emphasizing its height. It has been suggested that a structure of this size – without known parallel in Cyrenaica – is likely to have been intended as a royal tomb; the

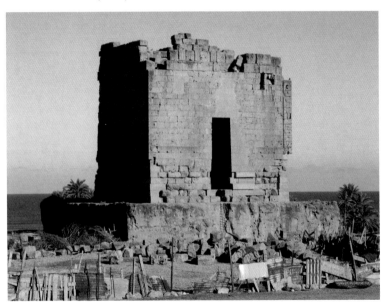

Fig. 68. Ptolemais: the 'Royal' Tomb.

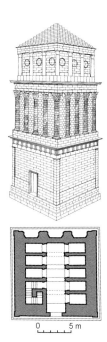

Fig. 69. Ptolemais: plan and reconstruction of the 'Royal' Tomb (from a drawing published by Sandro Stucchi).

most obvious candidate, in that case, is Ptolemy VIII Physcon who ruled in Cyrenaica alone from 163 BC, while his brother, Ptolemy VI Philometor, held sway in Egypt. Physcon acquired Egypt as well after his brother's death in 145, and would then have had no use for a mausoleum at Ptolemais; but it is typical of such structures that they were built with dynastic intent, to house large numbers of the founder's family over several generations.

While acknowledging the exceptional scale of this mausoleum, one should not lose sight of the presence of two other rock-platforms of similar size in the same quarry. Their tombs have entirely disappeared, but they too must have represented wealthy families of the Hellenistic period.

The Museum ★ ★

The museum display at Ptolemais has grown progressively, and not in any very systematic way, since it was first created. Some labels have been introduced by the Polish team which has been working on the site in recent years, but these were far from comprehensive at the time of writing. I am much indebted to the former curator of the site and museum, Abdussalam Bazama, for placing at my disposal his personal knowledge and recollection of the material, but where objects listed below are inadequately explained I must beg the reader's indulgence. The museum is composed of three rooms, as shown in figure 70; the objects are generally described in a clockwise order around the walls of each room, followed by those items in the centre of the floor. Many of the finest objects on display were found in the Colonnaded Palace (15), including numerous fragments of architectural ornament.

Left-hand room

1. Fragment of marble stele, showing a *quadriga* (four-horse chariot).
2. Reclining nymph in marble, a fountain-head from the Colonnaded Palace.
3. Feet only from a marble statue-group depicting Dionysos with a satyr with pan-pipes, dedicated by M. Ulpius Cominius (cf. item 64). From the 'Odeon' (25), second or third century AD.
4. Sandstone sarcophagus lid. A recent find.
5. Sandstone stele depicting a seated woman, from Barka (al-Marj).
6. A group of two Corinthian pilaster-capitals with some painted wall-plaster. From the Colonnaded Palace.
7. Lid of an Attic sarcophagus with reclining couple, an early find on the right bank of the Wadi Khambish. Second or third century AD. In the corner

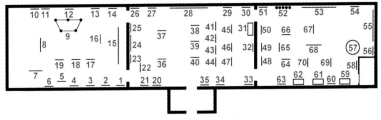

Fig. 70. Ptolemais: sketch-plan of the museum.

behind the sarcophagus, a sandstone column and capital on the floor, found close to the museum; the pieces above are from the Colonnaded Palace.

8. Part of an Attic sarcophagus depicting the legend of Achilles on Skyros, found in the Wadi Khambish (fig. 71). The hero is in the centre, wearing a *himation* but leaping up with a shield in response to the trumpet-call of the herald behind him, and thus revealing his identity (having been hiding in woman's clothing). The piece has been ascribed to the second quarter of the third century AD. The lid beside the museum (on the L, towards the side gate) may be the lid of this sarcophagus, or of one of the others found in the same area. On the end-wall behind are some small gravestelai: one showing a flask and strigils, one showing a bearded head with cap. High on the RH corner is a decorated cornice-fragment from the Colonnaded Palace.

9. Five stuccoed sandstone capitals on a frame: the figural Corinthian capitals are from the Colonnaded Palace (p. 84), the painted Ionic ones are unprovenanced.

10. Three items against the wall from the Colonnaded Palace: an engaged Doric column-capital, a small Corinthian capital and a block with painted wall-plaster.

11. Statue of a funerary goddess, from Barka (al-Marj). Probably Hellenistic.

12. Plain sandstone sarcophagus. Unprovenanced.

13. Part of a sarcophagus lid.

14. Ottoman grave-marker. From Ghut Qinubil, near al-Marj. High in the corner of the room is a cornice from the Colonnaded Palace.

15. On the wall between the doorways, and on the stand in front of it, are various Kufic inscriptions of Fatimid date from al-Marj al-Qadim. These were mostly uncovered during road-building and other operations in 1936; one of the

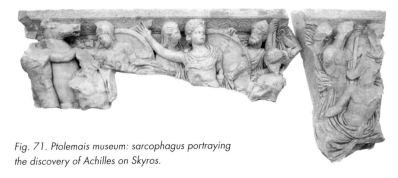

Fig. 71. Ptolemais museum: sarcophagus portraying the discovery of Achilles on Skyros.

blocks contains a reference to the late tenth-century Fatimid caliph al-Mu'izz.

16. Torso of a Roman emperor in local sandstone: a recent casual find reported by a shepherd.

17. Archaic funerary goddess, provenance uncertain. Fifth century BC.

18. Faceless archaic funerary goddess from Barka (Wadi Azziya). Late sixth or early fifth century BC.

19. Archaic funerary goddess, from Ptolemais (E side of Wadi Ziwanah). Probably fifth century BC.

Centre room

20. Two fragments of marble inscriptions in Greek mentioning an *akademarch*, head of the local ephebic organization. Found in the West Church; the left-hand fragment is dated AD 128–138, the right-hand one belongs approximately to the second or third century AD.

21. Small inscribed marble stele with pediment. This is a dedication by the *epheboi* of Ptolemais of 4–3 BC. Find-spot unrecorded. To the R of this and on the adjacent wall between the left and centre rooms are panels in Italian which describe the various sculptural riches (both Egyptian and Hellenistic/Roman) which were found in the excavation of the Colonnaded Palace.

22. Torso of a naked man, from the Colonnaded Palace.

23, 25. Two fragments of mosaic *emblemata* illustrating a cockerel and fishes, respectively. Found unstratified in the Colonnaded Palace (presumably fallen from an upper floor).

24. Geometric mosaic with central *emblema* of a Medusa head (fig. 72). Found in the Colonnaded Palace, room (e) (p. 83).

26. Headless seated female figure (Demeter?) in limestone. From the Colonnaded Palace.

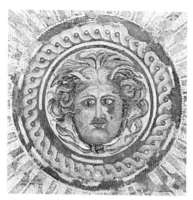

Fig. 72. Ptolemais museum: mosaic emblema *with Medusa head from the* Colonnaded Palace.

27. Christian funerary tablet commemorating 'the blessed servant of God, Julia.' Sporadic find; probably sixth century AD.

28. Mosaic of the Four Seasons, from the summer *triclinium* in the villa named after it (27: p. 94). Spring is at the lower left, with a shepherd's crook and a garland of flowers; Summer is in the opposite corner, with a garland of ears of corn; Autumn (upper left) clearly represents the vintage, while the head of Winter (lower right) is largely missing, though the heavy winter cloak is apparent. Datable between the first and third centuries AD.

29. Latin inscription from near the Arch of Constantine (2). This is a fragment of the original dedication of the arch, which has been shown to belong to the years AD 311–13. See also item 35.

30. Fragment of the Price Edict of Diocletian, found re-used face down as a paving slab in the Street of the Monuments, in front of the Late Baths (5). This was a vain, empire-wide, attempt to control inflation in AD 301, by posting maximum permissible prices for a range of about a thousand different products and services.

31. A case of pottery: that on the top shelf is from Barka, including painted vessels of the Classical period. The remainder is coarse ware from Ptolemais.

32. On the wall, a mosaic panel showing a lion devouring a donkey, from the Villa of the Four Seasons (27). Below, the lower part of a small marble statue of Demeter from Zawiyat Innablu and three small fragments of sculpture from Ptolemais.

33. Oversize marble head of Tyche from the Colonnaded Palace.

34. Large sandstone boundary-marker from the time of Domitian, found by the Taucheira Gate (30). Dated to AD 88–89, it records the restitution to the city of land previously acquired by private individuals. Several similar boundary markers are on display in the Apollonia museum: p. 285.

35. Small fragment of a monumental Latin inscription, another fragment of 29.

36. Large statue of Athena, slightly over life-size, from the Street of the Monuments (3).

37. Draped male figure, slightly over life-size, with a stack of scrolls (?) at his feet.

38. Draped (headless) female with windswept clothing in Pentelic marble, from the 'Odeon' (25): probably a Victory, and a Roman copy of an earlier original.

39. Oversize Pentelic marble statue of Claudia Euporiane as Demeter (no head but veiled and with ears of corn in her hand), identified by associated base, from the Street of the Monuments (3). Antonine?

40. Draped male in Pentelic marble, identified by associated base as M. Aurelius Flavianus, from the Street of the Monuments (3). Second half of second or early third century AD.

41. Headless marble figure of Artemis as huntress, from the Colonnaded Palace.

42. Torso only of a naked female: one of the Three Graces, from the Late Baths (5). First half of second century?

43. Figure of Dionysos (head lost during the Second World War), from the Colonnaded Palace. Flavian?

44. Small figure of a young satyr with club and wineskin, from the Colonnaded Palace (head lost during the Second World War).

45. End of a marble sarcophagus portraying Greeks fighting Amazons, an early find from Wadi Khambish. Second century AD.

46. Life-size Pentelic marble statue of Artemis, from the 'Odeon' (25).

47. Sarcophagus-fragment: festoons on the rear, Heracles on the angle, two erotes fighting over a palm on the end. An early find from Wadi Khambish. Second century AD.

Right-hand room

48. Tombstone of a gladiator, Hermes, found in or near the amphitheatre. He is armed as a *retiarius*, holding a trident in his left hand and with chain-mail armour protecting the arm and shoulder on that side. The nine palms either side of his name signify his victories. On the bottom of the stone, a second inscription records that he was formerly known as Philo (prior to becoming a gladiator). Second or third century AD.

49. Tombstone of a gladiator (unnamed) who died 'not, like the others, in battle, but from disease'. Found in or near the amphitheatre. Second or third century AD.

50. Tombstone of a gladiator, Hippomedon, found in or near the amphitheatre (fig. 73). He is heavily armed as a *secutor*, with a legionary shield and

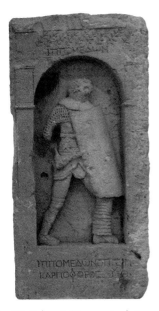

Fig. 73. Ptolemais Museum: tombstone of the gladiator Hippomedon.

53. Mosaic from the Villa of Orpheus (34), showing a winged figure (Autumn) holding fruit and with a *nimbus* behind her head; several crosses are also discreetly incorporated into the surrounding abstract composition. Compare item 55 below. Late fourth or early fifth century AD.

54. A small female marble figure on a plinth, with an elephant headdress and a leopard-skin around her shoulders, representing Africa or Libya. Not readily identifiable with a specific Ptolemaic queen. Findspot uncertain. Late second century AD.

55. This large mosaic was lifted from the Villa of Orpheus (named after it), excavated in 1960 close to the seashore (34) and no longer visible. The central scene (fig. 74), familiar from many representations, shows Orpheus clothed as an oriental (wearing a purple cloak and a Phrygian cap), seated and playing the lyre. Around him is an array of wild animals, all of whom

protection for his left leg and his right arm. He also wears a distinctive helmet, almost spherical, with two small eye-holes. A secutor would typically be paired with a retiarius (as no. 47); hence the helmet, designed to ward off the points of the trident. Hippomedon has also won nine fights, and was formerly known as Karpophoros. Second or third century AD.

51. Half of a semi-draped marble Venus. Findspot unrecorded.

52. A selection of stuccoed and painted columns from the Villa with a View (16). On the wall behind is a cast of a Hellenistic votive relief of a horseman, found in the villa excavations.

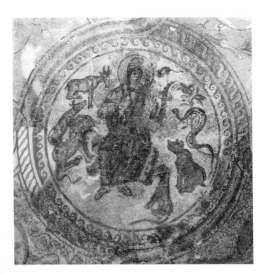

Fig. 74. Ptolemais Museum: central scene of the Orpheus mosaic.

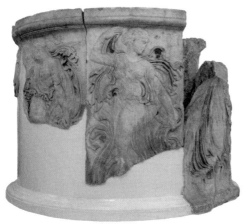

Fig. 75. Ptolemais Museum: Fountain of the Maenads.

59. Case of largely complete coarse-ware jars.

60. Very fragmentary over life-size female figure.

61, 62. Two cases of pottery from the Barka area, including a stone alabastron: mostly of the sixth and fifth centuries BC but including Roman lamps also.

63. Naked male torso.

64. Marble statue of Athena found in the portico of the 'Odeon' (25), dedicated by M. Ulpius Cominius (cf. item 3). Early second century AD.

65. Half-draped, headless statue of Venus, from the 'Odeon'.

66. Large draped headless female.

67. Headless Athena, from the N side of the Street of the Monuments (found in the E *cardo*, on the W side of the *tetrastylon*?).

68. Attic garland sarcophagus of the third century AD, found E of Wadi Ziwanah, re-used for a burial in the narthex of a recently-discovered church. Of the Roman period, with an eagle between garlands on the principal face; on the rear face is an urn and bosses between garlands, re-carved with a cross. The interior of the sarcophagus show signs of secondary widening. Next to the sarcophagus is a fragment of a lid, which was presumably found in association with it.

69. Naked male torso.

70. Life-size draped female in Pentelic marble. The body (wet, clinging drapery) is said to be of Venus, while the veiled head is of Demeter. Found outside the 'Odeon' (25).

are gazing at him in attitudes of rapt attention. The minor roundels and the triangular corner-panels of the composition show water birds going about their business amongst 'Nilotic' vegetation. The mosaic has been attributed to the late fourth or early fifth century AD, and is claimed by some to have Christian overtones. The halo or *nimbus* around the head of Orpheus is cited, the theme being related to that of the Good Shepherd. This association is perhaps reinforced by the mosaic on the adjoining wall (item 53), which comes from the same house.

56. A small burned marble figure of Venus, from the Colonnaded Palace.

57. The Fountain of the Maenads (fig. 75). This is a handsome copy of disputed date (opinions range from Hellenistic to Antonine) of a sculpture carved in Athens by Callimachus c. 405 BC for the choregic monument of Euripides. The fragments were found in the Street of the Monuments, close to the foundations of a fountain at (7).

58. Torso of Herakles, findspot unrecorded.

4 AL-MARJ AND SITES TO THE SOUTH-EAST

As one progresses eastwards from Benghazi towards the jabal, the land rises in two separate steps which are quite widely separated. The first of these steps is characterized by the vast plain of al-Marj, extensively cultivated today in large regular plots for both arable crops and soft fruits. The plain lies at a height of 280–350 m. The only major ancient settlement here was the city of Barka, succeeded by al-Marj which was itself refounded on a new site after a disastrous earthquake in 1963. Parts of the plain (particularly around the town of al-Marj al-Qadim) have always been subject to flooding; this was thought to have played its part when in 515 BC King Arkesilaos III took refuge there, placing his confidence in a warning by the Delphic Oracle to avoid 'the land surrounded by water' – which he mistakenly interpreted as signifying Cyrene with its abundant springs. The Oracle could not, therefore, be blamed for his subsequent assassination! (See p. 3.)

The red soil of the plain is fertile and has been the object of agricultural projects both in the Italian colonial period and subsequently. There is evidence of farming during antiquity, but little is now visible. To the N, the ground falls away quite steeply towards the coast and to the port of Ptolemais which undoubtedly grew up to serve the inland region. (It is of note that, of the ancient cities on the coast, Ptolemais was that which survived the longest into the medieval period: this presumably reflected its connection with Barka/Barqa which continued to be a centre of Berber habitation.)

To the S of the plain, the ground rises across rounded hills. Amongst these there are still valleys which are broad enough for cultivation and it is here particularly (around Zawiyat al-Qsur) that numerous fortified farms of the Roman period have been recorded and may still be found. The hilltop site of Qasr al-Jaballah, rather different in character, surely reflects military control of the zone from one of its high points. Yet further S, the land becomes progressively more arid as it slopes down away from the coast towards the desert. Here there was an important caravan route, probably more so in the Islamic period than previously, which linked the Syrtic Gulf (and pilgrims from the Maghrib heading for Mecca) with the Gulf of Bumba and Egypt. Settlement is confined to scattered watering-holes and alluvial fans capable of supporting seasonal crops. Much has yet to be learned about these settlements, in terms both of date and of the nature of their occupation (military sites, civil settlements, caravanserais).

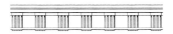

AL-MARJ المرج

Coordinates: N 32° 30.02', E 20° 53.52'
Directions: The new town (al-Marj al-Jadid), on the main road E from Benghazi and about 15 minutes' drive E of the Tukrah Pass, is unmissable. For the old town (al-Marj al-Qadim, to which the coordinates refer), continue eastwards on the main road for a further 5.4 km beyond the junction for the new town until you come to a cross-roads with a check-point. (For steam buffs, there is on the forecourt of a former

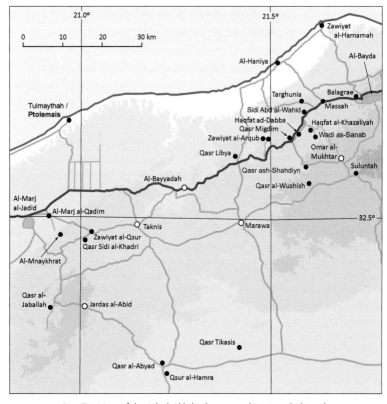

Fig. 76. Map of the Jabal Akhdar between al-Marj and al-Bayda.

filling station here an ancient steam plough-ing-engine, which appears to be a German Heucke model of the 1920s!) Turn south-wards here and you will come to the old town in a further 1.5 km.

There are today two towns of al-Marj, the Old (Qadim) and the New (Jadid). The old town was severely damaged by earthquake on 21 February 1963, and was replaced by a new founda-tion 5 km away: this is the burgeoning town through which one passes on the main E–W road today, distinguished in its time for possessing the first clover-leaf junction in Libya!

The old town is now a shattered rem-nant of its former self, with many build-ings in ruins. However, its history goes back to the mid sixth century BC, when the settlement of Barka was founded by Greeks from Cyrene, at a time of civil strife. Unlike the other Greek foundations in Cyrenaica, Barka seems always to have been a joint venture between the immigrant Greeks and the indigenous Libyans. We are told of this by the fifth-century BC historian Herodotus, who provides us with colourful stories of its early history and of internecine strife amongst the ruling dynasty of Cyrene. The economic significance of Barka in terms of its vast surrounding agricultural plain does not need to be pointed out to anyone on the ground; but the site is far from the sea and to the Greeks, for whom the sea was their principal means of communication, a port was necessary. It developed early a port on the coast to the N, but from the time when that city took the name of Ptolemais (in the late fourth century BC: p. 68) and was greatly developed, Barka seems to have been eclipsed by it. The Pentapolis, the Hellenistic federation of five cities, included Euesperides/Berenice, Taucheira, Ptolemais, Cyrene and Apollonia, but not Barka.

Nonetheless, the city clearly continued to exist and to flourish, for at the time of the Islamic conquest in the seventh century AD its capture was an early achievement of the invading forces. There is a clear implication that the inhabitants were less Hellenized/Romanized than those of the coastal cities, and that they could be more readily detached from allegiance to Byzantine rule. After the conquest, when travel by sea became more hazardous (and the Arabs were in any case not accustomed to it), the importance of Barka increased again, to the extent that it gave its name to the entire region – and Barqa remains the Arabic name for Cyrenaica today. Later on, we know that Barka was important to the Fatimids in the 10th century, and it was described by al-Bakri in the 11th as a prosperous city, exporting fruits, honey and wool to Egypt. In the 12th century, after the invasion of the Bani Hilal and the Bani Sulaym it was described as a much smaller, but formerly flourishing town. After that, it seems to have dwindled away completely. In 1852 the English traveller James Hamilton saw a castle which had recently been built at

Barqa by the Ottoman Turks, and which he observed to be composed of 'ancient materials dug up on the spot.' A new settlement was growing up around it. The castle collapsed in the earthquake of 1963.

There is nothing to be seen today of the antiquity or former importance of al-Marj, though both excavations and casual finds have shown that the old town does indeed stand directly on the site of Classical and medieval Barka. A number of fine Kufic inscriptions, comparable to those from Ajdabiya and almost certainly of the Fatimid period, are now on display in the museum at Ptolemais (p. 102). Before the earthquake, the mosque of the former zawiya at al-Marj was described as incorporating ancient columns, capitals and bases in its architecture. The building still stands, but was not accessible at the time of writing.

Rock-tomb of al-Mnaykhrat ★

This is a two-storey tomb, set into a hillside and entirely cut out of the rock face (fig. 77). In order to reach it, drive directly through the centre of old al-Marj. At the far end of the main street, you will have to turn L and then immediately R in order to pass round the former Italian railway station and a radio mast. Keep going in the same direction (approximately SSE) until you reach the edge of the jabal. The asphalt comes to an end about 3.6 km after passing the old railway station, but the unmade track beyond is readily negotiable in dry weather. Pass by a former firing range on your L, and at the foot of the escarpment turn L; continue in this direction for exactly 1 km, at which point you will find yourself at the mouth of the Wadi Taybsillu, with the rock-tomb

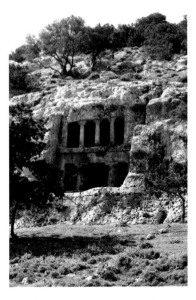

Fig. 77. Al-Marj: archaic rock-tomb of al-Mnaykhrat.

clearly visible part-way up the W bank. The coordinates of the tomb are N 32° 27.67' E 20° 55.24'.

The lower storey of the façade has a portico fronted by two stocky Doric columns standing on a plinth. The plinth is cut between them to make an opening into the portico. The upper storey takes the form of a loggia, with three slimmer square piers surmounted by barely articulated Ionic or Aeolic capitals. The walls of the portico are lined with seven carved stone *klinai*, couches for funeral banquets. Over the top of one of these (as in the early rock-tombs at Cyrene) a doorway leads into an inner chamber, off which opens a burial recess on the right-hand side. The loggia which constitutes the upper storey is purely decorative and there is nothing behind it. It is accessible only by means of a narrow path on the face of the hillside,

and there is no direct communication between the upper and lower floors.

The style of the architecture places this tomb somewhere in the later sixth century BC. The position is commanding and it would have been widely visible to people in the plain: we may reasonably assume that this was the resting-place of a person of great importance. Early modern visitors optimistically inferred that the toponym 'Mnaykhrat' was a corruption of the ancient Greek name *Menekrates*. Unfortunately – and this is a salutary lesson in this kind of speculation – the Arabic name actually means 'nostrils', an understandable description of the holes in the hillside!

QASR AL-ABYAD   القصر الأبيض
Coordinates: N 32° 10.68', E 21° 11.68'
Directions: The site is close to the triangular junction at al-Kharrubah between roads from al-Marj/Jardas al-Abid (NW), at-Tamimi/Makhayli (E) and Zawiyat Masus (S). The qasr may be found on the N side of the road to Jardas, at a distance of 250 m from the junction.

Fort, farm or communal refuge? ★
This is a spectacular building (The White Castle) some 26 m square at ground level (fig. 78). It stands to a height of 7 m, with thick walls of mud-brick, faced on the outside with a sloping outer skin of rough stonework. There is a single entrance, on the E side, and on each side there are four narrow windows, set high up. The interior of the building is now some 5–6 m above the external ground-surface; the surrounding walls extend higher, and on the N side may be seen voids still roofed by stone vaults. It is likely therefore that a lower floor survives beneath the rubble, and that there was a second tier of rooms above.

The only pottery which has been found here is medieval; the structure may therefore have been built in imitation of (late) Roman stone buildings further to the E (e.g. Qasr al-Maraghah, p. 310, and Qasr Wurtij, p. 318), but it is certainly not contemporary with them.

The Wadi Islan is capable of sustaining agriculture in this region, and this site is on an E–W route from the Gulf of Bumba to the Gulf of Sidra which skirts the southern edge of the Jabal Akhdar. (This acquired particular importance in the Islamic period as part of the pilgrim route between the Maghrib and Mecca.) It is likely that there was a permanent settlement of some sort here over a long period. The fort does not suggest high-level or 'official' military activity, and may have been a defence erected by the local community for its own preservation. In that regard, it may well have served also as a food-store, like the communal granaries found in the Jabal Nafusah of Tripolitania.

QASR AL-JABALLAH قصر الجبلّه

Coordinates: N 32° 18.05′, E 20° 53.84′
Directions: For convenience, it is assumed that a visit to this site will be combined with a visit to Zawiyat al-Qsur (p. 113). From the T-junction at this location, head SW, past Qasr Sidi al-Khadri, for a distance of 10.4 km. At N 32° 25.14′ E 20° 55.40′ you will reach a T-junction: turn L and follow this road southwards for a further distance of 14.0 km, until the road makes a bold turn to the E. At this point (N 32° 18.85′ E 20° 54.34′) an asphalt road veers off almost due S. Follow this road for just 2.0 km: the ruin is clearly visible on top of the hill on your R, and is best approached by means of the farm track on the S side of the hill. Park in front of the farm and ask permission, if there is anyone about.

Roman fort

This is an approximately square Roman fort, 39 × 39 m, atop an isolated hill which dominates the surrounding countryside. The external walls in rough

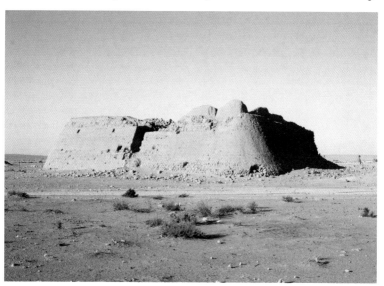

Fig. 78. Qasr al-Abyad.

111

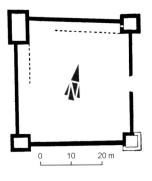

Fig. 79. Sketch-plan of Qasr al-Jaballah by Richard Goodchild.

ashlar masonry are well preserved, though more than one phase of work is apparent, with perhaps late repairs of inferior quality. The entrance was probably on the E side (though this is not now detectable) and the corners were protected by square or rectangular towers. Part of the NW corner-tower still stands to a height of some ten courses of masonry and close examination will show that part of a tall, narrow window is present. Little is visible of internal structures, though outside the fort, on the W side of the hilltop, stone door-jambs and other foundations indicate discrete rectangular buildings. Blocks re-arranged into elliptical outlines show that the site was used at some time after the Arab conquest as a burial-ground.

QASR TIKASIS   قصر تكاسيس

Coordinates: N 32° 12.90′, E 21° 24.14′
Directions: N of the road between al-Kharrubah and Makhayli: turn N at N 32° 11.31′ E 21° 24.12′ onto an unmade track; this is at 19.7 km E of al-Kharrubah and about 200 m to the E of a radio station. Proceed northwards for 2.8 km: this is rough and slow, but negotiable in a saloon car at the time of writing. The settlement is

clearly visible 600 m E of this point; from here it is probably just as quick to walk as to pick your way between the stones with a vehicle.

Roman/Italian military post

Here, as in many other locations, geography determined a suitable position for a defensive post, whether in the Roman period or in the 20th century. The site is on high stony ground overlooking the Wadi Samalus. Here there are ruins of an Italian military post; examination will show that at its SW corner this made use of a small rectangular building (11 × 10 m) of much earlier date, constructed in mud-brick, with a steeply sloping outer face of roughly squared stone blocks. Parts of the walls are still 3 m high. Immediately to the S of this structure are traces of other rectangular buildings; in the beds of the tributary wadis nearby there are also typical wadi walls, constructed across the beds of the wadis in order to delay the run-off of rainwater and so to assist in the cultivation of the soil. Potsherds of late Roman date have been found on the site, though it is impossible to say without excavation whether the defensive building (no more than a watch-tower) is of late Roman or early medieval (i.e. Islamic) date. The quality of stonework in the sloping revetment is certainly higher than that found in the post-Roman Qasr al-Abyad (p.110), 20 km to the W.

Some 400 m to the NW of the qasr, at N 32° 13.00′ E 21° 23.88′ and facing it in the bank of the wadi, is a rectangular rock-cut chamber-tomb with a round-headed door approached by means of a steep *dromos*; within is a rectangular chamber with a raised *loculus* in the entrance-wall, on the L. This is surely of Roman date.

QSUR AL-HAMRA القصر الحمر

Coordinates: N 32° 9.68', E 21° 12.07'
Directions: The site is close to the triangular junction at al-Kharrubah (N 32° 10.56' E 20° 33.40') between roads from al-Marj/Jardas al-Abid (NW), at-Tamimi/Makhayli (E) and Zawiyat Masus (S). Take the road S from here, for a distance of 1.7 km. The site lies approximately 200 m to the E of the road and to the N of a present-day farm. Ask permission before visiting. The Wadi Islan runs parallel to the road on the far side of the site.

Late Roman farms
Here, on the W bank of the Wadi Islan, an approximately triangular enclosure formed of rubble stone walls includes, at its N and E corners, ruins of two solid square buildings, the Qsur al-Hamra or Red Castles (fig. 80). These are represented now by rather shapeless cores of mud-brick, their stone facings having been appropriated to construct the modern building which stands between them. The northerly qasr, which stands within its own walled enclosure (perhaps once filled with surrounding rooms), still preserves part of its original

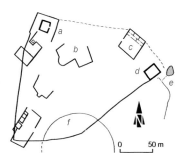

Fig. 80. Qsur al-Hamra: sketch-plan of the visible structures. (a) North qasr; (b) Recent cemetery; (c) Modern building; (d) East qasr; (e) Sink-hole/cistern; (f) Circular enclosure.

stone facing around the entrance on the E side. The main enclosure interrupts, and therefore overlies, traces of other ancient buildings; there is also a recent cemetery and, on the S side of the site, a large circular enclosure whose relationship to the other features is uncertain. A natural sink-hole in the limestone, just outside the E corner, has served as a cistern, for a mortar-lined channel has been constructed to divert rainwater into it.

Late Roman pottery has been found on the surface; like Qasr al-Abyad just to the N and Qasr Tikasis some 20 km to the E, this site may have been settled in the late Roman and/or early medieval periods.

ZAWIYAT AL-QSUR زاوية القصور

Coordinates: N 32° 27.97', E 21° 0.18'
Directions: The easiest way to find this area is to leave the main road E of al-Marj al-Jadid by the checkpoint at N 32° 30.89' E 20° 52.98' and to head S for al-Marj al-Qadim. After 1.3 km, at the cross-roads at the entrance to the old town, turn L and follow round the edge of the town, heading SE towards the jabal escarpment. Climb the pass and at a distance of 12.7 km from the cross-roads, you will come to a turning to the R opposite the small settlement of Zawiyat al-Qsur.

Area of ancient farms
The road which heads towards the SW at this point (towards Jardas al-Abid; if you continue straight on, you will come to Taknis) runs along a valley of good arable land which was evidently intensively farmed in antiquity from defensive residences situated on the higher ground on either side. Several ancient farms can still be made out: just two of them will be described by way of example.

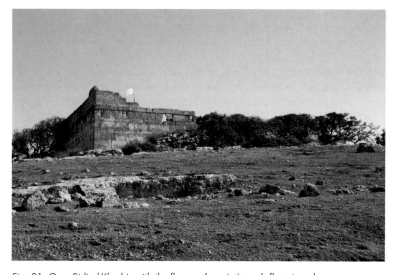

Fig. 81. Qasr Sidi al-Khadri, with the flag on the saint's tomb fluttering above Byzantine walls.

The little zawiya of **Zawiyat al-Qsur** (which takes its name from the plentiful ancient remains) stands on the hilltop at the road junction; it may readily be approached by a track on the S side. The ancient farm on the same hilltop was still described as an 'imposing castle ruin' in 1963, but has now been superseded by a modern farm. A few large squared blocks projecting from the ground are the only surviving signs of antiquity.

Qasr Sidi al-Khadri ★ (fig. 81) has fared somewhat better. This lies some 300 m to the S of the road, just 1.9 km from the junction. There is a short track from the road towards the qasr, actually leading to the saint's tomb which nestles against it; you can hardly miss the green conical roof and white flag. (These words were written in 2010: since then, many saints' tombs have been damaged or destroyed by Salafist fanatics, and Sidi al-Khadri may not have escaped.) The qasr is faced externally with handsome ashlar masonry with a projecting string-course between the floors, as at many other sites (e.g. Qasr al-Wushish, p. 125; Qasr az-Zaarura, p. 123). Internally, a number of arches are still preserved spanning ground-floor doorways; the plan appears to have taken the usual form of two storeys of rooms around a small central courtyard. There was a rock-cut quarry/ditch on at least the N and W sides of the building, but there is no sign of a sloping external revetment. The style of the masonry and the presence of a carved cross on one of the corners suggest a Byzantine date.

5 SITES BETWEEN BAYYADAH AND CYRENE

For this zone, continue to refer to the map in figure 76.

To the E of the plain of al-Marj, the ground begins to rise again, and the former Italian colonial settlement of D'Annunzio, now Bayyadah, may be taken conveniently to mark the transition along the main road from the plain in the W to the more broken ground to the E. The limestone hills here are deeply dissected by steep-sided dry valleys; the tree cover is more extensive, including both juniper, olive, Aleppo pine, Kermes Oak and Mediterranean cypress. The rainfall is good and, where the soil is deep enough, it has been cultivated through much of history. The combination of steep-sided valleys, difficult of access, and of caves and rock-shelters in the limestone, has made this an attractive zone for defensive settlement, from prehistory until modern times. Prehistoric sediments have been excavated in Haqfat ad-Dabba in the Wadi Kuf, and in the 20th century small bands of Libyans under the leadership of Omar al-Mukhtar sustained a lengthy and bloody resistance to Italian conquest in this area for some twenty years, making use of the same caves. The writings of Synesius of Cyrene (p. 8) give a vivid picture of life on a landed estate in this terrain in the early fifth century AD, and of the perils which the population constantly faced from predatory marauders. The great hilltop fortress of Qasr ash-Shahdiyn, possibly the *Bombaia* mentioned by Synesius, bears material witness to the investment which had to be made by any authority which wished to enforce its control over the area.

The route now followed by the main road directly across the gorge of the Wadi Kuf on a high suspension bridge was created in the 1960s. Its precursor took a lower course through the wadi and over a Bailey bridge, built by the British army during the Second World War to replace an Italian bridge which had been destroyed during the North African campaign. Even this road was built only in 1936. Prior to that, the main lines of land communication had passed either further to the N, along the narrow coastal strip (climbing onto the jabal to the W of Massah), or further to the S, approximately on a line through Taknis, Marawah and Suluntah to the Cyrene area.

As elsewhere in this guide, it is particularly true of the central Jabal Akhdar that the density of visible farms and settlements belonging to Classical antiquity is far greater than is represented by the selection presented here. Those listed are chosen partly at random and because they can be visited easily in clusters; they should nonetheless suffice to give an idea of the material heritage in which this landscape is so rich.

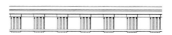

AL-BAYDA   البيضاء

The modern town of al-Bayda is largely a creation of King Idris in the 1960s, developed initially as a federal capital away from the rivalries of Tripoli and Benghazi. It takes its name from the Zawiyat al-Bayda (the White Monastery), the former site of which is now on the western outskirts. This was the first lodge in Libya of the Sanusi brotherhood, established in 1843. After Qadhafi's revolution the town lost its intended pre-eminence, but it has continued to grow apace. In so doing it has enveloped the historic monuments described below.

Sanctuary of Asklepios ★

On the N side of the main E–W road which leads westward from the modern town, a few metres to the E of the distinctive buildings of Omar al-Mukhtar University, is a walled enclosure with ruins of ancient buildings outside the wall and next to the road. This enclosure (entered most conveniently by the side-road which runs up its western side) contains the Sanctuary of Asklepios, the god of healing (at N 32° 45.65′ E 21° 42.93′). This was the focal point of the ancient settlement of *Balagrae*. The sanctuary was renowned in antiquity as a direct offspring of the cult centre at Epidaurus in the Peloponnese, and was said itself to have been responsible for another such foundation at Lebena in Crete.

Foundations of ancient buildings were found here when Muhammad Ali as-Sanusi was building the first lodge in Libya for his brotherhood nearby in 1843, and much masonry was removed by Italian troops constructing the barracks immediately to the W in 1915. More methodical excavations were subsequently carried out by the Department of Antiquities in 1920, and again, when al-Bayda was designated

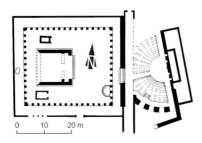

Fig. 82. Partial plan of the Sanctuary of Asklepios at Balagrae (Al-Bayda).

as the federal capital of Libya, in 1956. During recent years, the Department of Archaeology of Omar al-Mukhtar University (across the road) has been conducting training excavations on the eastern part of the site.

The sacred precinct (fig. 82) consists principally of a rectangular enclosure with internal porticoes on all four sides and with its principal entrance on the E. Within the central open space stood three temples: a large one on the central axis dedicated to Asklepios, flanked by two much smaller ones dedicated to his daughters *Hygeia* (Health) and *Iaso* (Healing). These have been stripped down to their foundations but are detectable beneath the remains of later buildings. Against the E portico is a small horseshoe-shaped structure in fine Hellenistic masonry; this may be the local counterpart to the circular *tholoi* which occur in many sanctuaries of Asklepios. (Unfortunately, we do not really know what these, often complex, buildings were for! In this case, it can hardly have enclosed more than a sacred well or a sacred tree.) Beneath the W portico there was a rock-cut cavity which is choked with column-drums and has not been fully explored: this may have been the dormitory where the sick were brought to sleep in the hope of a vision of the god and of being healed. The portico colonnades, in local limestone, are unusual in that three sides are in the Doric style, whereas the fourth, on the E, is in a version of Ionic. The corner problem is resolved through the use (not uncommon in Cyrenaica) of heart-shaped corner-piers. It has been suggested that the use of the Ionic order on this side implies the former presence of an upper storey (which would have masked the building to the E) though of this there is no direct evidence. From the

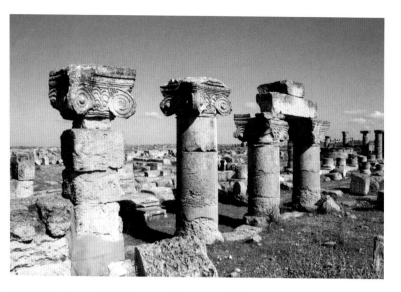

Fig. 83. Sanctuary of Asklepios: partially re-erected columns with curious Ionic capitals.

S portico there are two openings into an area of other buildings which has not been fully explored; but the wider of these is notable for its columns with Ionic capitals which have been said to bear stylized silphium plants (p. 11) between the volutes (fig. 83: stylized, yes – but even so, hardly silphium!). The reconstruction is puzzling, for there are actually five capitals, including one on the ground, and that which has been placed as an *anta*-capital on top of a square pier cannot have belonged there: there was perhaps therefore a porch with two rows of three columns in the openings.

Immediately to the E of the sacred precinct is a small theatre, facing E but on a slightly different alignment, probably determined by that of a street which runs behind the stage-building. The theatre had 16 tiers of seats, partly truncated towards the precinct; the two are connected by a passageway which runs beneath the seats of the theatre into the orchestra. On higher ground to the E of

this, across an ancient street, has been exposed a house with a Doric peristyle, beneath which is a huge vaulted cistern. The water could be drawn up through a handsome moulded well-head on the edge of the peristyle.

The origins of the sanctuary must go back to the fourth century BC: we know that the daughter foundation at Lebena existed at that time, and the place-name seems to be related to the Macedonian personal name *Balacros* – implying a connection with the arrival of Macedonians in the time of Alexander the Great (c. 331 BC). However, apart, possibly, from the *tholos*, what is now visible belongs to the time of the emperor Hadrian, whose name is inscribed on the architrave of the portico (laid out on the ground) and in the theatre. (Within the Temple of Asklepios has been found a fragment of the floor of an earlier – and smaller – predecessor.) This rebuilding may have been work carried out in consequence of the destruction wrought by the Jewish Revolt in AD 115. The theatre – and probably the sanctuary also – had gone out of use as such before the great earthquake of AD 365 (p. 7), for at that time an occupant of a modest dwelling built in one of its corridors was crushed by its falling masonry. We can be sure of the occasion, because the unfortunate victim was accompanied by a hoard of 259 coins which must have been in a box or purse. The latest of the coins was struck in 364. (A note of caution should, however, be inserted here: a recent study has drawn attention to the fact that many of the coins in this hoard were clipped to conform to a weight standard which was adopted only in 375!) Inscriptions, including the text of a sacred law regulating access to the sanctuary, and fine pieces of sculpture were recovered from these late structures during the earlier excavations. Further evidence leading to a similar conclusion has been found in recent excavations close to the eastern boundary of the site. Buildings here which were thrown down in the earthquake of 365 were already built of blocks taken from the (presumably) ruined temple precinct. The occupation in this area was also domestic or agricultural in nature, including an installation for wine-making (with pressing-floor and fermentation vats). In the N portico of the sacred precinct there is also clear evidence of later secular occupation, with an array of stone 'mangers' or troughs in the NW corner.

Houses bordering the present main road are also part of the surrounding settlement, which certainly persisted at least until the time of the Arab conquest; a house here with a central peristyle may go back to the early Roman period. Balagrae is referred to in the early fifth century AD by Synesius (p. 8). He writes on one occasion with a timeless complaint against local government cuts: the *Balagritae* had been a sturdy local defence force of mounted archers, but after a recent change of provincial governor their horses had been sold and they were now obliged to fight on foot!

There is a small museum in the side-road on the W side of the site, housing finds from the excavations, but this was closed 'for reorganization' at the time of writing. The Sanusi zawiya of 1843 used to be at the far end of the street.

Sirat al-Jamil: late Roman church/ farm complex ★

This complex is just N of the main road which runs from W to E through the centre of al-Bayda, about five blocks E of the Qasr al-Bayda Hotel, at N 32° 45.91' E 21° 45.03'. From the hotel, follow the main road E for about 500 m to the next major cross-roads, where the dual carriageway begins; turn L and then first R, and the entrance to the site will be found on the left-hand side of the road. The gate to the antiquities zone is separated from the road by an open space.

The archaeological enclosure here, excavated by the Italian Mission between 1966 and 1972, comprises two building-complexes (fig. 84): on the E a Christian monastery and on the W a farm building and winery. These are now engulfed by modern al-Bayda (and constantly under threat from the dumping of rubbish), but must be imagined as originally isolated buildings on high ground in the countryside. The farm (fig. 85) is the earlier structure, built in the second half of the fifth century AD. It had an entrance on the E side (a) which led directly into an internal courtyard; this was surrounded on three sides by rooms in two storeys, possibly with taller towers at the front corners (where the lower walls are more solid). In the NW corner of the courtyard is an aperture into a rock-cut cistern (b), which would have been fed by rainwater. Within the building can be made out a latrine (c: immediately on the R of the entrance), the staircase (d) which led to the upper floors and a wine-making installation in the W range.

The wine-making area was entered from the courtyard through a large doorway with a decorated lintel. Inside was a hall (e) whose ceiling was supported on two arches spanning the width of the room. This hall was paved with waterproof cement (*opus signinum*) into which was set an array of decorative motifs in mosaic chips, across the width of the room (not currently visible). Some of these incorporate unambiguously Christian symbolism. This room was initially unencumbered, but in a second phase eight large terracotta *dolia* were installed around its walls, held in place

by a mass of concrete rubble. Each of these fermentation vats had a capacity of around 750 litres. To the N was a second room for the fermentation and storage of wine, with eight more *dolia* around the walls, set partly into the rock beneath and partly again within an armature of concrete. The pressing-room (f) occupied the corresponding room to the S. Just inside the door on the R was a small trapezoidal basin for the treading of the grapes. The juice extracted here ran into a larger, adjoining basin which occupied the whole of the W end of the room, and in which was a raised circular plinth. Upon this plinth would have been placed baskets of trodden grapes for pressing, and this was achieved by means of a wooden press-beam, one end of which was set into a socket in the wall behind, while the opposite end was raised or lowered by means of a windlass. The windlass was anchored by means of two sockets cut into the rock of

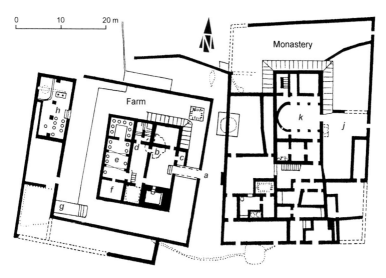

Fig. 84. Sirat al-Jamil: plan of the site. (a) Entrance to farm; (b) Cistern; (c) Latrine; (d) Staircase; (e) Fermentation hall; (f, g, h) Pressing rooms; (j) Entrance to monastery; (k) Basilica.

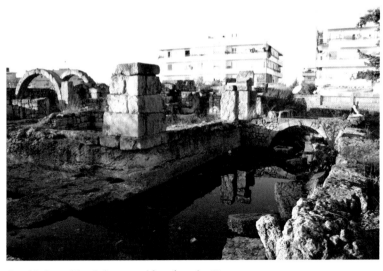

Fig. 85. Sirat al-Jamil: the moated farm from the SE.

the floor. The juice from both the treading and the pressing ran from the larger basin, through a tube formed by the neck of an amphora, into a collecting tank which was also cut into the floor.

The building is surrounded by a rock-cut ditch, which provided at the same time a source of building-stone and a means of defence. This was crossed at the entrance by a bridge; it was enclosed on the S and W sides by outbuildings and on the N and E sides by a plain boundary wall. There was an underground rock-cut chamber accessed from the SW corner of the ditch (g). This preserves interesting details of its use. In the E wall, on either side of the entrance passage, are six mangers for animals, cut in the rock. (These may not be original, but may relate to later use of the chamber as a stable.) In the W wall are two, possibly three, cruciform sockets for the end of a press-beam. A little way in front of each of them is a recess in the floor and a channel for the liquid to be collected and run off into a tank on the N side; in the

SW corner is a rock-cut bench which perhaps constituted a preliminary treading area. In the absence of nearby fermentation vats, it may be questioned whether this installation was used for pressing olives rather than grapes. In the ceiling is a central opening to provide daylight to the interior.

In the building outside the ditch at the NW corner (h), now reduced to its foundations, was another pressing installation for wine. A huge block with two holes in it once anchored the windlass which was used to pull down the press-beam, while in the floor were set up to sixteen *dolia* for the fermentation and storage of the wine.

The monastery was built some fifty years later than the farm. The core of the complex was a rectangular building three storeys high, in fine ashlar masonry with projecting string-courses. There was an arched axial entrance on the E side (j) which led directly into a small three-aisled basilica (k). The nave of the basilica was separated from the aisles by square piers and the apse was inscribed within the W end. Doorways leading off from the aisles gave access to flanking rooms, and a staircase in the NW corner led to the upper floors where the monks probably lived and had their refectory and dormitory. On the S side (less well-preserved) is an array of store-rooms, press-rooms, latrines and housing for animals and perhaps also a lay work-force. The entire complex is enclosed within a boundary wall.

During the life of both building-complexes, repairs were necessary and unstable walls were reinforced by mas-sive buttresses. This is a constantly recur-ring feature of late Roman buildings in the Cyrenaican countryside; it is likely in many cases to have been necessitated by earthquake damage, but in some it may simply have been a consequence of inad-equacies in the original construction. The buildings were certainly occupied until the Arab conquest in the mid-seventh cen-tury, and possibly beyond. The monastery had, however, lost its religious functions in the later phases, the church having become simply another storeroom for agricultural produce.

Tomb of Sidi Rafa

As one approaches al-Bayda from the W, immediately inside the ring-road and on the L as one proceeds towards the town centre, is a tree-lined cemetery with a domed tomb set back slightly from the road. The position is N 32° 45.46′ E 21° 43.90′. This dates back to the earliest years of the Islamic presence in North Africa, being the tomb of Ruwayfi ibn Thabit al-Ansari, one of the compan-ions of the Prophet. He became governor of Barqa and died in 675/6. The tomb was destroyed during military opera-tions in 1913 and completely rebuilt by the Italians (surely also more recently).

AL-HANIYA   الحنيه

Coordinates: N 32° 50.16′, E 21° 30.62′
Directions: This is reached from the main jabal road by leaving it at Massah, at the cross-roads where there is a pedestrian bridge. Turn to the NW (seawards), drive straight through the village, turn R at the T-junction at the far end and sharp left at the next intersection. The road winds down from the upper plateau and then passes in a fairly straight line across the lower pla-teau before descending easily to the coast. The distance from the main road at Massah to the cross-roads on the edge of the mod-ern village of al-Haniya is 15.3 km. The remains of the ancient settlement may be found by turning L at this point and follow-ing the road for another 2 km towards the W. (A turn in the opposite direction leads after 12.4 km to Zawiyat al-Hamamah: see p. 147.) Here a track on the seaward side leads to an abandoned beach-restaurant(?) which makes a convenient stopping-point at the W end of the bay.

Ancient coastal village

The site consists of a jumble of ruins around the E side of a small bay which is partially enclosed by promontories and by a small island. There is an extensive scatter of pottery dating from the Hellenistic to the Byzantine periods, together with masonry, including the broken vault of a large structure with waterproof plaster on the inside, which must have been a cistern. The densest concentration of pottery is on the rocky knoll half-way round the bay (to which the site coordinates refer). A little way to the W of this is a low rocky outcrop which projects into the sea and which is pierced by lined, rock-cut storage tanks, such as may be seen also at Zawiyat al-Hamamah and Apollonia (p. 279). Foundations on the island may repre-sent a lighthouse. Rock-cut tombs and sarcophagi have been reported near the settlement.

The ancient name which seems to fit best with the location of this settlement is *Aptouchos*, known as the location of a temple – perhaps even that which formed the backdrop to the *Rudens* of Plautus (see under Apollonia, p. 281).

MASSAH

مسه

Coordinates: N 32° 45.45', E 21° 37.20'
Directions: Massah (formerly the Italian settlement of Luigi Razza) is on the main jabal road between al-Marj and al-Bayda. For the ancient settlement, turn L at the crossroads immediately to the E of the pedestrian bridge (N 32° 45.03 E 21° 37.63); at the end of the road, turn R. This skirts the edge of the village; at the next opportunity, turn L onto the road for al-Haniya. After 500 m there is a track leading back to the L; there is also a temple-tomb in the field immediately adjacent. Park here and walk in a straight line along the track; the ancient ruins will be apparent all around you after about 200 m.

Ancient settlement ★

To the NW of the modern village there are very extensive traces of an ancient settlement, none of which has been excavated. Here it is possible to trace the outlines of a winding village street (fig. 86), buildings and cisterns. Several architectural tombs in the vicinity show that the settlement at Massah was both very early and from the beginning of its history very Greek. Its name was almost certainly *Artamis*, named (in the Doric dialect) after the sister of Apollo, the patron of Cyrene. The fertility of the land around it is sufficient justification for its existence and prosperity. That it persisted also into late antiquity is shown by the presence of a church. This is terraced into the hillside just below the crest, towards the S end of the settlement and just below a large, isolated carob tree (at N 32° 45.41' E 21° 37.23'). Immediately above it to the N are the remains of a square fortified building. This is a makeshift late-antique structure, but incorporates features of an earlier building on the same alignment. The church is now barely detectable

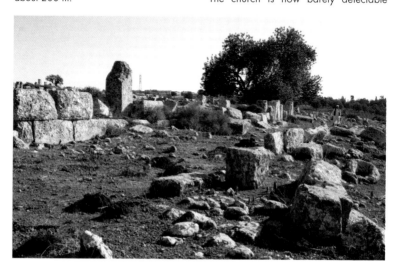

Fig. 86. Massah: a street of the ancient village.

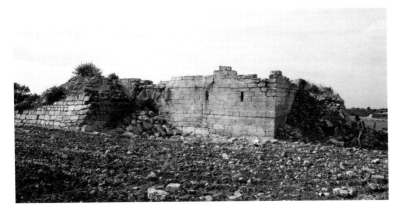

Fig. 87. Qasr az-Zaarura from the NE.

beneath tumbled blocks of masonry: the flanking arcades of the nave can be made out, with a secondary strengthening. The apse was initially at the E end, but after rebuilding was at the W end, and the nave appears to have been substantially shortened. However, the major interest of this tumbled ruin is in a complicated underground complex, once entered from the N aisle of the church but now inaccessible. It is composed of an underground courtyard 6 m square, surrounded by arcaded rock-cut galleries on all four sides. These include a room resembling a chapel, which perhaps housed the remains of some prominent Christian personage or saint.

In the landscape immediately surrounding the ancient village may be seen property boundaries in the form of lines of orthostats; these are the surviving skeletons of former walls or fences. A very fine example crosses a modern farmyard on the W side of the road to al-Haniya some 200 m beyond the track which leads to the main concentration of ruins. In the same farmyard is a well-preserved example of a temple-tomb of the fifth or fourth century BC. This takes the form of a rectangular stone chamber set

above ground on a stepped plinth and with a rendition in stone of a pitched, tiled roof. There is a single monumental doorway on one end, in imitation of a small temple. Several similar tombs stand out in the fields round about. Another monumental tomb, presumed to be of Hellenistic date, takes the form of a cube of masonry (containing the burial) formerly surmounted by an Ionic column; the capital and base now lie nearby, together with three drums of the shaft. The surrounding slopes are also pierced in places by rock-tombs.

Qasr az-Zaarura ★

On approaching Massah from the W, the fortified farm of Qasr az-Zaarura is visible on the hilltop to the R immediately before entering the modern village. To reach it, turn R immediately in front of the first buildings of the village on the R side of the road (at N 32° 44.91' E 21° 37.49') and turn R again after 120 m through a farm gate. The site lies in the middle of arable farmland: courtesy demands that one should call at the farmhouse before proceeding further. At the time of writing, the farmer was delighted that anyone should take an interest in 'his' ruin.

The ancient building (at N 32° 44.68' E 21° 37.41') has the form of a square with a single arched entrance on the E side. The original outside wall, visible to the N of the entrance (fig. 87), is of fine ashlar masonry in large blocks with horizontal string-courses at intervals. There are small slit-windows and on either side of the entrance-arch are stone 'curtain-brackets'; all of these architectural features are shared with other buildings in the region (e.g. Qasr Shahdiyn, p. 126; Qasr al-Wushish, p. 125; Qasr Zawiyat al-Arqub, p. 144). They have generally been attributed to the fifth century AD or later. Internally, several arches can be made out amidst the tumbled masonry: there were probably several rooms opening off a central courtyard, and there may be a staircase in the NE corner. At some point in the history of the building, it has been surrounded externally on all four sides by a massive sloping revetment of (less careful) ashlar masonry. A narrow passageway was retained for the entrance. To the R of the entrance, the (collapsed) revetment has been cleared away by the farmer, exposing the original masonry behind. At the E end of the N wall, jagged cracks running from top to bottom provide the explanation: this building had been severely fractured by earthquake, and the revetment must have been added to stabilize it. This combination of features is also widespread and is discussed in the Historical Introduction (p. 14). The catastrophe must have occurred at some point in the Byzantine period. A loose block on the ground by the NE corner bears a clearly chiselled cross.

Despite its handsome masonry, this building was probably a farm and not a military outpost. About 200 m to the ENE of the qasr both rock-cut vats and large buried *dolia* have been found, indicative of agriculture and the cultivation of vines and/or olives.

Tumuli

Bordering the ancient road from Artamis to Cyrene (closely followed by the modern road) there are a number of

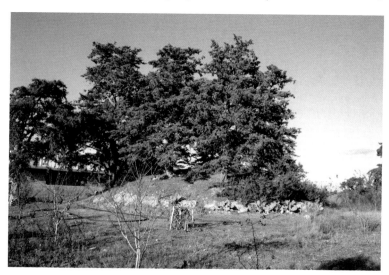

Fig. 88. Tumulus of the seventh century BC to the E of Massah.

tumulus-burials of the archaic period. The earliest of these is at a distance of 2.2 km from the E road junction at Massah. It stands on the crest of a low rise, and is easily visible on the N side of the road behind a hedge (at N32° 45.34' E21° 39.27'). The mound, surmounted by trees (fig. 88), is 19 m in diameter and ringed with a retaining-wall of squared blocks. It has been dated to the late seventh or early sixth century BC, a little later than the original Tomb of Battos in the Agora at Cyrene (p. 169). Another tumulus may be seen to the N of the road at Ain al-Balanj, a further 2.35 km to the E (at N32° 45.72' E 21° 40.68'). This is not obvious from the road, but lies about 60 m to the W of a minor road-junction. If you take the minor road, which curves round behind the tumulus, it can readily be found. This tomb is a much smaller structure, with an encircling wall of squared orthostats on the N side. The side towards the main road has been obliterated by the construction (in the Italian period?) of a small circular watch-tower. A third tumulus is to be found on high ground 1.8 km to the E of the last-mentioned and 100 m to the S of the main road. The enclosure wall of this mound is formed of regular limestone ashlar masonry; it is probably later than the other two burials, and of the fifth or fourth century BC.

QASR AL-WUSHISH ★   قصر الوشيش

Coordinates: N 32° 34.36', E 21° 35.50'
Directions: This site can be reached by means of a (currently) unsurfaced track leading S from Qasr ash-Shahdiyn (take the asphalted side-road which turns off just below the castle, and then turn left after 900 m: the total distance is about 6 km), but it will be found more easily from the road between Suluntah and Marawah.

From the junction with the road to Omar al-Mukhtar (just to the W of Suluntah) proceed westwards for 10.2 km. At point N 32° 33.81' E 21° 35.91', turn N onto an asphalted side-road. After 800 m, turn R at N 32° 34.07' E 21° 35.56' onto an unmade track; follow this for 850 m, with the castle clearly visible to the left of the track. Pass a track which heads deceptively towards it, and turn L on the rise beyond, at N 32° 34.47' E 21° 35.67', onto a track which leads directly to the entrance to a walled enclosure.

Late Roman castle?

As in so many cases in the region, this ancient building (fig. 89) has become the focal point of a Muslim cemetery, which in this instance is still in use: hence the modern enclosure wall surrounding the castle and the many graves marked by elliptical rings of stones. The building is preserved to its full height on the N side and on approximately half of the two adjoining sides. The walls are faced on either side with large, well-dressed ashlar blocks, and have a core of rubble. As in many other late Roman buildings, there are slightly projecting string-courses marking off the basement, the upper floor and the roof-parapet. The over-all size is small, some 15 × 13 m, and there must have been a single entrance, buried in the collapse of the S wall. The building, perhaps to be thought of as a watch-tower, is too small to have had an internal courtyard; the interior was roofed by three barrel-vaults running N-S, and was lit on both levels by narrow slit windows. There is no obvious surrounding ditch.

What is the date and function of this building? It shares a masonry style with Qasr ash-Shahdiyn and with the Fortress of the Dux at Ptolemais, and is therefore probably late Roman. It is inter-visible

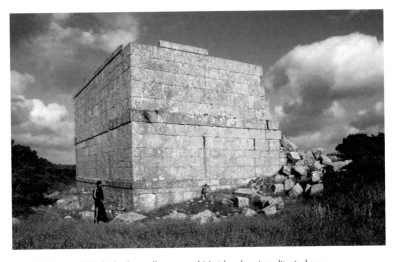

Fig. 89. Qasr al-Wushish: the well-preserved N side, showing slit-windows.

with Qasr ash-Shahdiyn, and was therefore perhaps military in purpose and related to the larger fortress. Qasr ash-Shahdiyn displays three phases of construction or reinforcement; it seems not implausible that the reinforcement followed upon earthquake damage. The state of collapse of one side of Qasr al-Wushish was perhaps brought about by the same event: one wonders whether the building was then considered beyond repair and was abandoned. (If this was indeed the case, excavation might provide some very informative evidence of both date and function.)

QASR ASH-SHAHDIYN ★ ★ قصر الشاهدين

Coordinates: N 32° 36.73', E 21° 34.68'
Directions: From the main road between al-Marj and al-Bayda, turn off to the S at the police post at N 32° 39.96' E 21° 32.53', 4.5 km to the SW of the suspension bridge over the Wadi Kuf. There is a fork here for the old road which goes along the bottom of the Wadi Kuf, but you want the turning at right-angles to the main road, which leads

to Omar al-Mukhtar and Suluntah. The castle stands on top of a hill which appears directly in front of you about 7.5 km from the turning; the road swings round to the L in front of it. It is easy to pull off and walk up the hillside.

Late Roman castle

This fine castle (figs. 90–94: Castle of the two eye-witnesses) is passed by many tourist coaches without so much as a glance; but five minutes' walk to the top of the hill to explore it will prove very rewarding. The hill is crowned by a huge rectangular keep, of which two storeys remain in many parts. It is built of limestone ashlar masonry with pronounced string-courses. The exterior has a forbidding aspect, being completely blind apart from a single arched doorway on the W side. The interior of the keep is accessible with care, but a hand-lamp is essential as it is pitch-dark and there are tumbled blocks and deep holes within. Examination has shown that there are three periods of construction. The earliest comprised a simple

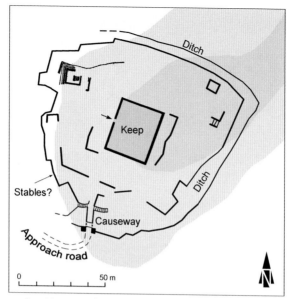

Fig. 90. Qasr ash-Shahdiyn: sketch-plan of general layout.

tower 14 × 13 m, with three vaulted chambers at ground-level accessed through a vestibule. (Compare Qasr al-Wushish, just a few km to to S: p. 125.) The original entrance of the first phase is clearly visible inside the later one (fig. 93): both arches are set in a moulded rectangular frame, and the inner one is enclosed between 'curtain-brackets' with huge hooks on the inner face. The central chamber beyond has numerous deep vats set in the floor: it may have been a storeroom, or these might be fermentation vats for wine.

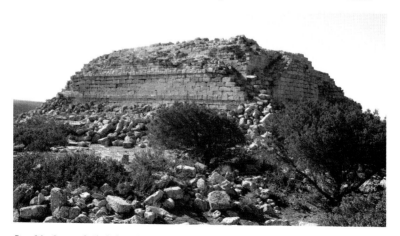

Fig. 91. Qasr ash-Shahdiyn: the keep from the E.

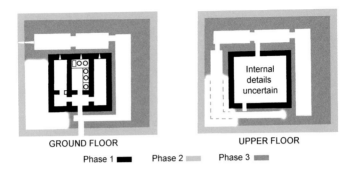

GROUND FLOOR   UPPER FLOOR

Phase 1 ■■ Phase 2 ▨ Phase 3 ▨

Fig. 92. Qasr ash-Shahdiyn: hypothetical phases of keep.

In a second phase the original building was surrounded by the outer curtain-wall that is now visible, enclosing an area of 32 × 27 m; finally (or perhaps at the same time), the intervening space was built up into long vaulted galleries on both the ground-floor and upper levels. (This is the phasing proposed

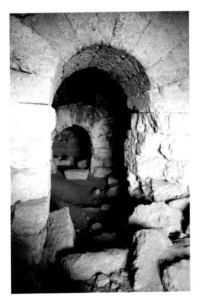

Fig. 93. Qasr ash-Shahdiyn: the interior, with the phase 1 entrance in the foreground.

by Richard Goodchild; Sandro Stucchi transposed the two latter phases, with the outer curtain-wall forming an added skin. This seems equally plausible.) There was presumably an internal staircase which is not now accessible.

The keep is, however, only the centre of an extensive fortified complex. The entire hilltop is ringed by a ditch, which is rock-cut but with an added revetment to the inner face of the outer bank in places. Several other buildings occupied the enclosure and numerous rock-cut chambers open off the inner face of the ditch. Some of those on the W side appear to have been stables: a large central space is ringed by stalls with mangers between piers, all cut out of the native rock (fig. 94). The ditch could be crossed only on the S side, by means of a sloping causeway of uncut rock which is interrupted only briefly, where there was presumably a drawbridge of some kind. There were flanking guard-towers on the outer edge of the ditch. In this direction at least one other rectangular building can be made out, but elliptical outlines of stones mark Muslim graves close to the approach road, which curved up from the W.

As at Qasr Migdim (p. 136), no excavation has taken place and the history of the complex remains uncertain in detail. The position offers evident military advantages, and military forces, particularly of the late Roman period, would have needed such strongholds to control the very broken ground of this region. As the Italians discovered in the 20th century, it provides excellent cover for small guerilla bands to penetrate deeply from the desert into the fertile upland and coastal zones; the writings of Synesius show that this was no less a problem in the fifth century AD. The first-period masonry has many features which are shared with demonstrably Byzantine buildings, such as churches, and the character of the latest work (together with the presence of Greek masons' marks) suggests that it is no later than Justinianic: a range of fifth to seventh centuries AD seems plausible for its entire history. As at Qasr Migdim, it is debated whether this was exclusively a military post, or whether this too was one of the monasteries (in this case *Dinarthison*) fortified by Justinian. No Christian features have been identified here. It

is perhaps a better candidate than Qasr Migdim for *Bombaia*, which is described by Synesius in the following terms. 'Bombaia is a mountain full of caverns, where art and nature have combined to form an impregnable fortress. It has been long celebrated, and justly: they often compare it to the subterranean vaults of Egypt. But today everyone admits that there are no walls behind which one could be safer than at Bombaia ... The moment one enters this place, one is in a regular labyrinth, hard to get through.'

QASR LIBYA ★ ★ ★   قصر ليبيا

Coordinates: N 32° 37.82', E 21° 23.77'
Directions: The site occupies a hilltop in the countryside to the N of the main E–W road and shortly to the W of the Wadi Kuf. It is necessary to turn N off the main road at N 32° 37.00' E 21° 24.00', where it crosses a ridge in a slight cutting at the village of Bir al-Mfawaz, which seems now to have acquired the name of Qasr Libya. There is a slip-road alongside the cutting, and the

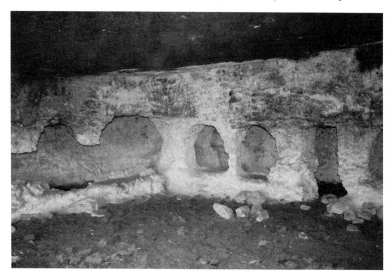

Fig. 94. Qasr ash-Shahdiyn: rock-cut stalls for animals.

junction will be found on the crest. Follow the side-road northwards for just over 1 km and turn L at the junction there. The little Turkish fort is now visible on the hill to your R. After 200 m there is an approach-road on the R which leads up to the gate. There is usually a guardian on the site.

The presence and character of the two churches on this rural site presuppose an associated settlement of some size in the late Roman period, though no formal exploration has been carried out. The ancient name of the settlement was probably *Olbia*. This seems to have been preserved in the Arabic toponym (which has now become assimilated to the name of the country, but was more accurately transcribed in the past as 'Elbia' or 'Lebia'). Traces of occupation in the neighbourhood go back to the fourth century BC. One of the panels in the nave mosaic of the East Church (below, p. 134) clearly names the settlement as the 'New City of Theodorias', after the wife of the Emperor Justinian. This seems to imply some specific imperial benefaction or sign of interest at that time.

The East Church was discovered by chance in 1957, and was excavated by the Department of Antiquities under Richard Goodchild. It became apparent that a second (West) church was incorporated into the small Turkish fort on the crest of the hill, and in subsequent years this was cleared of later accretions and partially restored.

East Church

Many tour groups are not shown the East Church, but though its excavated remains are now in a rather sorry state (the cover-building

Fig. 95. Qasr Libya: plan of East Church.

erected in the early years being now largely derelict), it is worth visiting in order to understand the setting of the remarkable mosaics which were found within it. It may be found by means of a path which leads away to the R of the fort (within the fenced enclosure), at a distance of about 100 m.

The church (fig. 95) faced W, and is entered by a doorway into the N angle-chamber beside the apse. The walls are of rather poor *opus africanum* construction, except on the N side where the building has been terraced into the hill-side and cut out of the living rock. The outer wall on the N side still showed substantial remains of painted plaster when first uncovered, including a representation of an *aedicula*, within which looped curtains framed a jewelled cross. Little of this now survives. The chancel, in front of the apse, is relatively small in this church. The foundations for the enclosing marble screen, together with the central altar-base, are still visible. The mosaic with which it was once paved has been lifted and is now displayed in the West Church. Its decoration is composed of jewelled crosses set in roundels, surrounded by figures of deer, smaller animals and partridges amongst trees.

The body of the nave was paved in part with marble slabs (mostly removed in antiquity, but evident from the mortar bedding beneath) and in part with a large mosaic measuring approximately 10.6 × 6.1 m. This mosaic was

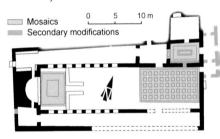
Mosaics
Secondary modifications
0   5   10 m

130

composed of fifty square panels. Problems of conservation did not permit retention *in situ*: the panels have been lifted individually and are now displayed on the walls of the little museum in the fort – most successfully – as a sort of picture-gallery. The cable-pattern border which linked the panels together does remain in place, creating a rather curious effect. However, the point to notice is that the mosaic is not axial to the nave, but is placed almost clumsily against its northern edge. A glance at the plan will also show that there is no narthex and no central entrance at the E end (though the plan does appear to show an external step or sill in the right place): instead, the nave arcades turn into solid walls about half-way along its length and there is a connected complex of rooms (not fully explored) in the NE corner. The exceptional interest of this part of the building was further emphasized by a third mosaic, in the room which occupies the E end of the N aisle. This mosaic has been lifted in its entirety and is now displayed on the floor of the museum. The over-all layout seems to imply that, in addition to the normal axial emphasis of the church (the panels of the main mosaic were so arranged that they would have been facing a person at the E end, looking towards the altar), there was some sort of secondary focus running across the E end. It has been suggested that there might have been a *martyrion* in the rock-cut room at the NE corner, but of any such feature there remains no trace.

The dating of the mosaics which adorned this building is not in doubt: two of them (the big mosaic in the nave, and that in the room to the N) were laid in the year AD 538/9, during the reign of Justinian. Is the church itself of this date, or might the mosaics have been inserted into a pre-existing building? This is a problem which archaeologists frequently have difficulty answering, and in the present instance it can only be said that there are differences of opinion; a date for the building in the second half of the fifth century has also been proposed, on the basis of the style of the masonry.

West Church ★

This church, which has survived to a considerable height within the body of the Turco-Italian fort, differs from many other Cyrenaican churches in two respects. In the first instance, it seems to have been built throughout in well-dressed limestone masonry, and secondly, its ground-plan (fig. 96) is not basilical but closer to the cross-in-square which becomes the hallmark of later Byzantine work in the eastern Mediterranean. There are therefore four rectangular angle-chapels, each communicating with the body of the church through two doorways, with flat lintels and relieving arches above. (The doorways on either side of the chancel at the E end are of different construction, and are secondary to the original design.) The inner walls of the NW chapel were removed in the Italian colonial period, and have since been reconstructed; it may readily been seen also that a number of modern windows have been closed up again. The main body of

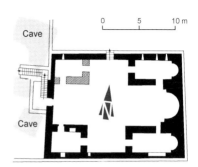

Fig. 96. Qasr Libya: plan of West Church.

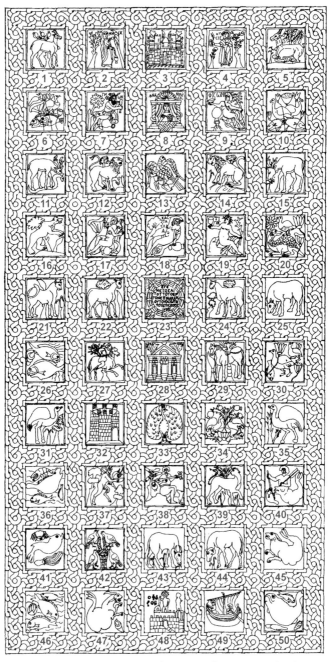

Fig. 97. Qasr Libya: scheme of the mosaic from the East Church.

the church has an inscribed apse at the E end, and so do the eastern flanking chapels. There were only two external doorways: that on the N side through which the church is now entered, and one at the W end which led originally only to an irregular rock-cut open space, off which opened three rock-cut chambers. One of these has at some time served as a cistern, but whether there was once a tomb in this area it is impossible now to say. The staircase in this area is modern.

The present roof of reinforced concrete has a simple tent-like appearance. However, springers for vaults which are still in place high on the walls show that each arm of the building (and presumably the corner-chapels) was roofed with a barrel-vault. The central feature over the crossing may have been a cross-vault or, more probably, a dome.

In view of the later history of the building, nothing has survived of its internal fittings or floor. The mosaic now set here has come from the chancel of the East Church: the space in the centre is where the altar stood, and around it there is on each side a roundel, bordered by a field of wild animals and birds in a wooded landscape. Three of the roundels contain jewelled crosses, and the fourth contains an inscription, which reads 'This work too came into being in the time of the very holy and pious bishop Theodoros.' (For Theodoros and the other inscriptions, see below.)

Examination of the fort shows more of the same massive ashlar masonry as that of which the church is composed; the round tower at the NW corner is visibly built on earlier square foundations. This suggests that the church was an integral part of a larger complex, very possibly a fort built in the Byzantine period for the same reasons that the Turks and Italians subsequently chose to maintain a military post here. It would therefore have been, in effect, the garrison chapel. To what date does all of this belong? There is, as usual, no direct evidence. Goodchild and Ward-Perkins seem to have assumed that this represented 'official' building-work, contemporary with the 'refounding' of the town in the reign of Justinian in the 530s; Stucchi argued that the architectural design (not all of which he had observed accurately) was more consistent with a date after 600.

The Mosaics ★ ★

The mosaics from the East Church are justly renowned for their intrinsic interest and for their virtually complete state of preservation. In view of the difficulty of maintaining the largest of them *in situ* on the ground, a particularly happy solution has been adopted of mounting the panels as separate pictures on the wall of the museum. In this way, they can been seen far more readily (and by many people at the same time), and their vibrant colours contrast strongly with the inevitably dusty appearance of the chancel mosaic which is now on the floor of the West Church. A short section of the cable-pattern border has also been lifted, and is displayed on the wall just inside the door on the L, in order to show the character of the border within which each of the panels was set.

The mosaic as a whole is composed of fifty panels, in ten rows of five arranged as shown in figure 97; they are now mounted on the wall in these rows. The first row (panels 1–5) was therefore nearest to the altar, and the viewer entering the church from the E would have first encountered row ten (panels 46–50). The range of subjects is wide, and at first sight a surprising mixture of pagan and Christian imagery. Much scholarly debate has been devoted to the symbolism of the mosaic, and of the juxtaposition of particular motifs, but inevitably this remains inconclusive. It should be noted that the craftsmen who laid these floors appear to have been responsible also for mosaics in both the known churches at Cyrene, the Central and East Churches at Apollonia, and those at Ras al-Hilal and Taucheira; in these mosaics the same panels and themes are combined in different ways, suggesting that there is not necessarily any symbolic relationship between them. The main points of interest are the following.

(3) A city gate flanked by towers and inscribed *polis nea theodorias*, 'the new city Theodorias' (fig. 98): presumably a reference to the settlement itself, named after Theodora, the wife of the emperor Justinian. Such a renaming would typically occur after a major benefaction, or after reconstruction following a disaster of some kind. (After damage by earthquake in AD 262, Cyrene was briefly renamed *Claudiopolis* after the reigning emperor Claudius Gothicus: see p. 149.)

(2, 4, 8) The panel depicting the new city is surrounded by three allegorical figures, *Kosmesis* (Adornment), *Ktisis* (Foundation) and *Ananeosis* (Renewal).

(7, 9, 17, 18, 19) Ananeosis is flanked by two personifications of rivers, depicted in the Classical style of a god reclining on a water-jar from which the river flows. The rivers are named as *Geon* and *Phison*, and they form a set with *Tigris* and *Euphrates* two rows beneath, being the Four Rivers of Paradise. In later Christian imagery they are not shown in this manner at all, but rather as a row of four gushing water-pipes. There is further interest in the depiction here, for in panel (18), between Tigris and Euphrates, there is a fifth water-source, identified as the nymph *Kastalia*. The name is associated with the spring at Delphi in Greece, and with another at Daphnae near Antioch. The reason for including either in this composition is wholly obscure!

(23) Close to the centre of the whole mosaic is a panel with an inscription within a wreath. It reads 'This work also came into being in the time of Makarios the most holy bishop in indiction year 3'. The date (within the 15-year cycle of indictions in the Church calendar) yields only one possible result within the reign of Justinian and Theodora: AD 538/9. (The indiction year begins on 1 September in this period.)

(28) shows the façade of a building, possibly referring (conventionally) to the church itself.

(32) is probably a representation of a fortified farm.

(48) The central panel at the base of the mosaic, and the first to greet the viewer (assuming that he enters on the axis, which the plan shows that he did

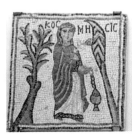 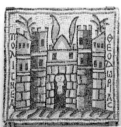 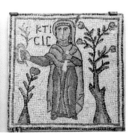

Fig. 98. Qasr Libya: panels 2–4 of the large mosaic in the East Church.

not do!) is a much-reproduced figure of the lighthouse at Alexandria (fig. 99). It is labelled *(h)o pharos* (The Lighthouse) and depicts the statue of Helios on top of the tower. There appears to be a second statue (unidentified) on the building behind. Helios has a sword (or an oar?) in his hand, and beneath it is an object which is perhaps the bronze mirror which was used to reflect the sun during daylight hours.

The remaining panels are filled with a wide variety of themes, drawn sometimes from life (animals and birds) and sometimes from mythology (the goat-footed god Pan in panel 37, sea-monsters in panels 40 and 47). Given the rather coarse measure of the tesserae, the figures are imbued with a remarkable sense of volume and character; sometimes, however, as in panel 20 depicting a crocodile, the artist was attempting to draw a creature of which he did not have an accurate idea.

If the extent of this mosaic seems impressive, it is worth bearing in mind that the mosaic in the nave of the 'cathedral' at Cyrene, now very fragmentary (p. 227), was laid in the same manner and was composed of 126 such panels!

On the floor of the museum is the mosaic which lay originally in the room at the E end of the N aisle in the East Church. This has a central panel with a Nilotic theme. This is common throughout Classical art and has no obvious Christian symbolism. Earlier examples in mosaic may be seen in Rooms 9A and 9C of the National Museum in Tripoli, and in the villa at Silin in Tripolitania, near Lepcis Magna. One of the most famous Nilotic mosaics of all may be seen in Italy at Palestrina (ancient *Praeneste*) to the E of Rome. The essence of these

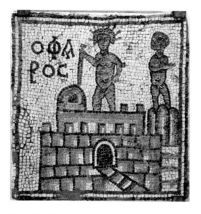

Fig. 99. Qasr Libya: panel 48 of the large mosaic in the East Church, showing the famous lighthouse of Alexandria.

scenes is life in the marshes of the Nile Delta, showing hunting and fishing amidst a landscape of reeds and lotus flowers, with occasional comic catastrophes when a cow is seized by a crocodile. Such an event is shown on the mosaic here, with the anxious owner of the cow attempting to retrieve his beast by pulling on its tail. Around its border, this mosaic incorporates three inscriptions. One of these reports the same date as that in the main mosaic, while indicating that bishop Makarios has been succeeded by 'the most holy new bishop Theodoros'. Another, originally in the doorway on the W side of the room (communicating with the adjoining room in the N aisle) has a quotation from the psalms, apparently modified to call for God's protection of his 'servant Theodoros the new deacon'. A third has another quotation from the psalms: 'Your witnesses were trusted; that greatly adorns your house'.

The inscriptions in all of these mosaics therefore represent a brief period of dynamic change in the settlement: at the beginning of the work Makarios is the bishop, and Theodoros his new deacon. Before the year is out and the work is completed, Theodoros is the bishop. The renaming of the settlement as Theodorias implies imperial interest. But were the mosaics an imperial benefaction? Given the fact that Justinian himself is not mentioned, while the names of Makarios and Theodoros are given some prominence, it is more likely that the bishops were the sponsors of the adornment, if not the construction, of the East Church.

QASR MIGDIM (BENI GDEM) ★   قصر المِقْدِم

Coordinates: N 32° 40.23', E 21° 32.32'
Directions: On the main road from al-Marj to al-Bayda, there is a police post at a junction at N 32° 39.96' E 21° 32.53'. Here the old road along the bottom of the wadi Kuf veers off to the R of that which now passes over the suspension bridge, and a third road, going off at right-angles to the R, goes past Qasr ash-Shahdiyn to Suluntah. On the opposite side of the main road is a track which winds round the hillside to the L and leads after 750 m, past a farm, to the castle.

Late Roman castle – or monastery?

The name of this castle has been variously rendered in the past. The version adopted here is that by which it is currently known in the district, and accords with the version Bu Migdem ('Abu' being a term of respect, 'Father').

Even in a ruinous state, this is still a very striking building, standing on high ground in the broken country of the Wadi Kuf (fig. 100). When one is travelling from Al-Marj towards al-Bayda, it appears suddenly to the left of the road, just after one has passed the right fork for Suluntah at a police post. The castle is a large rectangular structure, 44.5 × 22 m, of two generous storeys above a basement, surrounded by a wide ditch. It is built in well-dressed ashlar masonry with string-courses between the storeys. There are two square, projecting towers in the centre of each of the longer sides. That on the N is well preserved: its chambers were vaulted and its large windows could have served as firing positions for *ballistae* (catapults). The interior is obscured by fallen masonry, but the outer walls were built in two stages, having

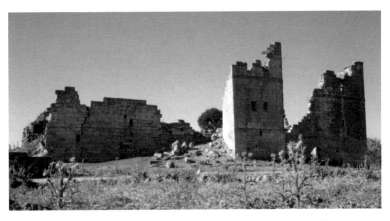

Fig. 100. Qasr Migdim, seen from the N in 2000 before the construction of farm buildings in front of it.

an added outer skin which implies two phases of construction. (The towers belong wholly to the second phase.) Perhaps the castle was increased in height, requiring thicker walls. The only visible entrance is an arched doorway on the N side, to the W of the N tower.

No excavations have been carried out here, though fragments of marble chancel-screens (such as those visible in the churches at Apollonia and al-Athrun) have been found nearby. The date and purpose of the building are therefore not as clearly defined as might be hoped. It is certainly late Roman, and it has been plausibly suggested that the two phases of construction belong to the fifth and sixth centuries respectively. The church fittings (now lost) indicate the presence of a church or chapel, and it has been argued by some that the building was the monastery of *Agriolode* which was fortified by Justinian in the sixth century. Others have proposed that it was the fortress of *Bombaia* described by Synesius in the early fifth. (See also Qasr ash-Shahdiyn, p. 129.)

On the slopes of the hillside below are extensive traces of a late Roman village, including rock-cut dwellings. In regard to these, it is difficult now to distinguish between excavations which were originally tombs, subsequently robbed and adapted as dwellings, and those which were devised as dwellings from the outset.

SIDI ABD AL-WAHID سيدي عبدالواحد
Coordinates: N 32° 43.67′, E 21° 34.76′
Directions: This small hamlet is sited just to the N of the main jabal road, approximately 3.5 km to the NE of the Wadi Kuf suspension bridge. The coordinates given are for the building described below: to reach it, turn W off the main road at N 32°

43.48′ E 21° 34.95′ and after 170 m turn R. After a further 400 m in a straight line, you will come to an open space and to a dividing of several ways. Park here, and the building described will be about 70 m ahead of you and slightly to the right.

Qasr Abayd, fortified farm
This is a small square structure built close to the crest of a ridge, heavily overgrown with vegetation and now largely surrounded by modern houses. It still stands 2–3 m high in good ashlar masonry, with a projecting stringcourse, narrow slit-windows and a single arched entrance on the SE side. In this respect it is surely of a type (and broadly contemporary) with Qasr az-Zaarura just 4 km to the E (p. 123) and perhaps Qasr al-Wushish (p. 125). Beneath the qasr to the E is a small quarry in which has been cut a large chamber-tomb containing eight *arcosolia*. To the N is a large rock-cut cistern spanned by two stone arches. There are further remains in this direction of both tombs and outbuildings.

Extremely ruinous traces of an ancient church were recorded in the vicinity in 1955.

SULUNTAH (SLONTA) ★ ★ سلنطة
Coordinates: N 32° 35.53′, E 21° 42.84′
Directions: Suluntah lies on the southerly road between Marawah and Faydiyah. In order to find the archaeological site, turn off to the N in the centre of the village at N 32° 35.34′ E 21° 42.94′; head N for about 250 m, go straight over the crossroads and then follow the road around to the L. About 100 m beyond the bend, there is a junction with a road approaching obliquely from the R. On the N side of this junction is an unremarkable wall with an

iron gate in it. This is the entrance to the site. If the gate is not open, and there is no one to open it, it is a trivial matter to go round the back, climb over the fence and so to unfasten the gate!

Native cult centre

On the hillside, tucked away inconspicuously on the edge of the modern village of Suluntah, is perhaps the most extraordinary of all the ancient monuments in Libya (fig. 101). Visitors to the National Museum in Tripoli will have seen (in Room 5) both photographs and casts of the bizarre sculptures carved here in the living rock. They occupy a small irregular space with a flat floor, in the middle of which is what appears to be the base of a column-shaft (or a circular altar). Both this and the presence of the sculptures have led to the inference that there was once a cave or rock-shelter here, of which the covering is now lost. However, looking at the site today, it is difficult to imagine how the mass of rock implied should have disappeared so completely.

The sculptures, cut into the natural limestone, consist of a wide variety of human and animal figures. There are groups of staring heads (curiously reminiscent of Celtic sculpture in NW Europe), crowds of small full-length figures, often making gestures of distress, a huge snake (fig. 102), and on the right-hand side something which looks like an altar-table (fig. 103): on the front are tiny writhing human figures, and on top are laid out four animals which look like pigs or boars. It is all a riot of carving. If it were recent, one might put it down to one individual's fantasy, but this is not an appropriate interpretation with regard to the ancient world. It is certainly a place of worship of some kind, and offering-tables (stone blocks with hollows carved in the upper surface) have been found in the vicinity. The recurrence of gestures of distress (figures with their arms raised) and the presence of pigs suggest a cult connected with gods of the underworld or the spirits of the Dead. We know from both Greek and Roman writers that Libyans (of various tribes) believed that when

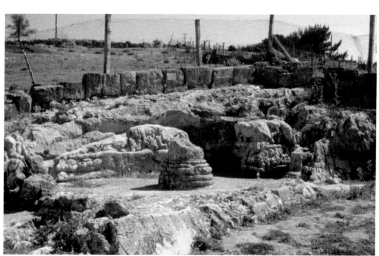

Fig. 101. The native sanctuary at Suluntah.

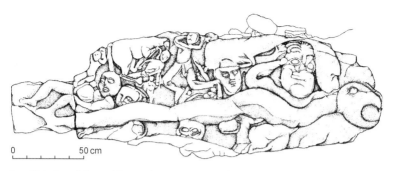

Fig. 102. Part of the rock-face in the sanctuary at Suluntah, showing human and animal figures and a huge snake. (Drawn by P. Giatti.)

they slept on the tombs of their ancestors they would be granted oracular dreams. It has even been suggested that the 'cave' of Suluntah would have been a place to seek such dreams. The setting hardly seems inviting!

To what date might it belong? It is certainly not in tune with the practices and imagery of Christianity or Islam. Nor does it fit readily into the 'Classical' tradition, though the linear decoration around the edge of the 'altar' resembles the bead-and-reel motif that is widely used in Classical architecture, and the column-base shows similar echoes. This is surely a 'Libyan' (i.e. indigenous) place of worship, developed during a period of familiarity with Classical forms. Scholars have pointed out contrasts in character between different parts of the carvings, and it has been suggested that while the 'Classical' elements are most closely paralleled in the second or

third centuries AD, the heads carved in the innermost crevice on the right-hand side may represent the beginnings of the sanctuary, and may be considerably earlier in date. Pottery has been found in the vicinity which is attributable to the fifth or fourth centuries BC and a coin of the fifth century BC has also been found.

In the immediate vicinity of the 'cave' with the sculptures have recently been identified around a hundred other workings of the rock with religious connotations. Many of these are rock-cut chambers approached by a level corridor or *dromos*. These are neither tombs as previously assumed (for they contain no burial recesses) nor habitations, but

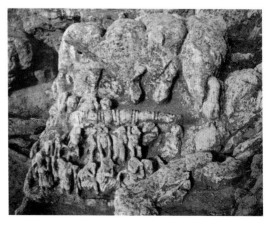

Fig. 103. Suluntah: an altar table with four sacrificial pigs?

places of worship like the sanctuary of Budaraj near Cyrene (p. 250). In many of these chambers there are niches in the walls for votive offerings or plaques. Also carved in various places upon the bare rock are lines of horizontal rectangular seatings, presumably *arulae* for the deposition of offerings. Parallels to these occur both along the road which lead southwards from Cyrene (p. 233) and in the sanctuary of Ain Hofra on the opposite side of the city (p. 252).

TARGHUNIA (طرغونيا) AND QASR NUWARAH (قصر نواره)

Coordinates: N 32° 45.15', E 21° 34.19'
Directions: On the main road between the Wadi Kuf and Massah, about 2.5 km SW of the centre of Massah, turn onto a side road at N 32° 44.23' E 21° 36.52', heading NW. After exactly 3 km, the road divides. Qasr Nuwarah may be found here behind the houses on the left-hand side of the road, at N 32° 44.96' E 21° 34.87'. For Targhunia, continue along the road, bearing L where it divides, and turn R 900 m further on. This road curves round to the R and the asphalt comes to an end after 250 m at the entrance to a walled Muslim cemetery. If the unmade track is followed along the ridge in the same direction, Qasr Targhunia may be found at the coordinates indicated.

Ancient settlement

This is a typical rural settlement, in a position which overlooks a route down from the upper to the lower plateau of the jabal. The presence of Greek, Roman and Islamic tombs indicates a long period of occupation. Today, the area is intensively farmed from scattered smallholdings. **Qasr Targhunia** is a substantial rectangular structure of ashlar blocks, partially surrounded by deep

cuttings in the native rock which represent a quarry/moat. Internally, it is filled with debris but it is possible to make out the flat, corbelled, ceilings of some of the ground-floor rooms. The date is presumably late Roman. Walls, cuttings in the rock and openings (into rock-tombs?) indicate an extensive ancient settlement on the slopes below. Below in the wadi, there are traces of an aqueduct fed by the spring of Ain Targhunia; in a building in this area was found a small altar dedicated to Apollo at the end of the fifth century BC. The Muslim cemetery on the ridge contains some very early burials (datable inscriptions belong to the ninth and tenth centuries AD); a few early tombstones have been arranged by the entrance to an inner enclosure where the early burials are located. Two further inscribed stones are on display in the museum at Cyrene (p. 250).

Qasr Nuwarah, a kilometre to the E, is behind a large new house, which encroaches to within a couple of metres of the ancient structure. The building is rectangular and formed of large, well-dressed ashlar blocks. Internally, it was composed of several vaulted chambers, one of which still survives intact and is in use as an outhouse. On the W side is a quarry/moat, full of recent building rubble, and in the bare rock beyond can be made out the cuttings of three ancient cist-graves. Just below the qasr on the S side is a large, rectangular underground chamber, within which can be made out the base of an olive-crushing mill and fittings for two lever-presses.

WADI KUF (وادى الكوف)/ WADI AS-SANAB ★ (وادي الصنب)

The main road between al-Marj and al-Bayda now crosses the Wadi Kuf at a high level on a handsome suspension bridge. The deeply incised limestone landscape is very striking; from above it is evident that the sides of the gorge (whose name means 'River/valley of the caves') house numerous rock-shelters. These have been used as residences or refuges from prehistoric until modern times, and an expedition into the bottom of the valley is well worth while. The downstream part of this drainage system is known as Wadi al-Jarjarummah where it reaches the coast, and some of the upstream features described below lie in a stretch which is known as Wadi as-Sanab.

The way into the bottom of the valley is to take the old road – still perfectly good – which branches off to the E of the upper road (coming from the W) at a junction (with police checkpoint) which also has turnings to Qasr Migdim (L: p. 136) and Qasr ash-Shahdiyn/Suluntah (R: pp. 126, 137), at N 32° 39.96′ E 21° 32.53′. Coming in the opposite direction (from al-Bayda) the old road drops away to the left at N 32° 42.60′ E 21° 34.23′, when the suspension bridge is already within sight.

Haqfat ad-Dabba prehistoric cave

To reach this site, take the old road through the bottom of the Wadi Kuf. The cave is on the NW side of the road at N 32° 41.00′ E 21° 33.78′; this is 3.4 km from the W end or 5.7 km from the E end of the lower road.

Haqfat ad-Dabba is a cave with prehistoric occupation, high on the walls of the Wadi Kuf system. It appears as an eyebrow in the rock face, some 60 m above the road and with a mud scree below it. Excavations were carried out here by a Cambridge University expedition in the 1950s, and yielded evidence of a distinctive Upper Palaeolithic

occupation which was consequently defined as the Dabban Culture. This could be dated only by reference to its presence further E in the excavated sequence at Hawa Ftiah (p. 297). New work has been carried out here in the last few years, again under the auspices of the University of Cambridge, with the aim of reassessing the previous findings and of obtaining new estimates of the age of the occupation.

Haqfat al-Khazaliyah: cult centre ★

For the exploration of the Wadi as-Sanab, leave the lower road through the Wadi Kuf at N 32° 42.39′ E 21° 34.61′, which is almost exactly 2 km from the northern junction with the upper road. Here will be found a track leading to the E, which is unsurfaced at the time of writing, but is well-graded and readily passable by ordinary vehicles; much of it may well be asphalted in the near future. Follow this track upstream for a distance of 3.4 km to point N 32° 41.74′ E 21° 36.04′. Here, on the slope above you on the right-hand side you will find a terrace of ashlar blocks, showing the drafted edges (anathyrosis) typical of Hellenistic work. This is in front of a rectangular courtyard, excavated from the rock. At the rear left-hand corner of this is a small cave, largely collapsed, but on the W wall of this are carved a number of simple, stylized ploughs (⌐). A larger cave, to the R of this, is entered from the courtyard through a large, plain rectangular doorway. It is divided internally by an anta in front of which is a square pier (carved from the rock) with a Doric capital. A recess on the R has a bench for offerings. Ploughs are carved on the E wall of the chamber (to the L of the entrance), and on the S and E faces of the pier.

The structure has none of the attributes of a tomb, and must have been constructed from the start as a sanctuary, dedicated presumably to a rural divinity concerned with the fertility of the soil: hence the images of ploughs. (See the similar rock-sanctuary to the SW of Cyrene at Budaraj, p. 250.) The masonry of the terrace and the style of the pier-capital suggest a Hellenistic date. At a later period there were half-hearted modifications, including the lowering of the floor inside the main chamber. An inscription in Greek characters on the S face of the pier, OCHNIOY+, appears to be a personal name ('of Osenios'), and the cross asserts a Christian association. This was perhaps an inhabitant of the cave in the Byzantine period, when it had ceased to serve a religious purpose.

Kaf al-Kibir and Kaf al-Khazin: ancient settlement★

From Haqfat al-Khazaliyah, follow the track for almost exactly 1 km further upstream, at which point (N 32° 41.48′ E 21° 36.28′) another track joins obliquely from the R. Take this track back along another tributary of the larger wadi, for a distance of 1.6 km. At this point (N 32° 40.83′ E 21° 36.53′) the huge natural cavern known as **Kaf al-Kibir** will be visible on the far (E) bank of the wadi. This is currently used as an animal pen and shows no sign of modification by the hand of man. A few metres to the R of this may be found an opening into another cave which still contains evidence of an oil-pressing installation. The cave is entered through a doorway on the W side. Inside, opposite the door, is the carved base of the mill for the initial crushing of the olives. One of the conical millstones was previously lying on the ground outside. The space around the mill is insufficient to accommodate an animal, so it must have been turned by human muscle-power. The pulp from the mill then had to be pressed. This took place at the right-hand end of the room. Here there is a socket in the wall in which to anchor the lever of the press;

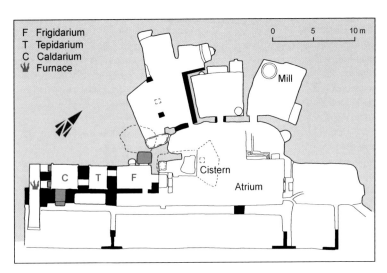

F Frigidarium
T Tepidarium
C Caldarium
♨ Furnace

Mill

Cistern

Atrium

Fig. 104. Wadi as-Sanab: plan of the bath complex at Kaf al-Khazin.

Fig. 105. Wadi as-Sanab: the bath complex at Kaf al-Khazin.

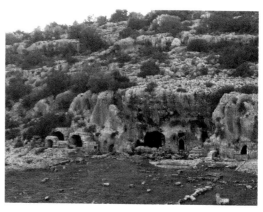

in front of that, beneath the beam, were the baskets of pulp. The oil which ran out was collected into a small rectangular basin carved out of the rock just to the L. From here it was transferred into a separating-vat, carved to the R of the mill; this communicates at a high level with a rectangular vat to its R, and ultimately with a cistern beneath. In this way the oil was separated both from the water which is also generated, and from any sediment. The sediment was eventually run off separately through a lower hole in the first vat. On the left-hand side of the mill was another set of decantation vats which functioned in the same way.

To the R (S) of the cave with the oil-press and slightly in front of it is a largely buried rock-cut cistern, whose broad flat roof is supported by a square central pier; above this, on the rock-face, is a little shrine-recess with a lightly carved pediment. About 150 m further on, another large rock-cut chamber incorporates a second oil-pressing installation. Yet further on and higher up the slope, at N 32° 40.78' E 21° 36.59', is an entrance to a tomb – probably later converted into a residence – with an arched doorway framed by projecting mouldings.

On the opposite bank of the wadi to this last, at N 32° 40.77' E 21° 36.51', is **Kaf al-Khazin**, part of a row of natural caves, the left-hand end of which has been adapted to accommodate a bath complex (figs. 104, 105). There are two rows of rooms,

one in front of the rock face (largely collapsed) and a second within the rock. The complex is entered from the N, across a rock-cut threshold which leads into an atrium. The atrium occupies the whole of the space in front of the cave, and is bounded at the front by a wall composed of stretchers. The southern part of the atrium overlies a rock-cut cistern with central pier. The cistern has a square mouth in the SW corner; it was fed by a rock-cut and cemented funnel on the rock above the cave, which channelled the rainwater into it. To the S of the atrium is a suite of three rooms comprising the baths proper, built externally of fine ashlar blocks. The first is a vaulted *frigidarium* (now roofless) with a cold plunge-bath in a rock-cut recess; from this one passed through a tiny doorway (once closed by a door) into the *tepidarium*. Fragments of *suspensurae*, the pillars which supported a heated floor, show the presence of heating, as do tubular terracotta flue-pipes in the four corners of the room. Another low passage (without a door) led from here into the *caldarium*, a small vaulted chamber with similar evidence of provision for heating and three small hot plunge-baths. Some of the wall-plaster still survives in this room, and on the

N side can be made out part of a simple decorative scheme of ribboned garlands in red and green. At the far end of this range, accessible only from the external courtyard, is the rock-cut furnace-chamber.

Opening off the main cave, which was possibly separated from the atrium by arches (now gone) are three inner chambers of uncertain purpose. The most southerly one is the largest, divided in two by an arcade on square piers. Its N wall, separating it from the adjoining room, is strengthened also by a revetment of ashlar blocks in front of the natural rock. The room has no visible means of heating, though the walls and floor are rendered and there is a waterproofed basin in the SE corner. It is possible that it served as a kind of Turkish bath, filled with steam by placing heated stones in the basin of water. The purpose of the other two rooms which open off the back of the cave is uncertain. At a later period, when the baths had gone out of use, oil presses appear to have been installed in the southern and central room, while a mill-basin has been formed in the floor of the northerly one. The name attached to the cave now ('Store cave') is of clear enough significance; in the not-so-distant past it has been used as a store for barley.

On the gently sloping rock surface, about 50 m to the E, is clear evidence of a wine-pressing installation, with a treading-bath and a pressing-floor, both with drains running into a deep collecting-vat; there is also a socket in the rock in front of the pressing-floor for the anchorage of the windlass which pulled the press-beam down. To the R of this, and slightly higher up, is the entrance to a tomb; traces can be made out of the original carved pilasters and lintel

which framed the doorway. Nearby, a long rock-cut channel collects rainwater off the hillside and feeds it into a cistern which has been refurbished and continues in use.

The features described above are difficult to date, but probably relate to an extended span of occupation from the Hellenistic or early Roman to the late antique periods. The date of the bath installation can be established only in the broadest of terms, by comparison with similar complexes elsewhere in Cyrenaica (Cyrene, Mqayrnis, Qabu Yunis) which are not themselves firmly dated. It is probably Byzantine.

ZAWIYAT AL-ARQUB زاوية العرقوب

Coordinates: N 32° 39.80′, E 21° 28.73′
Directions: Leave the main road between al-Marj and al-Bayda 7.5 km to the E of Qasr Libya, turning N into the village which now bears the name of Zawiyat al-Arqub at N 32° 37.48′ E 21° 28.22′. Bear round to the R, then turn L into the main street. From this point proceed northwards along the road for 4.7 km. On the crest of a narrow ridge, fork R; the zawiya is 350 m ahead, from which one may walk 150 m further to the E to reach the castle.

Castle ★

Here stands a substantial late Roman castle (figs. 106, 107). It occupies a commanding position with wide views and Qasr Migdim is clearly visible, some 6 km to the E. The building is almost exactly square; it is constructed with facings of large ashlar masonry and smaller rubble infill; as in the case of a number of other late Roman structures, the masonry has slightly projecting bonding-courses at intervals, which run through the thickness of the wall; two are preserved on the N side. It is aligned almost exactly

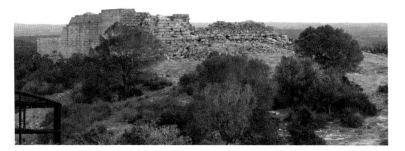

Fig. 106. Zawiyat al-Arqub: the late Roman castle.

with the cardinal points of the compass, and originally had a single entrance in the middle of the S side. The thickness of the outer walls is 1.6 m and on the N side parts still stand 5.5 m high; on the N and W sides can still be seen several narrow slit-windows.

Internally, the space is divided into a number of rooms, perhaps around a central courtyard. On the far side, opposite the entrance, is a solidly constructed apse, preserving even part of the semi-dome above it; the room of which it forms part was also vaulted (at a higher level), but the remaining rooms almost certainly had flat timber roofs. The presence of the apse and the general layout of the building have suggested to some scholars that it is a church or monastery, albeit unquestionably fortified. However, the facts that the apse faces N (not otherwise attested for a church in Cyrenaica) and that there is a complete absence of any specific Christian presence (by way of ornament or fittings) weakens this argument. On the other hand, the assumption that there was a central courtyard in front of an architecturally dominant vaulted audience-chamber makes perfectly good sense as a military structure.

The various flanking rooms are all solidly built, and all doorways are arched. Many of them are provided on either side with 'curtain-brackets' (p. 14). The E wing has been substantially modified at an uncertain date. It was originally entered from the inferred courtyard to the W, but in this later phase that opening was blocked and a new doorway was cut through the outer wall on the E side. The internal subdivisions (originally two wide arches) were also altered. The W wing is composed of a single rectangular

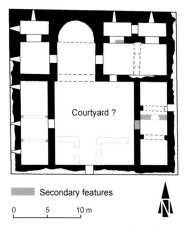

Courtyard ?

Secondary features

0   5   10 m

Fig. 107. Zawiyat al-Arqub: plan of the castle.

hall, into which in a second phase were inserted two slender arches spanning its width. The E wall was partly restored in this phase, but the doorway into the courtyard, with 'curtain-brackets', is original. In the remaining central area, there are traces of rooms on either side of the entrance, but these are irregular in plan and of poor masonry: they are certainly not original. It makes good sense of the plan that all of this should have been an open space; there would presumably also have been a (wooden?) staircase somewhere, leading to an upper floor.

The character of the building is undoubtedly late Roman, consistent with that of Qasr Migdim (p. 136) and Qasr ash-Shahdiyn (p. 126) in the same territory. On the saddle between the castle and the zawiya is a deep rock-cut cistern which has been refurbished and is in current use. About 20 m to the E of the castle are the roofless remains of a small square mosque, possibly of fairly recent construction; the mihrab is still visible.

Ancient village

The main ancient settlement here lay some 700 m to the W, on the terraced slopes which drop down on the other side of the ridge along which the road runs. The site is covered with dense scrub and fences also create difficulties of access; but here there are traces of a village of the Classical period, with a jumble of massive ashlar blocks, many standing arches, a couple of semi-domes (fig. 108), and wells and cisterns. Towards the valley-bottom, at N 32° 39.89' E 21° 28.21', is a small bath-building of concrete rubble, plastered on the inside. Two barrel-vaults are visible, belonging to heated rooms with vertical flues at the corners.

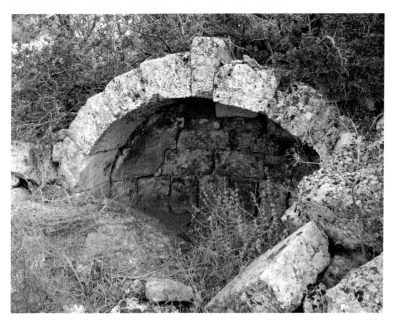

Fig. 108. Zawiyat al-Arqub: surviving semi-dome of an unexplored ancient building.

ZAWIYAT AL-HAMAMAH (PHYKOUS) زاوية الحمامه

Coordinates: N 32° 55.40′, E 21° 37.78′
Directions: Leave al-Bayda in a north-westerly direction (at N 32° 45.94′ E 21° 43.78′, a clover-leaf junction where the by-pass is incomplete), and follow this road as it winds down the upper and then the lower escarpments of the jabal. On reaching the narrow coastal strip, cross directly over the coast road and continue for a distance of 1.6 km, at which point the road crosses the mouth of a wadi before coming to an end at the zawiya. The settlement occupied the headland to your left and the coordinates given refer to the position of the church. The total distance to this point from the edge of al-Bayda is about 24 km.

Greek and Roman port

This site may be identified without hesitation as the ancient *Phykous*, referred to by a number of ancient writers between the first and fifth centuries AD; it was clearly a thriving port and town, serving like Apollonia as an outlet to the sea for Cyrene and the surrounding plateau. There are extensive remains on the headland of low walls, and on the waterfront close to the sandy beach on the E side are the outlines of warehouses, with an alley behind. At the western end of the beach, a bare rocky promontory is almost cut off on the landward side by an artificial cutting, probably a quarry which doubled as a defensive feature. On this promontory, a square masonry structure, perhaps the remains of a lighthouse, stands to a height of c. 2 m. Nearby, a series of deep ovoid storage-tanks (like those at Apollonia, p. 279) are cut in the rock. Further round to the W, extensive quarries (now flooded, presumably due to the sinking of the coastline) are visible. On higher ground, at the root of the headland, is the massive rectangular outline of a church; little internal detail can now be made out, apart from the S shoulder of an apse at the E end. Pottery collected on the site ranged from the fourth century BC to the sixth century AD.

Phykous twice makes a modest appearance in literature. Cato the Younger, fleeing from Julius Caesar with his fleet in 48 BC, was denied entry by Phykous when driven there by a storm. Much later, at the beginning of the fifth century AD, Euoptius, the brother of Synesius (p. 8), lived near Phykous, where apparently he managed to grow silphium in his garden. On many occasions, it was through the shipping of Phykous that Synesius sent letters to his friends overseas.

6   CYRENE ★ ★ ★

For the location of numbered monuments and features at Cyrene, the reader is referred to the general plan inside the rear cover, and to the more detailed area plans in figures 109 (p. 152), 131 (p. 184) and 136 (p. 194). There is also a key to the numbered locations opposite the general plan.

The visitor can hardly fail to be captivated by the site of Cyrene. The setting is unforgettable: on the edge of the upper escarpment of the Jabal Akhdar at a height of 600 m, one may look out northwards over the lower plateau to its abrupt edge, just 9 km away, where it drops another 300 m to the narrow coastal strip and the blue Cretan Sea. This was a bare and windswept hillside at the beginning of the 20th century, but thanks to the planting programme carried out by the Italians in the colonial period, it is now aromatic with pine and sighs in the breeze. Because of the pine woods, the different areas of excavation are now partly hidden from one another, increasing the apparent size of the ancient city and making its over-all layout difficult to grasp. It is with good reason been inscribed in the UNESCO list of World Heritage Sites, though it must be admitted that during the Qadhafi years it has not been managed to the standard which that calls for. It is to be hoped that, as with all other sites of antiquity in Libya, it will see better days.

Inasmuch as Cyrene was the first successful settlement founded in Libya by Greek colonists in the seventh century BC, and was the dominant city of Cyrenaica until the beginning of the fourth century AD, the history of the city is closely bound up with that of the region as a whole. For the broader perspective, the reader is referred to the Historical Introduction (pp. 1–17). Here I shall take up only those themes which are specific to Cyrene itself.

The historical account of the foundation of the city, related by the fifth-century writer Herodotus and corroborated by an inscription of the fourth century BC found in the Cyrene excavations (see p. 243, item 4.7), has already been related. But a city of such standing should have a divine foundation-myth also. The patron of the city was Apollo Pythios, the oracular patron of Delphi in Greece, and in this case he was associated with a nymph, Cyrene (or *Kurana* in the Doric dialect spoken there – I shall use this form to refer to the nymph, in order to distinguish her from the city). In the version told by the poet Pindar in his ninth Pythian Ode, Kurana was a young lady who disdained the domestic arts and preferred hunting wild beasts. Apollo chanced across her one day in the act of wrestling unarmed with a lion and was understandably impressed. In a moment of hesitation that is quite uncharacteristic of most such myths, he apparently asked the centaur Cheiron whether he should bed her immediately, or marry her first! Cheiron told him to do the honourable thing, and prophesied that he was to take her beyond the sea to a 'choice garden of Zeus', where she should become a queen of cities. Apollo whisked her off forthwith (presumably via the Registry Office) and lay with her that very day in Libya, where she remained to watch over the city that bore her name. The offspring of their union was Aristaeus, a minor god who was a shepherd, a beekeeper and the discoverer of the wonder-herb silphium.

The basic key to the location of the city will have been the perennial springs which gushed from beneath the cliff below the acropolis. It is on the high ground above that the earliest settlement will have been established: little of this area has been subject to archaeological investigation, but the pointers seem to be clear. The early settlement then expanded eastwards along the ridge, and the 'Street of Battos' (3) became the axis of its public and religious heart. Probably equally early was the initial development of the terrace below the springs into another sacred zone, with temples to Apollo and many other gods.

Extensive tracts of city walls are preserved, but the study of these is still in its infancy. Above the Sanctuary of Isis and Serapis on the acropolis (44), a section of defensive wall has now been attributed to the mid-sixth century BC. The account by Herodotus of the Persian attack in 515 BC suggests that the northern ridge, where the Temple of Zeus stands, was outside the walls at that date; the defences which now enclose it, and which are most widely visible on other parts of the site, are Hellenistic in date.

The city clearly expanded in the Hellenistic (Ptolemaic) and early Roman periods, but suffered a grave setback in the Jewish Revolt of AD 115 (see p. 6). In this great conflagration, it seems that virtually all of the public buildings were seriously damaged or destroyed. We are told that 220,000 people lost their lives. It took a long time for the public areas to be fully restored, but there are plenty of signs that by the later second or early third century there was considerable private wealth in the city; there are numerous instances of the amalgamation of several pre-existing properties into very luxurious residences decorated with mosaics on the floors and marble panelling on the walls.

In the chaos which affected the whole Roman Empire following the fall of the Severan dynasty in 235, the settled areas suffered from the opportunistic depredations of the tribes of the interior. These probably also took advantage of a natural disaster, an earthquake which appears to have struck Cyrene in 262 (if we can rely on a record of an event in that year which was alleged to have affected particularly the cities of Asia, but also Rome and Libya). In the Central Quarter of the city has been identified a defensive wall which was hastily constructed around this time from re-used materials (57: the blue line shown on the main site plan) and this has been associated very plausibly by Richard Goodchild with an inscription on display in the museum (p. 243, no. 4.5) which records the 'refounding' of the city in 268 as *Claudiopolis*, in honour of the emperor Claudius Gothicus. Such an event seems to imply major reconstruction, and perhaps new defences. It is also notable, particularly in terms of the building activity of this time, that the centre of public life had shifted definitively away from the 'Street of Battos' (3) on the acropolis ridge to a parallel axis along the Valley Street.

The next major archaeological horizon is marked by the earthquake of 21 July 365. This event has been discussed in the Historical Introduction (p. 7). While the damage recorded elsewhere cannot always be imputed to this event with confidence, there can be little doubt that Cyrene suffered badly. It was described a few years later by the historian Ammianus Marcellinus as 'an ancient but deserted city;' however, in the time of Synesius, a generation later, the city may have been past its days of greatness but was still far from dead.

A note of caution must be introduced at this point. Evidence of earthquake damage can on occasion be unequivocal, where for instance there is shattered masonry with crushed skeletons beneath. Epigraphic evidence, when recording reconstruction after earthquake or deaths of individuals in the disaster (as in the Tomb of Demetria, p. 238) may also be specific. But where the evidence is limited to fire, collapse and reconstruction, there are plenty of other reasons why this may have occurred. The consequences of the Jewish Revolt are a graphic illustration of this. The surrounding colonnades of the great Temple of Zeus (106) were felled on that occasion. It is clear that that was achieved through human agency, since the columns fell radially outwards: an earthquake would have caused them all to topple in one direction. The collapse of several of the major public buildings along the acropolis ridge and their replacement by dwellings described in deprecating terms by their excavators (prior to a further catastrophe which should be that of 365) has been widely accepted as evidence of an earthquake in or around 262. Similar evidence has been adduced from the American excavations in the extra-mural Sanctuary of Demeter (116). But the force of this kind of evidence is not entirely cumulative: it may be the archaeologist who is subconsciously willing a number of discrete events, separated by no great interval of time, into a single natural catastrophe. It could be so, but needs to be demonstrated in each case. It must also be admitted that much of the excavation carried out at Cyrene in the 1920s and 1930s was of a low technical standard and simply did not gather the kind of evidence (typically broken pottery) which we would now consider essential to the establishment of a convincingly narrow date-range for a destruction event.

The issue of dating evidence (or the lack of it) from old excavations also bedevils the next phase in the history of Cyrene. It is considered broadly true that the destruction caused by the earthquake in 365 served in a sense to mark the transition from paganism to Christianity. The old temples, already in decline, were not restored, but churches were built instead. Amid the ruins of the Temple of Zeus Lykaios (106), the reduction of the head of a cult-statue, and indeed of many marble columns, to tiny fragments suggests the hand of furious man rather than any kind of natural catastrophe; this has been interpreted as evidence of ritual purging of the temple ruins by Christians. However, it does seem quite clear that the Sanctuary of Isis and Serapis on the Acropolis (44) was restored after the earthquake, and that it continued to be venerated perhaps until as late as the sixth century AD. It has likewise been suggested that there were some pagan temples in the Sanctuary of Apollo which were restored or indeed first constructed after 365 (Temple of Zeus Ombrios, 86; Temple of the Petal Mosaic, 90; Shrine of Apollo Kitharoidos in the ruins of the former Fountain of Philothales, 94). The extent of the persistence of paganism here seems a little surprising, but unfortunately the confirmatory evidence of date probably does not now exist.

At the end of the Byzantine period, the positioning of the Central and East Churches (54, 110) and of the contemporary or later Qasr Shaghiyah (111) seems to imply that the centre of the remaining habitation was in the eastern part of the former city, and that the mid-Roman defences (57) had perhaps been relevant for only a short period of time. Qasr Shaghiyah has been attributed to an Arab date on structural grounds (though I am not convinced this is compelling); there is rather firmer evidence in the East Church of a late phase of secular use, which must surely post-date the Islamic Conquest. For how long after that there continued to be a community at Cyrene we cannot at present tell. The toponym 'Grennah', which still applied to the neighbourhood in the 19th century, clearly transmitted down the centuries the name of the ancient city. The rediscovery of the site by travellers, scholars and archaeologists has been described in the Historical Introduction (p. 15).

Apart from the re-use of some ancient tombs as residences, and from a single building on the slopes of the North Necropolis (p. 236), there was no habitation on the site when the Italians began to establish their military base at Cyrene in 1913. Subsequently, a small village by the name of **Shahhat** (شحات – now partly ruinous) grew up in the upper part of the Wadi Bu Turqiyah. In the 1960s, anxious to avoid the further expansion of this village, the Controller of Antiquities Richard Goodchild negotiated the creation of a new settlement to the S, beyond the walls of the ancient city. He could hardly have foreseen how this settlement would grow into the sizeable town that the visitor encounters now. Modern buildings have almost totally engulfed the South Necropolis of the ancient city and new measures of effective planning control are urgently needed to preserve the environment of this World Heritage Site.

The monuments described in the following pages are listed in a series of geographical zones. These start with the caravanserai and the principal monuments of the southern or acropolis ridge (Caesareum, agora, acropolis). Then follow the Central Quarter and the Valley Street, which lead naturally to the Sanctuary of Apollo below. After this, the order takes in the N and E parts of the site, including the Temple of Zeus. Next the areas immediately outside the walls are described, taking in the recent excavations to the S of the city, the South and North Necropoleis and the museum. Finally the two outlying sanctuary sites of Budaraj and Ain Hofra complete the tour. Cyrene is a hugely complex site, where intensive excavations have taken place for nearly a century. To study it in detail requires a great deal of time, beyond the means (and probably the interest) of many visitors. The reader is therefore advised to pay more than usually close attention to the star-ratings, and if pressed for time, to pass over those entries or monuments which are unstarred! In this way, I hope that those who wish to see the most impressive buildings will not be confused by unwanted detail while, on the other hand, the passer-by whose attention is suddenly caught by a particular feature may also find satisfaction.

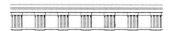

CARAVANSERAI ★ (1)

Most visitors to Cyrene will arrive from the main jabal road, turning left at a cross-roads and passing through the ever-growing village of modern Shahhat. The road through the village follows the line of the ancient approach from the E and was formerly lined with upstanding funerary monuments. Few of these are now apparent amongst the encroachment of new buildings, though the marble plinth of a fine circular mausoleum has been moved bodily from elsewhere to provide a feature in the centre of one of the roundabouts from which one approaches the ancient city. Passing beyond the succeeding roundabout, two columns flanking the road (again, a recent conceit) announce the antiquities zone. As one heads towards

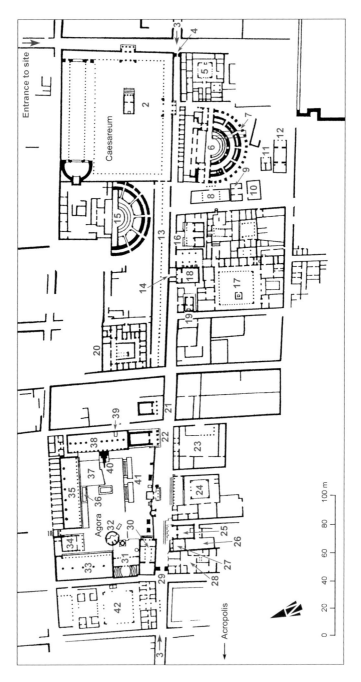

Fig. 109. Cyrene: the monumental zone along the acropolis ridge. (For the key to the numbered locations, see inside the rear cover.)

the trees (planted in the last century by the Italians and now a very endearing characteristic of the site) one cannot fail to notice on the right-hand side a fine ancient wall enclosing a huge rectangular space of some 2 ha which now serves excellently as a football pitch. The perimeter wall is Hellenistic in style, and is consistent with the expansion eastwards of the city in the second century BC: its masonry is like that of the Caesareum (2), which was first constructed at that time, and it is clearly also integral with the eastern part of the city's Hellenistic defences. The monumental nature of the enclosure, together with its evident absence of internal structures, identifies it with little doubt as a *caravanserai*, a place where visiting merchants from other places could make camp and gather together their travelling party and their beasts of burden before the principal gate of the city.

Within the enclosure, at a later date, was installed a range of six parallel but separate water-cisterns, the vaults of two of which are partially preserved. Beyond them and parallel to the city wall behind, is a seventh, reported to be intact but now buried and inaccessible. This is of different build from the others and appears to pre-date them. All of these must be of Roman, rather than earlier, date, but beyond that there is little agreement. Goodchild associated them with water-supply systems within the city of the second or third centuries AD; Stucchi and others have claimed that they reflect the (attested) shortage of water in Cyrene in the fourth century and that they were built after AD 365 in order to combat that and a perceived change in climate. To my mind, the similarity in construction to the cistern at Safsaf (p. 321), which is now known to have been linked to Cyrene, and the

orderly character of the masonry (cut for the purpose, with mason's marks, and not made from *spolia*) argues irrefutably for the earlier date.

THE ACROPOLIS RIDGE

Passing beyond the caravanserai, one shortly comes to a parking area on the L side of the road, with a ticket office which provides entry to a large enclosed zone of ruins (fig. 109), named here for convenience the acropolis ridge. The earliest settlement was at the far end of the ridge, but at an early date it expanded eastwards along a road which connected the spur to the main body of the plateau behind. As the city developed, so this area of both temples and major public buildings evolved progressively. By the third century AD, however, it was in decline and the principal axis of the city had shifted northwards to the Valley Street, an area which is today much more fragmented in terms of both exploration and accessibility to the visitor.

The entrance to this part of the excavations leads southwards along the street which heads for the South Gate.

Caesareum ★ ★ (2)

On the right-hand side of the street, as you enter the site, is a high wall from which projects a monumental porch. A fragmentary inscription over the inner side of this porch refers to a 'portico of Caesar', and the complex is therefore generally referred to as the *Caesareum*. On passing through this porch one enters an enormous rectangular piazza, surrounded on all four sides by Doric porticoes (fig. 110). This is the result of excavation and of painstaking reconstruction carried out by the Italians in the 1930s, and the effect is duly impressive. There is a similar porch on the S side, the

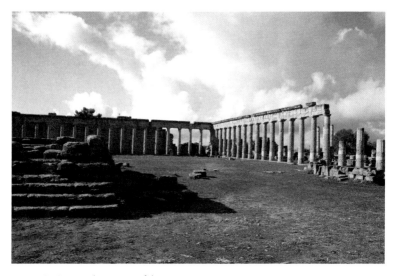

Fig. 110. Cyrene: the interior of the Caesareum.

inscription upon which commemorates a refurbishment by M(arcus) Sufenas Proculus, a citizen in the early years of the first century AD. However, the building is substantially older than that and is now believed to have been constructed as a *gymnasium* in the middle of the second century BC. We know from an inscription that Cyrene had a public gymnasium which was also known as the *Ptolemaion* (having been built by Ptolemy VIII?), and it may be the later rendering of this into Latin which has given it the name *Caesareum*. Behind the portico on the N side of the piazza there was originally a row of eleven rooms associated with its function as a gymnasium.

In the Flavian period (latter part of the first century AD) the entire complex underwent a change of purpose, becoming at that time a Roman forum. The rooms off the N portico were levelled, and a **basilica** was constructed which actually incorporated the N portico itself (presumably because of the rapid fall of the ground-level towards the N, which

would have involved massive substructures, had the building been extended further in that direction). The piazza presumably ceased at this time to have any athletic associations, and became a market area. The Capitoline Temple however, which one might also expect in a forum, is not to be found here; Zeus/ Jupiter, at any rate, already had a temple just up the road in the agora (25).

The complex suffered, along with most of the public buildings of Cyrene, at the time of the Jewish Revolt (p. 6), necessitating restoration in the time of Hadrian. A bilingual inscription honouring this emperor may be seen on a statue base in the apse of the basilica, which was apparently first constructed at this time. The apse was provided with niches for statuary, and two of the figures (Nemesis and Tyche) were found in the ruins; a yet later modification was the enlargement of the central recess from a plinth for statues into a judicial tribunal. A further addition to the layout in the second half of the second century was the

temple, the podium of which may be seen in the centre of the piazza. A colossal statue of Dionysos, found here in 1861, is a potent clue to its dedication. The temple is not accurately aligned with the piazza, which was initially a source of puzzlement to archaeologists. (Surely the architect was not so incompetent in laying it out? Was it in fact there first?) Recent excavations have shown that the solution to this riddle lies in the presence beneath of much earlier buildings on a slightly different alignment; the orientation of the temple was adjusted to make use of these structures for its foundations!

The monumentality of the area was already being impugned in the third century AD by the construction within it of modest shops in stone which gradually filled the space within the porticoes. One of these seems to have been a potter's workshop, yielding moulds for lamps and other tools. This degeneration apparently continued after the earthquake of AD 262, with further buildings constructed from fallen elements of the superstructure (fig. 111). In the fourth century, the area was taken over by the military. Nearly all of the late structures were dismantled by the excavators in the 1930s, in order to recover and replace fallen elements and to restore the complex to its 'former glory'; but in the SE corner may still be seen traces of the cavalry barracks, with beam-sockets for the roofs (at two levels), drinking-troughs for the horses carved out of architrave-blocks, and even some mosaic flooring.

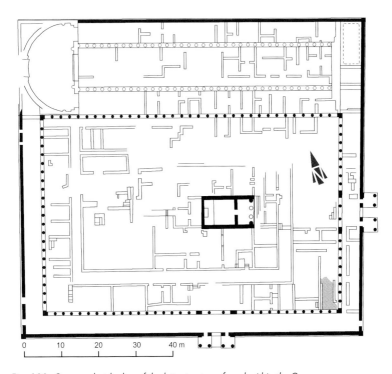

Fig. 111. Cyrene: sketch-plan of the late structures found within the Caesareum.

To this activity must also be ascribed the loopholes in the E wall at first-floor level, and probably the installation of the deep cisterns in the NE corner of the complex. After this, the final collapse and abandonment have been attributed to the earthquake of AD 365.

Finally, excavations beneath the centre of the piazza have revealed walls of very simple dwellings associated with pottery of the late seventh or early sixth century BC. This suggests that the early settlement, centred on the acropolis and the agora, had very rapidly expanded to considerable size. Stratigraphically, these are succeeded by two phases of more substantial buildings (of the fourth and third centuries BC) prior to the clearance of the area to construct the gymnasium.

Street of Battos (3)

On leaving the Caesareum by the S porch, one emerges onto one of the principal streets of the city, which leads from the acropolis, through the agora and past the Caesareum, to the countryside beyond. It is the line of this street that runs past the caravanserai (1), seen on the approach to the city. I shall refer to this, for convenience, as 'The Street of Battos', the name given to it by Richard Goodchild. The name (purely a modern convenience) is justified by the fact that it was evidently fundamental to the expansion of the early settlement eastwards from the acropolis hill, and that it came to represent the public life of the city. It passed through the agora, was bounded by numerous temples, and then passed by the public gymnasium of the second century BC and an important early sacred zone to the S of it (see below). In the Roman period, further expansion northwards of the settled area gave rise to a new major axis of communication

along the Valley Street, which led to the Sanctuary of Apollo and eventually to the port of Apollonia. As the centre of gravity shifted, so the Street of Battos and its associated monuments seem to have lost their status and to have become a much less dignified – not to say rundown – quarter.

Recent Italian publications name the street *Skyrotà*. This is derived, like Goodchild's choice of name, from the fifth Pythian Ode by Pindar, which celebrated the victory of Arkesilaos IV of Cyrene in the chariot race at Delphi in 462 BC. Pindar relates that the founder of Cyrene Battos/Aristoteles 'laid down a gravelled road (*skyrotan hodon*), straight and level, echoing with horses' hoofs in processions in honour of Apollo'. Scholars were long troubled by the problem that a route from the acropolis to the great Temple of Apollo below the springs (77) could never in any terms have been considered straight and level! This difficulty was resolved with the identification of one of the early temples in the agora as the Temple of Apollo Archegetes (30). It is also uncertain whether the term *skyrotos* is to be understood as a proper name rather than a description ('gravelled'), and I have therefore preferred to retain Goodchild's name, which has essentially the same significance.

East Propylaeum of public zone (4)

The formal 'public' area of the city was marked out in the Roman period by two *propylaea* or gateways set across the street, one at the SE corner of the Caesareum (4) and the other to the W of the agora (29). The eastern arch was initially flanked by engaged semi-columns on either side, forming a simple portal. Surviving fragments from the inscription indicate a date after the Jewish Revolt. At some time in the later second or third century AD, massive encasing piers were added, and the structure became a public fountain, with basins in semi-circular niches on either side of the E face. (Traces of both remain, though only that on the R is immediately evident.) Water was supplied, presumably from the cisterns by the E Gate (1), through conduits and clay pipes. In the fourth century, when the Caesareum had passed over to military use and a reduced defensive circuit was constructed, the space in front of the fountain was outside the defences, and a small gate was placed obliquely across the street leading southwards. Finally, at some later time, a limekiln (now removed) was established directly in front of the fountain-gate, showing that it had ceased to be any kind of thoroughfare at all.

House of the Doric Peristyle ★ (5)

This is a private house, not very helpfully named, since many houses at Cyrene have Doric peristyles! It comprises a neglected and essentially unpublished domestic complex with rooms opening off a peristyle in its eastern part. In its latest form, it probably incorporated several separate earlier properties, but was then a residence of some pretension: it is still worthy of exploration. On the E side, rooms open off the Doric peristyle from which it is named. This area shows typical characteristics of the late Roman period: the interstices between the columns have been blocked by a stone screen, and the S side of the portico is paved with a coarse geometric mosaic like those seen in the cavalry barracks in the Caesareum. Off this portico there is a room in which can still be seen extensive areas of painted wall-plaster in a panel-design of red,

yellow, white and green. Beyond this, in the SW corner, is a smaller peristyle, again with stone screens between the columns, but this time paved in the centre with mosaic in a diamond-pattern. There is a hole in the centre, from which was taken a portrait of a bearded man now on display in the museum (p. 250, no. 11.6). This was perhaps displayed beneath a film of water in order to enhance the colour. Further in this direction is a stable, with stone feeding or drinking-troughs for animals.

Returning northwards along the W side of the property, it is clear that there have been successive alterations and subdivisions of space. But one can make out here a large rectangular space (perhaps a courtyard but more probably a large hall) which was once lined with Doric semi-columns: it is possible also to make out windows and moulded door-frames.

Goodchild, in a brief reference to this complex, states that it was destroyed by fire. In that case, this is likely to have happened in the third or fourth century AD.

Theatre 3 ★ (6)

Across the Street of Battos from the Caesareum are the forlorn remains of a theatre, conventionally numbered 3. (Cyrene has a still-growing abundance of theatres, but they were not all fulfilling the same function at the same time!) The theatre is of Roman type and date, with a semi-circular orchestra in which there would have been seating for the wealthier citizens, separated by a parapet (partially restored) from the tiered seating of the *cavea*. It is almost identical in size and plan to Theatre 2 (15) but its date of construction is disputed. It seems unlikely that the two theatres would have been co-existent, but one strain of opinion argues that the construction of Theatre 3 in a previously open piazza followed the Jewish Revolt in AD 115. An alternative, which seems more plausible, is that Theatre 3 was constructed as a successor to Theatre 2, following the destruction of the latter in the earthquake of 262. The frontage onto the Street of Battos on the N is filled by a row of small shops. They were probably constructed around the same time that the porticoes of the Caesareum (above) were similarly being blocked up by the presence of shops.

Theatre 3 was systematically levelled in antiquity, which is why both the stage-building and all but the first five tiers of seats have disappeared. This demolition is presumed to have taken place when the Caesareum became a military zone and part of the city's defences in the fourth century. The latest structure found (now removed) was a limekiln built in the former *orchestra*.

Sacred zone behind Theatre 3

On the S and W sides, Theatre 3 is surrounded by a group of at least five small temples. All of these sanctuaries opened originally towards the E, onto what had been an open piazza, prior to the construction of the theatre. Recent excavations within Theatre 3 have revealed the foundations beneath it of a large **altar (7)** in the centre of the piazza, attributable to the fifth century BC, accompanied by votive offerings and pottery of the archaic period. This altar was slightly more than 30 m in length, and therefore comparable in size to the altar in front of the Temple of Apollo Pythios (76). The zone was therefore of religious importance from an early stage in the history of the city, and the modest temples now identifiable almost certainly had early antecedents.

The first building on the W side of the piazza was long described as an unusual two-winged temple but has now been re-interpreted very plausibly as a **hestiatorion (8)** or banqueting hall. It had a central projecting porch on the E side; this led to a paved courtyard, with a large marble base against the rear wall (constructed from re-used materials and therefore not original). Off this space opened two lateral halls on opposite sides, each fronted by two columns and two semi-columns. The building is of late Hellenistic origin, but was entirely rebuilt in the early first century AD and renovated at some point in the second century. In the late Roman period it was despoiled in order to build houses in the same area.

The **Temple of the Dioscuri (9)** is the principal temple of the group, being aligned centrally with the altar which is now beneath the theatre; it may be the oldest of the group. In its earliest form it was entered from the E and was composed of three successive rooms (two *naoi* and an *adyton*). The foundations are composed of small unshaped stones and associated finds indicate that it was constructed in the second half of the seventh century BC. The finds included a Chiot chalice with an inscribed dedication to the Dioscuri (Castor and Pollux). Two further phases of construction, in the sixth and fifth centuries BC and on the same plan, are represented by larger squared blocks with drafted edges and a raising of the internal floor-level. A subsequent rebuilding took place in the Roman period, perhaps in the second century AD. After the construction of the adjoining theatre, which almost completely blocked the approach from the E, the original doorway was closed up and a new doorway was opened in the centre of the S side. The inner *naos* now became a raised courtyard, leading into a pair of flanking *cellae*. Deep excavations beneath this paving (fig. 112) have exposed the earlier masonry and thick deposits of burnt material used to raise the internal floor-level. This contains much bone, exclusively of calves, and is thought possibly to represent the debris of sacrifices cleared away when the great altar was built.

The **Shrine of the Meander Mosaic (10)** is extremely ruinous. It is composed of a single room entered through a doorway, at one time with a Doric frieze of triglyphs and metopes above; there is a plinth for a cult-statue against the W wall. As in the case of the preceding temple, the entrance, originally at the E end, was moved to the N side when the building was reconstructed (presumably after the Jewish Revolt). It takes its name from the mosaic which covered the entire floor and which has been attributed to the end of the first century AD. The floor is largely covered

with the blocks of the S wall, which has toppled inwards (in the earthquake of 365?). A staircase in the SE corner perhaps post-dates this collapse.

The **Temple of Cybele (11)** is a recent discovery, having previously been concealed by the track of the Decauville railway. The form is of a façade with a Syrian arch, leading into a *pronaos* succeeded by twin *cellae*. (It has been suggested that the internal division is secondary, but this seems to me to have been fully bonded into the main structure.) The Syrian arch suggests a date in the middle or later second century AD. After the earthquake of 262, the internal walls were rearranged to create two small rooms on the N side and one larger one to the S. What had been the northern *cella* was stuccoed and became a cistern. The final collapse of the building is well dated by coins to the earthquake of 365. The dedication of the temple is presumed from the eleven statuettes of Cybele which were found,

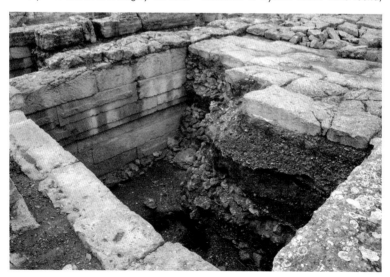

Fig. 112. Cyrene: excavations beneath the late paving of the Temple of the Dioscuri, showing earlier structural phases and fill of burnt offerings.

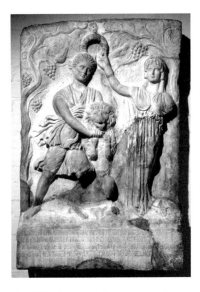

Fig. 113. The nymph Kurana strangling a lion while being crowned by the goddess Libya: a relief of the late second century AD found in the Temple of Aphrodite at Cyrene. (© The Trustees of the British Museum.)

still in a line, against the rear wall, together with many other fragments of marble and terracotta figures.

The **Temple of Aphrodite (12)** is early, with huge orthostats in its walls. It had originally a simple entrance leading directly into a *cella* with eight internal piers. In the Roman period it was rebuilt with an added porch at the front, with flanking internal colonnades to the *cella* and with a raised *adyton* at the far end. When the building was first excavated by Smith and Porcher in 1861 they found within it six statues and 29 statuettes. Ten of these represented Aphrodite, from which they deduced the dedication of the temple. Amongst the finds from this excavation was the famous relief, now in the British Museum (fig. 113, but with a replica in the Cyrene Museum: see

p. 239, no. 1.1), of the nymph Kurana strangling a lion and being crowned by the goddess Libya.

The area to the S and E of Theatre 3 is still under investigation at the time of writing. Beneath the E side of the theatre, a broad foundation running N–S has recently been identified as the eastern defensive wall of the city in the archaic period.

Stoa of Hermes and Herakles ★ ★ (13)

Looking W along the 'Street of Battos' from the Caesareum, the dominant feature is now the enormous wall of the Stoa of Hermes and Herakles, so named from the alternating figures of these two divinities which decorate the piers separating high window-openings. (Herakles has the beard.) This is the fruit of a massive work of reconstruction, carried out by the Italians under the direction of Sandro Stucchi following their return to Cyrene in 1957. The interior of the building (behind the wall) has still been barely excavated, but it is clear that it is integral in structure and date with the gymnasium known as the *Ptolemaion* and subsequently as the *Caesareum*. (Hermes and Herakles were particular patrons of athletic prowess.) The stoa was initially a *xystos* or covered running-track 123 m (approximately two-thirds of a stade) long.

In a second phase, presumably corresponding to the time when the Caesareum ceased to be a gymnasium and became a forum in the Flavian period, the track was converted into a stoa or portico with an internal colonnade, and it was only now that two doorways were cut through from the Caesareum at the E end of the *xystos*. It thus became a covered adjunct to the Street of Battos between the new forum and the older agora. In the fourth century, when this wall became part of the defences, a **tower (14)** was constructed part-way along the now-defunct street, completely blocking it. (The opening in the wall at this point may have been made now to provide access to the tower, but I can see no authority for the other two openings into the street.) Probably at the same time, most, if not all, of the windows were blocked up. As in the Caesareum, so here too the space within the portico had become cluttered with small structures during its later history. It is because the entire façade fell forwards across the street in the earthquake of 365 that it was possible to carry out a credible reconstruction.

On the pathway which leads through the stoa to Theatre 2, one can see both the masonry cast down by the earthquake, the columns of the internal portico and some of the walls of structures which encumbered the interior during the later history of the monument.

Theatre 2 ★ (15)

A narrow pathway through the stoa opposite a street junction leads through the tunnel of a *vomitorium*, into the *cavea* of another theatre (fig. 115). This is of similar size and character to Theatre 3 (6), but has been more extensively restored and in recent times put once more into use. Unlike Theatre 3, which was entirely built up on flat ground, Theatre 2 is built on ground which falls away to the N: the *orchestra* is therefore substantially lower than the level at which one enters the *cavea* through the *vomitoria*. A landing at this level, once fronted by a parapet, divides the upper and lower tiers of seats, whereas there is no parapet between the *cavea* and the *orchestra*. There is some evidence that there was originally a colonnade surrounding the top of the cavea, which would have made the theatre a prominent landmark.

The stage is fronted by a wall with alternating rectangular and semi-circular niches; its floor was always of wood.

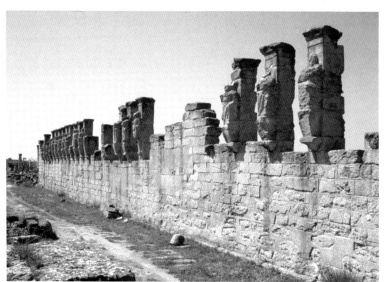

Fig. 114. Cyrene: the Stoa of Hermes and Herakles.

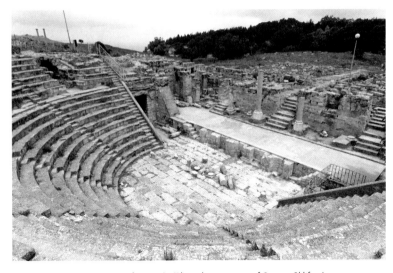

Fig. 115. Cyrene: Cyrene: Theatre 2. (Photo by courtesy of Steven Sklifas.)

The stage-building behind was pierced in the usual way by three entrances. The (wider) central entrance was flanked by Corinthian columns of red Aswan granite, and the two outer ones by Doric columns of white marble. These must have been a job lot, as they do not match one another for length and the shorter (granite) columns are raised on rather curious octagonal bases of Pentelic marble in order to make up the height. Similar bases may be seen at the foot of the stepped street to the W of Theatre 4 (see p. 192). Fragments found in the excavation suggest that there were two further tiers of columns above, and that the whole backdrop was extensively decorated with statuary, including figures of Apollo and seven Muses (of which four are displayed in the museum: see p. 249, nos. 10.13–16).

The ornamentation of the stage-building was all destroyed in a fire in the second half of the third century (perhaps due to the earthquake of 262). Subsequent to this, parts of the damaged structure were used to create simple rooms in the lower levels, connected to the Caesareum by a doorway which was cut through the intervening wall. This activity was associated by the excavators with the late military activity in the Caesareum and in the Stoa of Hermes and Herakles. The original date of construction of the theatre is not closely established. It has been cautiously attributed to the second century AD, and it may have been erected late in that century as a consequence of the conversion of the former theatre in the Sanctuary of Apollo (89) into an amphitheatre. The building has been described erroneously as an odeon, implying that it was roofed. In point of fact, there is no trace of such provision whereas there is evidence of a coherent system of rainwater drainage.

Return from the theatre to the Street of Battos. Facing you and extending towards the R is a complex area, originally two *insulae* of the city plan but combined into one to make a very luxurious

Roman house. Typically, the entrance to the house is framed by various public buildings which open onto the street.

Twin temples (16)

At the left-hand corner of the double *insula* stands a pair of identical small temples, side by side with a paved corridor between them. Their façades and frontal steps have gone, but within the westerly of the pair there is still the base of an altar against the rear wall. They are said to be of the second half of the second century AD, and it has been suggested that they were dedicated to Hermes and Herakles, patrons of the gymnasium – though it would be most unusual for Hermes to have had a second temple so close by (at no. 19).

House of Jason Magnus ★ ★ (17)

The name given to this complex (fig. 116) is derived from the inscription in mosaic of the neighbouring Temple of Hermes (19), a dedication by a slave of Tiberius Claudius Jason Magnus. The association would be plausible in terms of date and social status, and there is inevitably a structural relationship between the temple and the house behind it, but it cannot be pressed further than that. The complex, in its final form, is undoubtedly a single wealthy property; however, it is not surprising that, in order to create such a home in an urban quarter which had been long settled, it was necessary to buy up and combine several pre-existing houses. In this instance, even a former street was closed and incorporated into the property.

The main entrance, off the Street of Battos next to the Hall of the Orthostats (p), leads into an atrium (a) with a central *impluvium* (water basin) surrounded by six Doric columns. The Proconnesian marble facing of the door-sill alone survives; the surround of the *impluvium* is paved in mosaic. An image in the mosaic of a Nereid on a hippocamp together with a Triton has been lifted (note the square void) and is now on display in the museum (p. 250, no. 11.2); the atrium was also once embellished by an over-life-sized marble statue of Herakles. A stepped corridor (b) on the line of the suppressed street led upwards from the inner end of the atrium, through

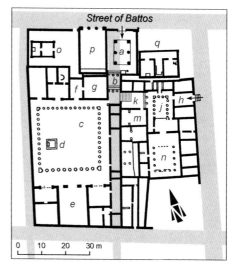

Fig. 116. Cyrene: plan of the House of Jason Magnus.

a Atrium
b Corridor
c Great Peristyle
d Lararium?
e Summer triclinium
f Vestibule
g Winter triclinium
h E entrance
i Peristyle
k Connecting hall
m Mosaic of the Four Seasons
n S peristyle
o Temple of Hermes
p Hall of the Orthostats
q Twin temples

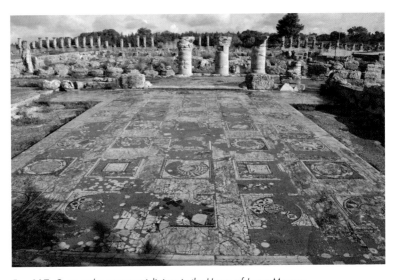

Fig. 117. Cyrene: the summer triclinium *in the House of Jason Magnus.*

two pairs of columns (presumably surmounted by arches) to a huge peristyle (c). This was lined on three sides by two-storey porticoes (Doric below, Ionic above) and on the fourth, towards the S, by a gigantic Corinthian portico, rising to the same combined height (over 6 m)! Three capitals from this side have been set up on column-drums by way of example. One of these formerly included what was said to be a portrait-head of Battos, the founder of the city. The portico along this side was also enlivened by statues of the Muses in Pentelic marble between the columns: one of these has been re-erected. A small shrine (d) in the garden of the peristyle was probably a *lararium*, a shrine dedicated to the gods (*lares*) of the owner's family.

The principal reception room of the complex, the summer *triclinium* (e: fig. 117), faced this southern portico. Its wide triple entrance and northerly aspect would have given it an airy and shaded character in the summer heat. The central part of the floor was

magnificently adorned with *opus sectile* patterns in a variety of Mediterranean marbles (fig. 118); the outer perimeter, which would mostly have been hidden by the couches of banqueters, was paved with relatively coarse and simple mosaic. The summer *triclinium* is flanked by other large rooms of uncertain (but surely formal) purpose, also paved with mosaic. The E and W sides of the Great Peristyle were originally lined by blank rear walls which faced in turn onto the flanking streets. After the incorporation of the adjoining property to the E (providing scope for the imposing atrium and stepped corridor), the space on the E side was used for further rooms opening off the E portico.

Towards the centre of the N range is a vestibule (f) with a favourite Roman motif in mosaic: the Labyrinth. The perimeter of the Labyrinth takes the form of a city (or fortress) wall. In the doorway stands Ariadne, holding the end of a thread; above her head is the inscription *Ep agatho* – 'Good luck!'

The main part of the floor is filled by a complicated meander pattern, bordering the (white) thread which leads eventually to an *emblema* in the centre showing Theseus slaying the Minotaur. This has been lifted and is now in the museum (p. 250, no. 11.3). A glance at the over-all plan shows that this must have been the original entrance vestibule from the Street of Battos, closed up when the new atrium (a) was constructed. (Note that the inscription and the figure of Ariadne face a viewer approaching from the N.) Now it leads only to a second *triclinium* (g), which will have served in the winter months or on occasions when use of the vast summer *triclinium* was not warranted. It was paved in a similar manner, with *opus sectile* in the centre and plain marble slabs around the three sides away from the door. The walls, initially plastered, were at a later date veneered with Proconnesian marble. On the opposite side of the vestibule, two further rooms were embellished with mosaic floors. The first

of them leads to two inner rooms, one of which contains an oven: this must have been the kitchen area.

The presence of two-storey porticoes implies an upper floor on at least the N side of the peristyle. Since none of the present rooms on the ground floor suggests the intimacy of domestic quarters, these may have been upstairs before the expansion of the property.

The E wing of the property was originally one or more independent houses. (Two peristyles on this side imply the possibility of two separate properties, but the original boundaries cannot now be determined with confidence.) The house towards the Street of Battos was initially entered from the N, but after the construction of the twin temples (q) in front, a new entrance from the adjoining street led through a vestibule (h) to a central peristyle (j). Directly opposite this entrance, a hall preceded by two columns (k) had perhaps once been a *triclinium*. However, after the unification of the properties across the intervening

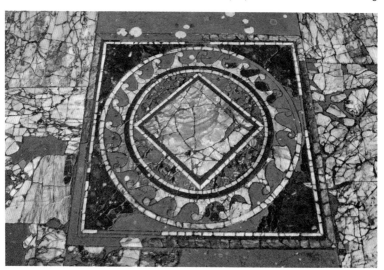

Fig. 118. Cyrene: detail of opus sectile *in the House of Jason Magnus.*

street, it was provided with a broad but steep staircase which connected it with the western part of the complex. A doorway in the S wall of this room gave access to a room (m) which still possesses (beneath a modern cover-building) a fine mosaic of the Four Seasons. The exceptional state of preservation of this mosaic is due to the fact that, some time after it was laid, the floor in the room was raised to match the levels in the W wing and it was simply buried beneath the infill. The square mosaic is primarily composed of a spiral guilloche, with figures of the Four Seasons at the corners and a figure of a Nereid riding a seahorse. (Unfortunately, from the windows which offer the best vantage-point, she is upside down! Even more unfortunately, it is reported that this mosaic has been one of the few archaeological casualties of the upheavals of 2011: parts of it have been cut out and stolen.) An archway marks off the further end of the room, where traces of stucco are still preserved. This can well be imagined as a bedroom. To the S of the first peristyle in the E wing is a second, larger one (n), off which, presumably, opened domestic quarters and service rooms. There was a water basin in the centre and there are signs here, as in a number of Cyrenean houses, that the spaces between the columns of the peristyle were subsequently walled up, perhaps to keep out the cold in winter. Waterproof cistern-plaster is apparent here even in the corridors of the peristyle, suggesting that the whole area was eventually converted into some kind of reservoir!

It is clear that in its latter phase, the House of Jason Magnus was divided into a grandiose W wing for public display and entertainment, and a more private E wing for the family and staff to live in. The style of the mosaics suggests that this phase belongs to the Antonine or Severan period, when Cyrene (like so many other North African cities) was at its most prosperous. Its magnificence suggests a member of the local aristocracy, but not necessarily that it was the residence of the local governor. The scale of the building, and the recovery from it of imperial statues, has suggested to some that it must have had some public function, and was perhaps even the Roman successor to the gymnasium which had been transformed into a forum at the end of the first century AD. (In view of the two *triclinia*, this does not seem an obvious inference to me.) At all events, it did not last long. It was destroyed violently – either by earthquake or by the hand of man – before the Caesareum was incorporated into the defences and the tower (14) was built across the former Street of Battos in the fourth century. When this occurred, its ruins were levelled in order to deny cover to attackers.

Hall of the Orthostats (18)

Immediately to the W of the entrance to the House of Jason Magnus is a large rectangular hall opening onto the Street of Battos. It is named from the large upright blocks of which its long sides are built. The hall is paved with a mosaic in a geometric pattern; this has caved in at various points under the impact of the roof which fell on it when it was destroyed. It was entered through a porch, but the façade, which must have fallen in the earthquake of AD 262, was wholly removed when the later defensive tower (14) was subsequently built across the street. The rear of the hall had a high podium across its entire width, and while the structure as a whole is not raised on a podium, there can be little doubt that it was a temple and that the podium served to display cult statues.

Temple of Hermes (19)

To the W of the Hall of the Orthostats is yet another temple, this time very small, free-standing and facing E within its own precinct or *temenos*. This is thought to have been Hellenistic in origin, and initially to have taken the form of a single room or *oikos*. In the Roman period, the building was subdivided by a new inner façade with a high sill; it is suggested that the outer part remained an open-air vestibule as in the Temple of Apollo in the Agora (30). The inner shrine, with a plinth for the cult statue, was paved with a very simple geometric mosaic incorporating the following inscription in large letters: 'I, Januarius the slave, have fulfilled out of my own means the vow which I made to the great god Hermes for the well-being and victory of Tiberius Claudius Jason Magnus.' We know that Jason Magnus was a priest of Apollo at Cyrene within the period AD 177–80; also that a Jason Magnus from Cyrene was a victor in the Olympic Games in 189. It seems likely that the inscription refers to this man.

House of Hesychios ★ (20)

To the N of the W end of the Stoa of Hermes and Herakles (reachable by various not very obvious paths) is an interesting late peristyle house which was once owned by a certain Hesychios. Its sole entrance was on the E side, from a side-street behind the stoa. As in many other cases at Cyrene, its initial excavation was poorly recorded and its chronology is now very difficult to determine. (There is also no authoritative plan, and descriptions are inconsistent!) However, it was possibly first built in the first century AD as a typical house with rooms opening off an Ionic peristyle, and a staircase on the E side leading to an upper floor. A cistern beneath the N range may not originally have been built over.

The house, as one sees it now, partially reconstructed, is in its late form (fig. 119). Controversy remains over whether this means between AD 262 and 365, or after the latter date. At this time, there was an entrance in the NE corner into a stable fitted with mangers along the N wall (a). A second entrance on the E side led through a generous portal into a vestibule with benches around its walls (b); from here one passed into the corridor surrounding the peristyle (c). The colonnade had by now been walled up, leaving only high lunette windows, which admitted light and air, but not too much! The northern side of the peristyle remained accessible, through a new and larger Doric colonnade, terminated at either end by engaged semi-columns against the flanking walls. Within the peristyle was constructed a fountain (d), decorated with a re-used marble relief showing a *quadriga* (now in the museum: p. 246, no. 7.10) and lined on either side by limestone columns, which presumably supported a pergola.

The northern corridor was paved with marble slabs, one of which proved to be part of an inscription of AD 238–44

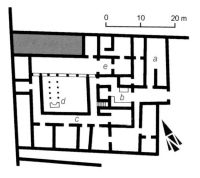

Fig. 119. Cyrene: sketch-plan of the House of Hesychios. (a) Stable; (b) Vestibule; (c) Peristyle; (d) Fountain; (e) Inscribed paving.

(suggesting that, at the very least, the late refurbishment was subsequent to the earthquake of 262). The S and W corridors, however, were paved with coarse mosaic: on the S side was a geometric pattern in black and white, enclosing inscriptions which invoke 'Good Luck' for Hesychios and his wife. The mosaic on the W side is polychrome and shows five medallions supported by crudely represented angels. The medallions enclose texts calling on God and Christ to protect various members of the family, including 'Hesychios the Libyarch.' The term 'Libyarch' probably signifies the president of the Council of the Two Libyas, a body originally connected to the imperial cult, but which still persisted in Christian times as an advisory body.

A room at the E end of the N corridor (e) has marble paving in which we see the name of Hesychios again, this time the invocation (despite a stonemason's error!) is 'Good luck to Hesychios the Younger!' This implies a further generation of the same family. To the N of this room is a small private bath suite.

So who were these Hesychii, and when did they live? Synesius of Cyrene (p. 8) addressed a letter to a friend of that name, and it is naturally a seductive solution to equate him with the owner of this house. Goodchild did so, but then changed his mind, since his soundings within the already-exposed building yielded no coins later than Constantius II (337–61); he therefore concluded that the occupation of the house came to an end with the earthquake of 365. Another possibility is that Hesychios the Younger was the father of Synesius (which would not be incompatible with the final destruction of the property in 365). A contradictory, but forceful, argument has been put forward by Denis Roques: he asserted that, since the Hesychios of the

mosaics was a Christian, he would not have held the office of Libyarch before it ceased to be connected with the imperial cult in about 400. Therefore, the latest phase of the house must post-date the earthquake of 365 and the owner WAS the correspondent of Synesius. Likewise, the style of the mosaics has been said to imply a date no earlier than the mid fourth century. At present, the issues must be considered to remain open!

Temple 'of the Muses' (21)

Continuing westwards along the Street of Battos, one now approaches the agora, once the heart of the ancient city. On the right-hand side of the next *insula* beyond the end of the Stoa of Hermes and Herakles, and immediately before entering the agora itself, one comes to the prostyle Temple 'of the Muses'.

This building was uncovered in 1915 by soldiers in search of building-stone. Its *cella* was paved with mosaic, the composition of which included (badly damaged) medallions with heads of the Muses, after which the building has been named. The temple was highly ornate: the porch was fronted by four Corinthian columns, so spaced that they probably carried a Syrian arch, and the podium was decorated externally with tragic masks carved in relief, separated by festoons (no longer detectable). The building has recently been dated to AD 180–190. In the last phase of occupation, the frontal steps were removed and the space was taken up by simple dwellings.

The Agora ★ ★

The visitor proceeding westwards now reaches the agora (fig. 120). While the initial settlement at Cyrene was on the acropolis nearby, the addition of the agora took place very early in its history, and it was for many centuries the focal

6 Cyrene: the acropolis ridge

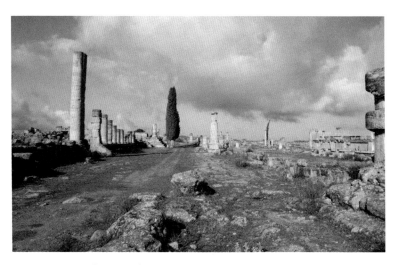

Fig. 120. Cyrene: the Street of Battos where it passes through the Agora. On the L are the façades of the prytaneion and the Temple of Zeus; on the R is the main piazza.

point of public and religious life. After the third century AD – perhaps after the earthquake of 262 – its status progressively declined, and as in the case of the Caesareum and the Stoa of Hermes and Herakles, its open spaces as well as its ruinous public buildings were encroached upon by a varied array of private houses. The result of these many layers of history, first built up and then destroyed, then excavated and selectively restored, is an effect that is visually very confusing. However, the agora zone has been more intensively studied and published than any other part of the city. Therefore, despite the 'non-scientific' character of the early excavations, the evolution of the zone is now reasonably well understood and it is possible to make sense of most of the buildings.

In a formal sense, the buildings on the S side of the Street of Battos are outside the agora, which occupied the space to the N of the street and lay at a lower level; nonetheless, it is clear from the functions of these buildings

that they constituted an integral part of its developed layout. The earliest structures to the N of the street belong to the late seventh century BC, whereas nothing on the S side of it is earlier than the fourth. This guidebook is not the place for an extended discourse on buildings which are no longer visible, but a quick thumbnail sketch may be helpful in setting the context. The earliest structures were a simple enclosure dedicated to Apollo Archegetes in the SW corner (beneath 30) and, on the E side, a little shrine dedicated to Opheles, a rural divinity with links to the Arcadian divinity Aristaeus (beneath 22). A little to the N of the latter was a tumulus in which was buried the founder Battos. During the sixth century BC, two *stoai* (beneath the later North Stoa, 35) were built and on the W side was added an open-air precinct dedicated to Demeter and Kore (beneath 33). In the fifth century, following the fall of the monarchy, the Tomb of Battos was destroyed, and subsequently re-constituted a few metres further to the

E; the shrine of Opheles was replaced by a Temple of Asklepios. On the W side, two buildings for public assembly, one perhaps a *geronteion* for the elders, appeared.

After the middle of the fourth century BC, a massive building programme began, funded by the wealthiest of Cyrene's citizens, which gave rise to many of the buildings that we can now see. The primitive shrine of Apollo Archegetes in the SW corner of the Agora was replaced with something more dignified (30) and most of the buildings on the W side were superseded by the substantial West Stoa (33). The N side of the Agora was extended northwards by means of a retaining wall and on top was built the North Stoa (35); on the E side, the Tomb of Battos was replaced again by a rectangular chamber-tomb within a

rectangular precinct (39). On the S side, buildings now rose on the S side of the Street of Battos: the *Archeion* (23), the (new) *Prytaneion* (24), the *Nomophylakeion* (26) and, in the second century, the Temple of Zeus (25). The two monumental altars in the centre of the piazza (41) have been attributed to the fourth and third centuries respectively; the new circular Shrine of Demeter and Kore on the W (32), the Monument to the Gods on the N (36) and the Naval Monument on the E (40) belong to the third or second centuries.

In the Roman period, there was much rebuilding, but relatively little that was new and monumental. A temple between the North and West Stoai (34) was an adaptation of an earlier building to house the imperial cult; the Temple of Opheles/Aristaeus/Asklepios in the SE

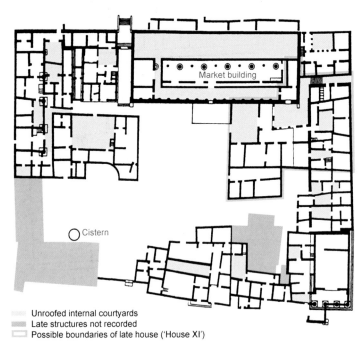

Fig. 121. Cyrene: plan of the agora zone in the late Roman period.

corner (22) was rebuilt in a very much grander style after the Jewish Revolt; and in the space to the N of that, where the Tomb of Battos had yet again been destroyed, a new E Stoa (38) was built. After the earthquake of AD 262, while buildings on the S side were refurbished in various ways, it seems that the heart of the former agora was in decay. Several of the temples went out of religious use, others were progressively superseded by modest houses constructed from reused materials; the North Stoa was rebuilt on a much reduced scale as a market-building.

The earthquake of 365 destroyed the remaining public buildings and terminated the civic and religious role of the zone. The market in the former North Stoa was restored, even including a *thermopolium* or fast-food shop; some houses of considerable pretension, with mosaic floors, invaded the ruins and the remaining open spaces (fig. 121). Because the uppermost layers were most extensively removed in the first excavations, the date and duration of this latest phase of occupation is controversial and difficult now to pin down. It may not have outlasted the middle of the fifth century AD.

The buildings on the upper terrace (the street) will be described first, followed by those on the lower terrace (the agora proper).

Temple of Asklepios (22)

This building, facing the Street of Battos and just across a side-street from the Temple 'of the Muses' is a tetrastyle prostyle temple of the second century AD. It was a fine example of the Corinthian style of the period, and was paved internally with a *trompe l'oeil* pattern in mosaic. An unusual feature is the octagonal bases beneath the columns of the façade.

The temple, constructed after the Jewish Revolt, succeeded a little shrine of the seventh century BC dedicated to the rural god Opheles, who is assimilated to the Arcadian god Aristaeus (offspring of Apollo and Kurana). This was sited a little further to the N, and faced N. The first shrine was replaced by a larger one, still facing N but now surrounded by a rectangular *temenos*, in the third quarter of the sixth century BC. About a hundred years later, this was replaced by a new building, larger again but still simple in design, now facing S; and a further rebuilding has been attributed to the second century BC. In its final, thoroughly Romanized, form, the size of the temple was increased such that it was now approached from the Street of Battos rather than the agora square, and the original dedication seems to have become further assimilated to the god Asklepios.

Archeion (23)

This is a public building, of which little detail is known, though it is asserted to have been added to the agora zone in the Hellenistic period. The name occurs in several inscriptions, and refers to the seat of one or more magistracies. Rooms open off the N and W sides of a huge peristyle, while in the NW corner was set a separate shrine, rebuilt in the second century AD as a temple of Athena, with a porch of the Corinthian order (one *anta* has been re-erected) and with a mosaic paving within. A fine Medusa head from this pavement has been lifted and is on display in the museum (p. 250, no. 11.7).

Prytaneion (24)

The *prytaneion* of a city was a civic building in which the sacred flame of *Hestia*, representing the focus of the city's identity, was tended and in which formal banquets and entertainments could be held (e.g. for visiting delegations). A primitive *prytaneion* – a relatively small building which accommodated a hearth of some sort – has been identified beneath the later extension of the Temple of Apollo Archegetes (30), but in the late fourth century BC a much grander building was erected on the S side of the Street of Battos. It is fronted by a colonnade rising from a flight of three steps. From this portico one entered a large peristyle, off which opened various rooms on the W side. These included a banqueting hall and, in the NW corner, the hearth for the sacred flame. The presently visible elements of the façade, with unfluted columns and Corinthian capitals, belong to a reconstruction following the Jewish Revolt.

Temple of Zeus ★ (25)

The next building which claims attention beyond the *prytaneion* stands on a high podium; it can only be reached by an extremely steep frontal staircase which

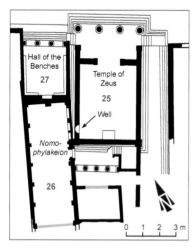

Fig. 122. Cyrene: plan of the Temple of Zeus and surrounding buildings on the S side of the agora.

obstructs the line of the street (figs. 120, 122). Its position over-all, seeming to have outgrown a site which was not big enough for it, reflects the nature of its history. Originally constructed in the second century BC, and even then squeezed into an inadequate space between the *prytaneion* to the E and the *nomophylakeion* to the W, it was initially a smaller building, raised on a plinth three steps high (detectable on the long sides) and with a tetrastyle façade in marble which projected less far forward. There is a curious void in the thickness of the *cella* wall on the right-hand side, which has been explained as a pre-exisitng sacred well associated with the *nomophylakeion* (see below).

Following the Jewish Revolt of AD 115, in which the building was evidently damaged, it was restored under Hadrian. At this time the podium was increased in height by a further course of masonry, the porch extended forwards and the vertiginous frontal stairway added, encroaching upon the street. As a concession to the virtual inaccessibility of this stairway, slightly more sympathetic flights of steps were inserted at either end of the façade, resulting in further encroachment on the side-street to the E. The new porch had Ionic columns and bases with Doric capitals! The cella was paved with a geometric mosaic, and against the rear wall was a substantial plinth for the cult statue. After the earthquake of 262, the temple was again restored, and at this time acquired, as a front to the statue-plinth, an inscribed slab which does not belong here at all. It records the erection of the arch (29), with statues, across the street at the W end of the agora zone by Hadrian and Antoninus Pius! Within the temple were found statues of Zeus (on display in the museum, p. 245, no. 7.3), of Athena and (possibly) of Hera (both in the British

Museum). These are of different styles and dates, and while it seems clear that the temple had originally been dedicated to Zeus alone, it is questionable whether in its later history it had become a Roman *capitolium*, dedicated to the Capitoline triad. A fourth-century coin of Constantius I was found in the excavations of 1915, but the temple probably met its end in the earthquake of 365.

Nomophylakeion ★ (26)

Behind the Temple of Zeus and eclipsed by it (fig. 122), is a rectangular building of a rare, but well-defined, type. Finds within it make it abundantly clear that this was the *nomophylakeion* or official archive of the city. A number of inscriptions commemorate dedications by the *nomophylakes*, the guardians of the laws, and the excavations also yielded many thousands of pyramidal clay seals. These bear impressions of the signet rings of the *nomophylakes*, and each has a hole in it; by this it was attached to the string which bound each scroll. The quantity of these seals shows that not only were laws stored here, but evidently many other documents, probably including property deeds, wills and the like.

The *nomophylakeion* was built in the fourth century BC, long before the Temple of Zeus, and originally had an open space to the E of it. The entrance was on the E side, facing a sacred well. When the temple was built in the second century, the original entrance was blocked, but access to the sacred well was maintained within the temple platform (see above). A new entrance to the *nomophylakeion* was made a little further to the S, and this was reached from behind the temple.

Various modifications and refurbishments followed. In the time of Domitian, a portico of three columns between rectangular pilasters was built in the entrance area, with a stone staircase leading to some sort of gallery or upper storey. (The present means of access to this area can hardly have been intended while the *nomophylakeion* was functioning as such. There appears to be a wide blocked entrance in the wall facing this portico.) Later in the second century, the internal long walls of the building were divided by added pilasters into a series of niches. A further modification was the addition against the N wall of a statue base framed by blind arches. Eventually, the whole was consumed by fire, the reddening effect of which upon the stonework is still readily apparent. Because of the unscientific character of the excavation (in 1919) the significant dates in the history of the building are far from certain; but its fiery demise was probably associated with the earthquake of 365. The wall at the southern end of the building is a late insertion, and its full extent beyond this point appears not to have been investigated.

Hall of the Benches (27)

To the W of the Temple of Zeus on the Street of Battos stands the Hall of the Benches (see fig. 122). This building, consisting of a single room opening onto the street through a typical porch of two columns between rectangular pilasters, is of uncertain purpose. It separates the *nomophylakeion* from the Street of Battos, and must therefore be either earlier or contemporary with it. At some point during the Roman period, the entrance in the façade was reduced to a narrow doorway and the inner ends of the long walls were lined with stone benches with elegant moulded legs. At a later date still a large – but crudely constructed – niche for a statue was inserted in the rear wall, projecting into the *nomophylakeion* behind. It may be presumed that the hall served as a meeting-place for a small body of persons representing a particular civil or religious function, but the nature of it cannot be determined.

The next building to the W, which occupies the remaining part of the *insula* which contains the preceding buildings, presumably also has its origins in the Hellenistic period. The visible remains have the appearance of a **peristyle house (28)** which, in this position, would surely have been occupied only by someone in an official position. However, no description or study of it has yet been published.

West Propylaeum of public zone (29)

The W end of the agora, and indeed of the entire public zone which started in the E at the Caesareum, is marked by a corresponding arch to that previously described (4). The stone paving of the Street of Battos is continuous between the two and extends for one more block to the W; beyond this point it had only a gravel surface. The arch, of which little remains, had a single narrow span and the piers were decorated on the outer face (that is to say, towards the acropolis) with a pair of three-quarter engaged Corinthian columns which have been partly re-erected. It was dedicated to Hadrian and Antoninus Pius, as we know from the inscription which was later re-used in the Temple of Zeus (p. 172), in AD 138. The re-use of the inscription suggests that the arch was not restored after the earthquake of AD 262.

Entrance to the Lower Agora

Having reached the western extremity of the agora, it is time to examine the main square and its associated buildings. It must be remembered here that, in late antiquity, the ruinous monuments of earlier periods were plundered for building material which was then used to construct houses. In the course of excavation, and of dismantling the later structures, much of this material was recovered, and subsequent study has enabled the earlier monuments to be (at least partially) reconstructed.

The lower part of the agora (the agora 'proper') was always separated by a boundary of some sort from the Street of Battos, which is on a slightly higher level. This boundary has been variously marked, but only the visible remains will be described here. From W to E, the boundary wall, which is of Roman date, is interrupted by a (reconstructed) semicircular *exedra* facing the *prytaneion*, which is Hellenistic or early Roman; next to this is the narrow *propylaeum* which constitutes the primary entrance to the lower part of the agora from the street. (Two other entrances appear to be casual or late.) This took the form (in the second century AD, succeeding an earlier Hellenistic structure) of a portal framed by square, fluted pilasters with Corinthian capitals. Note that the steps would have prevented the passage of wheeled traffic. Next come the very ruinous foundations of a small tetrastyle temple (dedicated perhaps to Hera, or to *Dea Roma*), the *cella* of which was in the agora, but the façade of which projected into the street. Beside this is the partially reconstructed Acanthus Column. This is a commemorative monument of the Hellenistic period composed of a fluted shaft rising from an acanthus calyx and surmounted by a (fragmentary) Corinthian capital: this was decorated on three sides with figures of Hekate, and on the fourth with an unidentified female protome. The agora square and the Street of Battos are given a certain sense of unity by their uniform paving of limestone slabs. This was laid

6 Cyrene: the acropolis ridge

in the time of Hadrian and in the course of restorations following the Jewish Revolt of AD 115.

Having passed through the *pro-pylaeum*, one may note against the N side of the boundary wall several reconstructed monumental bases. Two to the W of the semicircular *exedra* catch the eye in particular: these are thought to have been statue-bases of the late second century BC.

The description continues in a broadly clockwise sense.

Temple of Apollo Archegetes ★ (30)

This was one of the earliest sanctuaries in the Agora area. It started life in the seventh century BC as a simple open-air enclosure, along the walls of which were placed offerings to the god, usually in the form of (painted) clay vases, but also including polished stones and knucklebones. A dedication scratched on one of these vessels tells us that the

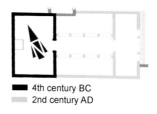

■ 4th century BC
▨ 2nd century AD

Fig. 123. Cyrene: plan of the Temple of Apollo Archegetes.

tutelary deity was Apollo, here in the guise of *archegetes* ('Principal Founder' or 'Leader of the Founders' of the city). In the second half of the fourth century a first temple was built (fig. 123), a room or *oikos* occupying about the western two-thirds of the former precinct and with a door on the E side. The temple was built of fine isodomic ashlar masonry (i.e. in which all the courses are of equal height) and provided with an ornate marble door-frame (fig. 124). There is a plinth for the cult-statue against the rear wall, with a small altar-base in front.

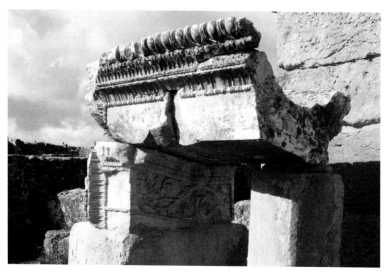

Fig. 124. Cyrene: detail of the rich architectural ornament from the door-frame of the Temple of Apollo Archegetes (fourth century BC).

In the second century AD, following damage to the temple in the Jewish Revolt, it was restored and extended in the form that can be made out now. In front of the earlier *oikos* was added a forecourt with internal porticoes along either side; access to this was through a vestibule with a wide opening onto the agora, divided into three by a pair of Doric columns between engaged semi-columns (a so-called 'Cyrenean' porch). The design is wholly unlike any other Roman temple of the period.

The temple appears to have lost its religious rôle after the mid-third century AD, and to have been adapted to secular purposes.

Assembly Building (31)

Immediately to the N of the Temple of Apollo are the scant remains of a hall which goes back to perhaps the fifth century BC, but was many times modified and refurbished. Throughout its history, however, it had internal steps, at first arranged on three sides of a rectangle and subsequently in curved rows facing one another. It had a single entrance in the middle of the long E side, and in the second or third century AD a full-length portico was added across the front. Against the centre of the rear wall there is still a marble plinth bearing a dedication to the emperor Hadrian in the year AD 118. It was an assembly building of some sort, but not large enough to accommodate the *boulé* or Council of the city, which numbered 500 members. It has been suggested that it might have been the meeting-place of the *gerousia* or body of elders, which numbered 101. In the late Roman period, this building also succumbed to subdivision into small residential units, and these internal walls now largely obscure its earlier character.

A *stele* inscribed with the Edicts of Augustus, now in the museum (p. 243, no. 4.4), was found in this building, re-used face-down as a door-sill.

Sanctuary of Demeter and Kore ★ (32)

The most distinctive monument on the W side of the Agora is a circular enclosure with high walls and two entrances on opposite sides (fig. 125). This, long thought to have been the Tomb of Battos, is now considered to have been an open-air sanctuary to Demeter and Kore (Demeter's daughter, also known as Persephone). The existence of coping-stones from the top of the perimeter wall shows that there was no roof. Within, a curved plinth now once again supports the seated figures of the goddesses which were found nearby. The lack of heads and of recognizable attributes prevents us from being certain which goddess is which, but the one on the left (who has cushions and a footstool) is perhaps the elder, Demeter. Before their feet are stone basins from which liquid offerings were funnelled into a room beneath. This crypt could be reached by a staircase hidden beneath a cover-slab. On the opposite side of the enclosure was inserted in Roman times an *aedicula*, in which two standing female figures may represent worshippers or may be further images of the two goddesses. The structure is believed to have been built around the middle of the third century BC, as a replacement (after an unexplained interval of a hundred years) for an earlier precinct of Demeter and Kore which disappeared when the West Stoa (33) was built.

Close to the sanctuary are the bases of several monuments. Notable is a handsome marble drum with a finely carved dedication to the goddess Libya on behalf of the well-being of the proconsul M(arcus) Pomponius Secundus; this was set up by his client, M(arcus) Messius Atticus, in the first century AD.

West Stoa (33)

The northern part of the W side of the agora is occupied by the West Stoa. When this was constructed around the middle of the fourth century BC, it swept away several pre-existing structures, including an early precinct dedicated to Demeter and Kore. Another casualty was a temple to the Dioscuri, which was now displaced into a simpler building in the basement at the N end of the portico (not now visible). The new stoa had frontal Doric and internal Ionic colonnades. Many of the intervals between the columns of the façade were closed up to head-height by stone screens: this has been taken to suggest that the stoa might have served as a place of assembly. About a hundred years later, perhaps under Magas, the stoa was rebuilt on nearly identical lines; a further rebuilding (with minor modifications) was carried out in the second century.

In the Roman period, restoration was called for following the Jewish Revolt, and the stoa appears to have retained its public function after the earthquake of AD 262. After that of 365, however, its interior was divided up into the rooms of several residential properties. These subdivisions remain, though parts of the front wall and internal colonnade have been re-erected, creating a rather confusing effect.

Augusteum (34)

In the NW corner of the Agora was built, in the last quarter of the second century BC, a monumental building, in effect a temple with columns on three sides and a rear wall on the fourth, but no internal structure. This was constructed to dignify a pre-existing, and presumably sacred, well-head (now represented by a rectangular void covered by a grid and surrounded by a modern wall). The columns had Ionic bases but Doric capitals.

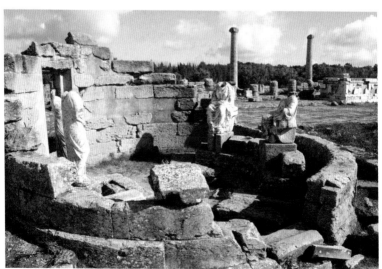

Fig. 125. Cyrene: the Sanctuary of Demeter and Kore in the agora.

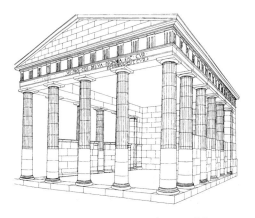

Fig. 126. Cyrene: reconstruction-drawing of the 'Augusteum' in the agora.

Around the turn of the era, this building was adapted to serve as an *augusteum*; that is to say, it was dedicated to the worship of the divinity of the Roman emperor, in conjunction with Apollo and Artemis. The adaptation took the form of inserting stone screens (as in the West Stoa) between the columns along either side (fig. 126). The sponsor of this modification, the proconsul Quintus Lucanius Proculus, put an inscription on the façade which claimed for himself the honour (and expense) of having erected the entire building!

After the earthquake of AD 365, when most of the public buildings in this area seem to have been abandoned to opportunist house-building, the Augusteum was refurbished as a *praetorium* or audience-chamber. A vestibule was created towards the front of the building by reducing the access between the columns to a double doorway and by inserting an inner wall behind, pierced by a re-used marble doorframe brought from elsewhere. At the rear of the audience-chamber was a large rectangular tribunal (accessed how?), separated from the body of the hall by a parapet made

from more re-used material. Here was found an interesting statue of the emperor Marcus Aurelius, composed of a second-century head set upon a later draped female figure, whose breasts have been re-shaped to suit! (This is on display in the museum: p. 247, no. 8.12.)

At a yet later date – and certainly by then having lost its original roof – the building was further subdivided to create a two-storey residence around three sides of an open courtyard.

North Stoa (35)

Already by the end of the sixth century BC, there were two simple stoai lining the northern boundary of the agora. In the third quarter of the fourth century these were replaced by a single, longer and wider, stoa, which involved the construction of a new terrace wall on the N (rear) side; this seems from now on to have served for commercial activities (in contrast to the West Stoa). At the same time, a stepped street was laid out at its western end, providing access to the agora from the lower ground to the N. (The entry of this street into the agora was embellished under the emperor Tiberius with a simple arch.) In the second century BC, the North Stoa acquired the scale and form which is still evident now from the two re-erected columns of its internal colonnade: its width was again increased by extending a basement northwards and constructing a row of twelve shops facing onto the adjoining street. At the upper level it now comprised a vast market hall, 53 × 21 m, with an internal Ionic colonnade and with Doric columns along the open front.

Around the turn of the era it was dedicated to Zeus Soter ('Saviour'), Rome and Augustus.

Restoration after the Jewish Revolt is suggested by a handsome marble inscription dedicated in AD 161 to the city by the governor G(aius) Claudius Titianus Demostratus. At some point in the third century AD, and plausibly in the earthquake of 262, this vast building lost its roof. The market was rebuilt within, using much of the length but less than half of the width of the standing shell; the surrounding spaces remained open to the sky (fig. 121). After the second earthquake, of 365, this diminished market was still retained, and bronze urns of the late fourth century found in an adjoining room suggest the presence of a *thermopolium* or fast-food outlet.

Monument to the Gods (36)
In front of the North Stoa stands a large plinth, to which have been restored numerous fragments of its former marble cladding. It is Hellenistic, but can be attributed only approximately to the third or second century BC. It is thought to have housed bronze statues of the major divinities of the city.

'House XI' (37)
In front of the eastern part of the North Stoa, and invading a considerable part of the paving of the Agora, are low walls which still demarcate a substantial house of the Byzantine period. As study of the preceding buildings has shown, much of the agora was invaded by such structures after the earthquake of 365, though most of them were removed by the excavators, in search of a worthy exposition of Cyrene at its best. The plan in fig. 121 gives a good impression of how the former monumental city centre had degenerated into a random array of residential properties constructed from re-used material. Yet the extent of the property outlined in green ('House XI' in the numeration applied by the excavators), with its mosaic floors and even a multiple latrine (just inside the entrance in the NE corner), shows that the houses of this period were by no means all wretched hovels!

East Stoa (38)
This is the latest of the stoai to have been added to the layout of the agora at Cyrene. Covering the latest representation of the tomb of the founder, Battos (and presumably structures to the N which have not been explored), it was built in the late second or early third century AD. By this time, temples were regularly of the Corinthian order; but here, presumably in order to sustain the architectural unity of the piazza, the internal and external colonnades had Doric capitals on top of Ionic columns and bases.

In the fullness of time, this stoa also was ruined and overrun by housing (see fig. 121). As in other cases, because of the nature of the early excavations, it is not now easy to determine whether this began after 262 or only after 365.

Beneath the foundations of the S end of the stoa may be seen the **'Tomb of Battos' (39)**. This was not the original tomb built in the early sixth century BC, which is known to have taken the form of a circular tumulus a little to the W of this spot; the structure now visible, a rectangular stone chamber with a pitched roof, was built at the end of the fifth century BC and stood in a rectangular enclosure (no longer visible).

Naval Monument ★ (40)
In front of the East Stoa stands a striking monument to a naval victory (fig. 127). Its position is assured from the base,

which stood within a basin of water; the elements of the upper part were all recovered from the walls of late buildings in the area. The representation is a typical Hellenistic motif: a figure of Victory, or *Athena Nike*, striding forward on the prow of a warship – identified by the ram at the bow, a bronze fitting designed to punch holes in the sides of enemy ships. The bow-wave beneath is symbolized by two dolphins.

It is has been argued that the monument was erected between 246 and 241 BC by Ptolemy III to commemorate a victory over Seleukos II of Antioch in the dynastic dispute known as the Third Syrian War. An alternative possibility is that it commemorates the victory of Berenice II against the forces of her mother Apama in the civil strife which followed the death of Magas in 258 or 250 BC. (See also p. 40, in regard to the relocation of Euesperides to Berenice.)

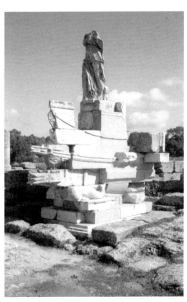

Fig. 127. Cyrene: the naval monument in the agora.

Monumental altars ★ (41)

Our circuit of the agora has caused us to skirt around one of the most prominent – and intelligible – features of the piazza. This is a pair of enormously long and high altars (fig. 128), and another such may be seen in front of the Temple of Apollo lower down the hillside (76). Like all of the other major monuments in the agora, the remnants of these altars have been painstakingly re-assembled from their scattered components. They do not stand directly in alignment with any temple nor do they follow the canonical practice of facing towards the East; rather, the earlier of the two (the more westerly) is aligned centrally with the North Stoa on the opposite side of the piazza. Both the altar and the stoa were dedicated to Zeus, so there was clearly a relationship between the two. Details of design suggest that this altar was built in the late fourth century BC or the first half of the third; the second followed not long afterwards. The dedication of the latter is unknown.

The altars were restored and rededicated in the Severan period but fell apart in one of the two great earthquakes, after which their marble facings were carried off for re-use in later buildings.

House by the Propylaeum ★ (42)

Moving westward along the Street of Battos, and leaving the agora zone by the W *Propylaeum* (29), one more large *insula* on the R has been extensively excavated (fig. 129). The excavator identified it as a gymnasium on the basis of a re-used inscription found there, but this interpretation is implausible. It seems, rather, to have been another very wealthy residence, like that of Jason Magnus further to the E (17).

The entrance was on the Street of Battos and took the form of a tetrastyle

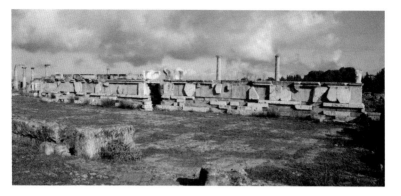

Fig. 128. Cyrene: the monumental altars in the agora.

porch leading into a spacious atrium. This was flanked on either side by largely symmetrical arrangements of six rooms each, with a staircase to an upper floor at the E end. From the atrium one passed through into a large Ionic peristyle, uniform on all four sides (i.e. not the 'Rhodian' type found in the House of Jason Magnus). This occupied the entire width of the *insula*. On the N side of the peristyle was again a symmetrical arrangement of large rooms, which must have been the formal reception rooms of the property. (The precise conformation of doorways in this area is not clear.) Beyond these was another peristyle which filled the remainder of the *insula*.

There are no records of the excavation of this *insula*, but what is visible is likely to belong to the prosperous times of the later second or early third centuries AD. Some later modifications in inferior masonry (particularly within the N peristyle) are apparent, but it is also evident that the house replaced smaller dwellings on part at least of the same plot. These were buried to a considerable depth when the whole area was brought up to the level of the Street of Battos. Beneath the northern range of rooms and the massive foundations of

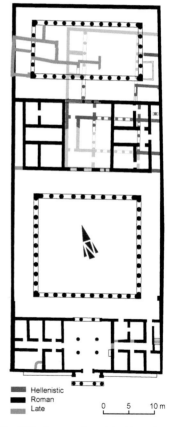

Hellenistic
Roman
Late

0   5   10 m

Fig. 129. Cyrene: plan of the House by the Propylaeum.

the N peristyle have been uncovered the remains of two Hellenistic houses. Each of these had a central colonnaded courtyard, flanked by rooms only on the E and W sides. An early mosaic, attributed to the second half of the third century BC, can still be seen in the more northerly of these houses next to the eastern street-frontage.

Acropolis ★

The Street of Battos now leads to the gate of the acropolis. The crest of the hill here was certainly the site of the earliest settlement, and was surely also the location in due course of the palaces of Ptolemaic kings and Roman governors. Yet, because of its obvious strategic value, it was occupied during the early years of Italian archaeological investigation by military installations. It was therefore off-limits to the archaeologists and its investigation has been much hampered as a result. The American expedition under Richard Norton carried out some explorations here in 1910/11: they uncovered part of a large Roman peristyle house and the foundations of a small temple, but neither offers anything to the passing visitor today. Their work did show, however, that the settlement on the Acropolis was laid out on a different grid from the later expansion of the city along the ridge to the E. (This is evident on the general plan of Cyrene inside the rear cover.)

The area is worth a brief visit, nonetheless, both to admire the solidity of the defences, which are well preserved here, and to see the Sanctuary of Isis and Serapis beneath the defensive wall on the N side. The extra walk is justified also by the panorama, which not only encompasses the surrounding countryside and the lower plateau of the Jabal Akhdar, but also serves to clarify the relationship between the quarter on the southern ridge and the sanctuary terrace below.

The defensive walls which are visible now appear mostly to be Hellenistic in date, with Roman refurbishments. (However, recent investigations in the Sanctuary of Isis suggest that some elements may go back to the sixth or fifth century BC.) The massive **Acropolis Gate (43)** is flanked by rectangular towers and was once spanned by an arch. In the time of the emperor Augustus, the proconsul Q(uintus) Lucanius Proculus restored the walls and recorded the fact on the gate. Blocks carrying part of this inscription lie on the higher ground on the L, just inside the entrance. The outer face of the acropolis wall has been exposed for a length of some 50 m northwards, as far as a tower at which it turns sharply to the W. In the opposite direction it has not been excavated, but it terminates in a tower, the surviving corner of which still stands over 11 m high above the Wadi Bil Ghadir to the S. At this point it joins the wall of the city. The course of the wall around the NE side of the acropolis is markedly irregular, and close to the E end it forms a sharp re-entrant, within which stands a place of cult of remarkable interest.

Sanctuary of Isis and Serapis ★ (44)

The re-entrant mentioned above encloses the foundations of a small temple facing outwards, with a porch of two columns *in antis* and a flight of three steps in front (fig. 130: a). At the rear of the *cella* is a statue-base with the imprint of the feet of two figures. From finds within the building, it is clear that this was a temple to the Egyptian gods Isis and Serapis, the presence of whose cult at Cyrene is well attested in the literary record.

This sanctuary area was first discovered in 1916, in the course of constructing military defences, which sought at this point to make use of the ancient acropolis wall. Only a small sounding was made at that time, resulting in the discovery of a remarkable cache of statuary. The area was subsequently exposed more extensively in 1935, and new excavations have been carried out by an Italian Mission since 2000. The foundations now visible belong to the Hellenistic period, with restorations in marble in the second or third century AD. However, deep soundings have shown that there was a sanctuary of some kind here as early as the beginning of the sixth century BC. At this time, the divinity worshipped was possibly the ancient Egyptian-Libyan moon-goddess, who only later became identified with Aphrodite and then with Isis. The foundations of the retaining wall behind the temple are now ascribed to the mid-sixth century BC, together with a steep stairway (b) which led down to the sanctuary from above. This stairway was blocked in the mid second century BC, when the acropolis was re-fortified and the new temple was built. The joint dedication to Isis and Serapis is assured by the evident double statue-base still visible within the temple, the discovery within the building of a bust of Serapis and the presence on a block beneath the statue-base of two symbols of a very worn hieroglyphic inscription. This change of dedication, and the new building, would certainly have been close to the interests of Ptolemy VIII at the time when he was established at Cyrene. The excavators reported that the walls of the temple showed the discoloration caused by intense fire – whether brought about by accident or as a result of ritual purging (by Christians, after the disaster of 365?) we cannot tell.

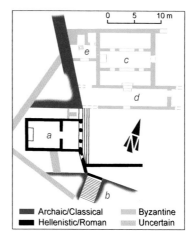

Fig. 130. Cyrene: plan of the Sanctuary of Isis and Serapis on the acropolis. (a) Hellenistic temple; (b) Archaic stairway; (c–e) Byzantine cult building.

Some time later, a new temple was built slightly to the N. It has the appearance of late and hasty work, being composed of small stones mortared with mud, standing on a foundation of large irregular blocks. Fragments of the earlier building, including a marble tympanum of the third century AD which had formerly been part of an *aedicula* enclosing the cult-statues, were also pressed into use. The form is not that of a Classical temple, but is composed of two 'cult spaces': there may have been here an adjunct to the earlier temple, of which this is the successor. To the E, and entered initially from that direction, is a basilical hall resembling a church (c): it is divided by piers and arcades into a nave and two aisles, and at the inner (W) end was a statue-base. Along the S side of this hall, and connected to it subsequently by a doorway, was a corridor (d) leading to a pair of small chambers set in the space between the main hall and the acropolis wall above. The first served as a vestibule, while the inner chamber (e) had a niche in its rear wall, and in front of this was found a square recess in the floor, sealed with a cover-slab and a layer of mortar. In the recess were found some carbonized remains, four hens' eggs, two late Roman terracotta lamps and five fourth-century Roman coins, the latest being of Constantius II (337–61). This appears to have been a foundation deposit and the new sanctuary probably post-dates the earthquake of 365. Also in this inner room were found no less than 22 complete or fragmentary marble sculptures and three inscriptions. The statuary included a group of the Three Graces and a priestess of Isis (in the museum, p. 247, no. 8.10), while the inscriptions included part of a Hymn to Isis. This was perhaps a cache of pagan statuary brought here for concealment from the Christians, but one piece, at the very least, must have belonged fundamentally to the late sanctuary, and may indeed have been inherited from the earlier. This is the remarkable coloured statuette of Parian marble depicting the goddess Isis, now on display in

the museum (p. 248, no. 9.27). This was found on its side in the niche, next to the base on which it had stood.

The chronology of this late sanctuary is very difficult to pin down, for lack of a stratigraphic record. It has been suggested that it persisted as late as the sixth century AD before being finally destroyed. Its destruction is attributed to the fervour of the Christians, but that too is speculation. The one thing that is clear is that this pagan cult survived and was revered at Cyrene long after most others had been suppressed. This complex and interesting zone is still in course of study, and the preceding account must be regarded as provisional.

House of the Dionysos Mosaic ★ (45)

After visiting the agora and the acropolis, it may be convenient to return to the entrance by the Caesareum before exploring other parts of the site. It is, however, possible to proceed directly downhill to the Sanctuary of Apollo. The best route for this is to follow the street which runs northwards between the

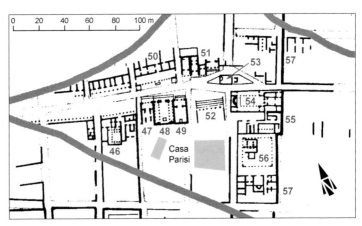

Fig. 131. Cyrene: plan of excavations in the Central Quarter.
(For the key to the numbered locations, see inside the rear cover.)

agora and the House by the Propylaeum (42). This will lead you across an unexcavated area to a point W of the Arch of Marcus Aurelius and Lucius Verus (61), where steeply terraced houses overlook the Valley Street as it descends to the sanctuary. In one of these houses (45), decorated with several mosaic floors in the late third or early fourth century AD, was found a mosaic depicting Dionysos and Ariadne; this is now on display in the museum (p. 250, no. 11.5). Because of the slope of the terrain, the house takes an elongated form with its rooms opening off a single corridor fronting the terrace, as if this were one side of a peristyle. The Dionysos mosaic was found in a room (the *triclinium*?) at the W end, where the walls still preserve part of a fine panelled decoration in stucco. From here you may pick your way, as in antiquity, either down steep stairways (to the R) into the Valley Street or down a ramp to the L which leads to the Fountain of Apollo (fig. 136). This zone is described below on p. 216 ff., as part of the Sanctuary of Apollo.

THE CENTRAL QUARTER

The description of the monuments now returns to the site entrance by the Caesareum and proceeds in a westerly direction down the valley of the Wadi Bu Turqiyah. This route collects together some rather scattered remains which are accessible in practice from different directions. (Those on the S side of the modern road are nominally enclosed within the acropolis ridge area, but at the time of writing the enclosure fence is decayed and may be crossed at several points.) The ancient topography is partly masked by the modern road and the 20th-century village of Shahhat, but in antiquity this was an important axis, leading down to the Sanctuary of Apollo

and thence, down the escarpment, towards the port of Apollonia. In Roman times this road became progressively more important than the 'Street of Battos' along the acropolis ridge and some of the latest monuments (e.g. churches) lie on or close to this road. They were built at a time when much of the acropolis ridge was abandoned and derelict. The excavations in this area were mainly carried out in the 1950s and 1960s by the Department of Antiquities, under the direction of Richard Goodchild.

Proceeding downhill from the car park by the Caesareum, one finds on the right-hand side of the road an area of excavations together with the excavation house of the Italian Archaeological Mission (Casa Parisi). The monuments of this area, known conventionally as the Central Quarter, are shown in fig. 131. One may enter the site at the Casa Parisi (passing to the L of the modern buildings) or more easily (at present) by scrambling through the fence at the western end of the enclosure, 150 m further down the hill. The layout here happens to encompass a major street-intersection and an awkward adjustment in the alignment of different parts of the street-grid of the city. The main valley street has a surface of rounded cobbles, and the roadway is flanked by broad, raised pavements. Visible at several points are openings into a huge vaulted storm-drain which runs beneath the street, finally coming out to the surface beneath the Baths of Trajan (pp. 195, 203). Towards the W (downhill), the road is flanked on either side by colonnades, of the Corinthian order and in white marble on the N side, but of the Doric order and in limestone on the S. The earliest inscription found in this area belongs to the year 10 BC, and it was probably not before this time that the area was first built up.

House of Domina Spata (46)

The westernmost property on the S side of the street, of which more than the frontage has been exposed, is a house which was probably built in the second or third century AD. The street frontage had eight doorways, most of which led into shops, though two of the rooms may have comprised stables with mangers. One of the central doorways led through into the house, which was arranged in conventional style around a two-storey peristyle. This was Doric both above and below: the lower order has been re-erected and the intermediate entablature is laid out at ground-level. On some of the columns from the upper storey were found incised graffiti, wishing good luck to *Domina* (Mistress) *Spata*.

Substantial later modifications re-arranged the rooms on the E side of the peristyle (with entrances flanked by half-columns of limestone which were stuccoed and painted red). The N wall of the peristyle was also opened up into an arcade, creating a double portico. Goodchild believed that occupation came to an end with the earthquake of 365; Stucchi believed the late alterations to have followed this event.

A glut of temples

The buildings of the next *insula* to the E project considerably further northwards into the street. Here are to be found three temples side-by-side. The first of these, **'Temple A' (47)**, of which one marble column has been re-erected at the head of the frontal steps, was much altered in late antiquity, with the insertion of internal walls; its original form and dedication are unknown. The adjoining **Temple of Commodus (48)** is of unusual form. The façade has three entrances through a front wall adorned with engaged Corinthian semi-columns, and the frontal steps are divided into three separate flights corresponding to these entrances. Internally, the *cella* is almost square and is divided, like a basilica, into a broad nave with flanking aisles. The limestone colonnades are of the Corinthian order, with 'Pergamene' capitals (one surviving). The inner faces of the outer walls are lined along both sides by continuous benches with projecting plinths and at the rear of the *cella* is a base for a colossal statue, once faced with marble. Fragments of this facing bear a dedication, datable between AD 185–92, to the emperor Commodus. Fragments of a colossal statue of Herakles were found nearby in the street: this was probably the cult statue, representing the emperor in his favourite guise. Two smaller bases apparently supported statues of Trajan, Hadrian and his wife Sabina (on display in the museum: p. 247, nos. 8.6–8).

Discoloration due to fire is apparent throughout the interior of the building, perhaps resulting from ritual purging of the pagan temple by Christians.

The third building in this row is a **Temple of the Nymph Kurana (49)**. The façade, of the Corinthian order, takes the typical Cyrenean form of two columns *in antis* between two engaged semi-columns. The identification rests on the presence of an aqueduct and of water-channels around the base of the cult-statue (not now visible), together with the discovery in the excavation of the street of a statue of Kurana strangling the lion, in which the lion's mouth is pierced as a water-spout. The statue has been attributed to the second century AD and the structural relationship with the neighbouring Temple of Commodus shows that to have been the later building.

6 Cyrene: the Central Quarter

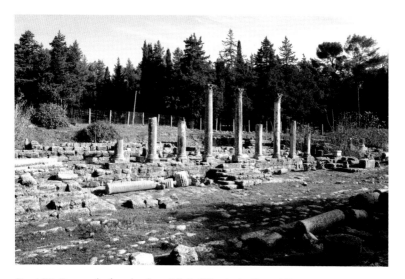

Fig. 132. Cyrene: the façade of a public building in the Central Quarter.

Facing these temples across the street is a **public building (50)** of some kind (fig. 132). It is fronted by a raised portico with ten columns of Proconnesian marble, which was accessible only by means of a small three-sided stairway in the centre, and by steps from side-streets at either end. (There are stepped plinths at either end of the façade, but these did not give access to the building since they stood in front of solid walls.) Behind this façade was possibly a late basilica, though what is visible now suggests a long history with various changes of use. There are extensive polychrome mosaics (of the second or third century AD?), overlaid by later walls which incorporate re-used *spolia* of high quality; the building has not been completely exposed.

Immediately to the E of the public building, and separated from it by a side-street, is a further group of **three temples (51)**, very ruinous and much altered in late antiquity (Temples 'F, I, G'). The first of these ('Temple F') had a façade of Corinthian columns of

cipollino marble, one of which lies at the foot of the temple steps. A graffito on this column, and others on a similar column, thought to have been removed from here to the Byzantine Baths in the Sanctuary of Apollo (66: p. 197), have been interpreted as having a Christian meaning, implying that the temple had been converted into a church – but the readings are far from certain.

On the S side of the street is a broad stairway and the colonnaded façade of what was clearly another substantial **public building (52)**. The columns are unfluted and the capitals Corinthian, but the core of the building has not been excavated. To the E of this, and of the temples described above, was a major street intersection of the city. The Valley Street is crossed at this point by the N–S street which runs from the S Gate, past the Caesareum (2) and towards the Temple of Zeus (106). Rather curiously, the thoroughfare is interrupted at this point by the remains, in the centre of the Valley Street which divides to pass around it, of a **fountain (53)**. The foundations enclose a semi-circular mosaic which originally adorned the bottom of the water-basin. The mosaic contains an inscription to the effect that the fountain was the gift of the decurion Sosibius Rufus, whose name is also recorded as a priest in the 'Grotto of the Priests' (92) in the Sanctuary of Apollo.

Central Church ★ (54)

On the SE side of the intersection lies the Central Church, a three-aisled basilica inscribed within a rectangle and with an apse at the W end. The church protrudes substantially across the N–S street, which must have gone out of use by the time that it was built. The apse is flanked by corner-chapels and there are two more at the E end of the aisles. In the centre of the E end was a triple archway supported on a pair of re-used columns; this led to a narthex-complex composed of several rooms, the layout of which is not clear. The apse was framed by a pair of grey granite columns; these have Corinthian capitals and stand on reversed four-way Ionic capitals of Proconnesian marble: all are re-used. The chancel occupied the full width of the nave in front of the apse. The foundations of the separating screen were found in position; other elements were returned to their original positions by the excavators, but have recently been overturned again. The posts which joined together the screen slabs take the unusual form here of square pedestal bases, on top of two of which stood squat and crudely finished columns of grey marble. (One of these, broken, now lies nearby.) In the centre of the chancel is the base of the altar, with sockets for the marble colonnettes which supported the altar table.

Both chancel and nave were paved with mosaics, certainly from the same workshop that created those in the East Church at Cyrene (110), at Qasr Libya (p. 133), Ras al-Hilal (p. 319) and elsewhere. That in the chancel is moderately well preserved: a jewelled cross with the letters *alpha* and *omega* is framed within a medallion and flanked by peacocks and other birds. The composition includes also the usual range of birds, fishes and animals in a 'Nilotic' landscape. The nave mosaic, on the other hand, is fragmentary; it included in its N border a lively hunting scene, which is on display in the museum (p. 250, no. 11.8).

Typically, the date of construction of the church is disputed. If the mosaics are original, then the building is Justinianic; if they are secondary, it could be as early as the mid fifth century. (No soundings appear to have been made beneath the floor, to determine the earlier history of the site.) There are certainly signs of later modifications, in the form of various inserted walls, and possibly the staircase in the SW angle-chapel. There are also signs that occupation in this area continued into the early Arab period.

Central Baths (55)

Tucked in to the E and S of the Central Church is a bath building. The excavator (Goodchild) considered it to be 'probably' later than the church, and possibly even to have continued in use into the early Arab period. Stucchi has argued, however, that part of a cold plunge-bath is cut by a wall of the church complex and that the baths previously extended into the area occupied by the rooms at the E end of the church. In either case, the baths were still in use after the construction of the church. The raised floors of three heated rooms are visible, and the *caldarium* is identifiable by the presence of small apses for hot plunge-baths on the N and S sides.

House of the Semicircular Couch ★ (56)

The remainder of the *insula* to the S of the Central Baths is occupied by a single residential property (which fills the space to the E of the Casa Parisi). The layout is somewhat confused by the unexcavated former line of the site railway, but its principal feature is a large 'Rhodian' peristyle like that in the House of Jason Magnus (17): this occupied the full width of the *insula* and initially had rooms opening off it only on the S side. When the colonnade of the peristyle fell (in an earthquake, that of 262?), two Corinthian capitals and part of the architrave above fell into a basin in the centre and remained there: they have now been set up on the stylobate. The decorative order was a thorough mixture of the Doric and Corinthian styles. On the S side of the peristyle was a central *triclinium* with flanking rooms, and a further range of private or service rooms behind.

The style of the architecture suggests a date in the Antonine period, broadly contemporary with the House of Jason Magnus; there are also parallels between the two properties with regard to the mosaic floors in the reception rooms. At a later period, presumably after the earthquake of 262, the property was renovated. This involved enlargement of the *triclinium* at the expense of the neighbouring rooms; it was also extended southwards into the courtyard behind, and within this extension was built a huge semicircular *kline* or dining couch in masonry. Perhaps at a similar period, on the N side of the peristyle was added a rectangular hall at a lower level, reached by a flight of steps. This had a stone paving and, down the centre, a row of stone feeding-troughs, suggesting use as a stable (as in many other properties of the period, both at Cyrene and at Balagrae).

Deeper excavations within the peristyle have shown that it succeeded and swept away smaller, but well-preserved, houses of the Hellenistic period: perimeter walling in finer-quality masonry is visible and there is also a remarkably preserved private bathroom containing a tub and a sitz-bath together with two basins or draw-holes from a cistern beneath, all with their original plaster rendering. A Hellenistic mosaic in another room shows a wave pattern.

Mid-Roman defences (57)

A final curiosity of this area of excavations is the presence, along the eastern boundary of the House of the Semicircular Couch, of a stone wall 1.75 m wide, running from the direction of the Caesareum, across the Valley Street (where Goodchild believed there to have been a simple gateway) and on northwards towards the Temple of Zeus. The wall, composed of re-used *spolia*, has been traced by Stucchi as far as the northern defences to the W of the latter (see the general plan inside the rear cover). This has the appearance of a defensive wall; Goodchild had no hesitation in associating it with the late tower (14) and other defensive modifications in the area of the *Caesareum* (2) and the Stoa of Hermes and Herakles (13). He further asserted that these defences were most probably erected in the aftermath of the earthquake of AD 262, when the city briefly took the name of *Claudiopolis* in honour of the emperor Claudius Gothicus (268–70), presumably in commemoration of its restoration. (The stone which records this event is on display in the museum: p. 243, no. 4.5.) A defence along this line would have excluded the eastern third of the ancient city. However, Goodchild also observed that the wall was partly overlain by the Central Baths.

This, together with the presence to the E of it of the East Church (110: probably the cathedral) and of an 'Arab' tower, Qasr Shaghiyah (111), suggests that it did not serve its purpose for long and that at a later date (after 365?) the city, or what was left of it, was once again occupying ground to the E. Despite their obvious interest, no detailed study of the defences of ancient Cyrene has yet been published, and this stretch remains a fragment in need of more extended investigation.

Market Theatre (58)

Leaving the area of excavations around the Casa Parisi and proceeding downhill, the modern road converges with the line of the ancient Valley Street. It will satisfy most visitors to view the next group of monuments on the S side of the street through the boundary fence; if you wish to examine them in detail, it may be necessary to enter the enclosure by the gate next to the Caesareum (though at the time of writing the fence is derelict).

The principal feature of this group is very evidently a theatre, known as Theatre 4 or as the Market Theatre (fig. 133), since it overlies an earlier market building. This was excavated by Richard Goodchild when Controller of Antiquities. Because of his early death, the information available about the structures is less complete that one would desire and there is scope for significant disagreement about both the nature and the chronology of the various components! The theatre superseded entirely an earlier building complex (described below) which is believed to have been destroyed in the earthquake of AD 365. Goodchild suggested that it was built in order to replace the theatre(s) on the Acropolis ridge (6, 15), which were destroyed in the same earthquake. However, it is now agreed that both of these buildings had either been dismantled or converted to other uses at an earlier date, so the motivation to construct a new theatre, in what was otherwise a period of decline, is unclear.

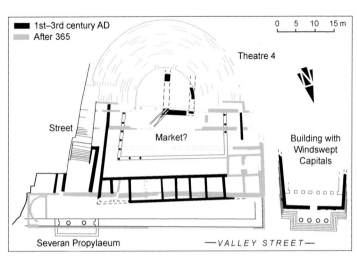

Fig. 133. Cyrene: plan of the Market Theatre and adjacent structures.

The semi-circular *orchestra* of the theatre was cut down through the paving of the previous building in order to make best use of the slope of the hillside. The *cavea* was ranged above, and the former stepped street on the E margin was adapted to provide access to the upper tiers of seats. (Of the seats themselves there is no trace.) The stage building was of simple rectangular layout, as was the *pulpitum* (the stage front). The latter was decorated with a row of re-used double-sided herms (re-erected after excavation but subsequently taken into store for safety); these are of second-century workmanship and presumably derive from the market building (see below). The seats of the *cavea* terminated around the *orchestra* in a flat platform and a parapet 1.35 m high, pierced by four narrow staircases. It has been suggested that this arrangement was secondary and intended to create a *kolymbethra* or pool for aquatic displays, such as may be seen in the 'odeon' at Ptolemais (p. 90). There do appear to be concentric cuttings for lower seats within the *orchestra*, but there is no trace of the waterproofing that one would have expected.

What lay between the stage building and the street in this period is difficult to say. Late walls at the W end suggest rooms opening onto the side street, while along the front there was some sort of linear hall, terminating in an apse at the E end. The foundations of the rear wall of this feature seem to respect the dividing walls between the shops which belong to the earlier period, implying that in some sense they continued to exist.

Beneath and in front of the theatre are traces of something entirely different. There was an approximately rectangular porticoed enclosure, with shops at least along the frontage of the street on the N side. Because of the steeply rising ground, there was probably only a terrace wall, rather than a portico, on the S side. The central space was paved, initially with limestone and subsequently with Proconnesian marble. (At the same time, the columns will have been replaced in cipollino marble: some of these have been re-erected.) In the centre, perhaps against the rear wall, was a rectangular building which is likely to have taken the form of a temple. Since all of this has been reduced to its foundations (which are, however, clearly recognizable by their yellower colour), much remains uncertain – such as whether the shops opened towards the enclosure or towards the street. Set into the limestone paving are narrow cuttings which accommodated lead water-pipes: one of these is still present. These are directed towards the central building, which must therefore have contained a water-feature. Goodchild interpreted these features as a market, with shops around the periphery and a fountain in the centre, which may also have accommodated a shrine to Hermes and maybe even a market office. The herms which were re-used in the theatre would also have been appropriate to a market complex. Stucchi, on the other hand, has asserted that the layout is typical of a temple precinct and that statues found in the vicinity suggest it was a temple to Asklepios and Hygieia; he believed that the herms could have delineated the boundary of the sacred area before the porticoes were built (in a second phase, corresponding to the marble paving). Goodchild's interpretation has subsequently been stoutly defended, and it certainly seems the more plausible to me. Amongst the arguments advanced in its favour is the absence of an axial entrance to the precinct in the centre of the shops fronting the street: this would be very unlikely in the case of a temple precinct, whereas it is not unusual for the layout of a market to be more flexible, with entrances at the corners. The original date of the market is probably early Roman, with a typical refurbishment in marble in the late second or early third century AD.

Severan Propylaeum (59)
On the E side of the Market Theatre was a stairway which led upwards in the general direction of the agora. Its alignment suggests that it existed before the construction of the market, though it was dignified, probably in the Severan period, by the addition of two columns of pink Aswan granite on octagonal bases of Proconnesian marble. At the head of the steps, behind the *cavea* of the later theatre, are ruins of an ornate building which perhaps gave added monumentality to the street at the upper level. The Valley Street in this section was fronted at the end of the second century AD by a terraced portico, with columns of cipollino marble identical to those used in the

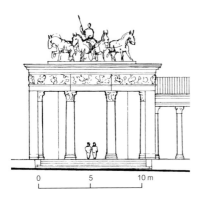

Fig. 134. Cyrene: reconstruction-drawing of the Severan Propylaeum in the Valley Street.

market building. Where the stepped street descended, however, there was a monumental feature now represented by very battered fragments and difficult to reconstruct. This was clearly a porch of some kind, which rose above the porticoes of the street and was decorated with a figured frieze. Beneath the frieze was an inscription honouring Septimius Severus; the date of the whole is around AD 203. This Severan *Propylaeum* was constructed in local stone faced with stucco. The opening was probably framed by two columns between two piers with engaged semi-columns or pilasters, though nothing of these remains. There are battered Corinthian capitals, carved with 'windswept' acanthus leaves: these, together with the sculpted frieze, have been set up under an inelegant cover close to the modern road. The inscription, in Greek, records the setting up by the citizens of Cyrene (at private expense) of a statue of Septimius Severus in a chariot. We may therefore assume that the statue stood above the porch, whose appearance may have been something like that shown in figure 134. The relief, in a gritty limestone which has eroded badly, portrays a heroized battle between Romans and barbarians, who may be identified by their 'Phrygian' caps as Parthians. Septimius is portrayed in the centre as a bearded horseman riding towards the right, but looking back towards the left. In the direction of his gaze is a Parthian horseman who is shying away from a youthful standing warrior with curly locks. This is Septimius' son Caracalla (head formerly restored, but now missing), and he is almost certainly balanced on the other side of Septimius by his other son Geta, now headless but also on foot and spearing a fallen victim.

Building with Windswept Capitals (60)

To the W of the Market Theatre are the partially excavated remains of another public building fronting the Valley Street. Its most distinctive feature was a projecting porch supported by four columns of local stone with shafts that were partly smooth and partly carved with spiral fluting. These were surmounted by Corinthian capitals with 'windswept' acanthus leaves like those used in the Severan *Propylaeum* (59). There can be little doubt that this porch, which represented an addition to an existing building, was constructed as a counterpart to the Severan *Propylaeum*, to give balance to the portico in front of the market.

The nature of this building is unclear, since the body of it lies unexcavated beneath the ordered blocks of its E wall, which have fallen across it in an earthquake. In its original form, it was built of carefully drafted masonry and had a frieze around the top of the wall in the Doric order. This may be attributed approximately to the first century AD. Subsequently (after the Jewish Revolt?), the façade of the building was replaced with a scheme of shallow pilasters on either side of a central doorway. This was of the Corinthian order, and pilasters on either side of the building probably masked the change of style. The paving inside probably belongs to this period. It is composed of alternating rectangular blocks of Numidian (yellow) and Phrygian (grey) marble separated by narrow fillets of Proconnesian. Later still, the tetrastyle porch was added in front, bringing the façade forward to the line of the portico in front of the market. Fragments of the cornice above the porch have been reassembled in front of the steps. This was surely part of a single scheme to regularize and monumentalize

this part of the Valley Street, dated by the Severan *Propylaeum*.

The building was evidently destroyed by earthquake and the excavator, Goodchild, was convinced that it was that of 365. Despite the presence beside it of the new theatre, the Building with the Windswept Capitals was left just as it had fallen, and the same was true of the portico in front of the market. The surface of the Valley Street was simply allowed to rise to a new level covering the debris.

Arch of Marcus Aurelius and Lucius Verus ★ (61)

Downhill from the Market Theatre there are, briefly, modern buildings on both sides of the road. The road then veers away from the line of the ancient Valley Street slightly to the right; on the S side at this point stands the re-erected lateral opening of a former triumphal arch. This was of conventional type, with a wide opening for the carriageway, flanked by two narrower pedestrian openings. The surviving lateral opening (fig. 135)

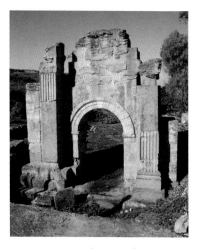

Fig. 135. Cyrene: the Arch of Marcus Aurelius and Lucius Verus in the Valley Street.

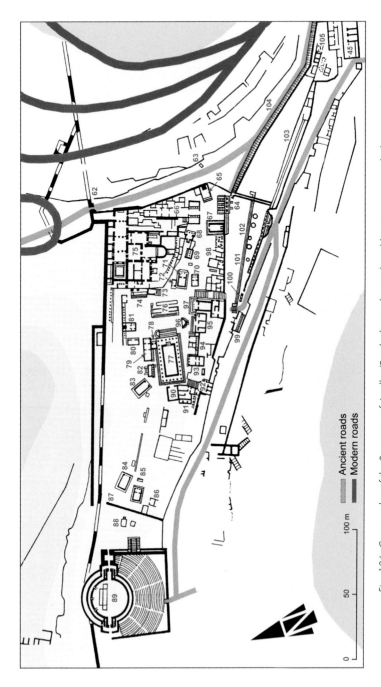

Fig. 136. Cyrene: plan of the Sanctuary of Apollo. (For the key to the numbered locations, see inside the rear cover.)

is framed between fluted rectangular pilasters with Corinthian capitals. The inscription above records its dedication by the city to the emperors Marcus Aurelius and Lucius Verus in AD 164–6. The arch marks the transition between the moderate slope of the Valley Street in the Central Quarter and the steep descent to the Sanctuary of Apollo below.

THE SANCTUARY OF APOLLO

Most visitors are likely to enter the Sanctuary of Apollo (figs. 136, 137) from the lower entrance to the main antiquities zone, opposite the bookstall and cafés. The route now described will start from here, will weave a way through the sanctuary area and will conclude by walking back up the Sacred Way towards the Arch of Marcus Aurelius and Lucius Verus (61). If, however, you are making your way down directly from the Agora, you will need to start with pp. 216–20, taking this section in reverse order before descending to the sanctuary area.

On entering the antiquities zone at the lower gate, one is passing through the **North Gate (62)** of the city, of which barely detectable foundations cross the path just inside the modern gate and ticket office. A modern footbridge then spans the major Roman drain which descended, alongside or beneath the Valley Street, from the Central Quarter. (This is visible if you drop down towards the R.) On the left-hand side of the modern path have been set up a number of statues, together with the original dedicatory inscription from the Trajanic Baths (75). At about 100 m from the entrance, where the space opens out, there is on the L a rectangular pedestal of masonry. This was surmounted by a column, presumably marking the ceremonial entrance to the city. Next to this base stands a **Roman milestone (63)**; the inscription on it, dated to AD 118 under Hadrian, records the repair by an army unit (whose name is lost) of the road to Apollonia, following damage inflicted in the Jewish Revolt. At regular intervals in

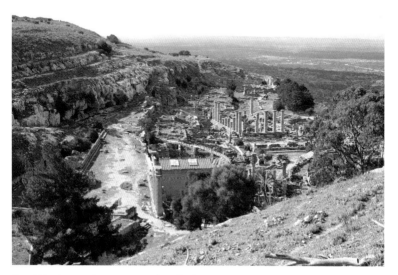

Fig. 137. Cyrene: the Sanctuary of Apollo from the east.

the rock-face along this stretch are openings into the huge storm drain mentioned above, which here is conveyed in a rock-cut tunnel beside the street.

Beyond this point, turn round to the right onto a broad, but tapering terrace. This is the Fountain Terrace, where the spring-line comes to the surface, providing the abundant water supply that was responsible for the presence of the Greek settlement (pp. 2, 149). Immediately on your R is a reconstructed portico of four Doric columns.

Greek Propylaeum ★ (64)

This is a reconstruction of the monumental entrance to the Sanctuary of Apollo which was built by the priest Praxiades in the second half of the third century BC. It took the form of a Doric porch with a pediment above; part of the dedicatory inscription has been restored on the architrave. On the N (downhill) side were three stairways enclosed between four fountains, fed from the Spring of Apollo. One of the stairways survives, together with parts of two marble fountains; the feet of a third are now in the *frigidarium* of the Trajanic Baths (p. 199). The *propylaeum* formed a link between the upper and lower terraces and was already a successor to earlier structures going back to the fifth century BC. At the earlier period, the Fountain Terrace had not formed part of the sanctuary, and the terrace wall and gateway here had marked the boundary between the two zones.

The Greek *Propylaeum* is believed to have stood until the earthquake of AD 365, after which many of its component parts were re-used in later buildings.

Temple of Aphrodite (65)

This small temple, just inside the Greek *Propylaeum*, is very ruinous. Its foundations are thought to go back to the fifth century BC, though the superstructure was rebuilt in the second or third century AD. The seated figure at the rear has been identified as Aphrodite, and this has been presumed to be the dedicatee of the temple.

Byzantine Baths ★ (66)

To the L of the Temple of Aphrodite and facing the Greek *Propylaeum* is the entrance to the Byzantine Baths, which superseded the earlier Baths of Trajan (75). (See fig. 139: the Byzantine Baths constitute phase 4 of the overall sequence.) Their construction made extensive use of materials taken from other buildings which had collapsed in the earthquake of 365. The entrance is in the same position as that which led into the earlier complex, though that is now most readily approached from the W side, and will be described later (p. 199). The new complex made no attempt to deal with the masses of fallen vaulting covering the ruins, but was constructed in the more readily cleared zone of the former *palaestra*. The entrance to the Byzantine Baths took the form of an open vestibule, flanked by two short porticoes (fig. 139). This stood forward of the earlier entrance, largely blocking the approach to the Roman *Propylaeum* (68), which was presumably ruinous and abandoned along with the rest of the sanctuary. Excavations beneath the floor of the vestibule make it awkward to explore; within, the plain columns with crude bases are late, while the fluted drums of marble which have been partly re-used in walls presumably belonged to the early Roman entrance. At the rear of the vestibule and to the L of it is part of the stairway within the original entrance (a).

Beyond the vestibule is the *apodyterium* (q), with a five-seater latrine at a higher level on the E side (r). The latrine still exhibits the lowest course of a corbelled stone roof. The two columns which have been re-erected on either side of the entrance to the *frigidarium* beyond are believed to have been brought here from 'Temple F' in the Central Quarter (51). One of them has several carved graffiti of Christian content in Greek (e.g. 'Lord help Januarius'), including a cross and a dove with a twig in its mouth: these are thought to relate to their previous position and use. The next two rooms, each with a cold plunge-bath on the R, seem together to have constituted the *frigidarium* (s). There is evidence here for the continued use and refurbishment of these baths in the early Islamic period, in the form of an Arabic inscription carved on the third of the four pilasters along the W side of the *frigidarium*. Beyond lies a succession of heated rooms (t, u, v), with hot plunge-baths and heating systems in varying states of preservation. Along the left-hand side of this area is a long service-corridor with stoke-holes, corbelled doorways and a corbelled roof (w).

Strategheion ★ (67)

Immediately to one's L, as one descends through the Greek *Propylaeum*, is the fully reconstructed building known as the *Strategheion*. This small treasury (repository for votive offerings) in the Doric style but with no colonnade, was originally built in the fourth century BC by three generals (*strategoi*). It was dedicated to Apollo as part of the tithe promised to him of the booty taken in a military campaign. This was fought against the Libyan tribes of the *Macae* and the *Nasamones*, extending the influence of Cyrene westwards into the Syrtic Gulf, in 308 BC. The building,

re-erected in 1934, was once used as a small museum, but is now permanently locked. There is evidence beneath the floor of successive periods of use and adaptation. These are related to an inscription on the statue base against the rear wall and another over the door, proclaiming that the building was rededicated by M(arcus) Sufenas Proculus to the (future emperor) Tiberius Caesar. This Proculus was also responsible for a restoration of the Caesareum (p. 153) and the inscription is datable in the period AD 4–14.

The temple fell in the earthquake of AD 365, and its fate is evident from the reconstruction. The uppermost parts of the structure fell first and became buried; the middle parts of the walls fell subsequently but were removed to build the Byzantine Baths (where they remain); the lowest parts of the walls remained in position.

Roman Propylaeum ★ (68)

Opposite the *Strategheion* and partly masked by the entrance to the Byzantine Baths, is the Roman *Propylaeum* (fig. 138), a further monumental entrance to the sacred zone, constructed in the second century AD following the Jewish Revolt. It is entirely Greek in character, with a tetrastyle porch of unfluted limestone columns with Corinthian capitals; these stood in front of two *antae* which enclosed a rear wall pierced by a single large portal. At the top of the door-jamb on the left-hand side of the portal is a metrical Greek inscription regarding the sacred marriage of Apollo and Kurana (p. 148). Steps behind the portal led down to the lower level beyond. The reduction in size of the portal by the insertion of inner piers supporting an arch has been tentatively assigned to the third century.

Gazetteer

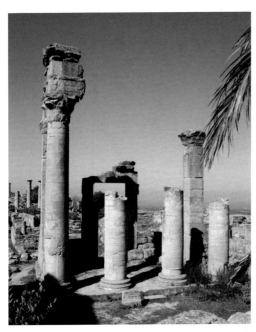

Fig. 138. Cyrene: the Roman propylaeum to the Sanctuary of Apollo.

Proceeding further towards the Temple of Apollo, one has to negotiate several more minor temples of which little more than the basic outlines are preserved. **The Temple of Athena (70)** is of Roman date (first century AD?), built on a podium six steps high. In front of the *cella* was a porch fronted by two columns *in antis*, with semi-columns on the inner faces of the *antae*. The temple was ascribed by its excavator to Persephone, the consort of Hades (to whom the temple next door was dedicated), but it has been argued more recently that it could have been dedicated to Athena. Persephone is apparently ruled out by the presence in front of the temple of an altar 'typical of Olympian gods'. In Byzantine times it became a residence for a mortal.

Given that the Roman *Propylaeum* can as easily be walked round as passed through, it is difficult to understand in what way it constituted a prescribed route into the sacred area.

Doric Fountain ★ (69)

Having passed through the Roman *Propylaeum*, one finds on one's L the remains of a charming and simple fountain, built in the Doric style in the third century BC. Set upon a base of three steps, a row of four columns *in antis* fronted a shallow basin of water. Behind this a parapet, divided into four sections by three columns, retained the main reservoir; from this the water poured through four spouts into the basin below. The water supply was brought by a channel from the springs above, and was led into the reservoir through an opening in the right-hand end wall rather than from the rear. It presumably served for the washing of pilgrims as they entered the sanctuary.

To the right of this is the **Temple of Hades (71)**, a slightly larger temple with a tetrastyle porch. The low podium with three steps all around it and the paired orthostats at the base of the *cella* wall on the S side indicate a Hellenistic foundation, and its original appearance will have been not unlike that of the *Strategheion* (67). In the Roman period, perhaps after the Jewish Revolt, it was substantially altered. The entrance to the *cella* was set well back between the side walls, which now became *antae* towards the front, flanking two columns; in front of these, another four columns (now

198

missing) constituted the new façade. Rather surprisingly (since Roman temples are generally set on higher podia than Greek ones) the floor was lowered in the course of these alterations. The dedication of the temple is presumed from the discovery within it of a statue of the seated Hades, with the three-headed hound Cerberus at his side.

Nestling against the rear of the right-hand side of the Temple of Hades, but facing in the opposite direction, is the tiny **Shrine of Serapis (72)**. Little can be said of its history, though it must post-date the adjoining temple and have undergone two modifications during its lifetime. Two short *antae*, terminating in semi-columns, were added to frame its façade, and then a portico was added in front of that. Within the shrine was found a headless marble statue that may represent Serapis, Asklepios or Zeus.

Before approaching the Temple of Apollo and the great altar in front of it, it will probably be convenient to continue round to the R to examine the remaining buildings in this area. Up against the boundary wall of the baths is the high podium of the so-called **'Shrine of the Dioscuri' (73)**, Castor and Pollux. Its association with an inscription recording the construction of a shrine to the Dioscuri, found in the baths, is far from proven. The podium of this small Roman temple is in fact composed of a somewhat earlier base for a votive sculpture, which had already been once enlarged. Frontal steps were added on the S side when it became a temple.

The first (northward) enlargement of the statue base had brought it into contact with the **Altar of Artemis (74)**. This was a long monumental altar, similar to that of Apollo but shorter and taller, set some way in front of the Temple of Artemis (79). The altar was built entirely

of local stone and was approached by three steps on the W side. The ends were decorated with carved finials: part of one of these has been found, depicting the Slaughter of the Niobids; this is now on display in the museum (p. 244, no. 5.4). (Niobe, a foolish mortal, had boasted that she had fourteen children, while the goddess Leto had only two, Apollo and Artemis. Apollo and his sister thereupon slew all fourteen with poisoned arrows.) The altar is probably contemporary with the temple, and hence of the fifth century BC.

Baths of Trajan ★ ★ (75)

The Baths of Trajan (fig. 139: lettered features refer to this drawing) are most conveniently approached at this point by means of a pathway to the N of the Altar of Artemis. This leads up a flight of modern steps and over a concrete bridge to the *natatio* and the later *frigidarium*. This never served as an approach in antiquity. The scale and former grandeur of the complex may be appreciated from here, but much of the central area is not accessible. We know from the dedicatory inscription, now set up beside the lower entrance to the site (p. 195), that the baths were completed in AD 98 under the emperor Trajan; also that they were 'destroyed and burned in the Jewish Revolt' of AD 115 and restored four years later under Hadrian. (This is recorded in an inscription now on the wall of the *frigidarium*: *tumultu iudaico diruta et exusta*.) They appear to have continued in use (with further modifications) until the earthquake of AD 365, at which time they collapsed, burying the rich haul of statuary that was eventually recovered by the 20th-century excavators. (It was the chance discovery here, in the winter of 1913, of the *Venus of Cyrene* – see p. 239 – which caused

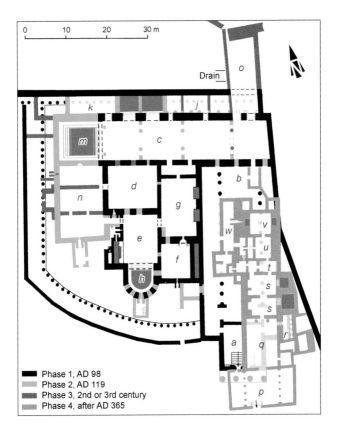

Fig. 139. Cyrene: plan of the Trajanic and Byzantine Baths in the Sanctuary of Apollo.

The Roman baths:		g	Frigidarium	*The Byzantine baths:*	
a	Entrance vestibule	h	Heliocaminus	p	Entrance vestibule
b	Palaestra	j	*Phase 2* apodyterium	q	Apodyterium
c	Apodyterium/*phase 2* frigidarium	k	*Latrine*	r	*Latrine*
		m	Natatio	s	Frigidarium
d	Tepidarium	n	*Phase 2* tepidarium	t, u, v	*Heated rooms*
e	Caldarium	o	*Phase 3* apodyterium	w	*Service corridor*
f	Tepidarium				

systematic excavations to be started and the military camp then occupying the site to be progressively removed.) After the earthquake, as already described, the baths were totally abandoned and the much smaller Byzantine Baths (66) were constructed where the *palaestra* had formerly stood.

Phase 1

The complex was constructed on the edge of the Sanctuary of Apollo and it certainly obliterated earlier structures, of which some elements are visible beneath the curved portico on the S side. (A recent find in this area was an hour-glass-shaped stone altar attributed to the Minoan civilisation, the first substantial evidence of contact with Crete in the Bronze Age.) The baths were surely built here in order to take advantage of the water supply, but such an establishment would never have been regarded as part of the sanctuary; it may well be for this reason that the complex is enveloped on the W side by a long curving portico. As previously mentioned, the baths were entered on the S side, close to but outside the Roman *Propylaeum*, by means of steps leading down into a vestibule (fig. 139: a). This led into a long *palaestra* or exercise yard (b), shaded by porticoes along either side. (Many of the column-bases are still in position, alongside the Byzantine Baths.) In the first phase, doors at the far end led into a long *apodyterium* (c) set at right-angles to the *palaestra*. At the far end of this hall, the bather turned L into a *tepidarium* (d) and thence into the *caldarium*

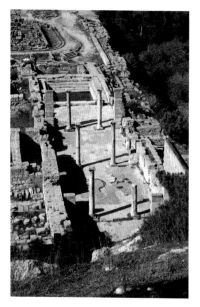

Fig. 140. Cyrene: the frigidarium *of the Trajanic Baths.*

(e), with a hot plunge-bath which had its own furnace. From here, a doorway in the E wall led into another *tepidarium* (f). From this room one could return northwards into the *frigidarium* (g), which had two cold plunge-baths in the E wall, fed from a cistern beside the *tepidarium*. Alternatively, one could proceed through another doorway into an unheated apsidal room facing S and provided with large windows (h). This appears to have been a *heliocaminus* or sun-room! From the *frigidarium* one might return, through a short vestibule, to the *apodyterium*. The S and W sides of the complex were separated from the Sanctuary of Apollo by a wall with a portico on the inside; on the N side this portico was carried along the terrace wall which also served as the city wall at this point.

Phase 2

Following the Jewish Revolt, the baths were enlarged within the over-all bounds of the property. First of all, a largely cosmetic alteration was the addition of a tetrastyle porch at the entrance to the complex (a). On the N side of the complex, the former *apodyterium* (c) was modified to provide a vestibule at the E end and a large new *frigidarium* in the remainder (fig. 140). In order to do this, the former portico alongside it was absorbed into the building, providing a new *apodyterium* (j), two cold plunge-baths and a latrine (k). The W wall was also dismantled and the hall extended further to the W in order to accommodate a *natatio* or swimming pool (m). The new *frigidarium* was further dignified (and strengthened) by the insertion of two archways supported by pairs of columns between pilasters. The flooring is partly of marble slabs and partly of mosaic, of which at least two successive layers are visible. A large new *tepidarium* (n) was

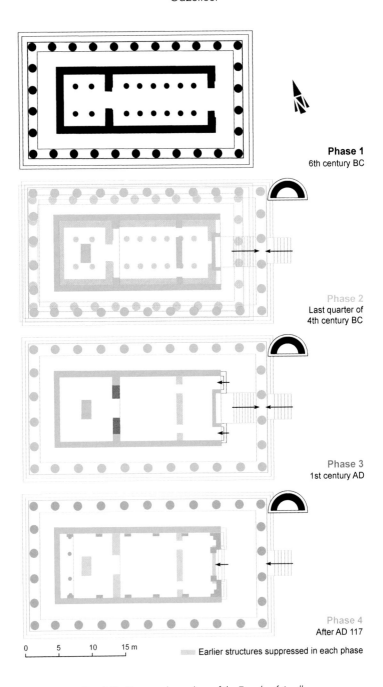

Phase 1
6th century BC

Phase 2
Last quarter of
4th century BC

Phase 3
1st century AD

Phase 4
After AD 117

0   5   10   15 m

Earlier structures suppressed in each phase

Fig. 141. Cyrene: phase-plans of the Temple of Apollo.

also added on the W side of the complex, and the internal circulation was modified by closing some doorways and creating others. In order to reach the *caldarium* (e), it was now necessary to pass through the new *tepidarium*. The S wall of the *caldarium* was broken down in order to incorporate the previous *heliocaminus* (h), into which was inserted a hot plunge-bath. The former *tepidarium* at (f) was suppressed, and the former *frigidarium* (g) was provided with a furnace and became a *tepidarium*.

Phase 3

The subsequent alterations designated as phase 3 in figure 139 may have been made over an extended period of time. A third *apodyterium* (o: reconstructed by the Italians as a museum but now closed) was added on the N side of the complex in the late second or early third century, to judge by the style of its mosaic floor. It bestrides the great drain of the Valley Street. Structural changes to the phase 2 *tepidarium* (n), involving its subdivision into three rooms, may have followed the earthquake of 262. At this time, the remainder of the portico against the boundary wall must have disappeared.

Altar of Apollo ★ (76)

Returning now past the Altar of Artemis, it is time to consider the central features of the entire sanctuary: the Temple and Altar of Apollo. The altar (76) stands to the E of the temple (77), aligned with it and equal in length to the width of the temple. Steps ran the full length of the altar on the W side, for the officiating priests. The upstanding altar was probably constructed at the time when the temple acquired its first external colonnade (see below, p. 204), in the late sixth century BC. It was built of local limestone, but of this only the lower part

now remains. The superstructure was rebuilt and faced in Parian marble in the second half of the fourth century BC by Philon, son of Annikeris (dedicatory inscription on the N end). The handsomely carved 'horned' finial which has been replaced on the S end is of this period. The altar has been extensively reconstructed by the Italians, who found the marble facings re-used in the paving of the Byzantine Baths (66). The size of it accords with ancient sources which tell us that a hundred bulls at a time were sacrificed in honour of Apollo.

The shorter foundation close to the E side of the present altar is all that is left of the very first altar, of the mid sixth century BC. Approximately half-way between the later altar and the steps of the temple may be seen a marble paving-slab in which are the remains of an iron staple. Circular wear to either side of this shows that there was here a large tethering-ring to which sacrificial animals could be tied.

Temple of Apollo ★ ★ (77)

Apollo was the patron and foremost divinity of the city of Cyrene, and the temple dedicated to him on the terrace beneath the sacred spring was one of the most important monuments of the ancient city (figs. 141, 142). The identity of this great building was established in 1861 when Smith and Porcher recovered from it a colossal statue of Apollo *Kitharoidos* (playing the lyre), now in the British Museum. In contrast to the Temple of Apollo in the agora (30) which celebrated his attribute as *Archegetes* (Founder), this temple celebrated the oracular Pythian Apollo, most famously worshipped at Delphi. It has a long and complex history, not free of controversy, extending across a thousand years. The account which follows is, I hope, at least plausible and intelligible.

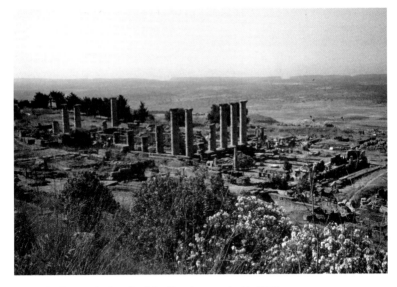

Fig. 142. Cyrene: the Temple of Apollo, photographed in 1972.

Phase 1

The first temple to Apollo built on this site has been ascribed to the mid sixth century BC. This building, detectable now by virtue of the blue-grey limestone in which it was built (visible on the N side of the *naos/cella*, inside the colonnade), consisted initially of a *naos* with an inner sanctuary or *adyton* at the W end. The upper parts of the walls were constructed of widely-spaced orthostats with an infill of mud-brick in between. Internally, both *naos* and *adyton* were divided into a nave and aisles by two rows of Doric columns, which were facetted rather than fluted on their shafts. These may still be seen, not in their original positions, but re-used as flooring-beams within the podium of the later temple. In the last quarter of the sixth century, a peripteral Doric colonnade or *peristasis* was added around the outside of the building; the column shafts were again facetted rather than fluted. (Note the two sizes of columns re-used as flooring-beams.) This is distinguishable from the original build by the yellow limestone from which it was constructed. The stylobate and some of the seatings for the columns at the E end may be seen at a low level, just inside the later colonnade and beneath the internal steps. A decorative element from the first *peristasis* which has survived is a handsome marble *akroterion*, the finial which stood at the apex of the pediment, in the form of a gorgon's face surrounded by volutes. This was re-used in the Byzantine period as a fountain-head and is now in the Museum (p. 242, no. 3.9).

Phase 2

In the last quarter of the fourth century BC, the temple was replaced in its entirety. The platform of the new temple was at a higher level, and it was in all respects slightly larger than its predecessor: its outline is that which survived through all subsequent phases. The columns were Doric, but fluted in the conventional manner. Since the excavation of the temple has removed any non-permanent surfaces within the *peristasis*, it is now very difficult to form any impression of the interior. It is clear, however, that anyone climbing the podium on the central axis would have found him or herself faced by a flight of steps leading downwards within, to a space beneath the front of the *naos*. This was perhaps the location of the sacred flame, which is described in a hymn by Callimachus as burning perpetually in honour of Apollo. For this reason, the *naos* was entered by two doorways on either side of this 'crypt' (not obviously detectable). Within, the former divisions were replaced by a vestibule or *pronaos*, from which two further doorways led into a smaller *naos*; at the far end, the *adyton* was demarcated only by a step and by shallow pilasters against the sidewalls. As a result of the lengthening of the temple, its platform at the front now impinged on the already-existing Exedra of the Palm of Leto (see below); it was probably in this phase that a narrow flight of steps was constructed in the centre of the façade, giving easier access to the raised platform. The date of the rebuilding is linked to the construction of the *Strategheion* (67), which incorporated in its foundations elements from the phase 1 temple. This must therefore have been ruinous or dismantled before 308 BC. Around the mid third century, a mosaic floor (in black and white stone with fillets of red terracotta) was laid in the 'crypt'.

Phase 3

This is represented only by internal alterations. The floors of the *pronaos* and *naos* were raised, necessitating extra steps at the two entrances, and the dividing-wall between them was removed. At the same time the entrance to the *adyton*

was made narrower. This seems to have taken place in the first century AD, presumably before a list of priests (which begins in AD 67) was carved on a doorframe of this period. (Blocks from this are now set up on either side of the entrance to the *naos/cella*).

Phase 4

This involved a major reconstruction of the temple after the Jewish Revolt. The unfluted columns which have been re-erected and which one sees now belong to this phase, though they stand precisely in the same positions as their predecessors. As well as the *peristasis*, part of the *naos* (or we may now call it a *cella* in the Roman fashion) was rebuilt. An inscription on the *cella* wall included the names of two priests and the erased name of the emperor Commodus. It seems therefore that the reconstruction was not completed until late in the second century AD. (It must, however, have been begun shortly after the suppression of the revolt, for a statue of Hadrian was found in the temple.) The reconstruction involved the suppression of the former 'crypt' and the creation of a central doorway into the *cella*. Within, its walls were embellished with pilasters and there was at the far end a shallow *adyton*, marked off by a single raised step and a Syrian arch.

Phase 5

A final phase (not illustrated) is very fragmentary and controversial. The original excavator, Luigi Pernier, suggested that after the collapse of the temple in the earthquake of AD 365, the floor of the *adyton* was raised yet higher above a newly excavated crypt at the W end (reached by a stairway visible just inside the N wall). He thought that these two chambers were reached by means of an external stairway in the W colonnade, which entered the building through a new doorway in the centre of the W wall. Because of the change of orientation, he inferred that this was a church. For lack of any carving or fitting suggesting Christian use, this interpretation has not been favoured. Sandro Stucchi, responsible for the reappraisal of the building upon which the account above is largely based, accepted the raised floor and the new crypt, but interpreted them as a larger and more elaborate *adyton* in the last phase of the temple before its collapse in 365. The coarse mosaic which survives against the inside face of the *cella* wall at a high level is also attributed to this phase, together with the late and inferior stairway (partly removed by the excavators) which spanned most of the eastern façade of the building, covering the earlier and narrower steps. The external structure in the W colonnade Stucchi identified as a small independent shrine.

Shrine and Exedra of the Palm of Leto (78)

Tucked into the narrow space between the Temple of Apollo and that of Artemis to the N of it, is a tiny shrine of Roman date in the form of a prostyle temple (with just two columns on the façade) *in antis* (78). In front of this, and respected by the front of the platform of Phase 2 of the Temple of Apollo which was cut to fit around it, is a semicircular marble foundation. This would normally be described as an *exedra* – a place for sitting out – but it is clear from the design that it never had a bench, but instead was enclosed by a metal grille across the diameter. The marble paving also shows a seating for a circular object, together with other sockets for metal inserts. We know from the Hellenistic poet Callimachus that Cyrene possessed a reproduction of the sacred palm tree of Leto, beneath which Apollo was said to have been born on the island of Delos. Callimachus describes in his *Hymn to Apollo* how the epiphany of the god was preceded by a vibration of the temple, the swaying of the Palm of Leto and the agitation of the Sacred Bay Tree. The palm and the bay must, therefore, have been within sight of worshippers in front of the temple. This monument, built perhaps in the first half of the fifth century BC and revered, both when the Phase 2 *Apollonion* was built and subsequently, has therefore been named, very plausibly, the Exedra of the Palm of Leto. It presumably enclosed a palm tree, surrounded by fronds or other objects, all in bronze. The position of the little Roman shrine next to it suggests that it too was dedicated to Leto.

Temple of Artemis (79)

On the N side of the Temple of Apollo stands the much more modest temple of his sister, Artemis. The core of the upstanding building is not closely datable, but the fact that its front was aligned with that of the Phase 1 *Apollonion* has been taken to imply that it was built before the other temple was rebuilt and extended forwards in the fourth century BC. It may belong to the early fifth century. It took the form of a simple *pronaos* and *naos*, both with central doorways and with no external *peristasis*. Instead, the doorway of the *pronaos* was embellished by a finely carved marble doorframe, possibly the first significant architectural use of marble in Cyrenaica. The walls of the temple are in fine ashlar masonry, with alternating courses of paired orthostats (with rubble infill) and of stretchers running through the thickness of the wall.

In the second century AD, in the time of Hadrian, a marble portico was added to the front of the building, with a typical Cyrenean arrangement of two columns *in antis*, with engaged semi-columns on the inner faces of the *antae*. The columns were fluted and stood on Ionic bases, but had Doric capitals.

Beneath the temple were found the foundations of an earlier building which perhaps belongs to the late seventh or early sixth century BC. This was almost square, but divided internally by two columns along the centre-line; the façade appears to have been pierced by four doorways. The plan seems to imply a double dedication, and since the structure predates the first Temple of Apollo, it has been suggested that this early shrine may have been dedicated to both Apollo and Artemis.

To the N of the Temple of Artemis are the bare foundations of a rectangular building with an entrance in the centre of the long side, facing E. Stucchi has suggested that this is of Hellenistic date and that it was perhaps a *lesche* (**80**), a social meeting-place.

The N side of the open space to the N of the Altar of Apollo is closed by a narrow portico, interrupted by the remains of a **Temple of Hekate (81)**. The portico is of Hellenistic date; its columns had Doric capitals and Ionic bases; at the right-hand end is a small room, probably for housing votive offerings, which is also Hellenistic. The temple, of which barely more than the foundations remain, is identifiable from a painted statue of the three-faced goddess Hekate, now on display in the Museum (p. 248, no. 9.17). An inscription records its construction in commemoration of Trajan's victory over the Dacian king *Decebalus* in AD 107. A second inscription records the reconstruction of the temple in AD 119 (following the Jewish Revolt), but the nature of this work is not evident from what remains.

Myrtle Bower ★ (82)

This monumental rectangular enclosure behind the Temple of Artemis has no entrance, but is in the form of a roofless Doric loggia, facing the Temple of

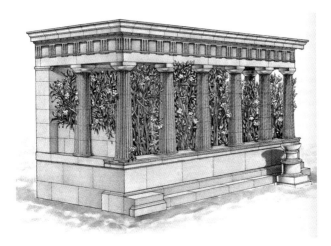

Fig. 143. Cyrene: reconstruction by S. Ensoli of the Myrtle Bower next to the Temple of Apollo. Drawing by A. Pagnini.

Apollo. Internal pilasters appear to have supported a timber pergola (fig. 143). The structure has recently been attributed to the mid-third century BC; it has been plausibly identified as the symbolic home of the myrtle-grove in which the sacred union of Apollo and Kurana took place (p. 148). The presence within it of a column-drum from the Temple of Apollo, felled in the Jewish Revolt, suggests that it was damaged at that time. The subsequent repairs may have included the addition of a cistern at the rear, for the watering of the myrtle.

To the NW of the Temple of Apollo, and at an angle to it which it shares with no other building, is the substructure of an **unidentified temple (83)**. This originally took the form of a rectangular building, whose walls were constructed from paired orthostats on either face, with a rubble filling in between. This technique occurs in a number of temples at Cyrene of the Classical and Hellenistic periods. At a subsequent time, the whole building was surrounded by a platform of three steps and the internal floor-level was raised correspondingly. The masonry of this period has drafted edges and looks Hellenistic. Immediately to the W of this building is a large square foundation with a bevelled edge, perhaps the base of an altar or a large statue. The foundation is cut by the secondary steps of the temple.

Western sanctuary area

At this point, it is probably convenient to strike out westwards towards the Greek theatre, before returning to examine the buildings on the S side of the sanctuary. On the way, one passes a less crowded, but perhaps less fully explored, area with some more small temples. For lack of better identifications, they have rather prosaic names.

West Temple 2 (84) is the most northerly of this group. It has been robbed to its foundations and little can be said about it. The presence of an altar in front of it may imply that it is indeed a temple (though the altar is not on the centre-line of the temple), and the three steps of its low podium suggest a Hellenistic date. In the second century AD (?) it acquired a colonnaded porch like its neighbour.

West Temple 1 (85) is a structure of the fifth or fourth century BC. It originally took the form of a plain rectangular *naos* without any colonnade, and with walls of paired-orthostat construction. In the second century AD it was reconstructed: some of the orthostats of the front wall were reused to build an inner partition between *pronaos* and *naos*, and a typical Cyrenean façade (two columns *in antis*, with half-columns against the inner faces of the *antae*) was added in front. There is again an altar in front of it, one of the horned finials of which is still present.

The **Doric Treasury (86)** is represented by a foundation of a plain rectangular building facing N. The orientation implies a *donarium* or treasury for votive offerings, rather than a temple which, given the choice, would always face E. It is thought to have been very similar in appearance and date to the *Strategheion* (67) at the other end of the sanctuary. At a very much later date, its ruins were used to construct a temple. The side walls persisted, but a new front wall was built from small irregular blocks; a new rear wall was also built substantially forward of the original line, containing a niche framed by two blocks of a hard shelly stone which is commonly found at Cyrene only in late (Byzantine) structures. The niche was plastered when excavated, and seen to bear graffiti, recording dates on which rain fell by the miraculous intervention of Zeus! Stucchi interpreted the new building as a **Temple of Zeus Ombrios**. Since the rear of the previous treasury was buried by a landslide, he attributed the temple to the period after AD 365, but no later than the end of the fifth century. Without more compelling evidence, it seems extremely unlikely that such a pagan temple would have been built at that time; rather, the fact that the temple was built after an earthquake is more likely to imply an association with that of 262.

Wall of Nikodamos (87)

The western end of the Sanctuary of Apollo is closed by a lofty wall running down the steep hillside. The excavators, who found the pitched coping-stones which originally crowned it, re-erected the wall with voids and concrete pillars where the blocks were lacking, creating a somewhat bizarre visual effect. An inscription on one of the blocks informs us that it was built by a certain Nikodamos; its construction is surely to be associated with the conversion of the adjoining theatre (intimately associated with religious festivals) into an amphitheatre (profane beyond redemption), which has been placed approximately in the second half of the second century AD. It should be noted that there would then have been no access through the wall where the modern pathway leads to the theatre, and that access to the (amphi)theatre would have been only along an upper roadway which passed above the sanctuary zone (fig. 136).

Beyond the Wall of Nikodamos, a small **shrine (88)** seems to have been cut off on the wrong side, and was perhaps out of use when the wall was built. It stands on a low podium, but had a narrow stairway across the front only, which suggests a Roman date.

Greek theatre ★ ★ (89)

This was the first theatre of Cyrene and it occupies a typically dramatic position, with views northwards over the lower plateau towards the sea (fig.

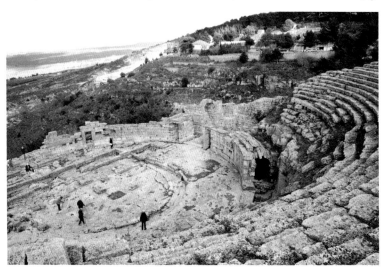

Fig. 144. Cyrene: the Greek theatre, later amphitheatre.

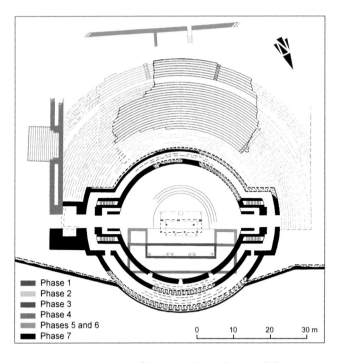

Phase 1
Phase 2
Phase 3
Phase 4
Phases 5 and 6
Phase 7

0   10   20   30 m

Fig. 145. Cyrene: plan of the Greek theatre, later amphitheatre.

144). It has a long and complex history, which is now divided into no less than seven phases, though a brief outline may suffice: figure 145 will hopefully help in the identification of the remains on the ground. The building started small and became progressively larger, often obliterating traces of the earlier phases. Because of this, and because the earliest phases are represented now by mere cuttings in the rock surface, the chronology is very approximate, based on dated parallels from other parts of the Greek world and on 'likely' occasions for modification.

Phase 1 is represented by three rows of sockets in the natural rock, close to the centre of the later arena. These are imagined to have corresponded to a wooden stage-building with a narrow

stage in front of it: this type of structure is attested elsewhere in the late sixth century BC. A second set of sockets indicates its replacement in **phase 2** by a similar, but larger structure, again of wood. This is not datable, but may belong to the fifth century.

Phase 3 brings with it the first stage-building in stone. This was a simple rectangular structure with a wooden stage against the front of it, for which sockets remain. To this phase are attributed the first traces (on the E side) of a curved *cavea* for the seating, 65 m in diameter. A date in the second half of the fourth century BC is guesswork, perhaps reinforced by the discovery in the ruins of some fragmentary capitals from the archaic Temple of Apollo: others were found in the *Strategheion*, built c. 308 BC (see above, p. 197). In **phase 4**, 'probably in the Ptolemaic period' (according to Stucchi, i.e. before 96 BC), the *cavea* was enlarged and extended forward: there are traces of the foundations of the retaining wall in the present E entrance to the arena. The cuttings for the lowest rows of seats, visible in the bare rock of the arena, also possibly belong to this phase. The stage-building was moved further to the N and was enlarged, enclosing the preceding structure entirely between its wings (*paraskenia*). (Thus the rear wall of the previous building was on the line of the front wall of its successor.) The masonry of this phase is distinguishable by its poorer quality. The stage-building will have had a plain façade with three openings.

Recent investigations have shown that the vertiginous 'stairway' on the E side of the theatre, far too steep for practical use, was a sort of pyramidal monument surmounted by a set of four honorific statues, the marble base of which still lies in the vicinity. The surviving inscription on the base is attributable to the third century BC.

Phase 5 is likely to be of early Roman date, for it represents a distinct 'Romanization' of the stage-building, whose façade was now embellished by paired engaged columns. At much the same time (it is suggested) the lower stratum of the surviving seating was established, and the *cavea* was for the first time enclosed by straight, rather than curved, walls. **Phase 6** is placed after the Jewish Revolt of AD 115 (for no compelling reason, other than that this was a period of renewal at Cyrene). The *paraskenia* on either side of the stage were extended towards the *cavea*, resulting presumably in a widening of the stage, but also in the closing of the *parodoi* which had previously provided access to the seating at the level of the *orchestra*. (How access to the seating was then provided is unclear: there may have been stairways in the now blind *parodoi*.)

The final **Phase 7** must have followed the preceding modifications after no great interval, having taken place before the end of the second century AD. Now the stage building was razed completely and the lower third of the *cavea* seating was removed in order to create an oval arena with a peripheral corridor and axial entrances to E and W. The building was thus converted into an amphitheatre, for a very different kind of entertainment, and the Wall of Nikodamos (87) was constructed in order to shield the Sanctuary of Apollo from the profane activities which now took place here. The only access henceforth was from above. In order to create an amphitheatre, where there was no means of introducing animals or fighters from a gallery beneath the arena, the peripheral corridor was essential. It was also decided to build a massive retaining wall on the downhill side, in order to create an appropriate arena. (There are other examples in the Greek world of theatre-to-amphitheatre conversions which did not go to such extremes, and made do with a semi-circular arena.) Above this, at least some rows of seating were provided; new seating was also laid in the existing *cavea*, directly on top of that of Phase 5. Much of this has long since collapsed down the hillside, and the movement would continue but for a major recent programme of stabilization, sponsored by the World Heritage Fund. When the amphitheatre went out of use we do not know, but it would obviously have been vulnerable to the seismic shocks which did such damage elsewhere in the city.

After the visit to the Greek theatre, the itinerary returns to the Sanctuary of Apollo in order to visit the monuments on the S side of the temple. Between the Doric Treasury already described (86) and the Temple of the Petal Mosaic which follows, there is an intermediate terrace wall, above which are several substantial buildings; however, I have found no published account of these and cannot offer any information about them.

Immediately behind the Temple of Apollo, and facing eastwards towards it, is a temple of unknown dedication which has been named the **Temple of the Petal Mosaic (90)**. This is of Roman date, built on a podium with frontal steps only but no colonnade. The *cella* is paved with a mosaic in which a panel of interlaced petals is enclosed within a border of diamonds. At the rear of the *cella* was a bench for the cult statue, and in front of that was found the base of a circular altar for burning incense. Stucchi, the only scholar to have written anything about it, ascribes the temple to the sixth century AD, which seems unlikely; it surely predates AD 365.

Immediately to the S of the temple just described (and structurally succeeding it) is a **Roman house (91)**, entered from the E side. This is an example of the invasion of the sacred area by housing, not unlike that described above in the agora (p. 171). It belongs to the late Roman or Byzantine period.

'Grotto of the Priests' ★ (92)

From the SW corner of the Temple of Apollo, an imposing flight of steps leads up to what must have been an important feature of the sanctuary. What we now find here is a more-or-less rectangular cave, rock-cut at the rear and built up in masonry at the front. Its interpretation remains somewhat uncertain, but like many other buildings, it has clearly had a long history involving changing uses.

It is not implausible that this was, in its early history, the oracular grotto from which Apollo Pythios spoke. A natural fault in the rock of the E wall has been artificially enlarged, and communicates with an array of cavities and passages above. The roof of the cave, which has been hollowed out into a regular rectangular chamber, is partly sustained by two square piers of living rock, carved above to represent timber framing. On these have been carved inscriptions of the Roman period, naming priests with the title *kallietes*. This term occurs elsewhere in the sanctuary, and is presumed to refer to a priesthood of Apollo.

The label at the entrance to the cave declares that it is a *mithraeum* or Temple of the Persian god Mithras. The change of use would have to have post-dated the inscriptions on the piers and would signify an important change (or decline) in the worship of Apollo. The chamber does resemble a Mithraic temple, in which one would expect (as here) raised benches along either side for the worshippers (accessed by narrow steps at the front); but that is the limit of the plausible evidence. There are no inscriptions relating to Mithras and no cult objects have been found in the vicinity.

There are further complications in the history of this cave, which is why it does not instantly satisfy those familiar with *mithraea*. The forepart of the roof collapsed on some occasion, and was reconstructed by building a façade of three arches to support a new roof. These arches have been re-erected by the excavators. It is also suggested that in the Byzantine period (after 365) the cave had a secular use and was adapted to become a *nymphaeum* or fountain in a private house. To this period are attributed the water-channels which run behind the benches and through five semi-circular features, where runnels perhaps encircled pieces of statuary. In this connection, the floor in the centre of the cave was lowered (which is why the 'benches' seem so improbably high), lined with water-proof plaster and paved with marble slabs in order to create a central basin. (This implies that the water feature occupied the central entrance – where there is indeed a drain – and that the *nymphaeum* could only be entered from the flanking entrances.)

Outside the entrance to the building, on the E side, is a small fountain formerly fronted by a pair of marble columns with 'Pergamene' lotus-and-acanthus capitals, probably of the third century AD.

Temple of Isis ★ (93)

Close to the S side of the Temple of Apollo, and facing N, is a Temple of Isis, which has been partially reconstructed. Its style of construction suggests that the *cella* (the rear part of the present building) goes back to the late fourth century BC, around the time when the *Strategheion* (67) was built. It was enlarged by the addition of a colonnaded porch in the time of Hadrian (recorded on the architrave of the façade). A further restoration in the time of Marcus Aurelius, by the priest Ti(berius) Claudius Battus, is recorded in an inscription on one of the column drums. Yet later, and probably after the earthquake of AD 262, the interior was remodelled, with the addition of benches on either side of the *pronaos* and the creation of a tiny *adyton* within the cella in order to dignify the statue of Isis which was found

within the building. In front of the steps are the remains of a small circular altar for burning incense.

The temple is believed to have been destroyed in 365. To the E of it are masses of fallen masonry, including both fluted and plain column-drums from the Temple of Apollo. (It is possible that these were stacked here by the excavators.)

Fountain of Philothales ★ (94)

To the E of the Temple of Isis, the retaining wall of the upper terrace was graced by a fountain in the form of a Doric loggia (fig. 146). The water-basin, partly rock-cut, was fronted by five Doric columns between end-walls with engaged semi-columns in the typical style of Cyrene; the loggia was apparently roofed with flat stone slabs. The inscription across the architrave names the donor as Philothales, son of Jason, and the monument has been attributed to the fourth century BC. Recent excavations have found traces of an earlier building, perhaps also a fountain but of the fifth century, in the same position. There can be little doubt that a fountain here, fed from the sacred spring above, would have played an important part in the rituals of the sanctuary.

The fountain was renovated in the second century AD and again in the third. It was probably destroyed by the earthquake of 365, after which a shrine dedicated to *Apollo Kitharoidos* was built in the ruins from entirely re-used materials and even with a cult-statue composed from parts of two different sculptures! (Was this the wretched successor to the great temple of former years? The statue is on display in the museum: p. 245, no. 7.7.) A new fountain was constructed, using a water-tank to the E of the earlier installation and the *akroterion* with the Gorgon's head from the archaic

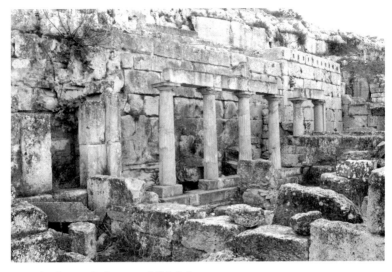

Fig. 146. Cyrene: the Fountain of Philothales.

temple (see pp. 204, 242) was pierced through the mouth and installed here as the fountain-head.

Temple of Apollo Nymphegetes (95)

To the E of the Fountain of Philothales is a long foundation fronted by five narrow steps. This was in the Hellenistic period another base for votive statuary; but in the reign of Marcus Aurelius it was adapted by Ti(berius) Claudius Battus (who also restored the Temple of Isis, p. 213) to constitute the approach to a small temple dedicated to *Apollo Nymphegetes* ('Leader of the Nymphs'). The dedicatory inscription, subsequently re-used in a late wall on the site, would originally have been placed across the architrave fronting the temple. This area was much altered by subsequent activity in the Byzantine period.

Exedra of Apollo Karneios ★ (96)

In front of the Temple of Apollo Nymphegetes and in a cardinal position with

respect to the Temple of Apollo Pythios (77) and its altar (76) stands a prominent votive monument. This consists of a semi-circular *exedra* with a projection towards the rear, on which stands a decorated marble plinth supporting a *meta* (column or marker) rising from an acanthus calyx; upon either end of the *exedra* is a passant lion. An inscription tells us that the dedicator was a certain Pratomades, son of Polymnis; it was probably built between 280 and 260 BC, since it appears on coins of Magas of that period. The *meta* is a device marking a focal point, and is particularly associated with the festival of *Apollo Karneios*; this originated at Sparta and was widely exported to other Doric states. Its significance here in Cyrene is undoubtedly to mark the point at which the first Greek colonists achieved their goal, under instruction from the Oracle of Apollo at Delphi. Apollo himself is represented on the figured plinth beneath the column, actually leaning on the *meta*! He is also associated in the foundation-myth, and here on the monument, with the nymph Kurana; there may also have been a myrtle tree in bronze, now indicated only by sockets in the stone for its attachment. The lions too are closely associated with the foundation-myth: both through the propensity of Kurana for tackling them with her bare hands, and for the story of how Aristoteles/Battos, the leader of the first colonists (p. 2) was cured of his stammer by an encounter with a lion!

After the earthquake of AD 365, the monument was converted into a fountain by bringing a water supply through the rear of the *exedra*, and building a parapet across the front in order to make a basin.

Temple of Jason Magnus (97)

To the E of the Temple of Apollo Nymphegetes is a Roman temple approached by a tremendous three-sided stairway. The practical reason for this is the lie of the land, which caused the *cella* of the temple to be substantially above the piazza in front of the Temple of Apollo; but a simple frontal stairway would have served the purpose and would have been less ostentatious! Unfortunately, we do not know to whom this temple was dedicated. We do know, from the inscription which formerly graced the façade and which has been recomposed at the top of the steps, that it was built in AD 176–80 by the priest Ti(berius) Claudius Jason Magnus out of the 'income' of Apollo. A mosaic in the *pronaos* of the temple records the name of another priest, Marcus Aurelius Euphranor, and is very similar in style to the mosaic in the Temple of Hermes on the acropolis ridge (19) which also names Jason Magnus and is responsible for the inference that he was the occupant of the sumptuous house next door (17).

Behind this temple, at a higher level and immediately beneath the wall of the upper terrace is a *hestiatorion* or hall for sacred banquets. This is of Hellenistic date, but shows evidence of two phases with a change of orientation (the entrance was first on the E and later on the N). In the later phase it had a white mosaic floor, of which traces remain.

'Agora of the Gods' (98)

This is the name which has been given, for convenience, to the space on the lower terrace between the Temple of Jason Magnus and the *Strategheion* (67). The name is justified by its occurrence at Thera and in another Doric foundation, Kameiros on the island of Rhodes. It presents an appearance of confused masonry, but much of this is composed of small altars or *arulae*. Many of these take the form of a single or double square, with one or two tray-like recesses in the top, on which a portable brazier would be placed. The dedication to a divinity might be inscribed on the altar, or on the brazier itself. The altars appear to be datable between the fourth and the first centuries BC; in the late Roman or Byzantine period, many of them seem to have been re-used to construct a building of three rooms. In this area was found the *stele* recording the will of Ptolemy VIII, in which he bequeathed his kingdom to the Roman Senate, should he die without an heir. This stone is on display in the museum (p. 243, no. 4.10).

In the same area (most readily understood from the terrace above) are the foundations of a Hellenistic building, facing N, with a Doric portico of Cyrenean type. This was perhaps a *lesche* like that near the Temple of Artemis (80). Squashed into the space between it and the terrace wall to the S are the remains of another temple, again with a

Doric portico of Cyrenean type, facing towards the E. An architrave block which may have belonged to it bears the titles of the emperor Trajan.

The circuit of the lower terrace is now complete. The upper terrace is a long, tapering space of relatively level ground immediately beneath the cliff face. This is where the groundwater comes plentifully to the surface. Its volume is reduced compared to ancient times, because much of the flow is piped off well inside the cliff, for use elsewhere; but there remains enough running water, in channels and reservoirs, to give an idea of how it must have been in antiquity. At certain times of year, one may also experience a deafening chorus of frogs croaking, greatly amplified by reflection off the rock face above! To reach this terrace, one may either return through the Greek *Propylaeum* (64), or climb the stairway beside the Temple of Jason Magnus (97). The features will be described from W to E.

Springs of Apollo and Kura★ (99)
The perennial water source beneath the cliff face was the prime reason for the Greek colonists to have chosen this site for their settlement in the seventh century BC. From the first, therefore, the source would not only have been sacred and an object of veneration, but also a daily necessity for watering both the human population and its flocks and herds. Only very gradually were these needs separated from one another and met in different ways. There were from early times two routes to the springs: one along the floor of the Valley Street and the other curving down from the agora and acropolis on a ramp cut into the rocky hillside. The ancient sources mention at least three features here: the Spring of Apollo, the Spring of Kura and

a *nymphaeum*. These may be identified now with varying degrees of confidence.

Immediately opposite the point at which the ramp from above terminates in a short flight of steps is a cave beneath the cliff face, which has at this point sheered off and partly blocked the access to it. This is thought to have been the Spring of Apollo. Beyond it to the W (to the R of a long rectangular basin) is a second cave which is identified by inscriptions as the **Spring of Kura** (a name from which that of the nymph Kurana is derived). Into the rock-face above the latter cave are carved various niches for statuary. The water which flowed out from here came from an array of clefts in the rock behind, which at different times were artificially enlarged and channelled together. The innermost part of the tunnel (not accessible) is largely artificial, and has been traced for some 300 m behind the rock-face. There are numerous graffiti carved on the walls, recording the visits of pilgrims; the earliest of these are Antonine in date. Within the cave is a deep reservoir, now in the form of two lobes. (Water still flows, though less profusely than it might, since much of it is now run off through pipes for current use.) These are not original. A new opening was cut through the rock face into the left-hand lobe probably in 19/18 BC by the priest Dionysios son of Sotas, who recorded work done on the spring. The opening gave access to a basin excavated on the inside, from which water might be drawn. At a later date, perhaps in the time of Marcus Aurelius, the much larger reservoir which one sees now was chiselled out of the inside of the cave, occupying both lobes. This put an end to the (presumed) use of the right-hand lobe as the *nymphaeum*, a place for *symposia* in the fifth century BC. Presumably at the same time, access to this reservoir and to the cave was blocked by a wall built across the front and by the excavation in front of that of a row of seven drinking-troughs.

The supply of drinking-water for the human population, assured by the work of Dionysios, was further elaborated by the construction, in front of his basin, of a much more substantial rectangular trough over 5 m long, partly rock-cut and partly built up. This was approached by a step and was fronted by a paved, walled enclosure in order to ensure its cleanliness and to exclude animals. A sleeper wall within the trough, upon which are eight square stone bases, provided a foundation for a roof supported by timber uprights. Wear on parts of the parapet caused by buckets being drawn up attests to the long and important use of this fountain, as do several inscriptions which record its cleaning or renovation at different times. Its original construction may be associated with a dedication of a fountain to Apollo *ktistes* (Founder) by a group of priestesses in the reign of Nero.

The **Spring of Apollo**, a few metres to the E of the installations just described, seems never to have been so extensively developed for public use, and may have remained more of a sacred shrine. Within the right-hand side of this cave are numerous small niches, of a size to accommodate small reliefs or portrait-heads. The spring was fed from a single cleft at the inner end of the cave. There is again a deep T-shaped reservoir which has been excavated within the cave, but there are not the extensive signs of wear associated with the drawing of water that are observable at the Spring of Kura. Indeed in the Augustan period, the spring dried up – possibly because its supply had been diverted by extended tunnelling operations behind

the Spring of Kura. Either then or later, a conduit was cut through the rock from the *Aqua Augusta* (see below) in order to provide a new supply to the Spring of Apollo. In the second or third century AD the Spring of Apollo was enclosed behind a precinct wall which was built across the front of it and pierced by three doorways. The latest of the graffiti within the tunnels (now connecting the two systems together) are datable to AD 285.

Fountain of Hermesandros (100)
Just to the E of the ramp which descends from above is a row of three limestone drinking-troughs, with a very worn relief on the wall behind showing oxen drinking. (The most legible part of this relief is now behind the oleander bush at the right-hand end.) This monument was set up by one Hermesandros to record the sacrifice of 120 bulls on the occasion of the festival of Artemis. This probably belongs to the early Hellenistic period, and served the practical purpose of the ritual washing of animals destined for sacrifice.

In front of the fountain is the end of the stone **Bench of Elaiitas (101)**, which extends for 89 m to the E, past the Greek *Propylaeum* (64). This was built in the second century BC by the priest Elaiitas and dedicated to Apollo. It presumably served as seating for those attending sacred festivals, when the procession would pass this way. Against the rock face behind the bench is a line of a further 21 drinking-troughs of Roman date, associated with (or subsequent to) the reorganization of the water supply in the time of Augustus. (See below: they were fed by adits connected to an aqueduct tunnel within the rock behind.) In the space between the bench and the drinking-troughs is a row of five beehive-like masonry structures structures. These are **Byzantine lime kilns (102)**, into which we may imagine much fine pagan statuary being cast in order to be burnt into lime!

Aqua Augusta (103)

Further to the E, beyond the end of the Bench of Elaiitas, are more cuttings beneath the cliff face, which may be explored with care. Here, in the time of Augustus, the proconsul C(aius) Clodius Vestalis built a new fountain, which was described in a marble inscription attached to it as the *Aqua Augusta*. A basin 74 m long was excavated beneath the cliff face (fig. 147), divided by square piers of living rock into 26 bays and fronted by a parapet with a capping of black basalt. In front of this was originally a built portico, of which no trace is now visible. The water supply was obtained from higher up in the Wadi Bu Turqiyah by means of a rock-cut conduit; at the downstream (W) end of the fountain, the surplus was carried in a further rock-cut channel to supply the Spring of Apollo and the drinking-troughs in between. The system had probably gone out of use at the time when the Stepped Portico was constructed (see below), because of the inherent hazards of the location (readily apparent from rockfalls), and perhaps because the water supply had been interfered with in the course of those works.

Stepped Portico ★ (104)

The *Aqua Augusta* just described is separated from the Valley Street by the line of a tall and unbroken wall, which has been re-erected further uphill by the Italian excavators. Against the N side of this wall was a stepped footway alongside the steeply climbing street, covered by a colonnaded portico; this extended all the way from the Arch of Marcus Aurelius and Lucius Verus (61) to the Greek *Propylaeum* (64). Its destination shows that it must have been constructed as a covered way to the Sanctuary of Apollo. The columns had

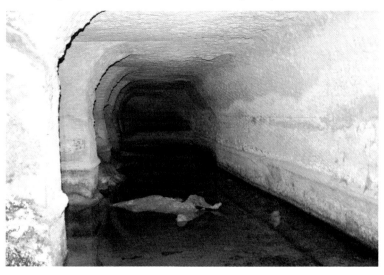

Fig. 147. Cyrene: part of the inner chamber of the Aqua Augusta *in the Valley Street.*

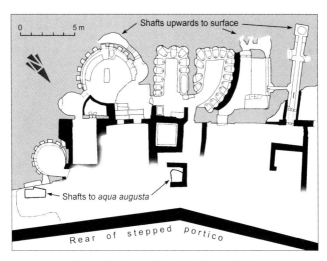

Fig. 148. Cyrene: plan of the Baths of Paris.

Ionic bases and Doric capitals. The difficulty of constructing a continuous colonnade on steeply sloping ground was overcome by building horizontal sections of open colonnade, the front of which was replaced by a plain wall where there were steps. The portico is potentially dated by fragments of an inscription which ran along the architrave, and which is now thought to belong to the reign of Antoninus Pius.

It is clear that the rear wall of the portico cuts off completely the long triangular space between it and the cliff face. Goodchild considered that this area, which included the *Aqua Augusta*, had become dangerous and was actually 'filled in' when the portico was built, but since the excavations in the 1930s took no account of stratigraphy, it is impossible to verify this. While this is a sizeable area, the construction of the portico certainly seems to have made it a barely accessible dead end.

On the opposite side of the valley, high up but beneath the modern road, is a long and confused series of rock-cut chambers. They look in the first instance like tombs, but given that they are within the Hellenistic wall circuit, they could only be such if they are of very early date. They do not, however, resemble the distinctive early tombs of the North Necropolis (p. 237). On the other hand, it is clear that they were used as troglodytic habitations during the life of the ancient city, and indeed until recent times. Most of them contain complex arrangements of rock-cut vats, some perhaps connected with either wine or oil.

Baths of Paris ★ ★ (105)

If you climb the Stepped Portico to its upper end near the Arch of Marcus Aurelius and Lucius Verus (61), you come to some terraced houses through which stairways lead upwards to the R and eventually to the agora. Conversely, if you have walked down from the agora zone (see p. 184), this is the point at which you will arrive.

Just below the top of the portico lies a hidden building complex of

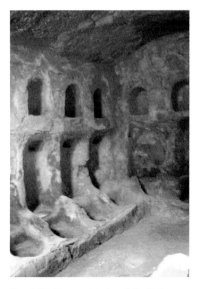

Fig. 149. Cyrene: interior of the Baths of Paris.

considerable interest and no little controversy: these are the Baths of Paris. They are on the S side of the Stepped Portico and can be reached only from above, by a steep modern stairway behind the rear wall of the portico. The complex (figs. 148, 149) is composed partly of built rooms out in the open, and partly of chambers excavated in the living rock. They are at a deep level in a space between the portico and the southern cliff face which is very narrow at this point. The structures show signs of lengthy use and alteration; but since they were excavated in 1934 without any observation of stratigraphy, many of the details (including the chronology) are difficult to unravel.

The essence of the various connected chambers, some rectangular and others circular, is that their walls are lined with seats or sitz-baths, above which are niches – often a small one suited to an oil-lamp and a larger one, perhaps for

a water-jug or for the user's clothes. In most of the rooms there appears to be either a raised basin or a carved trench into which, like a sauna, heated stones would be placed and water thrown over them to create steam. The water was obtained either from a well-shaft which reached down to the course of the *Aqua Augusta* below, or from a cistern fed by channels from the hillside above. A room at the right-hand end of the complex has a floor of coarse tessellation, in which white tesserae spell the name of Paris, son of Sammaios, together with a ribboned wreath enclosing a star and a *tabula ansata*.

So to what era does this strange complex belong? It is certainly a bathing establishment of some sort, and without further inscriptions it cannot be claimed that it served any but mundane purposes. Richard Goodchild drew attention to parallels in the Hellenistic world: he considered the baths to be Hellenistic, and to have gone out of use when the construction of the Stepped Portico at a much higher level surely buried them completely. Sandro Stucchi, on the other hand, responded that the baths were not buried by the portico and that 'the quality of the construction, decadent beyond all imagination, and the style of the lettering [in the mosaic] leave no room for doubt that the date of this complex is very late, and that it has nothing to do with the practices of Classical Greece.' Given that the Stepped Portico probably collapsed into a heap of rubble in 365, it seems to me that the depth of the baths makes it inconceivable that they should have been accessible, let alone first built, at such a late date. The cutting of a shaft at that time, connecting the baths to the long-forgotten conduit of the *Aqua Augusta*, is also not credible.

THE NORTH-EAST QUARTER

Within the circuit of the ancient walls, there remain a few scattered but important monuments to be described. They may readily be visited in conjunction with the museum, which is located just inside the eastern limit of the city. The fact that they appear scattered and isolated is more an accident of research than anything else, for there has been no systematic excavation of the northern ridge of the city, much of which remained a military zone until very recently. (A substantial temple was examined towards the western end of the ridge in 1926, but no trace of it is visible now.) The position of the E Church (110), which seems very likely to have been the cathedral of the city in the sixth century, is a long way outside the restricted defensive circuit which was built in the third (p. 189). There is also in this area a substantial building which was probably still occupied in the early Islamic period (Qasr Shaghiyah: 111). This implies that there was vigorous settlement in the vicinity in the latest phase of Cyrene's history, which invites further investigation.

Temple of Zeus ★ ★ (106)

The Temple of Zeus (figs. 150, 151) was in its heyday, and is again now, one of the most imposing monuments of Cyrene. Its collapsed ruins alerted early explorers to its size and importance; it was excavated between 1926 and 1942 and the impressive work of reconstruction (apart from the re-erection of one and a half columns by the British Army in 1957) has occupied the years 1967–2008. Its present appearance corresponds to no one phase of its history, but provides a vivid visual impression of its main features.

We know from a passage in the History of Herodotus that in the year 515 BC a Persian army passed through the city of Cyrene and then camped on the 'Hill of Lykaean Zeus.' At that point they regretted not having seized the city as they passed through it, and tried to return. However, the Cyreneans sensibly

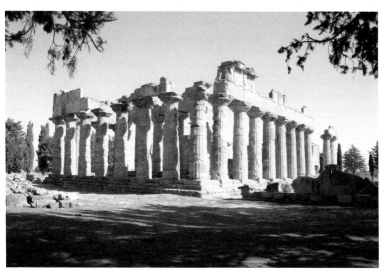

Fig. 150. Cyrene: the Temple of Zeus in the NE Quarter.

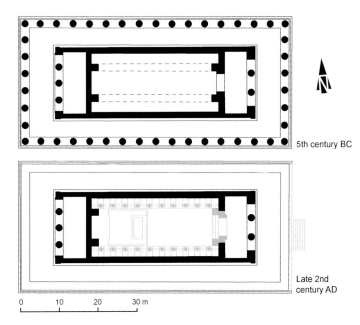

5th century BC

Late 2nd
century AD

0   10   20   30 m

Fig. 151. Cyrene: plan of the Temple of Zeus in the NE Quarter.

refused them entry a second time and, after an inadequately explained debacle, the Persians left and returned to Egypt (of which they were in control). This passage indicates that there was a sanctuary of Zeus outside the city at the time. Though small finds from the excavation do go back that far, current opinion of the architectural characteristics of the temple favours a date of construction around 500–480 BC.

The temple faced E and stood on a platform of three steps measuring 70 × 32 m: larger than the Temple of Zeus at Olympia, and almost exactly the same size as the Parthenon at Athens. The core of the early temple consisted of a *pronaos* with two columns *in antis*, a *naos* or *cella* which was divided into a nave and aisles by two-storey internal colonnades, and an *opisthodomos* fronted by three columns *in antis*. The

surrounding colonnade (*peristasis*) consisted of 8 × 17 columns of the Doric order, and its foundations were stucturally independent of the *cella*; it has therefore been suggested that, as in the case of the Temple of Apollo (77), the *peristasis* may have been a secondary addition. The geometry of the colonnades includes a range of optical refinements similar to those found in the Parthenon. The temple was built of the shelly limestone that is found in the immediate vicinity, and the subsequent excavation nearby of a hippodrome (108) probably made use of ground already quarried for the temple. This stone is not of very good quality, and renovations will have been necessary at various times. (One of the justifications given for the extensive modern reconstruction is that the if the fallen column-drums had been left exposed to the weather on their sides, with the bedding of the stone in the vertical plane, they would soon have broken up completely.) The size of the columns is impressive by any standard: the topmost blocks, which include the capitals, weigh about 17 tonnes each!

Surviving elements of the W (rear) pediment have been reassembled on the ground nearby. At the opposite end, part of the architrave from the E front has been reconstructed at ground-level, showing the lettering of a monumental inscription in Latin. This relates to a reconstruction which must have been carried out under Augustus. During the Jewish Revolt in AD 115, the temple was attacked and substantially destroyed. The columns of the *peristasis* were systematically undermined, and fell radially outwards around the building. (If this had been caused by an earthquake, they would all have tumbled in the same direction.) The strength of motivation of the furious Jews can barely be imagined, when one considers the risk to life of undermining these colonnades with hand tools! The fallen masonry was accompanied by a clear burnt stratum.

After the Jewish Revolt, a further reconstruction was begun, but the *peristasis* was never replaced. According to Sandro Stucchi, responsible for the detailed study and reconstruction of the building, a start was made at the NW corner, but the supervising architect mistakenly thought that the columns were ten drums high instead of nine, and the attempt was rapidly abandoned! The *cella*, however, was rebuilt. The internal wall-surfaces were veneered in marble and the previous internal colonnades were replaced by engaged orders along the walls. The shafts were of cipollino, and the bases and Corinthian capitals of Proconnesian marble. The reconstruction (or at least its completion) was

commemorated by an inscription carved on the internal architraves and repeated on the pediment of the *pronaos*, which now constituted the façade of the building. It is datable between AD 172 and 175, when Claudius Attalus was proconsul. At the front of the temple, the original stepped platform (*crepis*) was reshaped to form a vertical face with a narrow flight of steps leading to a lowered ground level. The steps were displaced southwards from the centre-line: this curious arrangement was presumably determined by the presence and significance of the small East Temple at this point, for which see below.

Another inscription tells us that, a few years later (185–92), a certain Menander was responsible for the construction of a huge platform at the rear of the *cella*, upon which was placed a replica (eight times life-size) of the famous statue of Zeus at Olympia, made by the sculptor Pheidias in the fifth century BC. The core of his throne incorporates some column-drums from the felled *peristasis*; the veneer of marble which covered this is still visible on the S side. Many fragments of the marble components of this statue (representing exposed flesh areas) have been discovered: the larger pieces now lie on the ground on the N side of the temple and various colossal fingers and toes are displayed in the museum (p. 247, no. 9.2).

The temple suffered catastrophic collapse once more in the earthquake of 365, but this was apparently not the end of its woes. The excavators found that the cipollino columns of the interior had been smashed into tiny pieces (now heaped outside by the colossal statue fragments), and one of the marvels of both excavation and restoration is the life-sized head of Zeus, now in the museum (p. 247, no. 9.1), which was found here and recomposed from more than a hundred fragments. Destruction of this kind has no natural cause, but must have been carried out deliberately, by human agency. The extensive reddening of the limestone inside the temple is also indicative of fire. The circumstance is believed to have been a ritual purging of the ancient pagan sanctuaries by the Christians, later in the fourth or in the early fifth century.

Buildings surrounding the Temple of Zeus (107)

Excavation around the Temple of Zeus has been too limited to reveal the full extent of the sanctuary or its relationship to the urban layout. However, a number of buildings have been uncovered in its immediate vicinity, which were presumably connected more or less directly with the cult of Zeus. Figure 152 provides an approximate sketch of these structures.

Immediately in front of the principal temple (a), and slightly to the N, is a small rectangular precinct (b), thought to be of Hellenistic date. This had a porch on the S side and contained within it a small Doric portico against its western wall. In the second century AD a little temple on a podium (the **East Temple**) was added within the precinct, with an altar in front of it, to the E. The presence

of this minor complex appears to have conditioned the curious off-centre stairway of the Antonine reconstruction of the Temple of Zeus and it has been suggested (though this is pure speculation) that, following the devastation caused by the Jewish Revolt, the little sanctuary served Zeus as a temporary home while the greater temple was awaiting repair. In the same context, it has been suggested that the handsome life-sized head of Zeus, found in the main temple in fragments and attributed stylistically to the time of Hadrian, may have been part of the cult-statue in this smaller shrine.

Near the NE corner of the main temple are the foundations of a small **Doric shrine** on an oblique orientation (c); this was probably a treasury, and it has been dated to the fourth century BC. Also in this area are remains of three further rectangular buildings (h, h) which have been identified as **hestiatoria**, or dining halls for ritual banquets. Two of them are orientated E–W and the third N–S. They are paved with mosaic, typically with a plain central area surrounded by a band of geometric decoration which is separated from it by strips of lead. In the northernmost of these, the parallel foundations are the remains of benches for the diners. These buildings are thought to have been built in the late third or the second century BC.

In the area of excavation, within the ring of trees which now surrounds the great temple, numerous other foundations have been exposed of buildings which were destroyed when its colonnades were felled by the Jews in AD 115. At the W end, notably, is part of a large rectangular structure on an axis which differs from that of the temple. No published account of these has yet been given.

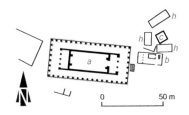

Fig. 152. Cyrene: sketch-plan of buildings around the Temple of Zeus. (a) Temple of Zeus; (b) East Temple precinct; (c) Doric shrine; (h, h) Hestiatoria.

Hippodrome (108)

To the E of the Temple of Zeus can be made out the long shallow depression of the hippodrome, running N–S. The initial date of construction is uncertain, though the presence of a central spine (verified by excavation) shows that it was still in use in the Roman period. The southern part was rock-cut, doubtless making use of an existing hollow, quarried previously for the construction of the temple. The racecourse is approximately 356 m (1,200 ft) long, with the starting-gates (*carceres*) at the N end. The curve of the S end is clearly visible, as are the cuttings for the seats on either side of the middle section. With regard to its initial construction, it may be remembered that Cyrene was famous for its horses in the fifth century BC and produced victors in the chariot races at the Delphic and Olympic games.

Temple of Eluet Gassam (109)

Clearly visible on a small eminence known as Eluet Gassam, to the N of the Temple of Zeus, is a fort built in the early years of the Italian occupation. This is constructed upon the foundations of a small temple facing E, which was recorded by Smith and Porcher in 1861. The masonry of its superstructure was entirely rearranged by the Italian engineers and only part of its foundations can now be made out. It is clear that the temple never had a surrounding colonnade, though the ground around it was, at least on the N side, built up to form a terrace. It stood on a platform three steps high, and appears to have had a porch fronted by two columns, possibly with engaged semi-columns on the inner faces of the *antae*, and a *cella* in which were seen two longitudinal foundations, perhaps for an internal colonnade. Certain details suggest that the temple may

have been built in the fourth century BC, with restorations in the first century AD. The dedication is unknown.

East Church ★ (110)

Close to the museum is an important but rather neglected building, which has remained partly exposed since antiquity. Limited excavations took place in 1917 and a more extensive examination was carried out in 1954–56 under the direction of Richard Goodchild. Further detailed study has been carried out in recent years. This is the East Church of Cyrene, and it was probably the cathedral of the city in the sixth century. Several phases of construction or reconstruction have been identified (see fig. 153); their chronology is subject to the same uncertainty and debate as bedevils most other churches in Cyrenaica.

Phase 1

The initial building took the form of a three-aisled basilica inscribed in a rectangle, with an apse at the E end flanked by wide corner-chapels. The perimeter wall is of coursed yellow-grey limestone, rather rough on the inside, and is easily recognized. The apse was pierced by a triple window, oddly off-centre (no longer easily made out). It will have been roofed by a semi-dome, and was fronted by two re-used columns, presumably carrying a triple arch. The nave was separated from the aisles by arcades carried on piers, some of which have stood since antiquity. At the W end was a narthex, divided into three spaces, corresponding to the nave and aisles. Access to the church was through at least two (probably three) doorways in the W end and possibly two in the N wall. No trace remains *in situ* of the chancel fittings of phase 1, which must have been obliterated

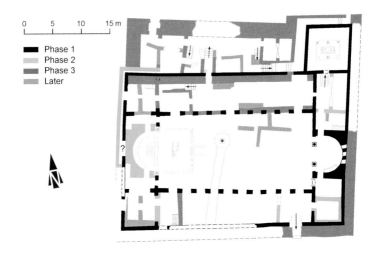

Fig. 153. Cyrene: plan of the East Church.

when the phase 2 mosaics were laid. At the NE corner a projecting chamber, which housed a baptistery in phase 2, may have performed the same function in phase 1, though this is not clear. (Despite straight joints, the structure is now considered original to the first building.) The whole of the E end is built over an earlier street which ran S from the hippodrome: soundings beneath the floor of the church have revealed the street-paving. As to the date of Phase 1, it is presumably pre-Justinianic, because of the stylistic associations of the mosaics of Phase 2; it has generally been attributed to the fifth century.

Phase 2

For reasons which are quite unknown to us, a major reconstruction of the church in the sixth century involved the reversal of its orientation, with the construction of a new apse at the W end in the centre of the former narthex. It was presumably a consequence of this, and of the suppression of the original entrance to the church at the W end, that a new

entrance was created at the E end of the S aisle. This involved steps down from the street into the aisle (to the E of the modern steps), part of which was now partitioned off to create a vestibule. At the same time, the corner-chapel immediately to the E was divided in half, with the southern room now becoming a porter's lodge. The northern room, presumably still a chapel, was paved with mosaic, as was the vestibule at the entrance. The mosaic in the chapel included an inscription naming a bishop Menas, who was presumably responsible for the work. Curiously, it faced the E wall, where there was never an opening from which it could be viewed!

Another major modification was the insertion of the visible components of a baptistery at the NE corner. The former NE angle-chapel was subdivided, and from the northern room a flight of steps, constructed of re-used marble elements, led up to the baptistery at a higher level. The baptismal tank was a re-cut Attic sarcophagus with a Dionysiac scene: most of its relief decoration was chiselled off, but traces of feet survive around its lower edge! Steps were carved in the interior, leading down into the water, but steps of wood would have been required in order to climb over the ends from the outside. The room as a whole was paved and the tank stood beneath an arcaded canopy supported by six columns.

The nave of the church was now paved with mosaic, in an array of rectangular panels like those found in the E Church at Qasr Libya (p. 133). However, while in that instance the mosaic was composed of 50 panels, here it was composed of 126 (14 × 9)! In the E apse (which was now enclosed by a metal railing) and in the chancel area, the paving was of simple *opus sectile*. The new W apse, flanked by columns matching those in front of the E apse (but here set into the angles), was largely filled by a *synthronon*. Much of this was built of masonry; only the uppermost tiers of seats will have been of wood. In front of the apse, the outline of the chancel screen can largely be made out, composed of posts taken from the chancel of phase 1. In the centre is part of a white marble altar-base, with sockets for colonnettes supporting the altar-table. At the E end of the N aisle, a fine mosaic with a Nilotic scene gave added emphasis to this area. A recess at this point in the later reinforcement of the N wall suggests that an object of veneration, a tomb or a reliquary chest, may once have stood here.

The style of the mosaics is clearly identical to those found at Qasr Libya (p. 133) and at Ras al-Hilal (p. 320), and therefore attributable to the reign of Justinian. The fact that the mosaic in the SE angle-chapel named a bishop implies that this was his church and therefore the cathedral. This is reinforced by the presence of the baptistery.

Phase 3

The next major change involved the addition of a rectangular extension on the N side of the building, and a reinforcement of most of its external walls. (Some reinforcement around the NW corner had already been carried out in phase 2.) As in other cases, it has been debated whether this was defensive in intent, or intended to prop up an ageing and unstable structure; the latter is probably the more likely. The addition on the N side was composed mainly of a long rectangular hall, accessed both from the N aisle of the church and (through a vestibule at the W end) from the street to the N. At the E end was a rectangular room with a staircase on the S side. There was clearly, from the start, an upper storey over the new structure and, either now or later, the N aisle of the church was strengthened and further staircases indicate an upper floor in this area too. Various subdivisions of the N hall are secondary, as were inserted walls in the N and S aisles which were removed in the course of excavation. These last indicate secular occupation, presumably after the Islamic conquest. Several rooms had at this time served for storage, for they contained *dolia* and stacks of roof tiles. However, not all of the alterations attributable to Phase 3 are as late as this, and it has recently been argued that the major features were contemporary with Phase 2. There are crosses carved on the masonry in places, and next to the doorway from the N hall into the church was found a holy-water stoup made from an upturned cylindrical (pagan) altar. It still bore its original decoration of garlands, but the top had been hollowed out and a Latin cross had been carved between the garlands.

A well in the centre of the nave appears to have been dug in the Islamic period, when it was surrounded by a raised platform and approached by a paved path between the structures which now encumbered the site.

This building, with its long and complex history extending into the Islamic period, offers compelling evidence for the vitality of this part of Cyrene when much of the rest of the city had been abandoned.

Qasr Shaghiyah ★ (111)

This is a fortified tower, more or less hidden in the trees. It was a prominent feature of the landscape in the 19th century, but much stone was quarried from its upper parts in the early years of the Italian occupation. In order to find it now, follow the modern road for about 150 m westwards from the East Church towards the Central Quarter. The tower will be visible on the high ground to the R, and may be reached through a gate immediately before a driveway. It had a single entrance on the S side, leading into a vestibule flanked by two small chambers, of which that on the L contained a staircase with access to a cistern beneath. Beyond was a long vaulted chamber, spanned by three pointed arches of late Roman or Islamic character, which appear to have supported a mezzanine floor. Examination of the structure showed that the SW corner had been rebuilt, together with the entrance doorway. Dating of the whole is very approximate, but this refurbishment is thought probably to have taken place after the Islamic conquest. An Arabic inscription was found on a fallen stone nearby.

BEYOND THE CITY WALLS

There are both buildings and tombs outside the walls of Cyrene on the S side. The modern road which curves round from the roundabout at the entrance to the ancient city passes by the funerary church on the L, and then swings SW to join the ancient road connecting Cyrene with Balagrae.

Funerary church (112)

This unexcavated building is more remarkable for its fancy arcaded enclosure wall than for what can be seen within. (There is, incidentally, no gateway into the enclosure, but it is not difficult to scramble over the wall.) It has been identified as a funerary church, inasmuch as its S aisle appears to be built over a tomb. This would also explain its presence outside the city in the necropolis. At the E end it has an apse with flanking chambers, inscribed within a rectangular outer wall.

At the E end of the site, some 70 m from the church and next to a modern building, are masses of fallen concrete which suggest the presence of a Roman bath building, perhaps belonging to a suburban villa.

The Southern Extra-Mural Sacred Zone

In recent years, extensive excavations have been carried out on the S side of the Wadi Bil Ghadir by a team from the University of Urbino under the direction of Mario Luni. A huge sacred zone is coming to light, occupied by several different temples accompanied by a theatre and other ancillary structures. Two areas suggest an association with the goddesses of rural fertility, Demeter and Kore ('The Daughter', an appellation used euphemistically in order to avoid naming her as Persephone in her other role as the wife of Hades) but the distance between them seems too large for a single sanctuary, and the relationship between the various scattered structures is still far from clear. The new excavations have brought to light the following components.

6 Cyrene: beyond the city walls

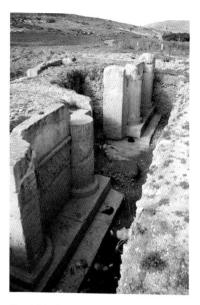

Fig. 154. Cyrene: propylaeum of the Sanctuary of Demeter S of the city.

Propylaeum ★ (113)

At the NE corner of the zone, and immediately next to the modern road where it joins the course of the ancient road from the S Gate, is a monumental *propylaeum* (fig. 154). This has been well preserved beneath some 3 m of alluvium which has collected in the valley bottom since antiquity. It is composed of two rooms flanking a central passageway. The outer face is framed by four Doric semi-columns with Ionic bases, while the inner face is simpler, with an angle-pilaster on either side of the opening. Sockets show that the outer portal could be closed by doors; when these were closed there was, however, pedestrian access through a doorway on the left-hand end. Adjoining the *propylaeum* is a modest but elegant **Doric stoa**, facing the road. This was fronted by three columns between semi-columns on the end-walls, and had a pitched roof composed of ten long slabs

of limestone. Both structures are said to be of the early Hellenistic period, though finds from the excavation suggest that the area was already frequented in Archaic times.

A little further to the S is a large square foundation, aligned parallel to the road. Its superstructure has been largely destroyed by ploughing, but it must have been a base for a statue or an altar. In a void between the blocks of its core was found a large terracotta vessel containing the bones of a piglet. This was presumably a dedication-offering: it has been suggested that the piglet reflects an association with Demeter.

Temple of Demeter ★ (114)

On the higher ground within the precinct is a fine Doric temple, the columns of which have now been partially re-erected. It has an unusual form (fig. 155), being prostyle (with columns only across the front) and hexastyle (with six of them). Internally, it was divided into a nave and aisles by two rows of Doric columns, originally two storeys high. Part of one row has been re-erected; the columns of the upper tier were smaller and monolithic. The style of the architecture and associated finds indicate a construction-date around 490–80 BC. An interesting detail which has emerged from the excavation is the demonstration

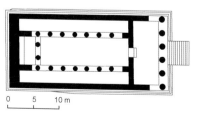

Fig. 155. Cyrene: plan of the Temple of Demeter S of the city.

that the lead used for clamps between the blocks of the superstructure came from mines in Attica (Greece). It should also be noted that traces of paint have survived on the blocks of the entablature. Within the temple and incorporated in its collapse were three statues, one of them of Demeter, the other two possibly Zeus and Athena. They were well-preserved, having stood between the columns of the *adyton* at the far end of the *cella* and having fallen when the building fell, without previous damage. Smaller objects found in a ritual deposit in the S aisle of the *cella* included terracotta statuettes (mostly of Demeter), 94 lamps (required for the nocturnal rites of the goddess) and bones of pigs mixed with ash and charcoal. Part of an inscription of the early first century AD has been recovered, which graced the façade of the building. The date is indicated by the name of the sponsor (of a restoration, presumably): M(arcus) Sufenas Proculus, whose name may also be seen on the S porch of the Caesareum

(2). The finds within the building suggest strongly that the temple was dedicated to Demeter and show that it was venerated from the late Archaic until well into the Roman period. In front of the temple have been exposed the foundations of its associated altar, which is contemporary with it.

Theatre 5 ★ (115)

Some way to the NW of the Temple of Demeter is a well-preserved theatre with at least 21 tiers of seats and a seating capacity of about 1,000 persons (fig. 156). Its flanks appear to be partly rock-cut, and are pierced by niches which once held votive statuettes and reliefs. The mosaic floor of one of the larger recesses in the E flank (a waterbasin?) incorporates a dedication to the nymphs. Numerous small votives, in the form of lamps, vases and terracottas, were also found in this area and are predominantly of Hellenistic date. The area in front of the *orchestra* is still in course of investigation, but it

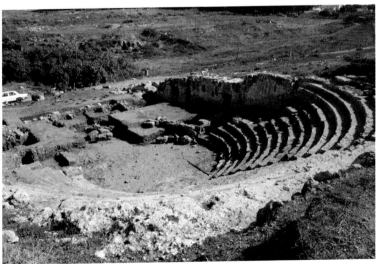

Fig. 156. Cyrene: Theatre 5.

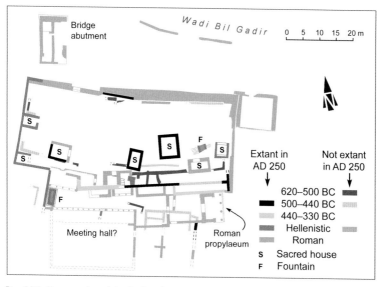

Fig. 157. Cyrene: plan of the Enclosed Sanctuary of Demeter and Kore to the S of the city.

is already clear that there was not a conventional Hellenistic stage-building. Likewise, the single central stairway through the seating is unconventional, and suggests a ritual use of the theatre (for ceremonies) which differs from that of more typical theatres. The lettering of a name carved on the front of one of the seats has been attributed to the fifth or fourth century BC.

On either side of the theatre are traces of numerous terraces and shrines. An *oikos* just to the W of the theatre has shallow rectangular niches in the walls to accommodate votive reliefs. To the R of one of these (on the right-hand side) are carvings of simple ploughs (⌐), similar to those recorded in the rural sanctuary in Wadi as-Sanab (p. 141). The alluvium washed down from above has buried many of these structures almost to roof-level, and if further excavations are carried out in this area they may well yield dramatic results.

Enclosed Sanctuary of Demeter and Kore (116)

On the steeper part of the hillside, to the NW of the recent Italian investigations, an American team excavated in the 1970s what proved to be an enclosed sanctuary on several terraces, dedicated to the worship of Demeter and Kore. (The enclosing walls, offering privacy for the rites celebrated within, are particularly characteristic of Demeter sanctuaries.) The area is now a confusing jumble of walls and terraces without much in the way of architectural pretension, not least because its superstructure was very largely removed in antiquity. The finds, however, were plentiful and remarkable.

The earliest structures appear to go back to c. 620 BC, very soon after the foundation of Cyrene. The phase-plan in figure 157 shows how the enclosed, but irregular, precinct developed. The earliest masonry is generally formed of uncut or roughly polygonal stones, while in the late Archaic/early Classical period fine

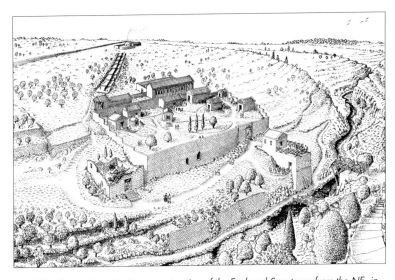

Fig. 158. Cyrene: imaginative reconstruction of the Enclosed Sanctuary from the NE, in about AD 200. The bridge across the wadi may already have gone out of use by this time. (Drawing by David Hopkins.)

ashlar masonry appears, often in the form of paired orthostats, each constituting one face of the wall, and with a rubble filling between the two. (This was widely used at Cyrene: see the Temple of Artemis, no. 79.) At this time the first of several one-room cells were constructed. Because they are now almost completely denuded, there is little that can be said about them; they were surely shrines of some sort, in which statues and other offerings might be displayed, sometimes on a bench running across the rear wall. (They are indicated as 'sacred houses' on the plan.) In the early years the offerings were mostly small objects (pottery, terracottas, lamps, small objects of bronze); later, these were largely supplanted by grander dedications: statues, reliefs and inscriptions. The inscriptions leave no doubt that the principal deities honoured here were Demeter and Kore.

The upper part of the sanctuary began to take on a more formal appearance in the Hellenistic period, with the introduction of a fountain and perhaps a precursor to the tetrastyle *propylaeum* which provided a grandiose entrance in the Roman period. Also in the Roman period, the western part of the upper terrace was occupied by a large building, perhaps a meeting hall, fronted on the N side by a Tuscan Doric colonnade; the body of the building remains unexplored. A further porticoed building on the lower level was linked to a bridge across the Wadi Bil Ghadir, which therefore provided a second access from the city to the sanctuary in addition to a road running along the S bank of the wadi. Figure 158 is an artist's impression of the probable appearance of the sanctuary from the acropolis ridge in the third century AD.

The evidence of both pottery and animal bones, discovered in large quantities on the site, shows that ritual meals were consumed here during much of its history, despite the absence of recognizable dining facilities.

Given the steeply sloping nature of the site, it is not surprising that it was badly affected by the earthquake of AD 262; there were traces of later activity and reconstruction subsequent to that event, but occupation seems definitely to have come to an end with the earthquake of 365. By no means all of this complex has yet been exposed, and its relationship with the area to the E is far from clear. A revived American mission is expected to resume work in the near future.

Southern temple precinct (117)

This bland designation is applied temporarily to a further area of new excavations, which are still in progress to the S of the Temple of Demeter (114). Here has been identified another large rectangular precinct, entered through a *propylaeum* next to the ancient road. Within have been found the remains of a Doric temple facing E, of conventional design, with a peristasis of 6 × 11 columns enclosing a simple *pronaos* and *naos*. The floor of the *naos* was paved, in its latest phase, with a polychrome mosaic of the Hellenistic period. In front of the temple, but close to the entrance to the precinct, are the foundations of a large altar, similar in size to that in front of the nearby Temple of Demeter and to that in front of the Temple of Artemis in the Sanctuary of Apollo (74). Opinions with regard to the date and life-span of this complex are hesitant at this stage; the temple was probably erected in the fifth century BC and the *propylaeum* appears to be early Hellenistic.

The latest excavations have revealed ordered rows of single cells within the northern and eastern boundaries of the precinct, not unlike the *oikoi* which are

appearing in the adjoining Sanctuary of Demeter and Kore. The function of these is not yet clear. Along the banks of the road, however, which is rock-cut in this stretch, are carved many votive niches or shelves (*arulae*), usually with a pair of shallow recesses in the floor, one of which may have a lidded cist within. Some of these cists have yielded miniature vases. Similar niches are present in quantity around the sanctuary at Ain Hofra (p. 253), and they bear a strong resemblance to the small votive altars found in the 'Agora of the Gods' in the Sanctuary of Apollo (98). There are further examples between the Temple of Demeter (114) and Theatre 5 (115). Inscriptions on the rock-face consist of personal names, presumably dedicators of the offerings placed there. The latest phase of this phenomenon is attributed to the Hellenistic period.

At the SE corner of the precinct, next to the road, has been found *in situ* one of many boundary stones which have been recorded in Cyrenaica, dating between the reigns of Claudius and Vespasian and serving to define former royal (i.e. Ptolemaic) lands repossessed by the Roman administration. The stone is inscribed in both Latin and Greek, and marks the beginning of the agricultural land outside the city. It is precisely at this point along the road that the tombs begin which characterize the entire periphery of Cyrene.

South Necropolis

The modern road S from the ancient city follows for part of its course the ancient road towards Balagrae, and is lined for a considerable distance with monumental tombs. The tombs which are most accessible are those in the North Necropolis (p. 235); but by following this road one obtains a good impression of the ancient landscape, with not only rock-cut and upstanding tombs, but also lines of orthostats which once delineated ancient property boundaries. At a distance of about 900 m beyond the *propylaeum* of the Sanctuary of Demeter (113), the modern road veers slightly away to the R of the ancient one, which continues in a well-defined cutting in the rock, lined with tombs of all sorts, for some 800 m. Where this tract begins, there is a Roman milestone to the L of the modern road, set up in the time of the Emperor Claudius. If you follow the modern road, taking the L fork when it branches, you will come out onto the main jabal road opposite a police station to the W of new Shahhat.

The 'new' village of Shahhat, which has grown up over the last fifty years, covers a considerable part of the South Necropolis. In places the ancient tombs have been spared, but in other instances some very interesting examples have been neglected or badly damaged.

One such is the **Tomb of Thanatos**. This was discovered only in 1971 in the course of development, and up to that time had remained completely buried. It is now enclosed within walls with no means of access, is overgrown and encumbered with rubbish. However, it is not irretrievable and, in the hope that it may in due course be cleaned up and made accessible, it is described here.

In order to find the tomb, take the side street which leads SW down the side of the Wahda Bank (at N 32° 48.72' E 21° 52.03'). There are fields on your R and buildings on your L. After 260 m, turn L, first R and again first L; after a further 50 m, the tomb will be found behind a wall on your R. It takes the form of a rock-cut tomb excavated in level ground. A stairway leads down to a complete underground peristyle courtyard, originally surrounded by five simple Doric columns, entirely carved from the living rock. An inner room is entered through a small doorway in the rock-face opposite

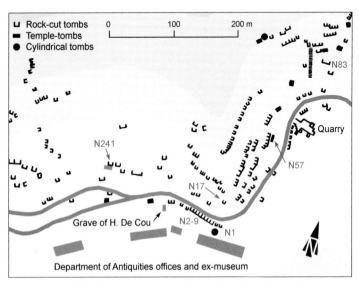

Fig. 159. Cyrene: sketch-plan of part of the North Necropolis.

6 Cyrene: beyond the city walls

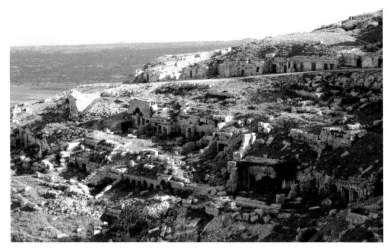

Fig. 160. Cyrene: the ancient road to Apollonia and the North Necropolis.

the entrance-stair; above it are several niches which would once have held statuettes or portrait-heads. The architecture indicates a Hellenistic date, though the niches for portraits must be a Roman addition. A subsequent modification (in the late Roman period?) is represented by waterproof plaster on all of the internal walls, when the tomb was converted into a cistern. Within the inner room was found a base upon which the customary half-figure of the Goddess of Death must have stood. It is inscribed with the name of the deceased, Deinis, son of Euryphon. Off this room, where traces of figure-painting were once visible on the walls (a figure labelled *Thanatos* – Death – gave its name to the tomb), open two funerary chambers with benches for the cinerary urns of the family.

150 m to the SE of this (continue in the previous direction, take the next L and the next R) was another fine tomb (catalogued as S388), described as having a courtyard, cut into a rocky slope, with a façade of a built wall with a Doric frieze, above which was a simulated Ionic colonnade set against another façade further back. Between the columns were inscribed bases for female funerary statues. This was reported as in course of reconstruction by the Department of Antiquities in 1975: it has now disappeared entirely beneath a rubbish tip!

North Necropolis

The cemeteries surrounding the city of Cyrene are amongst the most extensive of any city in the Greco-Roman World. The burials extend in time from the sixth century BC until at least the fifth century AD and embrace a wide range of structural types. (Most of the available space had already been taken up by the end of the Hellenistic period, and later burials mostly involved refurbishment or re-use of pre-existing tombs.) There are simple cist-graves, rock-cut chamber-tombs, monumental built tombs and upstanding sarcophagi. Tomb-façades often include niches of a size to receive portrait-heads of the deceased; these are additions of the Roman period. These types may be found widely in the Cyrenaican

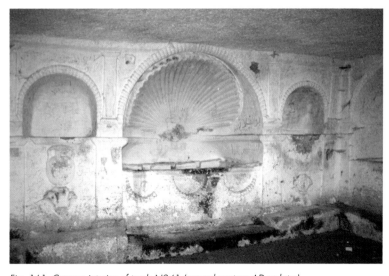

Fig. 161. Cyrene: interior of tomb N241 (second century AD or later).

landscape, and many other examples are described in this guidebook; but nowhere do they occur in such concentration as at Cyrene, where they extend over an area of some 20 sq km. The area which is most striking visually, and is easiest to visit, is the North Necropolis which extends down the N face of the upper escarpment, on either side of the (old) road to Apollonia (figs. 159, 160). A half-hour walk down the modern road from the entrance to the Sanctuary of Apollo will be enough to give a vivid impression of this city of the dead. The asphalt road follows the course of that established in the seventh century BC.

As you descend from the sanctuary and the adjacent cafés, the road curves round to the R and then to the L. Immediately, there are tombs cut in the rockface to your R and spreading down the slopes below to your L. Also above you to the R are the once-elegant offices of the Department of Antiquities, built in the Italian colonial period. (The little white-painted villa has had a long and

chequered career: it was built for Air Marshal Balbo when governor of Libya, was used by the British Embassy for some years as a country retreat, housed the library of the Department of Antiquities for a while and then caught the eye of Colonel Qadhafi ...) Below the next (embanked) curve to the R stands a roofless 'modern' building. This is known as the Mudir's house, and prior to the advent of the Italian army in 1913 was the only modern building in the entire landscape.

Immediately beneath this house is the entrance to a fine **rock-tomb** (catalogued as **N241**) which is a rare example of new excavation in the late second century AD. The entrance is plain on the outside, with two small windows on either side of the door; within is a rectangular chamber, carved to resemble a two-storey courtyard of a house with pilasters representing the colonnades of the peristyle. The most elaborate wall is that opposite the entrance (fig. 161), with an *arcosolium* recess for an inhumation crowned by a shell-head and flanked on either side by smaller recesses for offerings (or ashes?); urns are carved on the flat surface below. Each of the lateral walls has two more *arcosolia*, treated in a more simple fashion, and it is clear from added burial recesses in the floor that the tomb was used over an extended period. The left-hand *arcosolium* on the left-hand wall once showed painted decoration of the fourth century AD and of clearly Christian symbolism: a peacock in the semi-dome surrounded by fishes, and the Good Shepherd on the front of the sarcophagus, carrying a sheep and surrounded by others. Sadly, this is no more.

Beyond the next right-hand curve of the road is a row of eleven tombs together, which are amongst the earliest to be seen. Before you come to them, however, cast a glance upwards to the spur above the road. Here, just inside the wire fence, is the **Grave of Herbert De Cou**, the epigraphist of the American expedition who was shot dead at Cyrene in 1911. The grave takes the form of a chest-tomb with a headstone in the form of a tree-trunk with a scroll on it. On the rock-face beside the road, beneath the grave of De Cou, may be made out part of an inscription in Latin and Greek, identifying the tomb of Lucius Vibius Gattabus, a freedman.

Tombs N2–9 which follow, opening towards the road, have a façade composed of two or three columns between *antae* or responding walls. The capitals are Doric or Ionic, with a plain, heavy fascia above, on which the details of an architrave and frieze may originally have been painted. In the case of **N8** a carved pediment with *akroteria* is preserved (fig. 162); in the other examples, this may have been constructed in masonry that has now disappeared. Within the portico of each tomb there is usually a bench, perhaps for funerary meals, and above this there is a doorway which leads into the tomb-chamber behind. These tombs have been attributed broadly to the later sixth and fifth

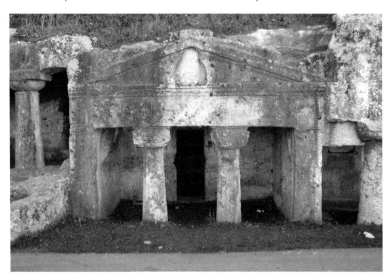

Fig. 162. Cyrene: tomb N8 (sixth century BC).

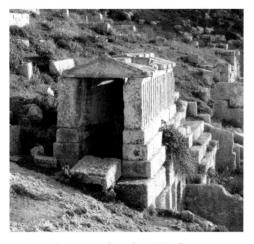

Fig. 163. Cyrene: temple-tomb N57 (Hellenistic).

examples from Cyrene and its neighbourhood. (A selection is displayed in the museum: p. 244.)

Further on, a little way below the road, stands the prominent silhouette of the upstanding **temple-tomb N57** (fig. 163), with pilasters carved along the sides in imitation of a wooden structure. This is again Hellenistic. A little way beyond N57, there is a large stone quarry above the road on the right; this too has been colonised by tombs.

Below the road, and on the outside of the next bend, is an area of burials which was examined in detail in 1957 and which is worth a visit. In the middle of the area, a wide rock-cut ramp leads down the slope between several 'courtyard' enclosures. Each of these contains several sarcophagi. These are cut from the living rock and are immovable, but they are fitted with lids in the form of pitched roofs. There are simple pyramidal finials at the corners, and in the centre of each lid is a square platform, often with a socket in it. It is presumed that this was the location for a bust of the 'Goddess of Death'. As you descend the ramp, pass around the first 'courtyard' on your R (from which a doorway leads into a rock-chamber with simple *arcosolia*) to the next 'courtyard' terrace (with lidless sarcophagi). In the rock-face on the uphill side there is again a doorway into a chamber-tomb, with a window immediately to the R of it. This is **Tomb N83**, with shell-head *arcosolium* recesses like those in N241, but less elaborately carved. The tomb is likewise considered to be of the late second century AD, with continuing use into the late

centuries BC. (Portrait-niches in some of the porticoes probably reflect continued use in the Roman period.)

Just above tomb N2 and below the former sculpture museum (in a suspended state of renovation) is the very handsome cylindrical **Tomb N1** upon a square base. The finds from the funerary chamber beneath belong to the mid fourth century BC, though the drum encloses a pre-existing rectangular temple-tomb. If you continue down the road from this point, where it curves to the L above a steep re-entrant, you will shortly see a bench below the road, strategically placed so that you can relax and take in the view. If at this point you look back towards the head of the re-entrant, you will see at the bottom of the slope the carved façade of the late Hellenistic **Tomb N17** (the right-hand one of a pair). Above the door are not only niches for portrait-heads but three actual sculptures carved in the rock-face: a draped pillar-herm (R), a pillar-stele (C, with later niches for portrait-busts cut out of it) and the 'Goddess of Death' (L), the strange veiled female of which there are so many fourth. It once displayed painted decoration on the furthest *arcosolium* to the right. There was also a painted inscription within, recording the interment of a certain Demetria and her son, who had both been killed in an earthquake. This was on the entrance-wall, and they must have been laid in the additional sarcophagi excavated in the bench on that side. A chi-rho symbol in the inscription demonstrates that they were Christians, probably killed in 365. Sadly, the only paint or epigraphy visible now is very recent, extensive and effected with a spray-can!

THE MUSEUM ★ ★

The museum is currently housed in a former warehouse close to the East Church (110: see the plan inside the rear cover). The present display was conceived in 1999 as a temporary arrangement of major items (primarily sculpture) from the last century of excavations on the site, intended to serve until such time as new permanent display areas (including the former museum and store buildings above the North Necropolis) could be made ready. The arrangement is therefore somewhat unusual, in gathering together a huge amount of material in a single roofed basilical space. The piers of the 'nave' have been used to divide the space into a succession of themed zones, moving in an anticlockwise direction from the entrance. Some, but not all, of the objects are accompanied by informative labels in three languages; but since these are not rigidly attached to the objects, they do sometimes become transposed and they must therefore be read with care! The numbering of the zones, and of the objects within each (as seen in 2010), is shown in figure 164 and is my own. I have supplied provenances and dates for the objects where I have been able to discover them.

Zone 1: objects in foreign collections, recent finds

The current display opens with casts of sculptures removed from Libya by foreign excavators. From R to L, these are as follows.

1. (On the wall) Cast of a relief showing the nymph Kurana strangling a lion. From the excavations of Smith and Porcher in the Temple of Aphrodite on the acropolis ridge (12) and now in the British Museum (fig. 113); c. AD 120–140.

2. Cast of a statuette of the nymph Kurana strangling a lion. From the excavations of Smith and Porcher in the Temple of Apollo (77) and now in the British Museum; probably AD 120–150.

3. Triumph! This is the Venus of Cyrene (fig. 165), first exposed by winter rains in December 1913 in the Italian military supply depot on the terrace of the Sanctuary of Apollo and very soon thereafter transported to Italy. She has spent many years as a prize exhibit in the Museo Nazionale Romano and was initially represented here by a cast. She was returned by the Italian government in 2008 and has at last taken her place in the Museum of Cyrene. This is a standing (rather than crouching) version of Aphrodite *Anadyomene* (rising from the waves), with her arms lifted away from the body in order to wring out her wet hair. The statue is considered to be a fine copy made in the second century BC of a lost original of the fourth century.

4. Cast of a small female figure found in the Temple of Eluet Gassan (109) and now in the British Museum.

5. (On pier) Cast of the head of a Hellenistic ruler, perhaps Ptolemy Apion. From the excavations of Smith and Porcher in the Temple of Apollo (77) and now in the British Museum; first century BC.

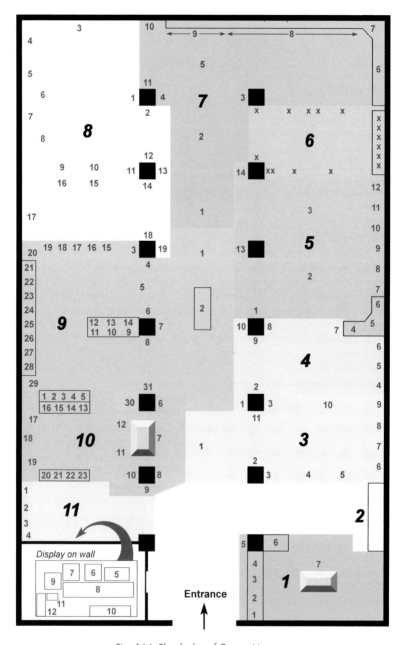

Fig. 164. Sketch-plan of Cyrene Museum.

6. Standing female figure about 1 m high, with traces of paint on headdress. Said to be a figure of Libya, found on the acropolis.

7. Attic sarcophagus with lid, from the Tomb of the Sarcophagi at Ain Hofra (p. 253). The scene on the front is Dionysiac, with the god Dionysos (with lionskin and attendant panther) accompanied by a flute-playing satyr, two dancing maenads and a lion. On the right-hand end are a satyr and a silenus; on the left-hand end is the sphinx and on the rear side are two gryphons, heraldically opposed; late second century AD.

Note how the surviving male head on the lid is only roughed out. These sarcophagi were fully carved at the quarry, but the masons there could not know the appearance of the individual by whom the work had been commissioned. It would therefore be necessary for the owner (or his heirs) to arrange for the head to be finished on arrival at destination. It is possible either that there was no sculptor locally who could do the work – or that the heirs, who had seen a good part of their inheritance swallowed up on the expensive tomb and sarcophagus, were not prepared to spend any more!

Zone 2: indigenous sculpture

A single glass case displays examples of what may be termed indigenous Libyan sculpture. While many other pieces on display show signs of local origin or of African influence within the broad environment of 'classical' style, these objects appear to be more distant from that world, and to give a stronger indication of underlying rural beliefs and practices. The items on display include a primitive statuette of a female divinity (the Libyan Demeter?) and a small limestone altar, both found in a rural sanctuary at

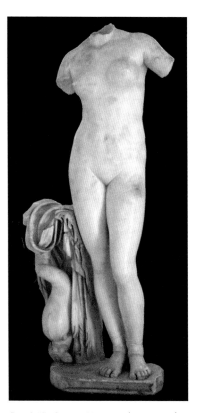

Fig. 165. Cyrene Museum: the Venus of Cyrene.

Martubah (SE of Darnah), which was unfortunately destroyed at the time of discovery (in the 1960s). There is also a fragmentary sculpture in Pentelic marble (i.e. an imported stone) of a ram carried on the head of a two-faced figure. The heads represent Libya on one side and Zeus Ammon on the other. Another piece is a (two-sided) Janus-head of Zeus Ammon. This deity will appear again repeatedly in zone 7 (below).

Zone 3: sculpture of the archaic period

1. Sphinx in Parian marble (fig. 166). This very fine piece, representing the Sphinx on top of an early form of Ionic

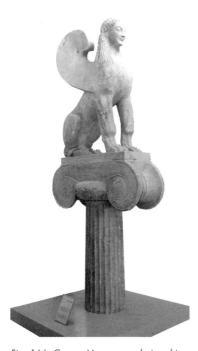

Fig. 166. Cyrene Museum: archaic sphinx.

with the possibility that the two together should be understood as Leto and her daughter Artemis. From the Sanctuary of Apollo, late sixth century BC.

6. Trunk of *kouros*. Findspot not recorded, c. 550 BC.

7. Trunk of *kouros*. Found near the Altar of Artemis (74), c. 540 BC.

8. Trunk of *kouros*. From the Sanctuary of Apollo, c. 540 BC.

9. Gorgon *akroterion* from the Temple of Apollo Pythios (77), re-used in the Byzantine period in the former Fountain of Philothales (94). The face has been mutilated by the piercing of the mouth to form a fountain-head, but note the drill-holes in the hair and around the face, which must once have anchored attached serpents in metal. End of sixth century BC.

10. Over life-size *kouros* (headless). From the same deposit as item 1, third quarter of sixth century BC.

11. *Kore* (headless). From the same deposit as item 1, c. 560–550 BC.

Zone 4: inscriptions

The site of Cyrene has yielded many hundreds of inscriptions, and many of these are still visible amongst the ruins. Others have been collected into the museum stores. A very small selection is on display here, either for their historical interest of because of the handsome quality of the lettering.

1. Square stele inscribed on the front with a list of gifts of corn from Cyrene to Greek cities during a famine in the third quarter of the fourth century BC. On two other faces are texts of a sacred law from the end of the fourth century BC. Found re-used in the *frigidarium* of the Byzantine Baths in the Sanctuary of Apollo (66).

2. Ephebic inscription listing *epheboi* and officials in AD 172–5. Found reused in the agora.

column, was probably originally a votive monument in a religious sanctuary. It was found to the E of the city, on the edge of New Shahhat, in fragments and buried in a pit, together with several other contemporary pieces of sculpture (see below, items 2, 9 and 10). It has been inferred that there was a temple nearby which had been desecrated by the Persian army during the events of 515 BC and that the broken *spolia* were subsequently buried here by the Cyreneans. C. 560–550 BC.

2. Life-size *kore* (headless). From the same deposit as item 1, 560–550 BC.

3. Trunk of small *kore*. From the Enclosed Sanctuary of Demeter and Kore (116), 560–540 BC.

4, 5. Two *korai*, forming a symmetrical pair: the first is thought to represent an older and the second a younger person,

3. A list of commanders of the army of Cyrene; the list extends onto the base beneath the stele. Found in the *pronaos* of the Temple of Zeus in the NE Quarter (106), c. 340–335 BC.

4. Large stele containing 142 lines of text in Greek. Four edicts of the Emperor Augustus promulgated in 7/6 BC and a fifth promulgated by the Roman Senate in 4 BC. These constitute revisions of judicial provisions in the province and other matters of empire-wide significance. They are important historical documents. Found reused in a late house in the agora.

5. Limestone inscription of the emperor Claudius Gothicus, recording his victory over the Marmaridae and his refoundation of the city (Cyrene) as *Claudiopolis*. Found on the 'western hill', i.e. somewhere on the acropolis ridge, c. AD 268.

6. Stele recording an edict (*diagramma*) of Ptolemy I in 321 BC establishing a new constitution for Cyrene. Found reused as a step in the *frigidarium* of the Byzantine Baths (66), which is responsible for the abrasion of parts of the inscribed surface.

7. Stele inscribed with a document of the fourth century BC which reasserts the rights at Cyrene of citizens of Thera, whence the original colonists had come. It incorporates the supposed text of the original decree of the seventh century BC under which the colonists had set out.

8. Tomb-stele commemorating a certain Paresia, daughter of Hephaistous and wife of Agathangelos, who died at the age of 'more than sixty' after enjoying various benefits in life. The first four lines of the text divided by a vertical palm frond, and there is a carved wreath at the bottom of the stone. This stele is a pair to a similar inscription in the courtyard in front of the museum entrance (immediately to the R of the door, between two headless female statues), which records another Paresia who was daughter of Hephaistous and Akrisios and who died at the age of four without ever having enjoyed the same benefits. The second daughter was presumably given the same name. Both stelai were found in the same tomb, and belong approximately to the second century AD.

9. Huge list, carved on a split column, of subscribers, with sums subscribed. From 'Cyrene', end of 4th century BC.

10. On a handsome stele with a pediment at the top, the will of Ptolemy VIII, made in 155 BC and under which he bequeathed his kingdom to the Roman people, should he die without a successor. This bequest took effect only when repeated on the death of his son, Ptolemy Apion, in 96 BC. Found lying face-down in the 'Agora of the Gods' (98).

Zone 5: Greek classical sculpture
There is inevitably some confusion between this zone and Zone 9 containing similar Roman sculpture, since most mythological pieces of Roman date are thought to have been based on Greek or Hellenistic originals. Thus, while displayed in this zone, item 13 is actually identified as a Roman copy of an earlier work.

1. Relief with carvings of a reclining banqueter on one side and of a gathering of medical divinities on the other. This was originally part of something larger (perhaps an altar finial) of c. 460 BC, cut down and reused with a laudatory dedication to Pausanias, a priest of Apollo, in the second century AD. From the Sanctuary of Apollo.

2. A copy of the of 'Perinthos Athlete', found near the House of Jason Magnus (17). Contemporary (?) copy of a Greek statue of the mid fifth century BC.

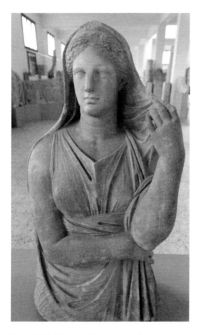

*Fig. 167. Cyrene Museum: veiled
Goddess of Death (early first century BC).
(Photo by courtesy of Steven Sklifas.)*

3. Torso of Boreas (with raised arm). Found in the NE quarter, second half of fifth century BC.

4. Limestone end-panel from the Altar of Artemis (74) depicting the Slaughter of the Niobids (p. 199). End of fifth century BC.

5. Archaic tombstone in local sandstone, with a warrior in a chain-mail helmet carrying a spear. From the E Necropolis, end of sixth century BC.

6. Tombstone of a warrior. Found in the area of the Temple of Zeus in the agora (25), late fifth or early fourth century BC.

7. Torso of another Perinthos athlete (compare item 2; headless). Findspot unrecorded.

8. Pair of sandstone funerary reliefs representing the myth of Admetos and Alcestis (Alcestis on the left-hand block

being conducted out of Hades by Herakles; the elderly Admetos on the other block in the presence of Hermes or Apollo). From the E Necropolis, late fifth century BC.

9. Small draped female figure: Kore/Persephone. Findspot unrecorded, second half of fourth century BC.

10. Head of Athena. Found in the agora area by the Americans in 1911, fourth century BC.

11. Headless draped female: Demeter. Findspot unrecorded, fourth century BC.

12. Small headless draped female: Demeter. No provenance or date.

13. Statue in Pentelic marble of Eros stringing his bow. From the Baths of Trajan (75), a Roman copy of a bronze by Lysippos of the fourth century BC.

14. Headless and armless statue of a charioteer (probably funerary). Findspot unrecorded.

Zone 6: funerary goddesses
This zone is dedicated to the peculiarly Cyrenaican form of funerary commemoration represented by the upper half of a draped female figure. (See fig. 167.) These figures occur in abundance at Cyrene, and have also been found at Barka and Ptolemais. (Compare the examples in the Ptolemais museum, p. 102 f.) The earliest examples, of the Archaic period, are faceless busts with a *polos* (a kind of pill-box hat). Subsequently, more of the upper part of the figure is represented and the *polos* is replaced by a veil. In the latest (Hellenistic and early Roman) figures, the facial details may be fully represented, though in one disconcerting figure on display against the outer wall, the features are masked but not hidden by a veil drawn across the face.

The display is arranged in an approximately chronological sequence running anticlockwise, with the earliest pieces against the pier on the R of this zone. These figures stood as markers on top of the graves or sarcophagi. They do not correspond to the practice of any other part of the Greek world. They are presumed to represent a divinity of some kind, though even that is speculation; they are generally referred to as the anonymous 'Goddess of Death'.

Zone 7: Hellenistic sculpture
This zone may be said to begin in the central nave; it is a somewhat diverse collection of different objects.
1.   Roman copy of a Hellenistic statue of Apollo, over life-size and remodelled from a statue of Asklepios (the original dedication survives on the back!). Pentelic marble, from the Baths of Trajan.
2.   Four-sided marble statue-base with charioteers on all four sides. The flat surfaces are covered with graffiti in Greek which appear to be ephebic: those which are legible consist of names and dates, one of which is possibly 19/18 BC. The original carved base must be substantially earlier. Found between the agora and the acropolis, and presumably

associated originally with a gymnasium.
3.   Statue of Zeus with the aegis over his shoulder and with an eagle at his feet. From the Temple of Zeus in the agora (25), first century BC copy of an earlier original?
4.   Over life-size statue of Alexander the Great (originally wearing an Attic helmet, presumably in bronze). From the Baths of Trajan (75), late Hellenistic.
5.   Seated figure of Demeter with head and body in different materials and possibly by different artists. Findspot unrecorded, Hellenistic body and Hadrianic head?
6.   Two panels of a Pentelic marble relief, showing Aphrodite and Eros with attendants. Found in the agora and thought to represent Berenice (wife of Ptolemy III) as Aphrodite, Hellenistic. Two of the heads have been damaged recently.
7.   Small seated figure of Apollo playing the lyre. Composed from an early Roman torso in Pentelic marble, conjoined to draped legs in a grey marble, thought to be of the second century AD. The head, which was also in the grey marble, has been missing since the

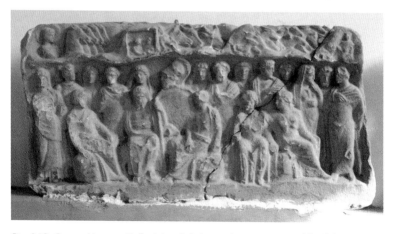

Fig. 168. Cyrene Museum: Hellenistic relief plaque showing an assembly of divinities.

Second World War. This statue served as the cult image in the shrine built over the Fountain of Philothales (94) after AD 365. (It is not clear why this is displayed in this zone.)

8. The end wall is filled with numerous examples of carved reliefs. These portray assemblies of divinities and are typical of rural sanctuaries in the Cyrene area. The reliefs are all very similar in character, generally constituting plaques in which the length is equal to twice the height. The compositions vary in detail, but a description of that illustrated in figure 168 (fourth from the R) will suffice to explain their general character. The principal scene appears to be located in a cave, above which the surrounding landscape is indicated, with the Sun rising in his chariot at dawn (on the L). Other animals or figures in the landscape appear to be still asleep, including a couple in a hut (?) and (at the R) a shepherd in a cave. In the foreground of the principal scene is Zeus Ammon, with ram's horns, seated upon a ram. He is facing towards two seated male figures (to the L); the outer, beardless figure, may be Apollo, seated on the omphalos which marks the centre of the world. On the other side of Zeus Ammon are two seated women, an older and a younger, interpreted as Demeter and Kore. The seated assembly is attending by a further fourteen standing figures, male and female and including a warrior with helmet and shield. The women typically wear a heavy, flattish cape over their shoulders, which seems to be a regional form of dress. None of these reliefs has hitherto been found in a secure archaeological context, but they are attributed with confidence to rural sanctuaries such as those at Ain Hofra (p. 252) and Budaraj (p. 250) and represent a fusion of Libyan and Hellenic

religious beliefs. They appear to range in date between the second century BC and the early Roman period.

9. Gathered to the left of the preceding are five fragmentary reliefs portraying horsemen and charioteers. That on the left-hand end was found in the agora.

10. Headless charioteer (?) standing on an unrelated base. The base is carved in low relief with a charioteer on the front face and a man leading horse on the narrow L side; the R side is plain. Later additions (on all four sides) are names and dates inscribed randomly in Greek; there is also (in larger letters on the principal face) a dedication to Hermes and Herakles. These are ephebic inscriptions and the block is clearly related to the gymnasium. The dates in the graffiti range between 12 BC and AD 29, though as in the case of item 7.2, the block itself must be several centuries older. Found in the House of Hesychios (20), reused in the fountain in the courtyard.

11. Altar-finial showing two apparently unconnected scenes. Aphrodite is seated in the centre, addressed on the L by Eros, who offers her a dove, and Hermes who observes. On the R, a poet with a scroll in his hand is instructed by a youthful (and rather smaller) muse. From the agora, second century BC.

Zone 8: Roman historical portraiture
1. Above: bust of Antoninus Pius(?). From the North Stoa in the agora (35). Below: head of Faustina the Elder. From the Twin Temples in front of the House of Jason Magnus (16), Antonine.
2. Portrait of a man. Found in front of the Temple of Apollo Pythios (77), Severan?
3. Female figure, fitted with a head that is too small and does not belong. From Balagrae; the head is considered Hadrianic.

4.   Headless figure wearing a toga. From the Caesareum (2), found with next, Flavian?

5.   Woman (priestess?). From the Caesareum, Flavian.

The next three statues, grouped together, were found in the Temple of Commodus in the Central Quarter (48), but are thought originally to have stood in the apse of the basilica in the Caesareum (2).

6.   Trajan.

7.   Head only of Hadrian.

8.   Vibia Sabina, the wife of Hadrian.

9.   Priestess of Isis (identifiable by reason of the 'Isiac knot' of the mantle in the centre of the chest). From the Temple of Isis in the Sanctuary of Apollo (93), Antonine?

10.   Priestess of Isis (headless). From the Temple of Isis on the Acropolis (44), Antonine?

11.   Bust of Marcus Aurelius. From the Temple of Demeter in the Agora (32).

12.   Late statue with the head of Marcus Aurelius on a female figure. Found in the Augusteum (34).

13.   Unidentified male figure.

14.   Portrait of a man. From the Sanctuary of Apollo, below the 'Grotto of the Priests' (92); Severan?

15.   Elderly priestess. From Balagrae, near the zawiya (p. 116), Hadrianic?

16.   Elderly priest. Found between the agora and the Caesareum, AD 270–80.

17.   Grave-stele of an athlete, Antonianos the Fool, of Ephesos. He holds a victor's palm and, above his head, possibly a jumping-weight such as are stacked beside him. From the North Necropolis, second quarter of third century AD.

18.   Bust of a priest. Found near the House of Jason Magnus (17), Antonine.

19.   Bust of Demosthenes. Found in the valley below the agora, Roman copy of an original of 280 BC.

Zone 9: Roman portrayals of divinities
Roman images of the Greek gods were often close copies of earlier originals. However, the uses of monumental statuary were becoming more varied, and statues of the most familiar deities served no less often as ornaments in public baths, than as objects of veneration in temples.

1.   Life-size marble head of Zeus, with painted details; reconstructed from over a hundred fragments. From the Temple of Zeus in the NE Quarter (106: p. 223); Hadrianic?

2.   Case containing various fingers, toes and a knee in marble of the colossal statue of Zeus, eight times life-size, which was installed in his temple in the NE Quarter (106) after the Jewish Revolt of AD 115. Other fragments remain on the site (p. 223). End of second century AD.

3.   Small statue of Aphrodite *Anadyomene* (rising from the waves). Findspot not recorded, Antonine.

4.   Aphrodite with triton and dolphin. From the slope to the NE of the agora, Roman.

5.   Three Graces. From the Baths of Trajan (75; another set is in the National Museum in Tripoli), Hadrianic?

6.   Small Aphrodite *Anadyomene*. Findspot unrecorded, probably Antonine.

7.   Large Knidian Aphrodite. From the Baths of Trajan (75), early Roman copy of a masterpiece of the fourth century BC by the Greek sculptor Praxiteles.

8.   An over life-size Hermes (identifiable by reason of the purse in his right hand). From the Baths of Trajan.

9–11.   Three statues of Asklepios, god of healing. Item 11 was found in the agora, and is attributed to the third century AD.

12–14.   Three figures of Hygeia (goddess of health, regularly associated with Asklepios): 12, findspot unrecorded,

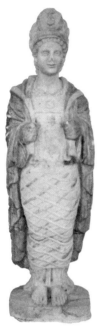

Fig. 169. Cyrene Museum: painted Roman statuette of Isis.

Roman; 13, from the Baths of Trajan, fourth century AD; 14, from the Agora, Roman.

15. Headless female figure: Athena, with the aegis reduced to a kind of scaly sash. From the Baths of Trajan (75), first century AD?

16. Helmeted head of Athena.

17. Sandstone three-way bust of Hekate, goddess of the crossroads, from her temple in the Sanctuary of Apollo (81). Note the red-painted flesh areas. The temple post-dates AD 107, but the sculpture looks as if it should be Hellenistic.

18. Kore/Persephone with double torch, marble head on limestone body. Recorded as 'from a well by Temple C' (where?), first century BC.

19. Dionysos. From the Sanctuary of Apollo, near the Temple of Isis (93), Antonine?

20. Female figure.

21. Headless figure of Artemis, over life-size. From the Sanctuary of Apollo, near the Temple of Hades (71), Hellenistic?

22. Hermes. Findspot unrecorded, early Roman?

23. Hermes. From the former Italian Ridotta Foligno in the NE Quarter.

24. Fragmentary figure of Dioscurus. From the Sanctuary of Apollo, Hadrianic–Antonine.

25. Dionysos. From the Sanctuary of Apollo.

26. Winged Nike. From the Sanctuary of Asklepios at Balagrae (p. 116), Roman, probably a copy of a work of the fifth century BC.

27. Painted statuette of Isis (fig. 169), from her sanctuary on the Acropolis (44: p. 184). Of Roman date, and surely repainted on numerous occasions, this shows a fascinating blend of Hellenistic naturalism with oriental or Egyptian stylization.

28. Statuette of Artemis, a copy of the 'Rospigliosi' type. From her temple in the Sanctuary of Apollo (79), Antonine?

29. Colossal figure of Herakles. From the House of Jason Magnus (17), Roman.

30. Knidian Aphrodite (see item 7 in this zone). From the Baths of Trajan (75), first century AD?

31. Over life-size statue of Dionysos, with panther. From the Sanctuary of Apollo, reconstructed from fragments; a Roman copy of a work of the fourth century BC by Timotheos.

Zone 10: other Roman ornamental sculpture
Plinth with five figures of small children:

1. Standing girl with jug.

2. Seated baby boy with a pigeon. From Balagrae 'near the zawiya', Antonine.

3. Sleeping Eros, lying on a lionskin. From the former Italian Ridotta Foligno in the NE Quarter.

4. Seated baby boy holding a ball and a tortoise. From Balagrae 'near the zawiya', Trajanic.

5. Support or table-leg decorated with two wrestling children (fig. 170); behind them on the pillar are strigils and a conch, symbolizing the gymnasium. Findspot unrecorded.

6. Satyr holding the infant Dionysos on his left arm, accompanied by a panther. From the Baths of Trajan (75), Antonine?

7. Attic sarcophagus with lid. The front portrays the legendary battle between the Lapiths and the Centaurs; scenes of Dionysiac revelry, involving satyrs, maenads and grape vines adorn both ends and the rear. On the lid is a reclining couple (the deceased) with very obviously unfinished heads, as on the other sarcophagus on display (zone 1, item 7). From the South Necropolis, second century AD.

8. Herm: a Roman copy of the *Hermes Propylaios* carved by Alcamenes for Athens in the fifth century BC. From the Temple of Hermes next to House of Jason Magnus (19).

9. Beardless herm: young Hermes? (Note the genitals: despite the feminine features, this is not a female!) From the Temple of Hermes, as the preceding.

10. Young satyr clothed in a pigskin. From the Baths of Trajan (75). The charming head was absent in November 2010, but hopefully is not missing

11. Table-leg carved with the figure of Marsyas, a foolish mortal, who challenged Apollo to a musical contest. His punishment was to be strung up (as shown here) and flayed alive! From near the Caesareum (2), second half of second century AD.

12. Table-leg decorated with a figure of Dionysos, accompanied by a panther. Note the traces of paint. Allegedly from the Sanctuary of Apollo.

13–16. Set of four Muses, part of the decoration of the stage-building in Theatre 2 (15), together with two further muses (Calliope and Thalia, of whom only the inscribed bases survive) and Apollo: from R to L Erato, muse of Lyric Poetry, with cithara (inscribed Melpomene); Terpsichore, muse of Choral Dance, with lyre (missing: inscribed Clio); Polyhymnia, muse of Sacred Poetry (correctly inscribed); Melpomene, muse of Tragedy, holding a tragic mask (inscribed Euterpe). The naming errors are original! Second century AD.

17. Ganymede with eagle. From Theatre 2 (15); second century AD.

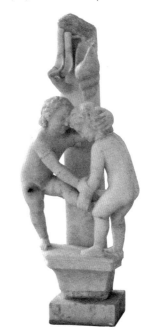

Fig. 170. Cyrene Museum: marble support or table-leg decorated with two wrestling children.

18. An unfinished frieze of divinities (L to R: Zeus, Hera, Apollo, Artemis, Aristaeus, Hygeia). From the agora.

19. Small group of Leda and the Swan as a table-leg. From the Valley Street.

20. Pan. From near the Caesareum (2).

21. Dancing maenad (headless). From the Baths of Trajan (75), Antonine?

22. Isis holding a baby. From her shrine near the Temple of Apollo (93).

23. Small headless female. From the Baths of Trajan (75), Hadrianic.

Zone 11: mosaics; late Roman and early Islamic objects

1. Very fragmentary *emblema* of the Three Graces.

2. Mosaic of Nereid and Triton (fig. 171). From the atrium of the House of Jason Magnus (17), late second or third century AD.

3. Mosaic of Theseus and the Minotaur. From the centre of the Labyrinth Mosaic in room (f) of the House of Jason Magnus (17), late second or third century AD.

4. Christian reliquary chest. From Qasr Stabulus, near the village of Omar Mukhtar, Byzantine.

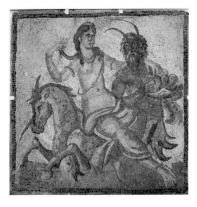

Fig. 171. Cyrene Museum: mosaic depicting a Nereid riding on a hippocamp, accompanied by a Triton, from the House of Jason Magnus.

5. Mosaic of Dionysos with his retinue and the sleeping Ariadne. From the House of the Dionysos Mosaic (45), second half of third or early fourth century AD.

6. Mosaic portraying a bearded head in a rhombus. From the House of the Doric Peristyle (5), third century AD?

7. Mosaic portraying Medusa head. From the Temple of Athena next to the *Archeion* in the Agora (23), mid-second to third century AD.

8. Part of border mosaic with hunting scene. From the nave of the Central Church (54), Justinianic.

9. Fragment of diamond pattern in black-and-white pebble mosaic. Said to be from Benghazi (Euesperides?), Hellenistic.

10. Limestone block with an Arabic inscription bordered by zig-zag or diamond ornament. Found in or near the East Church at Lamludah (p. 298).

11, 12. Two early Arabic tombstones from Targhunia (p. 140).

OUTER ENVIRONS OF CYRENE
Sanctuary of Budaraj ★

Besides the features previously described, there is to the S of the city, deeply hidden, an interesting rural sanctuary. It is hidden away on the precipitous upper slopes of the Wadi Bu Nabih. The visit is very rewarding, but **DO NOT ATTEMPT IT if you are not sure of foot or if you are nervous of heights!** In order to find it, follow the ancient road to Balagrae and turn R (asphalt road) about 400 m SW of the *propylaeum* of the Sanctuary of Demeter. Follow this road for just over 1 km until it turns a right-angle to the R at N 32° 48.60′ E 21° 50.67′. At this point, leave the asphalt road and continue straight on, taking the right

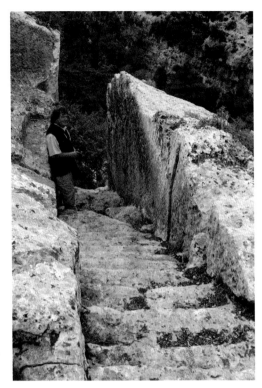

Fig. 172. Cyrene: rock-cut stair leading to the sanctuary of Budaraj.

fork immediately beyond, where the track divides; continue for about 400 m until the track divides again. If you are in a vehicle, park it here on the R, where there is a farmhouse and three monumental tombs. From here, walk on downwards and round to the R, keeping to the track on the flank of the Wadi Bu Nabih. The track winds down to a lower level; where it straightens out and passes to the R of a small re-entrant, leave it and find your way round towards the L. At a distance of about 100 m (at N 32° 48.80' E 21° 50.30') you should find a broad slab of bare rock, below which is the head of a rock-cut path which heads downwards and round to the L. (If you fail to find this easily, go back to the track and walk on: the path is clearly visible from further along the track.) Follow this path for a total distance of 120 m. About half-way down, it may appear to come to an end, but keep going in the same direction and you will find it again, finally descending in a beautifully rock-cut staircase (fig. 172) to the caves described below. The steps turn sharply to the R at the bottom. NOTE: the path down to the sanctuary is firm under foot, but is exposed (particularly at the bottom) above a perilous drop! The sanctuary is located at N 32° 48.79' E 21° 50.22'.

This is, like the Fountain of Apollo in the centre of Cyrene and the sanctuary of Ain Hofra to the E (p. 252), clearly a religious site associated with springs of water. In this instance, the tiny sanctuary occupies a concealed space cut out of the rock, high on the side of a ravine. On the hillside above is a collection tank for water, both run-off from the surface and from a spring, whence the water is channelled into a basin in a rock-cut chamber below. The principal chamber is more or less rectangular in plan, with chiselled walls and a flat roof. It is fronted by a narrow terrace, and this is reached by the fine rock-cut staircase which leads down from above. There are many graffiti carved into the walls, one of which tells us that the grotto was dedicated 'to the Goddesses.' The style of the graffiti is said to range in date from the fourth century BC to the Roman imperial period. The grotto was lined with benches, and a plinth (altar?) stands opposite the entrance; in the walls above are numerous niches of different sizes, presumably for lamps and for votive offerings. (Some of these would be well-suited to receive relief plaques of the kind now displayed in the Cyrene Museum: p. 246.) Amongst the graffiti have been recorded simple carvings of a plough (: no longer visible), an indication of the association of the cult with agriculture. (Note similar carvings near the theatre in the Southern Extra-Mural Sacred Zone, p. 231, and in the Wadi as-Sanab, p. 141.)

To the R of the main chamber, which goes back to perhaps the fourth century BC, is another cavern of similar form, with benches along either side, and a podium with a niche behind it at the inner end. This is clearly a later addition, since it is barely accessible by means of a narrow ledge which passes round the staircase. It shows signs of secondary modification within (the benches show signs of having been cut back) and it has been suggested that it was perhaps at first a *heröon* (shrine to a hero) dedicated to the veneration of Kotys son of Aristoklidas, whose name is carved in handsome letters on the front of the podium. The lettering is considered to be late Hellenistic. Subsequently, the *heröon* seems to have been adapted as a sanctuary similar to its neighbour. Here too there are graffiti cut into the walls, one of which records an offering 'to the Gods' by a certain Tiberius Claudius Istrus, who was a priest of Apollo in the second century AD.

As you stand outside, facing the entrance to the main chamber, there is to the L a smaller room of uncertain purpose,

which intersects it. Yet further to the L and not accessible from here is another cave; this is reached by its own stepped pathway. Internally, it shows no obvious signs of cult use, but it does contain remains of a pressing installation (for oil?). There are also tethering-rings cut in the ceiling. It is difficult to imagine the state of insecurity which would drive someone, not only to live here, but to bring down here their animals and their produce!

Ain Hofra ★

Ain Hofra is a sanctuary to the E of Cyrene, in the cleft followed by the new road down to the middle plateau, which passes to the E of the Temple of Zeus. It is built around a water source, like the Fountain of Apollo. In order to find it, leave the ancient city in the direction of new Shahhat and turn L opposite the Wahda Bank at N 32° 48.72' E 21° 52.03'. Follow this street to the edge of the village, and continue to follow it as it veers L. After a total of 950 m from the intersection, turn L off the asphalt road onto a track and then R in front of a farm after another 70 m. The track is unmade, but negotiable in a saloon car. From this point, follow it for a further 800 m; fork L where the track divides and after a further 100 m you will arrive at the most recent excavations, with a fine view towards the sea (at N 32° 49.55' E 21° 52.46'). The road brings you to the head of a precipitous ravine in the edge of the upper jabal plateau: the water emerges from beneath the cliff at your feet. Before descending – which is an awkward scramble whichever way you do it – the recent excavations by the University of Chieti above the cliff are worthy of attention.

First on the L is the monumental **Tomb of the Sculptures**, a lavish construction of the late second or early third century AD. The tomb is entered through a tetrastyle porch of huge Doric columns with plain shafts and Ionic bases. This leads through a triple doorway between massive square piers to a rectangular central chamber. Beyond this an inner chamber (seen through an axial window, but accessed only by means of a vestibule at one side) housed a vast Attic sarcophagus with an Amazonomachy scene (the mythical battle between the Greeks and Amazons). In the same chamber were found one female and two male life-size portrait statues and a small Attic sarcophagus with a portrayal on the lid of a child holding a dove. There was also a decorated marble cinerary urn. In the central chamber were found fragments of a Thasian marble sarcophagus. The excavations showed that the tomb had been damaged in the earthquake of AD 262; after this, it was adapted to house animals. In the earthquake of 365 the roof fell in, killing two adults, a child and several cows. (The date is assured by the presence of three coins of 364.)

Next to the Tomb of the Sculptures is the smaller **Tomb of the Sarcophagi**, composed of just two chambers. This was found to contain two sarcophagi, one Attic with dancing maenads (on display in the museum, p. 241, no. 1.7) and the other of Proconnesian marble, portraying the myth of Phaedra and Hippolytos. (See the example at Apollonia, p. 282.) The date is again considered to be late second century AD.

The sanctuary itself is characterised by terraces carved in the steep rock-face on the W side of the ravine, where the water emerges from beneath the cliff and is conducted away in two rock-cut channels. Here are carved over a hundred niches, singly or in groups of two or three, often with dedications in Greek to Zeus

Meilichios, to the Eumenides (Fates) or to heroes (now barely detectable). A small shelf below (frequently with two shallow recesses side by side) would presumably have served as an arula (miniature altar) for offerings. Various stepped paths lead down from the high ground above, past a rock-cut portico fronted by two rectangular piers with Aeolic capitals which must belong to the sixth century BC. The absence of an inner room makes it unclear whether this was a tomb that was never finished, or whether it served some other purpose. Further round to the L is a natural cave which is subdivided internally by rough stone walls: this is currently in course of excavation. The lettering of the inscriptions around the area shows that the sanctuary goes back at least to the fifth century BC. The cult is known from elsewhere (particularly, a large sanctuary at Selinous in Sicily); it is associated with purification and with the propitiation of the threatening power of the Underworld.

The road to Apollonia

The road to Apollonia shows traces of ancient settlement at many points, just two of which are described below. Until the advent of the Italians in the 20th century, its course followed mostly that established in antiquity. In the colonial period they devised a new descent from the lower plateau to the coastal plain (to the W of the earlier and steeper course); when the road was further upgraded in the 1980s, the city of Cyrene and a large part of the North Necropolis was spared (at a late stage of planning) by cutting a new route from the upper plateau to the middle level next to the ravine of Ain Hofra. The new road rejoins the old at a hairpin bend which, bizarrely, encloses a children's playground.

Qasr Shtillu

The road levels out where the school of Sambar stands on the N side of it. Just on the other side of the valley, one can clearly see the remains of a rectangular tower-tomb of Hellenistic date, around which a farm has been built in the late Roman period. Take the good gravel track which leaves the road on the E side of the school (at N 32° 50.24' E 21° 52.44'), follow this for 1.2 km and fork R where the track divides, towards a group of farm buildings. Leave your vehicle in the farmyard and make yourself known as a courtesy if there is anyone about. The ancient buildings are about 150 m to the E, at N 32° 50.78' E 21° 52.39'. They are composed of a large rectangular enclosure in well-cut ashlar masonry, built around the taller remains of a square tower-tomb of the Hellenistic period. The basal moulding of the tower-tomb is clearly visible. Within are traces of a staircase; it is calculated that there were five storeys

in all. The entrance was in the E side of the tower, and a rock-cutting in front of this indicates that the tomb-chamber was excavated directly beneath the tower and entered from the same side. With regard to the larger enclosure, no internal details are apparent but it has the general character of Byzantine farm buildings in villages such as Mqayrnis (p. 303).

Slightly more than a kilometre further along the Apollonia road from the school at Sambar, there is a new enclosure with a fresh water tank on the L side of the road. Almost immediately opposite is an extended area of ancient quarries and tombs. The tombs mainly take the form of sarcophagi cut from the living rock and fitted with lids, but there is also a denuded circular tumulus burial containing a rectangular central chamber surrounded by a circle of orthostats. This resembles the tumuli in the vicinity of Massah (p. 124).

7 APOLLONIA ★ ★ ★

The earliest settlement here cannot have long post-dated the establishment of Cyrene. Along the inhospitable coastline, this site offered the closest secure anchorage to the city on the plateau above. Pottery of the seventh century BC has been found on the site. For many centuries, it seems to have been known simply as the port of Cyrene. The name *Apollonia*, in honour of the patron god of Cyrene, is first probably attested in a fragmentary inscription of 67 BC, but it has been plausibly argued that it received its name and attained its independence from the greater city in the second half of the second century BC (see the discussion of the defences, p. 258). Later on, its name became *Sozousa* ('Saviour', feminine, as of the Virgin Mary): this had happened by AD 359, and has persisted through the later centuries of abandonment, becoming Susah (سوسة) when a new settlement of Muslim refugees from Crete was founded immediately to the W of the ruins in 1896. After the Italian conquest, military installations (known as Ridotta Roma) were built on the western part of the ancient site, and probably made extensive use of ancient building materials. These installations were progressively removed during the 1950s, and all that remains now is the former military hospital. This is immediately above you on the R as you enter the site: it was renovated in the 1960s as the site museum and has since again been abandoned.

Apollonia shared the fortunes of Cyrene for much of its history, but rose in importance in the Byzantine period, as Cyrene declined. It should have shared in the disastrous experience of Cyrene in the earthquake of AD 365, but of this little trace has been detected. Presumably because of its access to the sea and its readily defensible circuit of Hellenistic walls – in contrast to the unmanageable defences of Ptolemais – Apollonia succeeded that city as capital of *Libya Superior/Pentapolis* around the middle of the fifth century AD (p. 9). Of three copies found in Cyrenaica of the Edict of Anastasius (at Taucheira, Ptolemais and Apollonia), determining military dispositions in the province at the beginning of the sixth century, only that found at Apollonia (now in the museum, p. 285) was on marble. This has been interpreted as evidence of the higher status of the city at the time.

When the Arabs came in 642, the Byzantine governor put up no detectable defence at Apollonia, but abandoned it and retreated with 'his troops and the rich men of the province' westwards to Taucheira. This in turn was the last settlement on Libyan soil to be ceded to the conquering forces in 645. As on the other major sites of classical antiquity, so too at Apollonia there is evidence of continued occupation on a very modest scale in the Arab period (particularly in the West Church, p. 262). But with the total cessation of seaborne trade, the city had lost its *raison d'être* and it must have been reduced fairly rapidly to an insignificant fishing village.

The lie of the land has changed very significantly at Apollonia, and much of the ancient site now lies beneath the surface of the sea (fig. 173). While the city must have been severely damaged in the great earthquake of AD 365, this was certainly not the occasion when it sank, for it would not otherwise have become capital of the province at a later date. The date at which this seismic movement took place has not been closely determined, but it was certainly later than the mid seventh century AD.

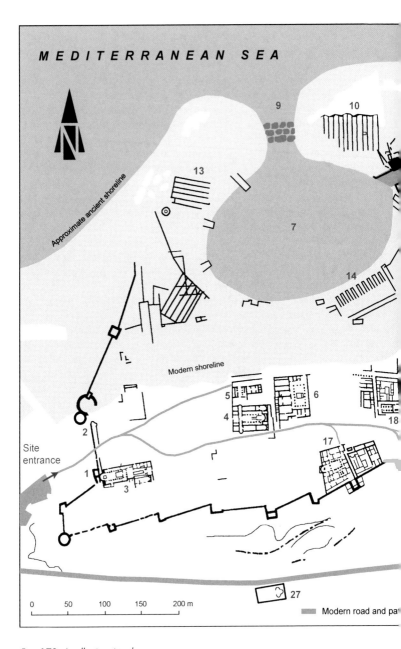

Fig. 173. Apollonia: site plan.

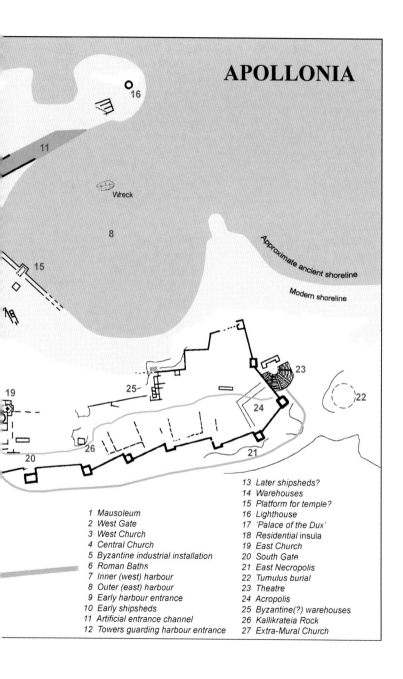

APOLLONIA

16

11

Wreck

8

Approximate ancient shoreline

Modern shoreline

15

23

19

25

24

22

26

20

21

1 Mausoleum
2 West Gate
3 West Church
4 Central Church
5 Byzantine industrial installation
6 Roman Baths
7 Inner (west) harbour
8 Outer (east) harbour
9 Early harbour entrance
10 Early shipsheds
11 Artificial entrance channel
12 Towers guarding harbour entrance

13 Later shipsheds?
14 Warehouses
15 Platform for temple?
16 Lighthouse
17 'Palace of the Dux'
18 Residential insula
19 East Church
20 South Gate
21 East Necropolis
22 Tumulus burial
23 Theatre
24 Acropolis
25 Byzantine(?) warehouses
26 Kallikrateia Rock
27 Extra-Mural Church

The site was visited and surveyed by the Beechey brothers in 1822, and the excavation and restoration of the East Church by Ettore Ghislanzoni took place almost exactly a hundred years later. Otherwise, archaeological explorations have been carried out there almost exclusively since 1955, by the Department of Antiquities (in the time of Richard Goodchild) and by French and American missions. Because of the prosperity of the city in the Byzantine period, when earlier buildings – redundant or ruinous – were extensively quarried for building materials, and because of the still limited extent of excavation (compared to Cyrene), the remains of its later monuments are very much better known than those which relate to its earlier history.

The numbering of monuments or features in the text which follows corresponds to that shown on the general plan in figure 173.

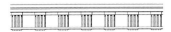

Coordinates: N 32° 54.06′, E 21° 57.90′
Directions: The co-ordinates are for the entrance to the site at the western end, next to the Manara Hotel.

Defences

The walls of Apollonia are well preserved above the present-day sea-level. They are essentially uniform in construction, and are now thought to have been built in the later second or early first century BC. It is also clear that a very major refurbishment was carried out in the Byzantine period, presumably following the earthquake of AD 365. The defences are distinguished by numerous projecting towers, of which twenty have been identified on the ground, at intervals of about 60 m. Many of these towers covered narrow postern gates adjacent to them, always on the W side. In the course of time, however, these gates were either widened into more significant thoroughfares or blocked up. It is notable that the masonry of the towers shows diagonal tooling on the faces of the blocks, whereas the blocks of the intervening stretches of wall are dressed smooth, with bevelled edges. The works were demonstrably contemporary, so this was perhaps done for purely aesthetic

reasons. The history of the South Gate (20) has been examined by the French team. Otherwise, the only major gate of the city of which there is any trace is the West Gate (2), on the foreshore to the L as you enter the site.

On the S side of the city, where the walls are built on the crest of the coastal ridge, their defensive value is enhanced by extensive quarrying of the bedrock on the southern slope. This quarrying (particularly apparent towards the E) must have been carried on through much of the city's history; it has created steep or vertical cliffs beneath the walls, convenient for the excavation of chamber-tombs. Some of these still serve as animal-pens. It was discovered in excavations made in 1965–67 that, wherever the defences were examined, they overlay burials of the sixth to fourth centuries BC. This shows that there was a flourishing, if smaller, settlement around the harbour long before any defences were built.

It is interesting that the over-all character of the defences of Apollonia is directed against attack by land, rather than by sea – in which direction the protection is considerably weaker. André Laronde has made a plausible case that Apollonia gained its independence from

Cyrene, acquired its own name and was fortified against possible attack *from that direction* in the time of Ptolemy Physcon. In 163 BC, he was granted rule of Cyrene alone while his brother, Ptolemy VI Philometor, acquired control of Egypt; Physcon persuaded the Roman Senate to support his claim against his elder brother to Cyprus. The Cyreneans took advantage of the dynastic squabble to make a bid for freedom, and revolted. The development of Apollonia, involving a new street layout, new defences and numerous other building projects, would have represented the promotion of a bastion which had remained loyal to Ptolemy in a territory of otherwise questionable allegiance.

Mausoleum (1)

As one approaches the site from the entrance, one is first presented with the western side of the city defences. The round tower of the West Gate (2) is prominent to the L on the sea shore, but the wall also stands high to the R of the path, and in an internal angle are remains of a square building, which was internally cruciform (see fig. 174). It was roofed with a central dome from which radiated four barrel-vaults, all supported on four internal piers. The ribs of the barrel-vaults are still in position. The chamber was entered through a doorway on the N side; in the opposite wall, partly cut out of the pre-existing city defences, was a round-headed recess or *arcosolium*. In front of this was found a broken Attic sarcophagus (now displayed in Room 1 of the museum, p. 282), which presumably once stood in the recess.

The building is certainly Byzantine or later in date. It is composed of reused blocks and the sarcophagus, of the second or third century AD, must have been plundered from an earlier tomb and

brought here. The sarcophagus was decorated with scenes in relief from Greek mythology, though it has been suggested that these were deliberately mutilated (as inappropriate?) when the sarcophagus was reused. The building was quite clearly a mausoleum, but how is it to be explained? If it belongs to the Christian period, it might perhaps have been the tomb of a martyr who was hurled from the wall to his (or her) death at this point; there are parallels for such tombs. Or does it even belong to the Islamic period? Architecturally, there would again be parallels. Sandro Stucchi suggested that the building was a *martyrion* associated with the West Church, immediately on the other side of the wall (3), and that it was reached by a late staircase which led up from the N aisle of the church (fig. 174: f), over the top of the wall and down again on the outside. This is not impossible, but the idea has not been warmly received by other scholars. There are no ancillary burials, such as usually cluster around the tomb of a holy man. It is perhaps more likely that this was the burial site of a prominent member of the Christian community, who wanted to be close to the West Church.

West Gate ★ (2)

This is a most unusual structure and, in its present state at the water's edge, very difficult to make sense of. On approaching from the W, the entrance was protected by a circular bastion on the seaward side. This was substantially refurbished in the Byzantine period and divided internally, at a high level, into small rooms; it yielded a small hoard of twenty coins, deposited immediately before the Arab conquest. On passing through the portal of the gate (blocked in the first half of the seventh century AD), there stood to the L a circular enclosure with a curving outer wall which formed part of the defences, but which is now largely destroyed by the sea. Against the inner face of the wall to the R are remains of several rooms constructed in the Byzantine period. The most northerly had two apses, each with a Maltese cross carved on the keystone (not now detectable), leading to the inference that the building served some religious purpose, perhaps as a *martyrion*. However, the presence of numerous arched recesses in the walls, like those interpreted as cupboards in the 'Palace of the Dux' (p. 271), would be consistent with a secular administrative rôle.

West Church ★ (3)

This complex was visible to the Beecheys in 1822, but was excavated by the Department of Antiquities only in 1958–9. The excavated area (figs. 174, 175) is most conveniently approached by a path (a) which leads to the street along its N side. About half-way along this, one steps down through an opening in a Roman wall which was cut through in the

Byzantine period and blocked up again after the Islamic conquest. In this way, one arrives at a broad flight of steps which marks the entrance to the narthex (b) of a westward-facing church, which nestles beneath the western defences of the city and indeed makes use of part of the city wall to support its apse. (The Hellenistic defensive wall is massively thickened on its inner face here, perhaps contemporaneously with the building of the church.) The narthex leads into a nave (c) and aisles, separated by re-used cipollino columns of various lengths (the shorter ones raised up on plinths), surmounted by arcades, of which numerous voussoir blocks are lying around. Some of the capitals above the columns are also re-used, but others are Byzantine and identical to those used in the Central Church (4). It is likely that there were clerestory windows above the arcades, but not a second storey. At the E end of each aisle was a corner-chapel or room, slightly deeper than the narthex in between and originally accessible only from the adjoining aisle.

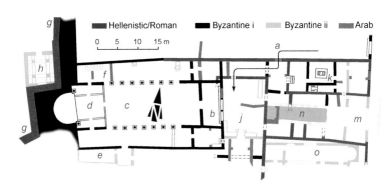

Fig. 174. Apollonia: plan of the West Church and adjacent mausoleum.

a	Pathway into site	f	Staircase	m	Antechamber
b	Narthex	g	City wall	n	Atrium with
c	Nave	h	Mausoleum		fish-tank
d	Chancel	j	Atrium/courtyard	o	Mosaic-paved
e	Sacristy?	k	Baptistery		hall

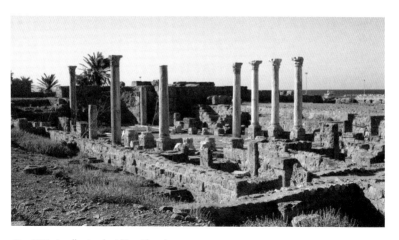

Fig. 175. Apollonia: the West Church.

The chancel (d) was set at the W end of the nave, in front of the apse. The footings for the enclosing screen are still in place. On the N and S sides, there were entrances corresponding to doorways in the walls which separated nave and aisles at this point; towards the nave itself, there is no surviving evidence for the usual screened passage. The chancel was handsomely paved with *opus sectile* or cut marble tiles. The central part of the pattern, with a cruciform design, has certainly been re-laid here from some other location in an earlier period; the diamond pattern around the edge is of lesser quality and was contrived to fill up the remaining space. The four bays of the nave immediately in front of the chancel were paved with marble slabs, and the remainder with mixed arrangements of tiles in local stone, as may be seen in several other Cyrenaican churches (e.g. at al-Athrun, p. 291). A sandstone block constituting the steps of an *ambon* was found displaced in the chancel: its original position is thought to have been in the nave.

The only subsequent modification, in the body of the church, which can be confidently ascribed to the Christian period is the addition of two rooms off the S aisle. The inner room of the pair (e) has a niche in the S wall and may have been a sacristy. In the N aisle is a flight of stairs (f) which ascends towards the city wall (g). It has been suggested that this was constructed in order to communicate with the (martyr's?) tomb on the other side of the wall (see above, p. 259), but neither its purpose nor its date can be determined with confidence. After the Islamic conquest, the nave of the church seems to have been deprived of its roof and to have become a dump for unwanted ecclesiastical fittings. The aisles, however, were subject to further modification (possibly including the addition of the staircase) and remained in use.

The structures to the E of the church were repeatedly altered and put to new uses over a long period of time, and are not now easily disentangled. The main outlines were established in the early imperial period, when this space may have been occupied by several adjoining properties. To the W of the buildings fronting the N–S street, there appears to have been a courtyard (j) with a surrounding corridor. When the church was built, this became an atrium, from which the narthex of the church (b) was entered through a broad opening, divided into three by columns. There was at this time no access to the street on the N, and the approach to the church must have been through the (unexplored) area to the S. Also when the church was first built, the northernmost range of rooms in what we may term the 'forecomplex' was adapted to accommodate a baptistery. This was approached not from the church, but by means of an opening into the street which now cut through the N wall of the Roman building at (a), and an outer and inner vestibule. The outer vestibule was paved with limestone and the inner one with mosaic; the baptistery itself (k), with a simple rectangular basin, shows traces of marble paving. In a little enclosure immediately to the S of the baptistery was inserted a water-tank, with a furnace beneath, in order to supply hot water to the basin; a connecting pipe runs down the wall. (Compare the similar arrangement in the East Church, p. 276).

At some date after the construction of the baptistery suite, but still within the Christian period, the space to the S was substantially remodelled in order to provide a grand axial approach to the church from the E. The floor level was raised by more than a metre and an antechamber (m) was created next to the easterly street-frontage, with steps and probably a porch projecting into the street. From this, one passed into an outer atrium which had lateral porticoes flanking a central water-feature (n). Amphorae set into its walls at certain points suggest that this was in fact a fish-tank. (Such recesses were provided for the fish to lay their eggs in.) Two breaches cut

through the earlier wall which had until then enclosed the inner atrium/courtyard (j) linked the new features to the church. Later again, a long narrow (audience?) hall (o) was constructed to the S of the new entrance; this had an apse at the E end and an antechamber at the W, and was paved with mosaic. This was clearly part of a more extensive complex which still remains to be excavated to the S of those structures now exposed. One may plausibly imagine an ecclesiastical residence.

The final phase of occupation identified in this area belongs to the Islamic period, and is a valuable sign of continuity, though it is at present impossible to say how long it lasted. The church clearly ceased to function for, as described above, the nave lost its roof and became a dump. However, other alterations attest continued interest in the area. Doorways were opened or blocked up, with the general effect of enclosing the area with a focus towards the S. Indeed, in the former atrium/courtyard (j) was installed a monumental entrance with a porch and flanking benches, which clearly led to a building of some importance outside the excavated area. Its purpose was surely official and, given its proximity to the city wall (and the staircase leading up to it, if this was added now), probably military. A further extension of the excavations here would surely yield valuable information about this little-known period.

What can be said about the dating of the ecclesiastical phases? Basically, that there is little agreement! They certainly represent an extended period of time, which may have begun before the accession of Justinian in 527 and certainly extended until the Arab invasion in 642. The mosaic in the baptistery

Fig. 176. Apollonia: plan of the Central Church. (a) Atrium; (b) Narthex; (c) Nave; (d) Martyrion? (e) Apsed hall.

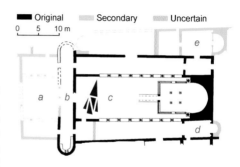

vestibule depicted a peacock and a partridge in the centre, with borders composed of vegetal elements and a procession of beasts. The style links it to the dated Justinianic series (e.g. at Qasr Libya, p. 133), though its quality is not so good. The fragments of mosaic in the apsed hall (o) are similar in style but clumsy; they are likely to be later.

Central Church ★ ★ (4)

This complex was initially excavated and restored in 1940, with further work taking place in the 1950s. The church (figs. 176, 177) is of typical 'sixth-century type', being externally rectangular, with corner-chapels flanking the apse on either side. The surviving fragments of mosaic (in the N aisle and the SE angle-chapel) also conform in style to the 'Justinianic series' in Cyrenaica. The nave (c) is unusually long, and the

arrangement of atrium (a) and narthex (b) at the W end is unusual, but what first strikes the eye of the visitor is the mixture of materials used for the (re-erected) columns of the nave. Four on each side are of Proconnesian marble, as are also the two either side of the apse, the smaller columns of the *ciborium* which once enclosed the altar and various other fittings. The style of the capitals, the crosses carved on the impost-blocks above them and the cross-on-orb motif carved on each of the columns (fig. 178) show that all of these fitments were part of a 'kit', made at one time and basically prepared in the quarry of origin. (Compare the West

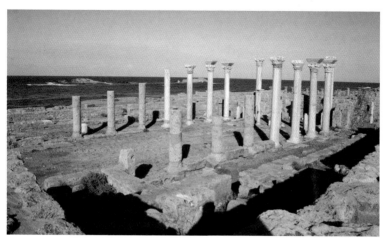

Fig. 177. Apollonia: the Central Church.

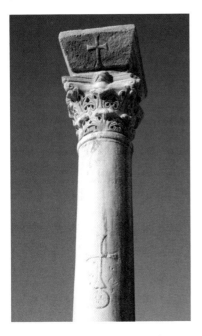

Fig. 178. Apollonia: Central Church, detail of column in the nave.

Church at al-Athrun, p. 290.) Note the column-bases, which generally are only roughed out, as they would have been in the quarry, in the (unfulfilled) expectation that stonemasons on the construction site would have finished off the detailed mouldings appropriately. The remaining three columns on each side of the nave are of local sandstone. These would have been faced with stucco, but the contrast would nonetheless always have been evident. Another curiosity, no longer apparent, is that the nave was paved partly with slabs of Proconnesian marble and partly with local stone. The arrangement was not symmetrical, with the marble being laid on the centre-line and on most of the N side. In both cases, the impression is inescapable that more marble had been expected, but that for some reason it did not arrive. Apollonia

is not mentioned in Procopius' work on the buildings of Justinian; while, therefore, the church may have been built during his reign, it presumably did not enjoy direct imperial patronage. Did some local patron initiate the project and run out of money part-way through? Were two shiploads of marble despatched from Proconnesos, of which one sank on the way and could not be replaced? We cannot know.

The discovery of a few voussoir-blocks suggests that the columns of the nave carried arcades; the roof will have been of timber, apart from a masonry semi-dome over the apse. Parts of the chancel screen at the E end of the nave have been replaced (randomly) in position. Sockets cut into the uprights on the N and S sides probably held hooks for chains across the side-openings, since they occur next to edges in which there are no slots for screen-panels. Sockets in opposing faces of the columns flanking the apse may likewise have contained fixings for a curtain. (It has been suggested that heavy wear on outer sides of the bases of these columns was caused by the curious peeping into the apse from behind the columns!)

There are structural indications of modifications to the original plan of the church, though these are not necessarily separated by any great interval of time, and may even represent changes of intention during the initial building work. The SE angle-chapel (d), entered through a wide arch, was unusually elaborate and its apse appears to be secondary. This is flanked by colonnettes, and by round-headed niches on either side. That on the L has a square recess in its floor, and the same may once have been true of its counterpart on the R. These perhaps held reliquary chests, and the chapel may have been a *martyrion*. Its floor was decorated with mosaic (now fragmentary) and traces of painted designs on wall-plaster were found both here and in the S aisle at the time of excavation.

On the N side of the church, the NE angle-chapel appears to have been simply a vestibule, providing access between the exterior, the N aisle and an apsed hall (e) at the E end of the added N wing. The hall was originally of two bays, with a wide arch between them. At some point this was closed up, dividing the space in two and creating a small doorway. Access was from the street and from the NE angle-chapel. The purpose of the hall, with traces of a stone balustrade across its apse, and of benches along either side, is unknown: it was not a baptistery. (A marble impost-block nearby, decorated with crosses and a small lion-head spout, has been hollowed out in the form of a basin; but this is not to be interpreted as a font.) To the W of the apsed hall was another longer and narrower hall with an apse at the W end, but this is very ruinous and nothing can be said of its purpose.

The W end of the complex has been extensively robbed, but its general outlines can be made out. The nave was preceded by an unusual narthex (b) with projecting apses at either end. The southern apse incorporates a stone throne with benches on either side of it, perhaps a place of teaching. Beyond the narthex, an atrium (a) is a secondary addition. This took the form of a paved courtyard, with colonnaded openings to the street and into the narthex, and flanking porticoes to N and S.

The building seems to have met its end as a result of deliberate action: a glance at the lower ends of the re-erected columns in the nave will show that they were felled like trees. This presumably occurred after the Arab conquest.

Byzantine industrial installation (5)

Between the Central Church and the shore lies a partially excavated complex of buildings, which was initially identified as a Byzantine bath suite. The excavation in the 1960s was motivated by the examination of the Roman Baths (below), which appeared to have gone out of service after the earthquake of AD 365, but then to have been adapted in part to accommodate large cisterns for a presumed successor installation. Unfortunately, the excavation was cut short by events associated with the Arab-Israeli war of 1967, and the southerly part of the complex was not excavated, making the interpretation of the rest more difficult.

In essence, part of an irregular layout, thought to be a bath building, was constructed (at a guess) after 365. This included two cold plunge-baths, a small sitz-bath and a cistern, probably associated with unexplored structures to the S. Water was provided by the late aqueduct identified along the W side of the Roman Baths (p. 269). Not long after, an extension was built to the E in fine squared masonry, ostensibly with *apodyterium* and *frigidarium* to the W, then a *tepidarium* and finally, at the E end, a *caldarium* with two hot plunge-baths flanking the furnace. However, if this was the intention, it seems that no floors were inserted and that construction was never completed. There are also aspects of the design, such as sub-floor flues in the '*tepidarium*' which communicate with the outside of the building as well as with adjoining rooms, which make the proffered interpretation improbable. At a later date, the unfinished E extension was blocked off and a paved, porticoed courtyard was created to the N of the old establishment, retaining the existing cold

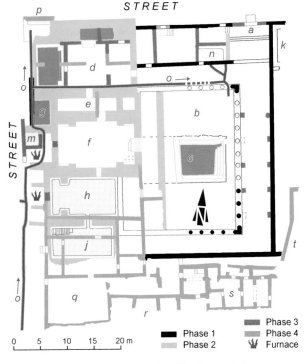

Fig. 179. Apollonia: plan of the Roman Baths.

a   Entrance
b   Peristyle
c   Basin / Natatio
d   Frigidarium
e   Tepidarium
f   Sudatorium
g   Water tank
h   Caldarium (later cistern)
j   ? (later cistern)
k   Latrine of baths
m   Cold plunge of later
    baths
n   Late latrine
o   Aqueduct
p   Byzantine fountain
q, r, s, t   Byzantine
    houses

plunge-baths within the portico. Yet further modifications suggested a change of use to modest dwellings.

The chronology of the whole was deduced from coins found in the various fills. These suggested continued occupation from the later fourth century until the Arab conquest. The search for a successor to the Roman Baths now points rather more plausibly to an area immediately to their W (p. 268); the structures described here are more likely to have been involved in some productive process requiring vats (perhaps the fulling of cloth). Along the northern edge of this complex is a fine stretch of what must have been the principal *decumanus* or E–W street of the ancient city; it is fighting a losing battle against the sea.

Roman Baths (6)

The presence of a large building on this spot was noted by the Beechey brothers in 1822, but much stone was removed in subsequent years (for the construction of

Susah in 1896 and of the Ridotta Roma in 1913). Limited excavations were carried out in 1947 (by the British) and in 1955–56 (by the French); a more extensive clearance was undertaken in 1962–65 by the Department of Antiquities, in the hope of unravelling the complex sequence of occupation on the site. Further targeted excavations were carried out by the French Mission in the 1970s. (See fig. 179.)

Phase 1
The complex is bounded by streets on the N and W; that to the N, now at the water's edge and partly eroded by it, must have been one of the principal thoroughfares of the city. It was paved in the Roman period, but where it has been cut through by wave action, a deep succession of earlier surfaces has been revealed. The earliest structures now visible in this area must have formed part of a wealthy peristyle house. The main entrance (a) was at the NE corner; this led up steps, through a lobby, to the peristyle (b). Some elements of the peristyle colonnades have been re-assembled in their original positions. The E colonnade was composed of fluted columns with Corinthian capitals. The capitals which survive show two different styles and are made from two different qualities of stone: those in soft sandstone are late Hellenistic in style, while those in a harder stone are most readily paralleled by examples at Cyrene of the Antonine period. They appear to indicate a refurbishment rather than a radical change. The N and S colonnades were composed of smaller columns, apparently of the Ionic order on the N and of the Doric order on the S. (This seems distinctly bizarre, and may represent a misinterpretation of the evidence: it is perhaps more likely that the Ionic columns, none

of which was found *in situ*, belonged to an upper storey.) The peristyle was therefore of the kind which Vitruvius calls 'Rhodian', the E side being taller and fronting the *triclinium*. There are several examples of such houses at Cyrene and Ptolemais.

There is no trace of the original W side of the peristyle. On that side it is cut off by a foundation which surely carried a wall and formed part of the later bath building; it may be presumed that the original peristyle extended further to the W. In the centre of the space which remains is a *natatio* or swimming-bath (c). The position of this is not symmetrical to the supposed peristyle, and it is curiously out of square at the W end. Close examination has shown that it originally extended further to the W. It was therefore part of the Phase 1 layout before being adapted to the purposes of the baths. The fact that it is later fed by a water-channel of Byzantine date shows that it had a lengthy existence.

It must be noted that beyond the outer wall of the peristyle itself there are no certain traces of contemporary rooms, even though the N façade facing the street has been attributed to this phase. Was this really a house? It has also been argued that it was a monumental *palaestra* enclosing a *natatio*.

Deep excavations within the peristyle have demonstrated that it was laid out in the late first century BC or the first century AD, succeeding earlier structures which included a votive deposit of miniatures vases of perhaps the fourth century BC.

Phase 2
Major changes were made when a bath suite was created on the western part of the property; this is thought to have taken place between AD 75

and 125, by analogy of design with other bath buildings of known date. The Antonine date attributed to the second series of Corinthian capitals in the peristyle may therefore relate to the construction of the baths, or to a hypothetical refurbishment after the Jewish Revolt. The baths were entered from the N portico of the peristyle. Here was the *frigidarium* (d), with two cold plunge-baths. It was paved with a geometric mosaic. From there, one passed through a narrow *tepidarium* (e) to a hot dry room (*sudatorium*, f). This was heated by a furnace outside the W wall. The raised floor of this room has completely disappeared, though a few *pilae* were found in the SE corner. It appears to have been systematically removed at a later stage in the history of the building, for at that time a doorway was cut through the E wall, and led down by means of some inserted steps to the floor of the hypocaust. (This floor was broken up only in the excavations of 1954–55, in a fruitless search for Egyptian antiquities beneath!) To the W of the *tepidarium* was a water tank (g), the outer wall of which is composed of Hellenistic masonry surviving from an earlier building.

To the S of the *sudatorium* lay the hot steam room, the *caldarium* (h) and possibly a further room beyond (j). The arrangements here have, however, been largely obscured by the creation of a huge double cistern in these spaces at a later date. The blocked furnace-arch can be made out in the W wall of the *caldarium*; immediately to the E of that, between the projecting piers on either side of the room, was the hot plunge-bath.

A latrine at the E end of the N frontage (k), supplied with water from the *frigidarium*, must belong to this phase.

Phase 3

At an undefined date, perhaps after the earthquake of AD 365, the baths went out of use, probably as a result of cracking of the concrete structure, which is still apparent at some points. The original entrance to the property was made narrower, and a ramp was installed in front of it. The E range of the peristyle was reinforced by the insertion of five arches, presumably carrying a new upper floor within the portico. In the *frigidarium*, the plunge-baths were filled in and the mosaic, which shows fire-damage, was buried beneath a layer of soil and a new plaster floor. The space was variously subdivided by inserted walls in poor rubble masonry. Where the furnace of the *sudatorium* had been, a basin was installed (m), which was initially interpreted as a public fountain. However, further excavation has shown that this is approached from the W by steps which lead both up to it and down into it. It must therefore be a cold plunge-bath belonging to a new building immediately to the W, which succeeded the wrecked baths on the present site. It was at this time that the *caldarium* and the adjoining space were excavated and converted into a large cistern, perhaps in order to supply the new installation.

Phase 4

The latest phase of occupation belongs to the latest history of the city, in the sixth or seventh century AD. Further alterations were made in the N range which incorporated (on a late floor in the former *frigidarium* and in a late stairway leading in from the street) a number of fragments of a marble inscription recording the Edict of Anastasius (p. 285). They must have found their way here long after the inscription (of c. AD 500) had ceased to be of interest. Also in the N range, a small latrine was installed (n), supplied with water from a refurbished aqueduct (o) which ran down the street on the W side of the property. Apollonia had no springs within its walls, and was supplied externally by a single aqueduct bringing water from high in the Wadi Susah to the S. The aqueduct was readily visible until the beginning of the 20th century, but almost all trace of it has now disappeared. It was located by excavation to the S of the city walls, not far from the 'Palace of the Dux' (17), and must somehow have traversed the coastal ridge in a tunnel; however, this has not yet been located. As well as the latrine, the aqueduct was connected to a public fountain at the NW street-corner (p) and to the *natatio*, showing that this was still in use, presumably as a cistern. It should be noted that the aqueduct circumvented the plunge-bath of the later baths (m), showing that they were still in operation at the time when the aqueduct was refurbished in the sixth century. The southern part of the bath-complex was stripped of its masonry, the deep cisterns were filled in and several houses of varying size (q, r, s, t) were constructed in poor re-used materials.

The port

After visiting the Roman Baths and before exploring the 'Palace of the Dux', the high ground in front of the latter offers a good vantage point from which to consider the ancient port, and what has happened to the shoreline since antiquity. Underwater investigations and surveys were first carried out in the 1950s by a team of divers from Cambridge led by Nic Flemming; more extensive work has been carried out since 1986 by the French mission under the direction of the late André Laronde. What is visible beneath the surface of the water varies considerably from one season to

the next, but we now have (thanks to the French), quite a complex picture of the development of the port.

What is visible offshore now is two rocky islands, and some small reefs further towards the W (and towards the modern harbour), resulting from a sinking of the coast by some 3.80 m since late antiquity. But the ancient shoreline depicted in fig. 173 shows that there was formerly a landlocked anchorage **(7)** in front of the larger (western) island. This island was joined to the mainland by a narrow spit, and to the E was a larger bay **(8)**, open towards the E but still protected from the NW. During the early years of the city, access to the western harbour was directly from the N, through a gap between the islands **(9)**. At an unknown date, shipsheds were cut into the native rock on the inner slope of the western island **(10)**. In calm weather, the upper ends of these can still be seen; there were ten of them, each approximately 6 m wide and up to 40 m long, sloping down gently towards the water. Here warships would have been pulled up out of the water and under cover. They had surely been constructed before the next major development in the port, which logic associates with the construction of the defences in the late second century BC.

At this time an artificial entrance channel **(11)** about 14 m wide and 2 m deep was cut through the spit of land on the E side of the original harbour, guarded at the inner end by two massive towers **(12)**, which may well have been part of the defensive circuit. At the same time, the original entrance on the N side **(9)** was closed up by the dumping of tonnes of massive rectangular blocks. This will have increased the security of the harbour from attack both by the elements and by hostile shipping.

In the early Roman period, quays were constructed on either side of the entrance channel, at its inner end. This enabled merchant ships (for the first time?) to tie up for unloading, rather than having to be beached or unloaded into lighters. This development, which extended across the lower ends of the former shipsheds, indicates quite clearly that they had gone out of use by then. Numerous structures are likely to be associated with this period, including possibly some further shipsheds on the W side of the harbour **(13)** and warehouses on the S side **(14)**. In the open E bay, a platform projects from a harbour wall or esplanade **(15)**, perhaps signifying the former presence of a temple. The

easternmost point of the eastern island **(16)** is thought to have been the site of a lighthouse.

The entrance-channel to the harbour must have been regularly dredged, for in the bottom was a layer of silt corresponding to a short period of disuse in about the fifth century AD. At some point in the sixth or seventh century, perhaps in the face of imminent attack from the Arabs (or the Persians in 618?), the channel was deliberately blocked by the tipping of tonnes of mixed building rubble. Also in the Byzantine period (and perhaps again due to preoccupations with defence), the outline of the coast was much altered by quarrying activity. This cut away large parts of the

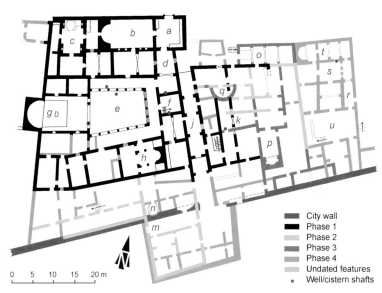

Fig. 180. Apollonia: plan of the 'Palace of the Dux'.

a	Waiting-room	h	Chapel	p	Office?
b	Audience-chamber	j	Corridor	q	Foundations of apse
c	Store-room with oven	k	Arched entrance to	r	Vestibule of E building
d	Lobby		E wing (Phase 1)	s	Courtyard/light well
e	Courtyard	m	Postern gate	t	Audience-chamber
f	Staircase	n	Oven	u	Courtyard
g	Banqueting hall	o	Store?		

270

outer faces of the islands and buried other parts of the former port facilities beneath spoil heaps.

The exploration of the port by divers of the French Mission in the 1980s yielded much pottery which had fallen into the water in the course of commercial activity (and which demonstrates the trading relations of the city). They also found in the E bay **(8)** the remains of a sailing ship about 20 m long, probably an abandoned hulk which sank through decay in the second century BC.

'Palace of the Dux' ★ ★ (17)

This complex (fig. 180), sited against the city wall, was partly visible in 1822 but almost wholly obscured in the early 20th century by the Ridotta Roma. The Italian structures were dismantled and the area excavated by the Department of Antiquities under Richard Goodchild between 1959 and 1962. Consolidation and a small amount of reconstruction were carried out at the same time.

It was clear from the finds associated with the structures now visible, that they belong wholly to the late fifth to seventh centuries AD. This prominent part of the coastal ridge will certainly have been built upon earlier in the history of the city, but the excavations did not seek to go down to earlier levels. Goodchild pointed out that the western limit of the complex, which forces it out of an otherwise rectangular layout aligned on the city wall, is the only feature which conforms to the earlier street layout to the N (e.g. to the E of the Roman Baths). He therefore inferred that its line was determined by the presence of an earlier building on the adjoining site to the W, which was still functioning when the 'palace' complex was built. He also inferred that the extent of the building, its prominent position and its internal character

implied a public function of the highest order: it was therefore almost certainly the residence of the provincial military governor (the *Dux*) in the latter years of the city. We now know from an increasing number of other examples (including the House of the Triapsidal Hall at Ptolemais, p. 77) that many of the very rich of the Byzantine period occupied houses with precisely the same characteristics. We may not doubt that the occupant was a person of great power in the community, but he was not necessarily the governor; and while we may entertain the image of the future empress Theodora frequenting these halls as the mistress of the governor, Hekebolios, this too is far from certain!

Phase 1

The principal doorway into the complex is on the N side, and is dignified by flanking mouldings. This leads into what is clearly a waiting-room (a), lined with benches, where clients would wait for an audience with their patron. The imposing character of the residence was emphasized by similar mouldings flanking each of the doorways which led to rooms beyond. Most clients would get no further than the room immediately to the R (b), which is equally clearly an audience-chamber. The patron would appear through the doorway in the apse at the far end, and would receive his clients while seated there on a throne. The cupboards along the walls, which have slots for shelves and doors, would have held documents and records. Beyond the audience-chamber, in room (c), were further cupboards, and into this an oven was later inserted.

If one was more privileged, one might by-pass the audience-chamber at the entrance and pass through the door straight ahead and through an

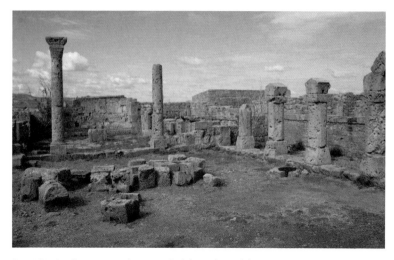

Fig. 181. Apollonia: central courtyard of the 'Palace of the Dux'.

intervening lobby (d) to the peristyle (e). This was a courtyard of some pretension (fig. 181), though the stocky proportions of the re-erected arcades are more reminiscent of a medieval cloister than of a classical peristyle. This impression is reinforced by the presence of crosses carved in low relief within pediments on the lintels of doorways. One should not, however, impute a particularly religious function to the building because of these crosses: this is simply the ornamental language of the age. Much, if not all, of the complex was two storeys high, though nothing of the upper floor survives. Access to the upper floor was by way of a wooden staircase, the stone base of which (f) is visible in a room on the E side of the courtyard. Beneath this staircase is a draw-hole for a cistern; there are others in the adjoining lobby (d), in the peristyle and in its N portico. All open into a single rock-cut cistern beneath, which was fed with rainwater by means of a downpipe in the SE corner of the courtyard. The major reception rooms opened off the central peristyle.

On the axis at the W end was a large apsed hall (g), open to the peristyle through two columns which were taller and more widely spaced than those of the peristyle. The floor of the apse was raised, it was roofed by a semi-dome and in front of it was a stone table, of which the top is now missing. This grand space, rising to the full height of both storeys, was probably a banqueting hall. It is flanked by rooms on either side which were perhaps offices.

There were further large reception rooms on the N and S sides of the peristyle, but of greater interest is the presence in the SE corner of a private chapel (h). It was entered through two doorways (now reconstructed) on the S side of the peristyle. The central part of it, including the apse and the short nave, was clearly vaulted. (The fallen concrete was removed in the course of excavation.) The remainder, comprising aisles and a narthex, presumably had a lower tiled roof on timber rafters. More or less in the centre of the chapel, between the columns, was found a marble reliquary chest which is now in the museum (p. 283). It had been broken open and there was no trace of its original contents. The chapel must therefore have constituted a *martyrion*, housing the relics of some saint acquired to add lustre to the household. Again, we know that aristocratic households of the period did have private chapels, so its presence is not necessarily exceptional, despite the fact that this must be almost the only one known.

The rooms so far described constitute the original 'public' or formal parts of the dwelling. On the E side, they are bounded by a corridor (j), which perhaps led initially to a tower and postern gate on the city wall. Beyond this lies a smaller rectangular building which has undergone modifications now difficult to disentangle. In its first phase, this had rooms on its western side and an open courtyard to the E. The rooms were linked to the courtyard by a triple arched entrance (k). The piers which line the corridor on either side indicate support for an upper storey which presumably joined the two buildings together. This was accessed on the E side by a stone staircase. One may imagine that the eastern part contained the private quarters of the owner and his family.

Phase 2

Subsequent modifications can be distinguished in part through changes in constructional technique. Walls of small squared stones were succeeded by others built of harder but less-well-trimmed boulders from a wadi-bed; at a still later juncture there was a reversion to squared stones of smaller calibre than before. Phase 2 involved a further eastward extension of the E building and the construction of additional rooms between the W building and the line of the Hellenistic city wall to the S. Goodchild's interpretation of

many of these features was conditioned by his assumption that he was dealing with the governor's palace and that there was therefore a strong military presence. If that was not the case, a household of such wealth would none the less have had a substantial domestic staff. The 'palace' is set against the city wall at a point where a tower was to be expected, but of the Hellenistic structure no trace was found, apart from a small unexplained dog-leg in the course of the wall itself. In Phase 2 a new tower projected beyond the wall, with a small postern gate (m) on the W side. The rooms immediately to the N appear to have provided services to the house, and the presence of an oven (n) suggests a kitchen.

Phase 3

Further extensive modifications were made to the E building. In front of it, on the N side, was built a large room (o) which was perhaps a store. The internal arches indicate the presence of an upper storey, as does the base of a staircase at its W end. The former courtyard was now largely built over, including an apsed room (p), perhaps an office, and further rooms against the city wall. The layout on the N side was now largely obstructed by the insertion of a semicircular stone foundation (q), which only makes sense as the support for an apsed room on the floor above. Fallen architectural elements in this area (voussoir blocks, piers, cornices) suggest that this was a room of considerable pretension.

Phase 4

This is characterized principally by the addition of a further self-contained house on the E side of the complex. This was more modest than its neighbour, but still reflects an owner of some standing. The entrance on the E side led into a vestibule (r), from which one might pass north-wards, through a corridor whose arched windows looked into a small courtyard (s), to an apsed audience-chamber (t – later subdivided). In the opposite direction, one entered a courtyard (u) which provided access to the other rooms of the ground floor and had a staircase to the floor above.

At approximately the same time, the tower projecting across the city wall was substantially strengthened (and enlarged?) and the previous postern gate was blocked up.

The excavation as a whole produced abundant pottery and coinage, which indicated a period of occupation from the later fifth or early sixth century until the time of the Arab conquest. There was no evidence of violent destruction, but some of late 'squatter' occupation which may belong to the period after the conquest.

Residential *insula* (18)

The *insula* immediately to the W of the East Church was excavated by a French expedition in 1954–55; no report of this excavation has been published. Its appearance is generally residential, and some vats suggest perhaps the

fermentation of wine. But there is certainly also something grander towards the S end, where there are large door-mouldings and a column-base. Sandro Stucchi saw here a Byzantine temple of Isis, by analogy with the late structures beneath the acropolis of Cyrene (p. 182), but this seems fanciful. Several slabs of pink Aswan granite found loose in this area belong with others found in the East Church (see below).

East Church ★ ★ (19)

The East Church, illustrated in figs. 182 and 183, was the first monument to be systematically excavated at Apollonia, by Ettore Ghislanzoni in 1922. It is one of the few in Cyrenaica the origins of which can be attributed with confidence to a pre-Justinianic date. It also makes use in part of a very much earlier building, the drafted masonry of which (apparent particularly on the street-frontage to the W) identifies it as Hellenistic. Its orientation seems to have been N–S, with its principal entrance on the N side. Its northern façade (the shallow decorative pilasters of which are partly preserved) was later converted into the atrium of the church, with its entrance in the same position. New excavations by Laronde suggest that the space immediately to the N or E may have been the agora of the city, in which case this may have been an important public building, and the church which succeeded it may have been the cathedral.

The precise date of the church has been hotly disputed, opinions ranging widely within the fifth century. The layout, distinctively different from the

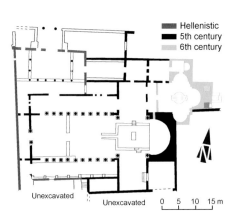

Hellenistic
5th century
6th century

Unexcavated

Unexcavated

0   5   10   15 m

Fig. 182. Apollonia: plan of the East Church.

7 Apollonia

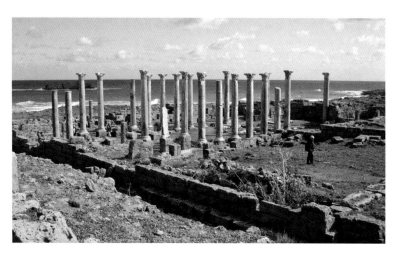

Fig. 183. Apollonia: the East Church.

definitely Justinianic churches, involved a three-aisled nave with transepts at the E end and a single apse. The existence of the earlier building presumably conditioned the provision of an atrium on the N side and of a very narrow narthex – not giving access to the street – at the W end. Extensive use was made of second-hand building materials, particularly apparent in the non-matching cipollino columns of the nave. Several of these are raised on square sandstone plinths in order to make up the requisite height.

The atrium, entered from the N through an added porch with two columns *in antis*, constituted the principal entrance to the church. It had internal porticoes on three sides, with columns of local sandstone bearing arcades: the voussoirs of these are laid out on the ground and the column-capitals are of late Roman manufacture. On the S side, openings led into the narrow corridor which served as a narthex at the W end, and directly into the N aisle of the nave. The columns of the nave, crowned by Corinthian capitals of the second or third century AD, probably carried arcades.

At the E end, the nave is separated by a central crossing from the apse and from the two flanking transepts. The nave aisles are clearly separated from the transepts (by a wall on the S and an archway on the N), and in the central space the transition is emphasized by the framing of the crossing between four tall cipollino columns which are set in from the lines of the nave colonnades.

In the centre of the crossing was the chancel, a raised rectangular enclosure surrounded by marble screens. Traces of two periods of work (and of mosaic) are detectable, with steps up to entrances on the N and S sides as well as the long entrance-passage towards the nave. The base of the altar is composed of two cipollino slabs, sawn from a column, with seatings for six colonnettes which would have supported the altar-table.

The apse was paved from the first with mosaic, of which about two thirds are preserved. The style is earlier than, and quite different from, that of the more common Justinianic pavements, being composed of a grid-pattern of squares, with circles enclosing rosettes at the intersections. The squares are filled with single abstract or animal motifs. A blocked doorway in the N flank of the apse once communicated with a room on that side and was suppressed when the baptistery was inserted.

The S transept preserves extensive traces of mosaic flooring of two periods. The earlier (with an abstract pelta design) must belong to the original construction of the church, while that which has been laid immediately on top is quite clearly the work of the same craftsmen who laid mosaics at Qasr Libya, Cyrene and Ras al-Hilal in the time of Justinian. The later mosaic is composed of sixteen square panels in a grid, separated by guilloche patterns and surrounded by a continuous inhabited scroll. Three of the best panels (Noah; a leopard; a man carrying a rabbit) have been lifted and are on display in the museum (p. 283); others show the same range of motifs as at Qasr Libya (p. 133) and elsewhere. An angle-chapel (perhaps a *martyrion*) fills the space between the S transept and the apse. The orientation of the mosaic panels was such that they should be viewed from the W (i.e. when facing the chapel).

On the N side of the apse, the baptistery belongs unequivocally to a second phase of construction. This is shown both by the distinctive ashlar masonry of its inner walls (with alternating courses of taller and lower blocks) and by the use of white lime-mortar for bonding, which occurs nowhere else in the complex. The baptistery as we see it now must have replaced a simpler angle-chapel (possibly also a baptistery) like that on the S side; but the new arrangement is placed within a grander 'triconch' room with three apses. There would have been small columns framing each of the apses, which presumably had semi-domes. The room as a whole cannot have been vaulted or have had a central dome, since the walls are not substantial enough to take the weight: it must have been roofed in wood. The baptismal basin was originally circular, but was then enlarged to its present square shape, lined with marble and with steps on opposite sides. Water for the basin was provided from a high-level tank behind the central apse on the N side. This supplied a lower barrel-vaulted tank behind the S side of the apse, which was placed above a hypocaust in order to heat it. The hot water was fed from this tank, by means of a duct, into the baptismal basin. There can be little doubt that the new baptistery was constructed in the time of Justinian, though Apollonia is not mentioned by Procopius amongst the building works of that emperor.

Amongst the architectural elements found loose in the church when it was excavated were a number of marble impost-blocks made from re-used statue-bases and stelai bearing inscriptions. These include a dedication to Apollo of the fourth century BC, a list of priests of Apollo (now on display in the museum, p. 285) and two which honour emperors of the late fourth/early fifth centuries AD. Their presence contributes to the inference that the church is sited partly in or next to the former agora of the city. Other notable elements still scattered around the church and in the *insula* to the W of it are large slabs of polished Aswan granite, some of which bear letters of a Latin inscription. These are thought originally to have been the facing of a large honorific statue-base of the Augustan period (in the agora?).

Immediately to the SE of the East Church, and towards the South Gate of the city, the French have explored a large cistern, which has long been visible. This appears to have lain beneath the southern end of a courtyard of a grandiose building (up to 50 × 40 m in extent) on the same alignment as the church – suggesting that, in the later years of Apollonia, there were other grand residences besides the 'Palace of the Dux' excavated by Goodchild.

South Gate (20)

From the East Church, the recommended course of the visit follows a track southwards by means of a low saddle and through the South Gate in the defences. This has been examined in recent years by the French team under André Laronde, and has been shown to have been a larger thoroughfare than the postern gates which are associated with many of the towers. Even so, at some 3.50 m wide and set at a right-angle to the line of the wall, it did not encourage large volumes of wheeled traffic!

The tower and gate were constructed in the late second century BC. The tower projects fully to the S of the wall on both sides, and between it and the curtain on the E side was a small postern, while on the W side was the wider opening. Towards the end of the first century AD, a new sill was set in place a full metre above the original one, and the fill in between was found to contain a couple of blocks from the parapet of the tower. This seems to imply that there was both early damage to the tower and a prolonged period of disuse, to account for the blocks remaining undisturbed and for the rise in level. The gateway was again modified in the third century, with the insertion of additional rooms against the N face of the tower, blocking the postern and rendering the larger gate impassable to wheeled traffic. At a yet later stage, this addition was demolished and the entrance restored (again at a higher level); the last alteration in this long sequence was the reduction of the gateway to a narrow postern. It may be supposed that this took place in the seventh century before the arrival of the Arabs.

East Necropolis (21)

From the South Gate, the track runs eastwards immediately below the city walls. The ground to the N rises progressively higher towards the acropolis, and the slopes below have been extensively quarried for building stone, thus increasing their defensive value. Into these quarry faces have been cut chamber-tombs. Their contents have long since been cast out, and many of them are

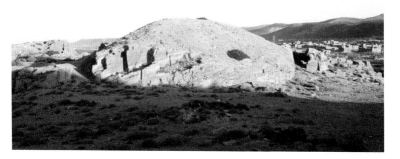

Fig. 184. Apollonia: possible burial-mound to the E of the city.

still used as animal pens; they are likely on the whole to belong to the Hellenistic and Roman periods.

Beyond the point where the acropolis walls turn away towards the sea, the lower ground opens out. The way to the theatre is round towards the L, climbing up again towards a low (modern) wall on the horizon with an opening in it. But before following that, note that in front of you rises a large **circular mound (22)**, which is easily mistaken for a natural feature (fig. 184). Sandro Stucchi has identified this as a tumulus burial, surrounded by a rock-cut pathway 100 feet in diameter, and with a terrace for funerary ceremonies on the SE side. The hypothesis has not been tested by excavation, but Stucchi has suggested that this intriguing structure is more probably an archaistic creation of the Hellenistic period (i.e. a Hellenistic fake!) than a genuinely archaic feature.

Theatre ★ ★ (23)

The theatre of Apollonia (fig. 185) lies in an unusual position, outside the city walls and nestling beneath their eastern face. The path below the city walls brings one to a point where a (modern) wall with a single entrance is visible on the horizon to seaward. Head for this opening and enjoy the panorama which suddenly opens before you! The presence of a theatre at this spot was noted by early travellers and it was excavated by the Department of Antiquities in 1961–63. Its construction is contemporary with that of the city wall (late Hellenistic) and its architect was faced with the choice, on rather unsatisfactory ground, of building up a mass of soil on the eastern side to support the seating (vaulted substructures for theatre seating do not appear until later) or of cutting away large quantities of bedrock on the W. His solution was a compromise,

with roughly half of the seating cut out of the rock and half built up, at the same time sacrificing some of the theoretical seating capacity on the W. There were thirty tiers of seats, without any dividing *diazoma* or landing. The *orchestra*, in Greek style, was a complete circle, to which the stage-building was tangential on the far side. The original stage-front (*proskenion* in Greek or *pulpitum* in Latin) was decorated with engaged Doric columns, of which fragments remain.

Towards the end of the first century AD, the stage was brought forward as far as the edge of the seating, and the stage-building behind was replaced with a taller and more massive structure. This carried an inscription in honour of the emperor Domitian which can be dated to AD 92–96. At the same time, the two lowest rows of seats in the *cavea* were removed and replaced by a stone screen (in order to make more space for dignitaries in the *orchestra*, and to save them from contamination with common citizens!). The excavators inferred that further modifications were made in the second century AD, probably involving the use of marble. However, in the Byzantine period any such material was carried away, presumably for reuse elsewhere, and the remaining lower courses of the stage-building were overlaid with late rubble walls belonging to a structure which had no connection with the earlier use of the site. Traces have been recorded of names inscribed on the risers of the seats in various places. They are, however, too poorly preserved for any inference to be drawn with regard to date.

While we cannot but admire the landscape setting of this evocative theatre, it should be remembered that at the time when it was in use the sea may have been some 50 m further away, and the sound and sight of it would have been

7 Apollonia

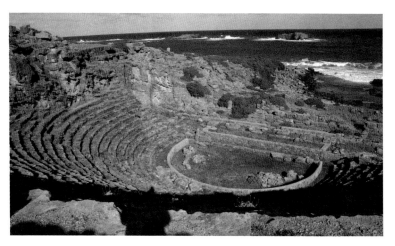

Fig. 185. Apollonia: the theatre.

diminished by the bulk of the intervening stage-building.

Acropolis (24)

The highest ground within the city is at the extreme eastern end, above the theatre. It is possible to scramble up here from behind the uppermost seats. (Just one loose block, appropriately placed, would make it a lot easier!) This is not a large area, and the limited excavations which have taken place suggest that it did not receive monumental treatment. What is visible indicates a quadrilateral enclosure of the Byzantine period with rooms set around a courtyard; this was probably dedicated to the needs of defence rather than anything else. A rock-cut cistern within the enclosure will have collected rainwater for immediate necessities; an overflow led northwards through the enclosure wall to a larger, stone-built, cistern on the slope below.

Warehouses? (25)

To the W of the acropolis, where the rock is now cut away in vertical faces towards the beach, one finds a row of rock-cut chambers facing seawards. The French expedition of 1954 carried out excavations in this area, but no account has been published. The chambers resemble warehouses. A rock-cut water-channel running across their rear walls may have served simply for the drainage of groundwater; sockets in the rock-façade indicate roofed structures once built in front. Further round to the E is a large area of quarries, now invaded by the sea. Here too is a series of huge ovoid plaster-lined vats. These are similar to those seen on many rural sites where there is evidence of oil or wine processing, and it should be remembered that when in use, they were farther from the sea (and higher above it) than they are today.

Kallikrateia Rock (26)

Beyond the low ground of the East Church and the South Gate, the ground rises again in the eastern part of the city The most prominent element in the nearby landscape is a small rocky knoll which appears to have been quarried away on every side, in addition to having suffered natural collapse, perhaps in the earthquake of AD 365. Cut into the knoll, below the summit, are remains of a modest chamber. This was originally accessible only from above, through a shaft with foot-holds in it, and appears to have served as a storeroom for a Byzantine look-out tower on top of the knoll. There are few traces of its superstructure, but the stone disk which served as a rolling door (compare the East Church at Lamludah, p. 298) still lies nearby. However, cuttings in the rock, close to the mouth of the shaft which leads into the storeroom, comprise three *arulae* or altar-tables: rectangular tablets with raised edges for offerings to a divinity or to the dead. (Compare the many examples in the Southern Extramural Sacred Zone or the Sanctuary of Ain Hofra, both at Cyrene, pp. 233, 253.) One of these bears an inscription on the edge, in lettering which has been attributed to the third century BC. It reads 'of Kallikrateia'. This was once taken to name the titulary of a local cult; but recent excavations by the French team, on the N side of the knoll, have shown the nearby presence of a religious sanctuary of some kind at least from the fourth century BC. A quarry here became a *favissa* or dump for offerings, in which was found much pottery and many terracotta figurines. These included both male and female figures (some of the females holding a silphium plant), and have close parallels amongst finds from Cyrene: a multiplicity of deities seems to have been honoured. Numerous further *arulae* have now been found, cut in the rock. In the late second or early first century BC, the area was levelled for a building, of which one room had a mosaic floor in a disposition which implied a dining room, perhaps a *hestiatorion* for religious banquets. In the time of Augustus, this in turn was superseded by a larger terrace of unclear

purpose. However, the number of coins found in the fill suggested to the excavators that they were placed there deliberately and that the site continued to have some religious association. The appearance of this zone now emphasizes the difficulty of excavating and interpreting the remains on these rocky surfaces.

A further votive deposit consisting of several hundred terracotta figurines was found beneath the nearest tower of the defences. These have been attributed to the first half of the fourth century BC and must be associated with the same cult activity.

Extra-Mural Church (27)

About 100 m to the S of the city walls, and now just on the S side of the village street which runs eastwards from the Manara Hotel, are visible parts of an ancient rectangular building in substantial ashlar masonry. Within the outer walls on the street corner may be made out the outline of a *triconchos* or (club-shaped) triple apse. The building has never been excavated, and until 1994 the western half of it was still an occupied dwelling; it seems very likely, however, to be another Byzantine church. (For the *triconchos* form, see the baptistery in the East Church at Apollonia (p. 274) and the 'House of the Triapsidal Hall' at Ptolemais (p. 77).

East Fort

On the next headland to the E of the city (at N 32° 54.15′ E 21° 59.19′, almost exactly 1 km from the theatre), there are traces of a fort, pottery from which shows that it was built, or at least occupied, during the later fourth or early third century BC. At this time, before the city's defences were built, it would have provided a visual link between the city and the coastline eastwards towards Ras al-Hilal, providing advance warning of any hostile approach. The fort was constructed partly by cutting back the native rock surface, and it is the walls of chiselled rock, including slit-windows, which now reveal its former presence.

West Necropolis

All that is visible of the western necropolis is a few rock-cut tombs beneath the western wall of the city, now arranged into a tasteful garden facing the Manara Hotel. The hotel itself was built (contrary to planning law) on the necropolis in 2000, and resulted in the mechanical destruction, without adequate record, of some twenty cist graves. The contents of the tombs were recovered by the Department of Antiquities, and included much Greek pottery of the fourth century BC. Many other tombs have also been destroyed by modern buildings in this area. To the W of the modern harbour enclosure, a perforated rock standing up in the water marks the position of a chamber-tomb which subsequently found itself in a quarry: the surrounding rock was cut away but the tomb itself was respected. Since the time when the quarry was cut, the land has sunk, leaving the tomb now standing bizarrely in the sea.

Two further monuments, to the W of the ancient city but now within the area of modern settlement, are of importance and are still traceable on the ground.

Extra-mural Doric temple

This building is now reduced to cuttings in the bare bedrock which represent the seatings for a substantial temple, facing E. It may be found off the old road into Susah from the W (either go straight on when approaching the town, rather than veering away to the R or, from the other direction, take the road W from the S

end of the garden piazza which was the centre of the 1896 settlement). On the N side of this road is the walled former Catholic cemetery, still with a roofless chapel in the centre; walk down the E side of this enclosure and round to the L. The remains will be found approximately 100 m to the W of the NE corner of the cemetery, at N 32° 53.90′ E 21° 57.22′. The few tumbled blocks of the superstructure which remain include a Doric capital. There is meagre evidence to suggest that it was built in the fourth or third century BC, but a later date in the Hellenistic period has also been argued. Its complete removal down to the bedrock most probably took place during the Byzantine period, when it was no longer venerated as a place of worship and was seen merely as a convenient source of building-material.

There is no direct evidence for the dedication of the temple. It has been argued that the temple of Venus on the coast near the harbour of Cyrene, which provided the setting for a play by the Roman playwright Plautus (*Rudens*, The Rope), may have been this building. The association would be pleasing, but the temple may equally have been in the vicinity of another outlet to the sea from Cyrene, Phykous or Aptouchos (see pp. 147, 122), further to the W.

Stadium

Vertical cuttings in the rock, close to the shore and resembling an ancient quarry, actually define the E end of a stadium (running-track), 150 m to the NE of the extra-mural Doric temple and about 60 m from the sea (at N 32° 53.95′ E 21° 57.29′). The track is lined on either side with stepped seating, at first handsomely rock-cut and then further to the W, where the natural rock falls away, constructed of the same material. In the rock-cut sector, there are five tiers of steps on the S side and three on the N; on the N side the seats are approached by a ramp leading down from the direction of the city. Cut into the rock-face at the E end is a rectangular chamber, typical of tombs; however, its precise axial position suggests that it formed part of the amenities of the stadium. The narrowness of the track (13 m, in contrast to a general range of 20–30 m) is exceptional and the length is unknown, but there can be little doubt about the identification. As to date, the second century BC has been proposed on the basis of a coin found in the foundation-material. Other foundations observed nearby, but not yet further investigated, suggested the possibility of an extended athletic complex.

As in the case of the Doric temple, it appears that all loose building-material was removed for reuse elsewhere in the late Roman period.

Museum ★

The Apollonia Museum (formerly just inside the entrance to the site) is now in the previous *municipio* of Susah, in the village and not more than 100 m from the Manara Hotel. It is by no means always open, but enquiry at the entrance to the site will usually produce a custodian with a key. The material is not all labelled, and the labels which do exist are by no means accurate: I have done my best to identify the objects on display.

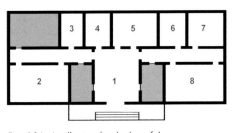

Fig. 186. Apollonia: sketch-plan of the museum.

For the layout, see figure 186. On the steps is a plain Roman sarcophagus in Pentelic marble, recovered from an Italian building in the village.

Room 1 (hallway)

In the centre of the hallway immediately inside the entrance stands a very fine Attic sarcophagus (imported from the Pentelic quarries near Athens) which has been attributed on stylistic grounds to the late second century AD. It was found in the late mausoleum beneath the western city wall (p. 259), where it had been reused. Little of the lid has survived, but the sarcophagus is otherwise well-preserved. The carved scenes depict the myth of Phaedra and Hippolytos. In a nutshell, Phaedra is the second wife of Theseus, and Hippolytos is his son by an earlier liaison. Phaedra falls in love with Hippolytos; he virtuously rejects her advances; she, in a rage, reports to Theseus that he has raped her; he, in a rage, curses Hippolytos in the name of Poseidon (with whom he has such an arrangement). When Hippolytos is practising in his chariot along the sea-shore (as young men do), Poseidon sends a monster out of the deep which frightens the horses; the chariot overturns and Hippolytos is dragged to his death. Phaedra commits suicide, either beforehand (leaving a mendacious suicide note for Theseus) or afterwards (out of guilt?). On the front of the sarcophagus, we see Phaedra seated at the L and facing away from the other figures. In the centre, now almost entirely missing, stood the figure of Hippolytos, being entreated on behalf of her mistress by an aged nurse, who is between the two and bowing towards Hippolytos. All of the other figures are hangers-on!

The scene on the left-hand end is very difficult to interpret, and even more so to fit into the legend. A seated, bearded figure at the L, with a club, may plausibly be seen as Herakles, but whether the others can be identified as Phaedra, Hippolytos and Theseus (also with club) is very questionable. The figures on the right-hand end are even more enigmatic and need not detain us. The rear face of the sarcophagus, which the sculptor doubtless expected to be of limited visibility or interest, is carved in low relief with a hunting scene. This is apparently common on sarcophagi illustrating the Hippolytos myth, and the figures have no specific associations.

On the walls on either side of Room 1 are personifications in mosaic of *Ktisis* (Foundation, on the R) and *Kosmesis* (Adornment, on the L) from the nave of the church at Ras al-Hilal (p. 320). Against the rear wall are two headless statues of draped female figures found in the East Church at Apollonia, approximately dated Flavian (L) and Antonine (R) respectively.

Room 2: Christian antiquities
Here may be seen more mosaic panels in the same style as those in Room 1 from Ras al-Hilal and those from Qasr Libya which are dated to AD 538/9 (p. 133). A fragmentary square panel showing Noah releasing the dove from the Ark is from the S transept of the E Church at Apollonia, as are three other small panels, one with a leopard, one with a man with a rabbit and one (from a border motif) with a man standing between bunches of grapes. In the left-hand corner of the room, beneath the window, is a limestone chancel-screen panel and two chancel-posts from the church at Ras al-Hilal. At the opposite end of the same wall is a small marble reliquary chest

from the chapel in the 'Palace of the Dux' at Apollonia (p. 273). The lid was once decorated with inlaid metal crosses, and was fastened down with bronze bolts. There is a small opening through the lid, in the centre of the ridge. The type has parallels in Greece, Asia Minor and Syria, and seems to have been a 'standard' product of a single (as yet unidentified) quarry. The pier in the centre of the room holds two marble chancel-screen slabs from the East Church at al-Athrun (p. 292) on the side towards the window; on the opposite side are two smaller slabs (source not known to me) together with a marble platter and a semi-circular 'sigma' altar table from al-Athrun. From the East Church at the same site are the two small column-capitals on top of the pier. Also on top of the pier are four small amphorae (source unknown) and a curious inscribed *pithos* found in the 'Palace of the Dux' at Apollonia (p. 270). The lettering on this object, impressed before it was fired, includes a Christian invocation ('Lord help …'). On a shelf between the two doors are a limestone relief and two fragments of a marble plaque (neither of which I have been able to identify).

Room 3: pottery
There are examples here of Greek black-figure and red-figure vessels, probably from the sixth century BC onwards. A case in the far corner contains grotesque masks, animal heads and the like in terracotta: these are from braziers (small cooking-stoves) of the Hellenistic or early Roman periods (not Christian, as indicated by the label). Inside the door on the R is a case of lamps, mostly Greek or Hellenistic, with some of Roman imperial or Byzantine date on the bottom shelf. The remainder of the pottery is mostly from tombs around the city, and particularly in

the vicinity of the city walls towards the SW corner (see p. 258). In the corridor between rooms 2 and 3 are further cases of terracottas and miniature vases. These are typical of votive deposits of the Hellenistic period, of which several have been found at Apollonia (see pp. 267, 280).

Room 4
Many of the objects displayed here derive from the French investigations in the harbour; they include lead anchor stocks and other items of ship's tackle. There are also cases of small objects in metal, glass and worked bone, as well as terracotta figurines. In the far corner are bronze pulley-wheels found in a quarry near Apollonia (possibly of recent date).

Room 5: sculpture
There are several examples here of funerary busts of the 'Goddess of Death', as seen in profusion at Cyrene (see p. 244), and in the centre of the room a headless Athena (found under water, second century AD?) and part of a semi-clothed male figure. There is also a small painted *aedicula* or shrine in sandstone. Between the doors is a fragmentary grave stele showing a female figure (L), facing a large chest with a lidded cup beneath it (findspot unrecorded, probably late fifth century BC). In the left-hand corner, an altogether finer (but fragmentary) piece of marble sculpture is part of a colossal figure of Cybele seated on a throne and attended by lions: the hindquarters of one of the lions and part of the throne are preserved (findspot unrecorded).

On the walls of the corridor in the right-hand half of the museum are four sections (behind glass) of stucco from the church at Ras al-Hilal marked with early Arabic graffiti: one of the texts is datable to AD 722 and another appears to refer to a monastery (p. 320 f.). Also in this corridor is a long inscribed marble lintel with a cross at the left-hand end. This was found (despite the label) in a building in the Turkish village of Susah; the inscription, in letters attributed to the sixth century, is an invitation in verse to baptism. It may have come originally from the West Church.

Room 6
This contains further examples of sculpture in marble, limestone and sandstone, with examples of very fine architectural mouldings and of stucco and painted plaster. There is also a display of vessels in alabaster. None of this material is labelled.

Room 7: inscriptions
Most of the items here are labelled. Going round the room in a clockwise direction, they are as follows.
1. Sandstone milestone of the Tetrarchy (AD 293–305) marking mile XV from Cyrene. Findspot unrecorded, but the location should have been slightly to the E of Apollonia.
2. Marble statue-base inscribed on the front with a secondary list (of *epheboi*?) in various hands. Findspot unrecorded, but probably from the E Church (19), probably first century AD.
3. Socketed statue-base in hard, bluish stone, with a Greek dedication in verse by Eupolemos to King Magas and to the god Ares. Found reused in a Byzantine house in the E part of the city, probably 275–250 BC.
4. (In the corner) Sandstone block with crude Greek lettering, the tombstone of Theuxenos of Barka, son of Diokrates. Findspot unrecorded, first century BC or AD?
5. Marble grave-stele with pediment and wreath, commemorating several members of a Jewish family. Note the

names Salo, Jesus and Marin; they lived for 45, 8 and 87 years respectively. Findspot unknown, probably first century AD.

6. In a glass case are fragments of an Edict of issued by the emperor Anastasius (AD 491–518) concerning military dispositions in the province. Other copies of this decree have been found at Ptolemais and at Taucheira, but these fragments are of higher quality and suggest that they represent the 'master copy' of the decree. Apollonia was probably therefore already capital of *Libya Pentapolis* at the time. Most of the fragments were found reused in late walling overlying the Roman Baths (6), but one came from the 'Palace of the Dux' (17): the building upon which the text was originally displayed was presumably somewhere between the two.

Across the right-hand end:

7. On the wall, a sandstone panel with a carved cross. The upper lettering signifies 'Ch(risto)s ni(ka)' - 'Christ conquers', while below are Alpha and Omega. Found in Byzantine buildings to the W of the East church, sixth century AD?

8. Sandstone boundary marker, recording the recovery of former royal (i.e. Ptolemaic) land by the Roman state in about AD 74, through the agency of Q(uintus) Paconius Agrippinus, a legate acting on behalf of the emperor Vespasian. The Latin text is on the principal face; the Greek translation appears below it and continues onto both sidefaces of the stone. Found at Ras al-Hilal. (Compare the recently discovered example at Cyrene, p. 233.)

9. (Across the corner) Lower part of a grave-stele in white marble. The names listed are Jewish, and the two surviving dates of death are in AD 62 and 69/70. Found in the Central Church.

On the wall next to the door:

10. Sandstone boundary-marker. On the broad face (originally the rear of the stone) can be made out traces of a Latin inscription which is probably similar to that on item 12 (below) recording a lease of public land in the time of Vespasian (AD 69–79) to a certain Apollonius. On the narrow right-hand edge is part of a Neronian inscription in Greek, dated 54–55 and recording the recovery of public land from private hands. This would also have been written in Latin on the principal face (now the rear), which has been sliced off. Found reused in a house close to the Extra-Mural Church (27).

11. Inscribed sandstone block with part of a Latin building inscription, dated AD 122–3. Reused as a step in the Central Church.

12. Sandstone inscription in Latin: a boundary marker from the reign of the emperor Vespasian, recording lands belonging to the city rented out to Apollonius, son of Paraebatas. Found in the Filtro area, to the S of the main road.

On a plinth in the centre of the room:

13. Three marble impost-capitals from the East Church. They have all been cut from an earlier stele listing priests of Apollo, suggesting that there may formerly have been a temple of Apollo in the vicinity. The lettering of the list suggests a date in the first century BC or the first AD. One of the blocks also has a much later honorific inscription (in big spindly letters) on the upper surface, probably datable to AD 395–408 but still pre-dating the use of the block in the church.

Room 8

This is dedicated to an ethnographic collection from the surrounding neighbourhood, showing traditional arts and crafts. On either side of the further door to this room are wooden paddles on which are written texts from the Quran.

8 MINOR SITES BETWEEN CYRENE AND DARNAH

To the E of Cyrene the landscape changes progressively once again. As one proceeds along the main road, the terrain, which continues to be dominated by dissected limestone, becomes drier and harbours less vegetation. The Jabal Akhdar maintains a steep scarp along the coast, but inland the second scarp, upon the northern edge of which Cyrene was situated, gradually melts away. Towards the E it turns imperceptibly into the stony ground of the Marmarica, while towards the S it merges into the vast plain of the Libyan Desert. There are villages and other signs of ancient settlement, such as monumental tombs, in this area, close together on the higher ground near Cyrene, but more scattered in the drier zones. Along the southern edge of this zone, as in the case of zone 4, I have included a few sites which were outposts of settled life in the Classical period and/or watering-points on the later pilgrimage-route which passed S of the jabal between Ajdabiya and Tubruq.

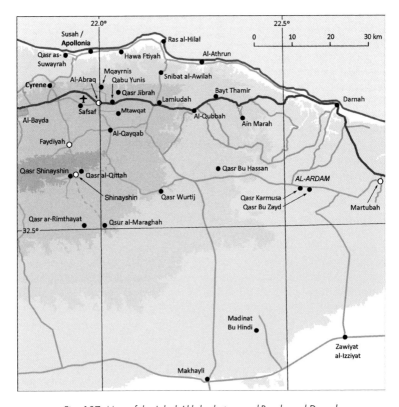

Fig. 187. Map of the Jabal Akhdar between al-Bayda and Darnah.

AIN MARAH (HYDRAX) عين ماره

Coordinates: N 32° 44.90', E 22° 23.21'
Directions: The village of Ain Marah lies about 2 km S of the main road from al-Bayda to Darnah. There are two turnings, of which the more westerly runs along the bottom of the valley, past the springs. The more easterly, recommended here, leaves the main road at N 32° 46.57' E 22° 22.98' and runs along the ridge into the main street of the village. Follow this until you come to the mosque.

Roman castle

On open ground to the SW of the mosque in the centre of the village are the last sorry remains of an ancient fort, one of many guarding the approaches to the Jabal Akhdar on the eastern side. When visited and surveyed in 1950, it was described as 34 m square and surrounded by a deep vertical-sided ditch, in the outer faces of which there were rock-chambers. It had outer walls of small, well-coursed blocks, with a single entrance on the SE side. Beneath the centre of the fort was noted a large rock-cut cistern. The cistern is still in use, but otherwise very little is visible amidst decayed recent buildings and others that are coming into existence. This is particularly unfortunate, since it was identified in 1950 as probably belonging to the same class as the interesting Roman castles at Qasr al-Hunayah (p. 31) and Qasr ar-Rimthayat (p. 312).

Ain Marah, whose ancient name was *Hydrax*, is mentioned in a letter of AD 411 written by Bishop Synesius of Ptolemais (see p. 8). He describes an occasion when he had to arbitrate in a dispute between the bishops of *Erythron* (al-Athrun, p. 289) and *Darnis* (Darnah, p. 325) over the fort at Hydrax, which was 'an abandoned heap of ruins' in the highest part of the village, having been destroyed by an earthquake. In the face of a threat of barbarian invasion, this ruin had acquired new strategic value, since it could be repaired and put back into use as a defensive strongpoint. The fort lay within the territory of Darnis, but the bishop of Erythron had attempted to claim it as his by the device of consecrating a small room in the ruin for Divine Service. In the event, Paul of Erythron admitted his deviousness and retracted his claim; his colleague and adversary, Dioscurus, then magnanimously agreed to sell him the property and all were content.

The 1950 expedition recorded that the NW and NE walls both showed outward bulges, and that on the NE side part of the inner face of the ditch had caved in. They inferred that this was the result of seismic shock; if it occurred substantially before the visit of Synesius in 411, it seems entirely plausible that the damage should have been caused by the great earthquake of 365. The ditch is wholly filled in and now only a single stretch of the NW wall is visible. However, the part which survives does show a marked outward bulge which could have been caused on that distant occasion.

AL-ARDAM الاردام

Coordinates: N 32° 35.53', E 22° 30.92'
Directions: This is an area of scattered modern settlement on the inland road between Martubah and Lamludah. From the centre of Lamludah, head S; after 4.5 km (at N 32° 44.47' E 22° 7.55') fork L (i.e. NOT for al-Qayqab); after a further 20.3 km (at N 32° 36.41' E 22° 14.74') fork L again (i.e. NOT for Makhayli); 26 km beyond this point you will see a turning to the L for Darnah, the position of which (denoted by

the coordinates above) provides a useful base-point for locating the two monuments described below.

Qasr Bu Zayd

At 5.2 km E of the Darnah fork, turn S off the asphalt road onto a track. Follow this in a south-westerly direction past some modern buildings for some 600 m. The ruins of a temple-tomb are visible as a substantial monument at N 32° 34.80′ E 22° 34.02′ (fig. 188). The tomb stands on a podium of five steps and is built of blocks with drafted margins in typical Hellenistic style. The W wall shows that the superstructure had square pilasters at the corners and four Doric engaged semi-columns on each side. The tomb has been extended on the E side, possibly forming part of a farm building in a later period; as at the nearby Qasr Karmusa, there were perhaps originally three doorways and three funerary chambers.

There is barely any trace of ancient habitation in the vicinity, though pottery of the first and third centuries AD has been found on the site. This was perhaps the location of the ancient settlement of *Mandis*, but clearance of the area for a military camp in the 1970s may well have swept away much of the evidence. Some of the fallen blocks have been arranged into ellipses, marking Muslim burials of uncertain date.

Qasr Karmusa

At a distance of 2.6 km E of the Darnah fork, and on open ground 450 m to the S of the road, at N 32° 35.01′ E 22° 32.48′, are to be found the foundations of a Hellenistic temple-tomb with a broad rectangular podium rising in five steps (fig. 189). Three entrances on the E side (largely collapsed) cut through the uppermost steps and lead into three funerary chambers. The central chamber has two flat cover-slabs, resting on a corbelled course of blocks beneath, still in position. The ceiling of the central chamber seems to have been higher than those of the lateral ones. On the N side, some scattered blocks lying nearby show that there was once a circular upper storey embellished with twelve Doric engaged columns. There was a circular boss on the wall in each space between the columns. The tomb has been attributed stylistically to the third or second century BC.

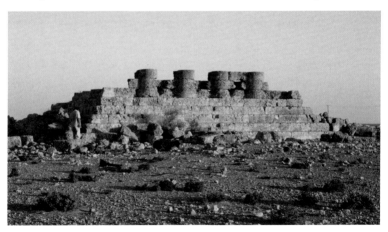

Fig. 188. Qasr Bu Zayd: Hellenistic temple-tomb.

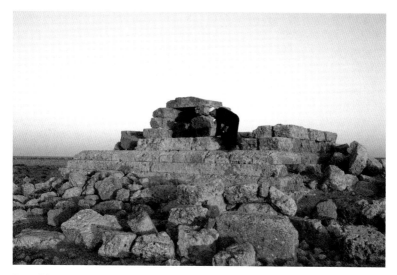

Fig. 189. Qasr Karmusa: Hellenistic temple-tomb.

AL-ATHRUN (LATRUN) الاثرون

Coordinates: N 32° 52.38', E 22° 16.60'
Directions: Travelling eastwards along the coast road from Ras al-Hilal, at a distance of 8.4 km from the junction with the road which climbs up to Snibat al-Awilah and Lamludah, turn off to the L onto the older road which passes between scattered houses. (The present road now by-passes it on the landward side.) The columns of the W church will become apparent, silhouetted against the sea; 1.2 km from the turn will be found a footpath down the side of a field, which leads to the archaeological site. This is enclosed by a high red-painted wall with a single gateway (to which the co-ordinates given refer); there should be a custodian present or in the vicinity.

Ancient town

Al-Athrun perpetuates in its name the ancient settlement of *Erythron*, and the reason for its presence here is the abundant spring of fresh water in Wadi al-Athrun. The town enjoyed the fertility of its immediate surroundings, and had

access also to the plateau above. It is not mentioned before the Roman period, and there is no archaeological evidence of earlier occupation. We know of at least three bishops of Erythron between AD 365 and 411 – at the latter date in connection with a dispute between the bishops of Erythron and Darnis (Darnah) over territory on the plateau at Hydrax (Ain Marah, p. 287). For this affair we have the report of Synesius, bishop of Ptolemais (p. 8), who was called upon to arbitrate. The presence of bishops at Erythron presupposes some measure of size and importance for the settlement, which should be thought of as a town rather than a village.

The coastline to the W of the mouth of the Wadi al-Athrun is composed of jagged cliffs; the superimposed rock strata of white limestone and brown tufa make a startling contrast with the blue of the sea. Along the cliff-top are traces of a small settlement, part of which has probably been lost long since to the sea. The main area of the settlement is now enclosed by a modern wall. Immediately inside the entrance gate, on the L, are the well-preserved and partly reconstructed remains of a small church. This is the westerly of two churches here. As one proceeds along the path towards the East church, ancient pottery is abundant on the surface and cuttings in the cliff face indicate rock-cut rooms (perhaps more probably than tombs, since they are within the settlement). The larger East Church stands on higher ground and current excavations in the vicinity by a French team are uncovering further buildings (see below). On the narrow headland to the N of the East church and on the W side of a deeply incised inlet, there are traces of a fortification of the Hellenistic period, protected on the inland side by a ditch. It has been suggested that there is a further defensive ditch, enclosing the settlement area as a whole on its landward side, but this is not now obvious on the ground.

The two churches were first discovered in the course of road-building activities in the 1950s; they were initially excavated then on behalf of the Department of Antiquities. In recent years the site has been revisited by a French team under the late Prof. André Laronde: they have carried out extensive reconstruction of the West Church and at the time of writing are conducting further excavations next to the East Church.

West Church ★ ★

This is the smaller of the two churches, and it faces W. (See figs. 190, 191.) It is, typically of many Cyrenaican churches, inscribed within a rectangle (measuring 26 × 15.65 m); there is a narthex immediately inside the entrance at the E end and an apse set between flanking chambers at the W end. The outer face of the N wall (towards the sea, where the ground falls away) is supported by a sloping revetment which is a secondary addition. Within the narthex there is, on the right-hand side, a cistern-head made from an unused impost-capital. The centre has been pierced through, but the outer profile shows how such elements were received from the quarry, roughed out but with no detail yet carved. The cistern beneath was fed by means of a channel leading in through the E wall of the church. Beneath the S side of the narthex is another opening, initially interpreted as a cistern but found in recent excavations to be an undisturbed tomb containing several bodies. These were laid mostly in the extended position and with the head to the W.

The body of the church is separated into nave and aisles by a row of columns on each side, raised on a low plinth. (Perhaps the architect wanted more height than the supplied columns afforded.) There was access between the nave and the aisles at either end, but this was prevented in between by the plinth and by decorated marble screens, some of which have been re-erected. The columns were surmounted by Corinthian capitals and impost-blocks. There are no traces of voussoir blocks, so the colonnades must have supported a flat architrave; above this was a second order of columns with Ionic capitals (now stacked

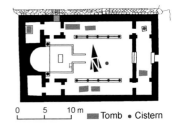

Fig. 190. Al-Athrun: plan of the West Church.

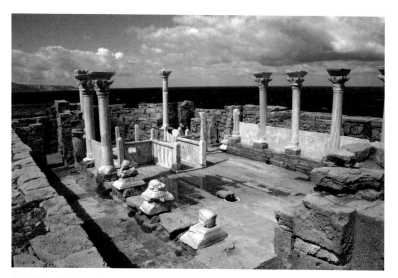

Fig. 191. Al-Athrun: the West Church.

in the SW angle-chapel), linked by a balustrade of sculpted panels. Near the centre of the nave is an opening into another cistern (also fed by a conduit beneath the floor, leading in from beneath the E door of the church). Towards the apse, the typical arrangement of chancel, enclosing screen and altar are sufficiently well preserved to be easily understood. The nave and chancel are paved with fine marble slabs, and just within the chancel on the S side are sandstone steps which once led to the *ambon*. The apse, on the other hand, was not paved; a slight offset and four sockets in the thickness of the wall suggest the former presence of a wooden *synthronon*.

The angle-chambers at the W end were each approached through vestibules in the aisles paved with blocks of stone forming octagonal patterns. (Parts of the N aisle were paved in the same manner.) The angle-chamber on the S side was featureless, but the vestibule was fitted with three wooden doors; this area probably comprised a lockable

sacristy or treasury. The N angle-chamber is paved partly with large slabs and partly with the same octagonal pattern. Against the W wall is an upstanding box-like structure within which was found only earth and a few unidentifiable bones. It was not original to the design, but had surely once housed a reliquary. The room became a *martyrion* for the veneration of a local saint. In the outer N wall of the vestibule on this side, an arch is built into the wall at a low level. This can never have been an opening, and is probably a relieving-arch set into the wall to carry its weight over some weakness in the bedrock.

In the N aisle, cover-slabs revealed the presence of two tombs, but though the covers were largely in place, the tombs beneath were found on examination to be empty. Likewise in the S aisle, rather more damaged by the collapse of the building, were found two tombs containing several empty stone ossuaries.

The walls of this church were plastered throughout, while the columns and many of the fittings were of grey-white marble, either from Proconnesos on the Sea of Marmara near Constantinople, or from quarries on the island of Thasos. They make a stunning impression in the sunlight today. Unlike the hotchpotch of re-used materials from earlier buildings which compose many early churches in North Africa, we have here, quite clearly, a uniform set of brand new, high-quality components. The presence of crosses and orbs show that they were intended, from the first, for a church. We know, in fact – particularly from the evidence of a shipwreck found off Cape Marzamemi in Sicily – that complete marble 'kits' of church fittings were supplied from the quarries. At the fullest, these would include columns, capitals, screen panels and uprights, colonnettes for the altar canopy (*ciborium*) and steps for an *ambon*. The W church at al-Athrun is the finest example

of such architecture hitherto found in Cyrenaica.

Who could afford this, and when? Because of close affinities between the two churches on this site, the question is best deferred until after the description of the East Church.

East Church ★

About 200 m to the E of the West Church lies a second church, of very similar design but larger (32 × 21.5 m) and facing in the opposite direction (fig. 192). This building is less well preserved, having been in a more prominent position and therefore more evident as a potential source of road-building material. The path brings you to the NW corner of the building and to a small doorway into the N end of the narthex. There was originally an axial entrance in the W wall, but this was closed up in subsequent modifications of the narthex, which

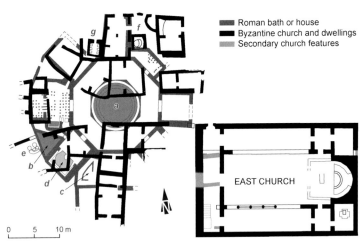

Fig. 192. Al-Athrun: plan of the East Church and neighbouring buildings.

■	Roman bath or house
■	Byzantine church and dwellings
■	Secondary church features

0   5   10 m

Roman features:		Late features:	
a	Natatio	e	Oil press
b	Cistern	f	Bakery
c	Latrine	g	Pottery kiln
d	Dining couch		

included both the insertion of a stone staircase on the S side and the insertion of other blocking walls. The narthex led to the nave and aisles through three marble-framed doorways, whose sills (of sandstone) are still in position.

The nave was paved with large marble slabs, and the aisles with patterns of smaller sandstone blocks, like those seen in the West Church. In similar fashion, the nave was separated from the aisles by marble colonnades, the intervals of which were closed by marble screen panels. (Some of these are on display in the museum at Apollonia.) The elements found on the site indicate that there were two orders of colonnades, the lower Corinthian and the upper Ionic, both with impost blocks. Scholars are divided as to whether these orders carried arcades or flat architraves – and the same issue arises with regard to the West Church. It has been argued that impost-capitals occur *only* with arcades; however, no single relevant voussoir block (of which there would have to have been many) has been found on the site of either building. It seems rather more likely, therefore, that the colonnades carried flat (timber) architraves.

The outlines of the chancel at the E end of the nave are clear, as are those of the altar-base within it. Some of the fallen elements in this area must have belonged to an altar-canopy (*ciborium*). Within the apse there is, for once, clear evidence of a *synthronon*, with stone footings in addition to sockets in the wall above for the wooden benches. A central platform in the stonework (with a corresponding gap in the sockets on the wall behind) suggests the position of a bishop's throne.

The angle-chambers on either side of the apse were each preceded by a vestibule. That on the N side had an earth floor and was featureless apart from an external doorway through the E wall of the building (blocked in a later phase). That on the S side was clearly more important; both it and its vestibule are paved with sandstone slabs, and the door-sills communicating with the nave and the S aisle show that these openings could be closed by wooden doors. In the angle-chamber was a small cruciform baptismal basin; this was partly dismantled at a later stage and converted into a reliquary recess.

The architecture, the marble fittings and many of the details (such as the patterned sandstone floors) of the two churches at al-Athrun are so similar that they must be closely contemporary in date. They also display a much higher quality of materials and of craftsmanship than most of the other known Cyrenaican churches. The latest publications favour a date at the end of the fifth century or early in the sixth for their construction. It is quite clear that both churches substantially post-date the fourth- and fifth-century bishops known to us. Who would have sponsored such expensive work at that period, we simply cannot tell. It seems generally to be agreed that the East Church, larger and more prominently sited, was the cathedral, and the that the West Church was a *martyrion*, built specifically for the custody and veneration of the relics of a saint. Furthermore, it is suggested that, perhaps in the face of external threat, the West Church was later abandoned and its relics transferred to the former baptistery of the East Church. The final phase of occupation of the East Church appears to have been secular: various additional walls subdivided the interior, and some of the chancel screen slabs were reused as paving. This presumably took place after the Arab conquest.

New excavations

Evidence for an episcopal throne in the East Church suggested that there should be an episcopal residence nearby. Recent excavations immediately to the W of the East Church (still in progress: fig. 192 is based on a plan published in 2011) might reasonably have expected to find it. Instead, what has come to light has been a remarkable octagonal bath complex with a history which extends from the third century AD until the eighth. The central feature was a stepped circular basin or *natatio* (a), surrounded by an octagonal portico: this was the focal point of a bath building of the third century AD. Heated rooms with floors supported on brick *pilae* are visible on the W and NE sides; on the SW side is a large triangular cistern (b) and a latrine (c). Alterations in the fourth century involved filling in a *frigidarium* (?) with a cold plunge-bath on the SW side, and transforming it into a dining room with a raised semicircular couch (d: as in the House of the Semicircular Couch at Cyrene, p. 189). The property was now, if not before, part of a substantial private house.

In the Byzantine period, when the East Church was built, the complex must have been in ruins. Some of its masonry was removed to build the church, but some surviving rooms were adapted to new purposes. The layout as a whole changed completely, with modest buildings on either side of a street leading to the church. A room where the triangular cistern had been contained a pressing installation for oil (e); across the street, on the N side of the former baths, was a bakery (f: with an hour-glass corn-mill and an oven) and a potter's kiln (g).

On the return from here towards the site entrance, if you keep to the high ground close to the boundary wall, you will see clear signs on the bare rock-surface of a level street, curving between various unexplored buildings.

AL-QAYQAB القيقب

Coordinates: N 32° 43.52′, E 22° 1.31′
Directions: Approaching al-Qayqab from the N (via al-Abraq), turn R at the triangular junction at N 32° 43.53′ E 22° 1.49′; after 250 m turn R onto an unmade side-street: the entrance to the castle is 150 m directly ahead.

Ottoman castle

Al-Qayqab perpetuates the name of the ancient settlement of *Agabis*, but nothing from Classical antiquity is now detectable. Its principal interest today lies in the presence of the only castle of the Ottoman period that survives in Cyrenaica (those at Benghazi and Darnah having long since been demolished, and that at al-Marj having been destroyed in the earthquake of 1963). This building was constructed in 1852 by the local governor, Abu Bakr Bay Hadduth. It was taken in hand by the Department of Antiquities in the 1960s, when modifications of the Italian colonial period were removed and it was restored as an ethnographic and natural history museum.

The castle is a single-storey structure in the form of a hollow square with round corner-towers. There is a single entrance on the S side, flanked by two British cannons of 1825. In the courtyard are a few busts of the 'Goddess of Death', which have almost certainly been brought from Cyrene. The displays within are dusty and unloved.

AL-QUBBAH القبة

Coordinates: N 32° 45.80′, E 22° 14.92′
Directions: Al-Qubbah is now a sprawling settlement on both sides of the road from

al-Bayda to Darnah. In order to reach the spring described below, it is necessary to turn off this road. If coming from the W, turn R at N 32° 45.97' E 22° 14.91' and then L; from the opposite direction, turn L at N 32° 45.93' E 22° 15.13' and then R. This will bring you to a shaded avenue of ficus trees which passes in front of the spring.

Ancient fountain-house ★

There is a considerable modern settlement here now, but the interest lies in a plentiful spring which gushes out from the base of a north-facing cliff. This was given monumental treatment when a portico built in front of it, formed of huge square stone piers with simple flaring capitals and massive flat lintels above (fig. 193). The simplicity of construction makes the portico difficult to date: it has been ascribed by Sandro Stucchi to the second century BC, but I see no reason why it should not be several centuries older. The spring has been modified and canalized in

modern times, and the little arch in front of the ancient fountain-house is a slightly unhappy pastiche; it was apparently constructed with the aid of voussoir blocks brought from Bayt Thamir! An even more unhappy addition is the recent spray-painted epigraphy.

The portico is now the only substantial ancient monument here, though a Doric frieze-block lying on the ground at the left-hand end suggests a later modification. The cliff-face further to the L is marked by tombs and rock-cut stairways.

BAYT THAMIR   بيت ثامر

Coordinates: N 32° 47.45', E 22° 18.68'
Directions: The ancient settlement lies on high ground just to the N of the main road from al-Bayda to Darnah, 6.5 km to the E of al-Qubbah and immediately to the E of the modern village. There is no archaeological zone, and the ruins lie amongst modern farms.

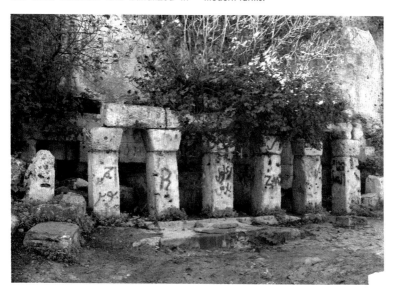

Fig. 193. Al-Qubbah: the ancient spring.

Ancient village

Here are extensive traces of an ancient settlement, identified by most recent writers with *Palaibiska*. This was a village mentioned by Synesius (p. 8) in connection with an ecclesiastical dispute concerning Erythron (al-Athrun, p. 289) and Hydrax (Ain Marah, p. 287). The site may be approached from the S by means of a farm track. At the time of writing, the current occupants of the land are ploughing it up with considerable diligence, and the evidence of ancient settlement is progressively diminishing. There are traces of farm buildings with olive-presses, of pointed arches and of rock-cut tombs, probably mostly late antique. However, some tombs with architectural façades in the Doric order must belong to the Hellenistic period. (One of these, close to the Tomb of Oedipus, is described below.) In front of the modern farmhouse on the top of the hill are several column-shafts belonging to a peristyle and indicating a former residence of some pretension.

In a slight hollow on the eastern side of the hill, at N 32° 47.49′ E 22° 18.72′, can be made out the outlines of a **Byzantine church** of three aisles. The N wall has a broad sloping revetment. Various architectural elements are recognizable, including a fine door-lintel near the E end, carved in relief with a cross-in-circle between vine-scrolls.

A boundary stone found on the site shows that in the Ptolemaic period there was a royal estate in the vicinity. Several tombs are reported to have funerary busts of Libyan appearance and the population was clearly mixed.

Tomb of Oedipus ★

One of the tombs, cut into the face of an ancient quarry, preserves painted decoration from which it has been named the *Tomb of Oedipus*. This tomb lies 150 m due N of the church, at N 32° 47.57′ E 22° 18.73′ on the N slope of the hill. It is in a farmyard, and though once protected by an iron gate it is now threatened by rubbish, and

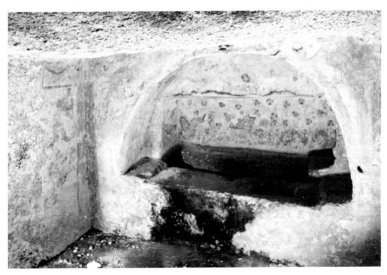

Fig. 194. Bayt Thamir: interior of the painted Tomb of Oedipus.

access may be impeded by a barrier of spiny brushwood.

A plain doorway, with two niches to the L of it on the quarry face, leads into a rectangular chamber (fig. 194). On the far side is an *arcosolium*: a semi-circular vaulted recess, long enough for a body, is cut out of the rock at table-height, with a rectangular cutting in its floor to hold a corpse (with or without a coffin). This wall, and part of the flanking walls on either side, have been treated to painted decoration bordered by wide red stripes. On the lower part of the rear wall are traces of vegetal decoration and of a male figure; in the angles above are peacocks, which together with floral motifs on the underside of the vault and in the rectangular panel behind the burial recess are commonly used to suggest the paradise beyond the grave. There is also figural decoration above the rectangular panel, but this is very difficult to decipher. The decoration on the flanking walls is divided on either side into three panels, one above the other. On the right-hand side is *Oedipus and the Sphinx*, at the top; beneath this is *The Flight of Aeneas and Anchises from Troy*, and a damaged picture which has been interpreted as *The Punishment of Sisyphus* (on his knees, attempting to roll his stone uphill). On the opposite wall, starting again from the top, is an unidentifiable armed warrior advancing to the R; a warrior driving a chariot, perhaps *Achilles dragging the body of Hector around the walls of Troy*; and *The Punishment of Ixion*, who is bound perpetually to a wheel of fire.

This combination of motifs is familiar in pagan funerary contexts. Oedipus, by vanquishing the Sphinx, represents the conquest of Death; the legend of Aeneas and Anchises stands for piety and for the wanderings of the soul; the punishments

of the giants in Hades have obvious significance for evil-doers. The tomb has been attributed to the fourth century AD.

The wall of the quarry to the L of the painted tomb is also pierced by an arched opening into a large family tomb. Above the doorway is an array of no less than nine niches for portrait-heads; within are two successive rectangular chambers with various recesses set in their walls.

On the opposite side of the farmyard (about 40 m to the NE of the Tomb of Oedipus) is the entrance to another rock-tomb. This has a carved rectangular portal framed by engaged Doric semi-columns; within is a rectangular chamber with benches around three sides and two-tier recesses for corpses in each wall. The left-hand recess in the rear wall has only been marked out, suggesting that the owning family died out before the tomb had reached its full capacity! The style of the portal suggests that this tomb was first constructed in the Hellenistic period.

HAWA FTIYAH   هوا أفطيح

Coordinates: N 32° 54.01′, E 22° 3.08′
Directions: At a distance of 8.3 km to the E of the cross-roads at the centre of the modern town of Susah, pull off the road at N 32° 54.25′ E 22° 2.98′. Here will be found a rough track leading uphill towards the very visible mouth of the cave. It is no more than ten minutes' walk. This is privately farmed land, and there are sometimes animals penned within the floor of the rock-shelter. Please respect the rights of the farmer!

Prehistoric rock-shelter

Here is a great rock-shelter in the limestone escarpment of the jabal, with an opening sufficiently wide that it can be seen from far away. Indeed, it is difficult to form an idea of the scale of it, even when standing within the opening, when the lip of rock is some 60 m above your head! This was identified as a likely site of early human occupation, and a deep excavation was carried out in the inner part of the cave by a Cambridge expedition in the 1950s. The excavators dug through 14 m of deposits, revealing a continuous sequence of occupation from the Middle Palaeolithic (about 80,000 years ago) until the Neolithic Period (about 7,000 years ago), with a smattering of Greek, Roman and Byzantine material. This has long been regarded as the most important such sequence established in North Africa. At the time of writing, a new expedition under the leadership of Prof. Graeme Barker (also of Cambridge University) has been re-excavating the earlier trench, extending it and carrying out, at the same time, a wide-ranging surface survey of prehistoric occupation in Cyrenaica. Scientific analysis of the newly collected material, in the light of advances made in dating techniques over the intervening fifty years, now suggests that the sequence extends over a much longer time-frame than had been estimated by the earlier excavator, Charles McBurney. The new data suggest that the prehistoric occupation began perhaps as much as 200,000 years ago and ended about 6,000 years ago.

LAMLUDAH　　　　　لملوده

Coordinates: N 32° 46.76', E 22° 9.26'
Directions: The ancient site lies to the E of the modern village, on the NE side of the junction (to which the coordinates refer) between the main road from al-Bayda to Darnah, and the minor road which leads northwards to Ras al-Hilal.

Ancient village ★

This extended settlement (fig. 195) has been noted by many travellers, but no excavation has taken place apart from a very limited (and largely unpublished) sounding by Richard Goodchild. A new examination of the site, by an Italian team from the University of Chieti, began in 2008. It is generally agreed that it corresponds to *Limnias*, a road-station listed in the Antonine Itinerary of the early third century AD. The ruins are enclosed within an archaeological zone at the junction where the minor road for Ras al-Hilal leaves the main jabal road; the entrance-gate is at the road-junction. There must have been a significant road-junction here also in Classical times. As usual, the ruins that are visible belong mainly to the latest, i.e. Byzantine, phase in the history of the settlement. We know that there was a bishop here in the Byzantine period. In the middle of the enclosed area is (as usual) the outline of a 20th-century Italian fort. The vegetation on this site is particularly dense and spiky, for which reason one should remember the possibility that there are snakes!

East Church

This forms a prominent rectangular mound, a short distance to the NE of the modern road-junction. The outer wall stands to a height of 4–5 m, and the interior is filled with rubble up to the crowns of the arches of the nave arcades: excavation within would be laborious, but surely rewarding. The original outer wall was composed at the corners of a single thickness of massive ashlar blocks, almost certainly derived from earlier buildings, while the straight runs in between were filled in with a core of rubble faced with smaller blocks. The apse (towards the W) was also built of large ashlar masonry. In this instance, the entire circuit of walls was strengthened at a later date by a massive sloping revetment. The corners were again faced with larger blocks than the straight runs in between. As elsewhere, the state of the original walls strongly suggests earthquake damage which needed urgent support. The original entrance at the E end was reduced in size at some point: within the original arch has been inserted a much lower and narrower one, that was barely passable. This seems to have been done for reasons of security: close inspection will show the presence behind it of a rolling-stone door, still in its slot! Internally, chambers may be detected at the four corners of the building; that at the SE corner was at some point lined with waterproof cement and converted into a cistern.

Two buildings to the E of the church have been associated with it, but this seems entirely speculative. Sandro Stucchi suggested that a square building with a corbelled (false) dome was a baptistery. (Corbelled domes are attested extremely late in the Byzantine period, if they are not to be seen as definite evidence of Arab work.) A little further away is the base of a rectangular tower. It has been buttressed in the same manner as the church and it has a single entrance facing towards it. The function of this tower is far from clear.

Press building

The uprights of oil-presses are visible on many parts of the site (nearly fifty have been recorded), as are crushing-mills and pressing-stones with grooves around the edge. In the 1950s Richard Goodchild carried out a small excavation to the N of the 'tower' near the East Church. This exposed about 70 m of a street running N–S, and on the W side of it (about half-way along) a well-preserved complex for the production, not of oil, but of wine. In one room are two presses and a treading-floor, all with channels leading into vats beneath, for the pressing of the grapes. The presses differ from those used for oil-making, since they deal with smaller volumes of material to be pressed (the already-trodden skins of the grapes) and require less pressure than olives. The upright in which the end of the press-beam is anchored is a single tall block with a blind socket in it, rather than a pair of uprights with two or more sets of holes for an adjustable fulcrum height; and the counterweight to which the windlass is anchored in order to pull down the press-beam is set in line with the beam, rather than at right-angles to it. This is a convenience which allows the installation to be fitted into a smaller room than otherwise. Further along the street frontage is a fermentation room with rows of perhaps two dozen large *dolia*, sunk into the floor, for the

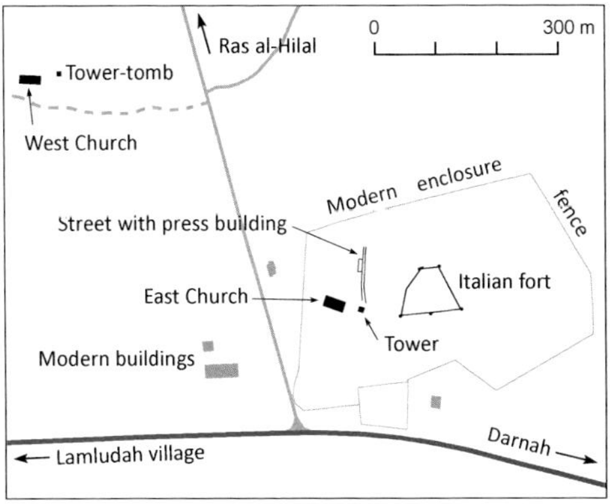

Fig. 195. Lamludah: sketch-plan of the settlement.

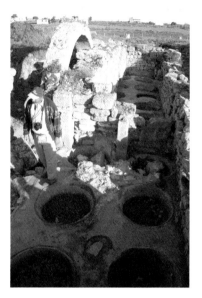

Fig. 196. Lamludah: wine fermentation vats.

fermentation of the wine (fig. 196). This room was originally spanned by a double arch supported by a central pier; at a later date it was subdivided and some of the *dolia* were buried by the inserted walls. A room behind the fermentation vats (i.e. further from the street), and much obscured by vegetation, appears to have stone cupboards all around the walls, and must have been a storeroom.

It is clear from inserted walls, one of which partly overlies the *dolia*, that there is more than one period of activity here, and that the second is probably not connected with wine production. No direct evidence of date has yet been put forward, though the materials used suggest that the first period is of Byzantine date; this is reinforced by the presence of two carved Maltese crosses on the parapet of the press-enclosure at its NW corner. The second may be also, but it may equally belong to the Islamic period.

In addition to these buildings, there are within the archaeological enclosure extensive traces of houses, often with the skeletons of arches still standing and with the uprights of oil-presses visible amongst the ruins. Note that here, as on many other sites, the arches of the late Roman period are often slightly pointed, rather than semicircular.

West Church and tower-tomb

Outside the fenced area to the NW are two further monuments of interest. The West Church lies amid patches of ploughsoil and bare rock to the W of the road to Ras al-Hilal: follow this road for 500 m from the junction. Almost opposite a track leading R to a farm is a lesser one leading L; take this and the church will be found to the R of it at a distance of about 250 m. Unfortunately, much of its masonry was dismantled in the 1970s in order to build a modern enclosure wall. It was of 'standard' Byzantine design, being rectangular in outline with a western apse placed between corner-chapels. The apse is preserved up to the first two courses of the semi-dome which covered it, and on the N side can be seen two limestone column-drums, still in position where they flanked the entrance to the northern chapel. At the E end it is still possible to make out the outlines of an entrance-vestibule between flanking rooms. The principal interest of this building, however, lies in its position. It is some way from the heart of the settlement, amongst tombs and directly over the top of a rambling rock-cut tomb-complex. This was accessed through a sunken courtyard – probably a former quarry – on the S side of the church, approached by a monumental flight of steps. Openings in the rock wall gave access to several interconnected chambers with piers supporting the roof.

Nothing now visible within the tomb-complex is of obviously Christian character, but it seems inescapable that the church was built directly above in honour of some venerated person who was believed to have been buried here.

A few metres to the E of the church is a square structure of massive ashlar masonry, possibly approached by steps on the E side. This appears to be the remains of a Hellenistic tower-tomb. (Compare the examples at Mtawqat, p. 309, and Qasr Shtillu, p. 254.) To the S of this, a ring of ashlar blocks perhaps marks a cylindrical tomb of the Hellenistic period. In this direction there is also a rectangular quarry.

MADINAT BU HINDI   مدينة بوهندي
Coordinates: N 32° 15.88', E 22° 25.16'
Directions: From the cross-roads at Makhayli, head E for 18.7 km, to N 32° 10.80' E 22° 29.36'. Turn N and follow this road (which leads to the marabut of Sidi al-Lahlafi) for 10.9 km to N 32° 16.07' E 22° 26.67'. At this point, a small double hump on the otherwise featureless western horizon is a suitable target to aim for, some 2.5 km to the W. From this point on, there are tracks, but **a 4-wheel-drive vehicle is definitely advisable**.

Late antique or early Islamic village

The last part of the route described above, after leaving the asphalt road, crosses a wide alluvial fan which is susceptible of cultivation in an otherwise stony pre-desert landscape. On the W side of this are the ruins of a substantial village, composed of buildings of rough stones, more or less laid in courses. Some of these courses are stacked obliquely on edge, with the course above leaning in the opposite direction in a vertical herring-bone pattern (fig. 197). It is evident that individual rooms were roofed with false domes, formed by flat courses of slabs corbelled progressively inwards (like the *trulli* of Puglia in Italy in more recent times). Corners of buildings tend to be reinforced by the use of larger blocks. The over-all layout may be described as

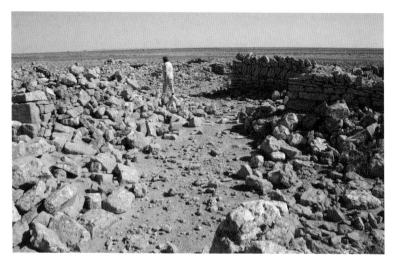

Fig. 197. Madinat Bu Hindi: a street in the village.

'organic', with winding irregular streets between the buildings. On the W edge of the settlement is a caravanserai of trapezoidal form with longer sides of 80 m and shorter ones of 56 and 51 m. It has two entrances, on the E and the W. Its wall is of small blocks reinforced by larger masonry at the corners; internally there are signs of a smaller enclosure and of a series of rooms.

The date of this settlement has not been established; it is probably early Islamic. The presence of herring-bone patterns in the masonry of some of the walls, together with the use of false domes, have been taken as evidence of this, but these usages are not themselves firmly datable. In the course of a brief reconnaissance in 2010 no diagnostic Roman pottery was found, but no glazed medieval wares were found either.

MAKHAYLI (MECHILI)   المخيلي

Coordinates: N 32° 9.55', E 22° 17.05'
Directions: The ruins described below lie to the E of the modern settlement, but about 800 m to the W of the Makhayli cross-roads and 250 m N of the E–W road. The co-ordinates are those of the supposed bath house.

Ancient settlement

There are wells here, and one would have expected a Roman outpost at this point, though nothing identifiably Roman has yet been reported. The presence of a fort was reported by al-Bakri (writing in 1068, but based on 10th century sources) and mud-brick ruins may relate to this. On open ground between the wells and the village mosque are walls of rubble masonry which enclose an (older?) structure of mud-brick. This consists of three small rooms in line, of which the central one still possesses about half of its roof. This is in the form of a dome, but is composed of flat courses of bricks, corbelled progressively inwards. This form of false dome occurs (in stone) also at Madinat Bu Hindi (above), a settlement 17 km to the NE, and in a late Roman church at Mqayrnis, not far from Cyrene (p. 306). Sandro Stucchi identified the

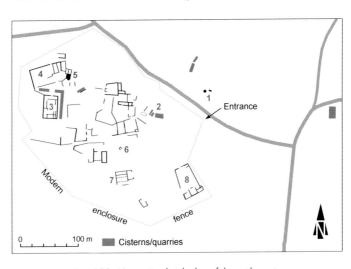

Fig. 198. Mqayrnis: sketch-plan of the settlement.

building (probably correctly) as a bath-house, but it is impossible to say whether it is late antique or early Islamic in date.

On higher ground, a few metres to the N of the bath-house, stands a single round tower. This is all that remains of an Italian fort.

MQAYRNIS (MGHERNES) مقيرنيس

Coordinates: N 32° 48.99', E 21° 59.73'
Directions: Head E from the Cyrene cross-roads for a distance of 6.9 km. Turn here onto a side-road leading N; there is a mosque just to the E of the turning. At a T-junction after 800 m, turn R. Follow this road, through a stony but fertile landscape with many traces of ancient habitation, for 4.6 km to N 32° 48.51' E 21° 59.76'. The buildings of the ancient village will be clearly visible on the higher ground to your L. Turn N onto an unmade but good farm track. After 800 m turn L again, and after a further 150 m you will find the entrance to the antiquities zone on your L and two ancient tombs above you to the R.

Alternatively (if approaching from the E) turn N at the E end of al-Abraq village, at N 32° 47.03' E 22° 00.49', then W after 2.2 km. From here, after 1.3 km, you will reach the same farm track heading N. The coordinates given for the site are those of the gate into the enclosed zone. (If closed/wired up, it should be possible to open it without difficulty: please leave it as you found it.)

Ancient village ★ ★

This remarkably well-preserved ancient settlement (fig. 198) lies 13 km due E of Cyrene, on the edge of the upper escarpment of the Jabal Akhdar. It was noted and sketched by 19th-century travellers, and it has been noted and photographed in the 20th century; but it has never been studied in detail. The

name of the settlement – a small town – is unknown to us, though an inscription found re-used in the Italian fort at al-Abraq almost certainly comes from this site. It indicates that it was sufficiently important in the late first century BC to have its own magistrates. Tombs in the vicinity, together with the style of some of the masonry, indicate that the settlement goes back at least to the Hellenistic period; the presence of a church indicates that it was still flourishing in Byzantine times. Most of what is now visible is likely to belong to the latter period.

The core of the site is enclosed by a fence, but cuttings in the rock and other features indicate that the settlement extended beyond this area. There are also lines of orthostats marching across the landscape which demarcate ancient property boundaries. An exploration of the site will reveal a number of large buildings, some of which appear to be farms. These take the form of squarish enclosures with high walls of ashlar masonry; sometimes a broad carriage-entrance can be made out. Internally, there is a division between an outer enclosure for livestock (with stone mangers or drinking-troughs) and an inner part which is residential. Beam slots in the inner faces of the walls indicate that many of these buildings were two storeys high. The following features are worthy of note. (Numbers refer to the sketch-plan in fig. 198.)

Tombs (1)

Similar to the handsome cylindrical tomb N1 at Cyrene (p. 238) is a (smaller) example here which is perhaps also of the fourth century BC (fig. 199). This tomb has the interesting characteristic of an internal peripheral corridor, entered through a doorway on the E side. (This would have provided for the ritual perambulation around the

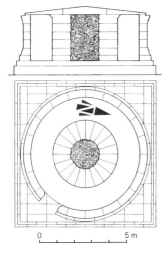

0 _____ 5 m

Fig. 199. Mqayrnis: reconstruction-drawing of a circular tomb of the fourth century BC.

tomb, which recurs in descriptions of funerals from Homeric times onward.) Immediately to the E of this tomb is a rectangular temple-tomb of unusually short proportions (which accentuate its height). It stands on a plinth of five steps (compare Massah, p. 123, and Snibat al-Awilah, p. 322), but the entrance doorway is placed entirely above the steps rather than cutting through them, resulting in a low funerary chamber. The sides of the tomb are carved with recessed panels, creating an impression of pilasters around the walls. This monument is placed tentatively in the third century BC.

Cisterns (2)

The track into the site leads onto a large expanse of bare limestone, which is characteristic of many sites on the Jabal Akhdar. Part of this expanse has been carved out into vertical-sided rectangular basins resembling swimming-pools. The primary function of these basins appears

to have been as sources of building material; however, their excavators appear to have been sensitive to their potential both for defence (when they form 'moats' immediately surrounding individual buildings) and for water storage. Both secondary functions seem to be represented at Mqayrnis. One of the basins in this area still has cover-slabs over it and must have served as a cistern, while on the western part of the site the 'citadel' (see below) has a moat on two sides which, while not constituting a complete defensive structure, was surely conceived as having a defensive role.

To the W of the cisterns is an area of buildings which still stand to a considerable height, and which comprise one or more large properties (probably farms).

'Citadel' (3)

Yet further to the W is a rectangular complex (fig. 200), whose entire perimeter wall is preserved, in places to a height of several metres. It was entered through a single arched doorway on the N side, and it is surrounded on the N and E sides by a neatly square-cut quarry/moat. This is interrupted in front of the entrance. Internally, the crowns of numerous arches can be made out amidst the fallen blocks and the bushes. Sandro Stucchi believed that this was a church, since it corresponds in mass to many such buildings. However, there is no sign of an internal apse and the inference suffers from the (to me, fatal) objection that the complex is aligned N–S rather than E–W. I have therefore retained the appellation 'citadel' used by some earlier writers: the solidity of the structure and its evident separation from other buildings suggest a special role, but it may just have been the most imposing of the farms in the group, with rooms opening off a central courtyard.

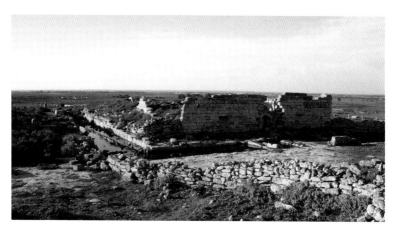

Fig. 200. Mqayrnis: the moated 'citadel' from the NE.

Hellenistic building (4)

A few metres to the N of the 'citadel' is a large rectangular enclosure. The outer face of its wall shows that the blocks of which it is built have the drafted edges which are typical of the Hellenistic period. In view of the longevity of the settlement, this structure was undoubtedly modified during the course of its existence; but it shows that when the monumental tombs were constructed there were already large buildings in the settlement, perhaps very similar to those of the Byzantine period which are now more apparent.

Baths (5)

The baths (figs. 201, 202) are small but remarkably well preserved. They consist of an *apodyterium* divided in two by a wide arch and entered originally through three arches on the W side or a single arch on the N. To the S of this are three rooms entered in sequence, whose roofs are still intact. The first, presumably a *frigidarium*, is barrel-vaulted; from this one proceeded to the *tepidarium*, covered by a dome of concrete rubble and with a projecting semi-dome over a

plunge-bath on the E side. From here one must have continued through a doorway (now buried) to the domed *caldarium*, which was provided with three such projecting semi-domes, again presumably over plunge-baths. One of these plunge-baths has recently been excavated, showing that the building has a considerable depth of fill internally. The

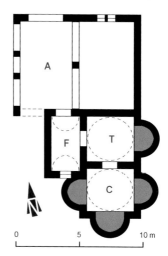

Fig. 201. Mqayrnis: sketch-plan of the baths.

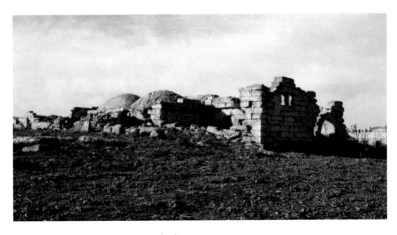

Fig. 202. Mqayrnis: the Byzantine baths.

undersides of the domes still have their original render of pink plaster. In the corners can be seen recesses, where terracotta flue-pipes once vented the smoke from beneath the heated floors out through the roof. Both the domes and the barrel vault of the *frigidarium* are pierced by several small square skylights. The external stoke-holes remain buried.

This little complex has been attributed to the Byzantine period, but the date should perhaps be regarded as provisional.

A few metres to the E of the baths can be made out remains of an oil-pressing installation, with an anchor-block for the press-beam and the base of a circular crushing mill.

Rock-tomb (6)

On the eastern part of the site, in a shallow quarry, is a rock-tomb accessed from a rectangular *dromos*; this leads through a doorway framed by carved mouldings into a single rectangular chamber. The tomb was presumably outside the area of settlement at the time of its construction: it may be Hellenistic or early Roman.

Church (7)

This building is readily identifiable from the arcade on the N side of the nave, which is clearly visible as one enters the archaeological zone. Many other details of the building are unclear. The nave can, however, be made out, separated from the aisles by rows of rectangular piers; those on the N side still carry their arcade. At the E end, a central doorway can be made out, implying that the apse was towards the W (though no trace of this is visible). In a second phase the church was drastically remodelled: the outer walls were reinforced and the nave arcades walled up, leaving a small central space with now unconnected flanking rooms, apart from a small doorway leading into the former N aisle at the W end. It has been argued that this phase belongs also to the Byzantine period, on the basis of a lintel with a (defaced) cross on it. This is hardly conclusive and it should also be noted that the rooms constructed in the N aisle were roofed by means of corbelled (false) domes. This is a roofing technique which may be exclusively post-Byzantine. (See under Madinat Bu Hindi, p. 301).

South-East Building (8)

At the SE edge of the enclosed zone is a large trapezoidal enclosure, dominated by a tower and perhaps other buildings on the SE side. This is presumably another large farm.

MTAWQAT   لمطوقات

Coordinates: N 32° 45.67', E 22° 2.46'

Directions: Head E from the Cyrene cross-roads, and at the beginning of the village of al-Abraq, at N 32° 47.03' E 21° 59.51', turn S onto the road for al-Qayqab. After 2.0 km, turn L and follow this road for 4.4 km until the asphalt comes to an end. The church will be visible 500 m to the SSE of this point; from here it may be reached in a few minutes on foot, or you may follow the unmade track to the E for 300 m and then fork R in order to get closer to the ruins.

Ancient village with church

The principal monument here is a large, three-aisled church situated in gently rolling country with a typical thin covering of soil over the limestone bedrock. It sits on a denuded rocky shelf overlooking a shallow valley to the S. There are many traces of an ancient settlement in the vicinity, though its name is unknown.

Substantial upstanding walls of the church are still visible, though no excavation has taken place here. Three distinct phases of construction are detectable.

Phase 1

This seems to have been a conventional church of rectangular plan, 31 × 18 m, with an apse between angle-chambers at the E end and a narthex extending the width of the building at the W end. The outer SW and SE corners still stand as skeletal remains some 8 m high, built in large blocks of well-dressed local limestone (fig. 203); the main parts of the walls were of smaller stones with a rubble core, and have largely fallen away. Visible details within which belong to this phase are the apse (including several courses of the semi-dome which covered it, and the crown of which was evidently well below the height of the external walls), much of the inner wall of the narthex, and most of the piers of the arcade on the S side of the nave. The

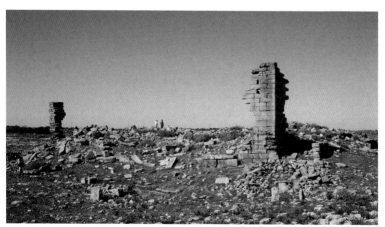

Fig. 203. Mtawqat: the upstanding corners of the church.

central part of the narthex wall, opening into the nave, was pierced by three arches of which the central one was wider than those on either side.

Phase 2

At a subsequent date, possibly as a result of earthquake damage, the N side of the church was partly rebuilt; at the same time, the building was extended northwards at the E end. This work was carried out in alternating tall and short courses, again of finely dressed limestone masonry. The NE corner was substantially remodelled, with internal walls (and arched openings) in different positions from before – but without excavation the details are unclear.

Phase 3

Straight joints show that, structurally at any rate, the W, S and E walls were enclosed yet later in substantial revetments, partly vertical but sloping inwards at the NW and NE corners. Where this was built against the phase 2 wall at the NE corner, the N wall of the phase

2 extension leans markedly outwards, showing the clear necessity of the work to stabilize a precarious building. On the same three sides there is a rock-cut ditch nearly 5 m wide; on the N side there are two open rectangular cisterns. Of uncertain date and character is a curious feature in the W end of the nave, close to the entrance from the narthex. Only partly visible amidst the rubble is an oval feature supported on arches and columns. The architraves across the top of the feature are composed of re-used colonnettes and fragments of decorated chancel-screen slabs.

In the absence of excavation, much concerning this church remains to be guessed, though answers may well lie beneath the surface. The layout (apsed nave inscribed within a rectangular outline) is generally agreed to be characteristic of sixth-century churches in Cyrenaica. The refurbishments and the sloping revetments surely suggest repairs following a natural disaster. As on many other sites, the question arises as to whether the ditch is original or secondary, and whether it is

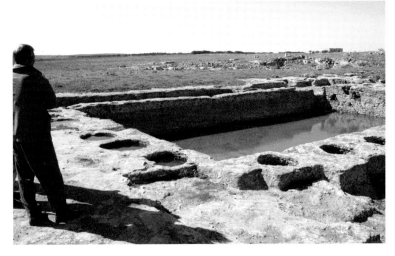

Fig. 204. Mtawqat: rock-cut tanks and vats.

Fig. 205. Mtawqat: the uprights of an ancient olive-press.

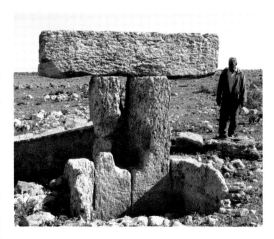

intended to be defensive in nature (see p. 14).

Roughly 150 m SE of the church is an area of quarries (with rock-cut tombs) and huge **rectangular tanks** – probably also quarries in the first instance. The largest of these (fig. 204) has an array of rock-cut circular vats around it and clearly served some industrial or agricultural purpose which is now difficult to divine.

Over a stretch of some 400 m across the lower ground to the SE of the church, there is a scatter of ruins suggesting a number of substantial **olive farms** with multiple oil-pressing installations. These are evident both from the distinctive uprights which anchored the press-beam (fig. 205: systematically different in design from those found in Tripolitania), and from the circular bases of crushing-mills. Some of these were turned on edge and found a secondary use as uprights. One of these farms (at N 32° 45.60' E 22° 2.67') incorporates a **Hellenistic tower-tomb**. This was a rectangular structure of ashlar masonry (without drafted edges) three storeys high.

QABU YUNIS   قبو يونس

Coordinates: N 32° 47.06', E 22° 1.63'
Directions: Head eastwards a distance of 15.3 km along the main road towards Darnah from the Cyrene cross-roads. The archaeological zone, enclosed by a fence, will be easily visible just 80 m to the N of the road.

Ancient village

This is the site of an ancient village, which has never been studied in detail. The area of orthostats and tumbled blocks is extensive; three upstanding monuments are worthy of notice.

At a street intersection stands a single span of what was once a **four-way arch** (*tetrapylon*: fig. 206). It is of limestone ashlar masonry, virtually without architectural embellishment, and is presumed late Roman. (Despite its modest character, this is still quite an unusual feature for a small settlement.)

To the E of this are substantial remains of a **bath-building**. This consists of three rooms in line, entered from the N, of which the second and third are heated; a fourth is at right-angles to the others. The building is of small ashlar masonry with larger blocks at the corners; the roofs took the form of barrel-vaults, which rose from a bonding-course of slabs which run through the thickness of the walls and project slightly on either side. The rooms were vaulted at differing heights which decreased from the entrance, and a 19th-century drawing shows part of an upper storey. Internally, vertical slots can be seen

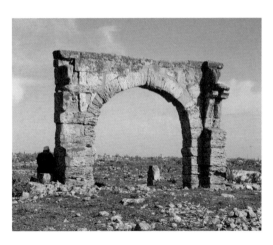

Fig. 206. Qabu Yunis: the tetrapylon.

all, but as you come out of the village it suddenly turns into a wide graded track which passes through rolling countryside, sometimes covered with dense scrub, sometimes utterly bare. **It is rough at the time of writing, and definitely requires a robust vehicle** – but it may in due course receive an asphalt surface! Follow this track for 15.5 km. At this point the Roman building will be clearly visible on low ground to the L of the road; the Italian fort lies on higher ground, closer to the road but 400 m further on.

where the flues from beneath the heated floors ran up the wall.

On the W side of the settlement can be made out the mass of a large rectangular complex surrounded by a ditch. Numerous arches are evident in the interior, but no detail of the plan is clear. It has been claimed that this was a church; it is at least aligned approximately E–W, but no trace of an apse is visible. It seems similar to the 'citadel' at Mqayrnis (p. 304) and subject to the same uncertainties of interpretation.

QASR AL-MARAGHAH قصر المراغه

Coordinates: N 32° 30.93', E 22° 0.26'
Directions: From the Cyrene cross-roads, head S to the village of Faydiyah at N 32° 41.36' E 21° 54.63' (12.2 km). Merge here with the road from al-Qayqab, which comes in from the L; after about 300 m, just before the rise, fork L onto a minor road. Follow this (still heading S after a few bends) for 7.4 km to the hamlet of Shinayshin at N 32° 37.63' E 21° 55.46'. The next bit is tricky, but only briefly! The asphalt road follows a long curve to the R, but you should aim to fork off to the L, still going directly S, between the houses. It hardly looks like a road at

Ancient farm and modern fort

This location is known now as Qsur al-Maraghah (in the plural) because of the presence of two 'castles' here. Between them, they provide a rather neat demonstration of the difference between a military post and a farm. The more southerly structure (which we may call 'B') is surely a relic of Italian military occupation, marked by a rectangular enclosure with round corner-towers. It is built of small loose stones, with some internal structures – possibly only walls protecting tents – of similar build. Occupation is represented by rusting tin cans. The position is on high ground with good views around. In contrast, the ancient building (A), which was described by Richard Goodchild as 'a simple watch-tower 15 m square, with a high revetted talus on the inner side of a very broad surrounding ditch' is sited some 18 m lower, in a hollow where it is overlooked (fig. 207), but closer to the floor of a nearby wadi with a potentially arable alluvial floor. There are indeed wadi-walls upstream of the site and at the point where it is crossed by the road to the N. This was surely therefore a farm and not a military post, despite its small size which can only have allowed for a few rooms and no central light-well.

The ancient building is very similar to those at Qasr Wurtij, just 16 km to the NE (p. 318), and Qasr Bu Hassan (p. 315). At first sight, it appears to be built of rough stones which form a sloping revetment around all four sides; there was a wide ditch all around it with a counterscarp on the outer edge. On the S side there was a narrow entrance, approached by a causeway across the ditch which led, not directly to it, but to the SW corner of the building. Goodchild regarded the building as Byzantine; however, as at the other sites, there is an original inner structure with vertical walls of good ashlar masonry on the

outside, smaller ashlar work on the inside and a fill of rubble in between. Amongst re-used materials lying on the surface are two pieces of a Doric cornice-moulding. Pottery found on the site ranged from the first to (at least) the sixth century AD, implying a long period of occupation. The sloping revetment is clearly secondary, and was perhaps added as a result of earthquake damage (or a fear of it; see p. 14).

QASR AL-QITTAH   قصر القطة
Coordinates: N 32° 37.88′, E 21° 56.54′
Directions: From the Cyrene cross-roads, head S through Faydiyah towards Shinayshin, as in the directions for Qasr al-Maraghah. Immediately before arriving at Shinayshin, turn L at N 32° 37.70′ E 21° 55.49′ onto what is now a good graded track (possibly soon to be asphalted?). Follow this eastwards for 1.7 km. The watchtower stands on a bare rocky spur just 100 m to the N of the track.

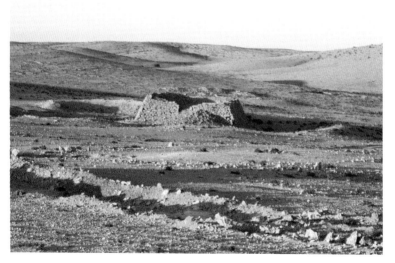

Fig. 207. Qasr al-Maraghah A, the Roman farm.

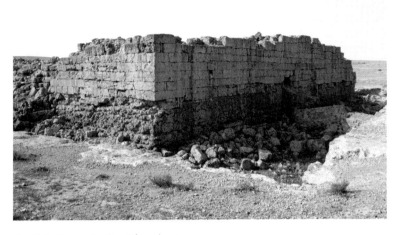

Fig. 208. Qasr ar-Rimthayat from the N.

Ancient watch-tower

This is a minor monument, but one easily included in an excursion to the Shinayshin area. It is a small rectangular building, approximately 8 × 6 m and in good ashlar masonry, which still stands to a maximum of seven courses high. It is too small to be anything other than a watch-tower (or a tower-tomb?). The masonry looks Roman rather than Hellenistic (there are no drafted edges) or Byzantine (there is no sign of a projecting string-course).

QASR AR-RIMTHAYAT قصر الرمثايات
Coordinates: N 32° 30.81′, E 21° 56.99′
Directions: As for Qasr al-Maraghah, head southwards from the Cyrene cross-roads, through Faydiyah to the hamlet of Shinayshin. On arrival at Shinayshin, remain on the asphalt road, which curves to the R, past the village. After 1.5 km there is another small group of buildings on the R, and a turning to the R at N 32° 37.05′ E 21° 54.82′. Continue straight on for 1.3

km, and take the R fork when the road divides at N 32° 36.44′ E 21° 54.47′. After a further 4.4 km, the asphalt comes to an end at a low earth dam. From here on, there is a multiplicity of tracks and **a 4-wheel-drive vehicle is strongly recommended**. The distance from here to the castle is about 8 km on a bearing of 148°: it is possible to follow a reasonably straight course towards it, and this will take about 45 minutes. As you approach, the handsome ashlar masonry of the castle is clearly visible from a distance.

Roman castle ★

The terrain that one passes through to the S of Shinayshin is initially fertile, rolling countryside, with scattered pine trees and extensive areas of cereal crops. The more southerly part of the route, beyond the end of the asphalt road, has large areas of bare limestone; there are, however, still areas of cultivated alluvium in the wadi-beds. Some of the wadis show signs of walling along their edges, typical of cultivation in antiquity, and it is likely that there are many ancient sites in the area to be discovered.

Qasr ar-Rimthayat is an impressive building, undoubtedly military, built in a slight hollow on high ground (fig. 208). An enclosure wall of good ashlar masonry, approximately 33 m square, rises flush with the inner edge of a rock-cut ditch, square in section and about 7.5 m wide. On the SE side the ditch was interrupted by an entrance causeway; on the opposite side, it was interrupted by a narrow wall of living rock, which has now collapsed. The purpose of this may be deduced by reference to Qasr al-Hunayah to the S of Ajdabiya (p. 31), which undoubtedly belongs to the same class of building. At that site, storerooms and stables opened into the ditch and there was also access to it by means of a ramp and external underground chambers. No such features are visible at Qasr ar-Rimthayat, but the ditch is sufficiently obstructed by fallen debris that their presence cannot be excluded. Examination of the interior

shows that, as at Qasr al-Hunayah, there were rock-cut chambers below ground-level. Partial breaks in the ceiling reveal two such chambers which are still accessible. That which is better preserved (fig. 209) is square, with a central pier supporting the ceiling. Because of the debris which has fallen in, the floor is not apparent, but the chamber may have been about 3 m high. For the same reason, it is not possible to say whether this chamber communicated directly with any other, or whether there was a staircase down from the ground-level. No doorway is currently visible, but an original square hatchway in the ceiling may suggest that access was by means of a ladder.

Close to the causeway across the ditch is a cluster of Muslim graves, two of which lie within a recently-constructed walled enclosure. The bare limestone surface around the castle is also marked by an extensive array of circular enclosures around 20 m across, defined by low walls of rough paired orthostats with a

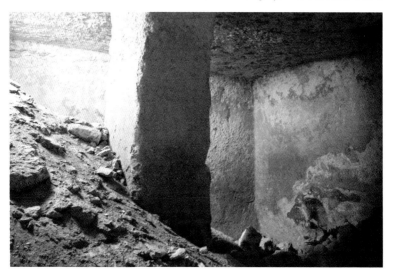

Fig. 209. Qasr ar-Rimthayat: underground chamber.

smaller rubble infill. Each of these enclosures contains a single underground chamber approached by a stepped *dromos*. These chambers show no distinctive feature within (neither burial recesses nor pressing installations), though some tethering-rings carved in the ceilings were noted. The enclosures are surely ancient and presumably contemporary with the castle. They may have been simply animal pens; but they probably served also for human habitation. A local population perhaps gathered around the fort either for protection or for its economic benefits.

Datable pottery collected on the surface here belonged exclusively to the second and third centuries AD.

QASR AS-SUWAYRAH   قصر السويره
Coordinates: N 32° 53.51′, E 21° 54.37′
Directions: The site is approximately 7 km to the W of Apollonia along the coast, and 800 m to the W of the nearby desalina-

tion plant. Coming from Apollonia, turn R at the checkpoint beneath the climb (at N 32° 53.26′ E 21° 55.95′) and follow this road, beyond the end of the asphalt and past the desalination plant, for exactly 3.0 km. From this point, the monument is just over 200 m S of the road. There is no path towards it, but the ruins are unmistakable when you find them.

Dovecote
These ruins are of interest for their unusual character rather than their magnificence. A mass of fallen blocks of carefully cut sandstone (fig. 210), on the edge of a terrace some 35 m above sea-level, reveals the location of a cylindrical *columbarium* or dovecote which once housed around 1,200 nesting-holes around the inner face of its circular walls. It must have stood some 8 m high, and will have been a striking landmark (fig. 211). The sill of the entrance is towards the terrace edge, so that it could not be reached without a ladder.

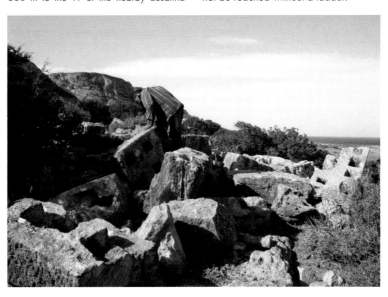

Fig. 210. Qasr as-Suwayrah: fallen blocks of an ancient dovecote.

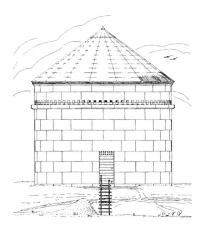

Fig. 211. Qasr as-Suwayrah. (Reconstruction-drawing of the dovecote by G. Hallier.)

The stonework of the dovecote is similar to that of the Hellenistic defences of Apollonia. It has therefore been suggested that this was not a private venture, but that these were birds sacred to a god, whose sanctuary may have been nearby. There are traces, some 50 m to the W, of a rectangular farm building, together with a rock-cut pressing-stone and vat; but these are not built to the same quality, and may be unrelated.

QASR BU HASSAN   قصر بوحسن

Coordinates: N 32° 38.00', E 22° 18.82'
Directions: From the centre of Lamludah, head S; after 4.5 km (at N 32° 44.47' E 22° 7.55') fork L (i.e. NOT for al-Qayqab); after a further 20.3 km (at N 32° 36.41' E 22° 14.74') fork L again (i.e. NOT for Makhayli); 6.0 km to the E of this point, turn L onto a track which leads after 2.4 km to two modern farms on the N bank of the Wadi al-Hiyshah. The ancient building stands about 200 m behind the one to the W, and now has a steel water-tank on top of it.

Fortified farm

The ancient building is a rectangular structure approximately 15 × 10 m, standing 2–3 m high. It is composed, at first sight, of sloping external walls in large uncut blocks of stone. No entrance is currently detectable, but on top of the mound it is clear that the sloping outer walls represent a revetment added to an original structure in good ashlar masonry. On the S side of the building, a modern cistern-head is very probably sited over an ancient cistern. There is no ditch around the building, but there are signs of an outer enclosure-wall, faced with large irregular stones, on the N and W sides.

In character, this building seems to be identical with the nearby Roman farms at Qasr Wurtij and Qasr al-Maraghah.

QASR JIBRAH   قصر جبْره

Coordinates: N 32° 48.33', E 22° 2.77'
Directions: Head eastwards from the Cyrene cross-roads towards Darnah, for a distance of 18 km. Here, at N 32° 47.46' E 22° 3.15', turn L onto a straight track running due N. The surface is graded but not asphalted; however, it is good enough for a saloon car. After 1 km the track turns westwards and after a further 600 m there is a fork. Take the right fork – the qasr is by now unmistakable beyond some modern buildings – and this will lead in about 500 m to the ruins.

Ancient village ★

This site does not benefit from an archaeological enclosure and is on the land of a present-day farm. Visitors should therefore show due courtesy to anyone they meet, and should respect the wire fences which may need to be climbed in order to explore the site!

As at Mqayrnis (p. 303), here too the scattered ruins of an ancient village include signs of relatively wealthy houses or farms. These are probably mostly late Roman in date, though the best-preserved building – **the qasr** – is in magnificent ashlar masonry with drafted edges, suggestive of a Hellenistic date. This is certainly a farm: within, it is divided approximately into two halves. In the eastern half, drinking-troughs for animals are cut into the thickness of the perimeter wall at the NE corner (fig. 212); above, rows of sockets for joists show that even this part of the complex was two storeys high. The western part shows internal subdivisions and must have been the residential area.

Immediately to the N of the qasr, orthostats appear to delineate a large **oil-processing complex**. This comprises a rectangular enclosure in which a number of oil presses may be recognized by the socketed uprights which anchored the press-beam, and sometimes by the pressing-stone (on

which the baskets of crushed olives were placed) in front. Further exploration will show that there were several other such installations in the settlement, and a number of upturned bowl-shaped mill-bases may be seen. On the highest point of the site is a rectangular structure, partly built of re-used blocks; the lack of any sort of architectural embellishment suggests a **watch-tower** rather than a temple or tomb.

Associated with the settlement are numerous **monumental tombs**. These take the form here of giant sarcophagus-tombs, of the Classical Greek or Hellenistic period. Superficially, they are not unlike temple-tombs (such as those at Snibat al-Awilah, p. 322), but here they are clearly carved to represent sarcophagi with lids, rather than petrified buildings with roofs (fig. 213). Each stands on a high, stepped podium, in one end of which is a doorway leading into a funerary chamber

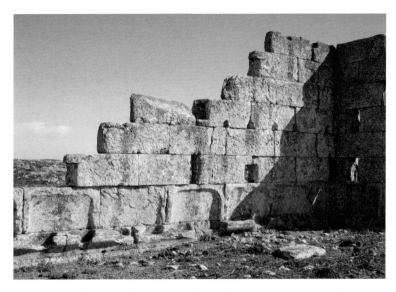

Fig. 212. Qasr Jibrah: drinking-troughs for livestock inside the best-preserved farm building.

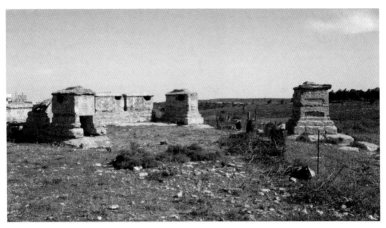

Fig. 213. Qasr Jibrah: giant sarcophagus-tombs.

beneath. The body is sometimes carved as a stone sarcophagus, and sometimes as a wooden chest with feet at the corners. It has a separate lid which covers an upper chamber. The podium is often carved out of the native rock beneath. The largest concentration of tombs is now in a farmyard, and resembles nothing so much as an array of huge petrified hen-coops! One of the tombs has three small niches carved on one side, as if for portrait-heads of the deceased: this perhaps indicates continued use of the tomb during the Roman period.

The track which leads northwards past the farm degenerates in quality; it is satisfactorily passable only in a four-wheel-drive vehicle. You may also find a locked gate further along (which is passable on foot). An expedition in this direction is, however, worthwhile, for at a distance of 1.9 km from Qasr Jibrah, at N 32° 49.15' E 22° 3.33', may be seen a huge portal composed of monolithic limestone uprights with a flat lintel. This goes by the name of **Bab Tawkharah** ★ (fig. 214). It appears to stand isolated in the landscape, but

as you approach it is clear that at this point an ancient road curves to the R in front of the portal and descends through an artificial cutting to the level below. Beyond the portal is a platform of bare rock with a magnificent view northwards over the lower jabal towards the sea. In the rock surface are cuttings for presses

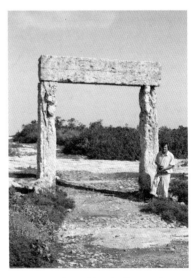

Fig. 214. Bab Tawkharah: the tantalising portal of a vanished Roman farm estate!

317

(oil or wine?) associated with collecting vats. This was evidently the site of a farm in the classical period.

QASR SHINAYSHIN   قصر شنيشن

Coordinates: N 32° 37.25′, E 21° 54.73′
Directions: As for Qasr al-Maraghah (p. 310), head southwards from the Cyrene cross-roads, through Faydiyah to the hamlet of Shinayshin. On arrival at Shinayshin, remain on the asphalt road, which curves to the R, past the village. After 1.5 km there is another small group of buildings on the R, and a turning to the R at N 32° 37.05′ E 21° 54.82′. The monument described below stands on the crest of the hill which overlooks these buildings.

Roman farm

On a bare rocky knoll here stands a small rectangular building (approximately 14 × 10 m) in large blocks of ashlar masonry, of which a few remain in position. There was no surrounding ditch, and the position of the entrance cannot be made out, but on the S slope of the hill is an array of cuttings, caves and perhaps foundations of buildings. Towards the bottom of the slope is a small perennial spring.

QASR WURTIJ   قصر ورتيج

Coordinates: N 32° 35.35′, E 22° 9.43′
Directions: From the main road between al-Bayda and Darnah, turn S at the modern village of Lamludah (at N 32° 46.75′ E 22° 8.59′: this is the road that leads to Martubah). After 4.5 km, where the road divides, fork L; after a total of 29 km from Lamludah, turn R at N 32° 36.80′ E 22° 13.55′. Follow this road WSW for 7.3 km. You will now see the castle prominently above the road on the S side and some 400 m from it. There is an unmade track here which leads towards it.

Roman farm – or military post?

This is a hill-top building with a fine view over stony desert country. The qasr is rectangular, with rounded corners. At first sight, it appears to be built of uncut stone blocks, massive at the base but progressively smaller higher up, with sloping outer faces. However, a closer inspection on top of the mound shows that this is a revetment added (after an earthquake?) to a pre-existing building with vertical walls (as at Qasr al-Maraghah, p. 310, and Qasr Bu Hassan, p. 315, which it closely resembles). These have an outer facing of well-fitted ashlar blocks, an inner face of smaller squared blocks and a fill of rubble in between. There is even a small exposed area of painted wall-plaster on the inner face. On the SE side, a straight edge suggests the position of the entrance. The over-all size is small and the style of the original masonry (so far as it is visible) would be consistent with almost any date in the Roman period. Pottery found in the vicinity belongs to the first century AD and to the Byzantine period. There was possibly a ditch or some kind of outwork surrounding the building and there are several rock-cut cisterns. Within one of these have been reported painted and incised inscriptions of specifically Christian import.

The terrain in the immediate vicinity is stony, but there is potentially arable ground in the wadi-bed just 500 m to the N, and there are traces there of ancient wadi-walls. The practical inference is that this was a farm, but that the building itself was sited on high ground in order to have a good view over the approaches from the E. The building at Qasr al-Maraghah 16 km to the SW (p. 310) is very similar in character, but is sited in very much the wrong position to be anything other than a farm.

RAS AL-HILAL   راس الهلال

Coordinates: N 32° 54.77', E 22° 10.14'
Directions: The church described below stands on high ground on the headland of Ras al-Hilal, immediately above the little quay on its eastern side. To reach it, it is necessary to turn off the coast road to the L (travelling eastwards) as the road descends to approach the holiday village and beach; the turning (at N 32° 54.59' E 22° 9.78') is recognizable by the old stone bridge of earlier years. Follow this side-road towards the headland for about 700 m, and then turn R onto a very clear unmade track; this leads after a further 200 m to a farm building; the gate into the archaeological enclosure is to the R of this.

Byzantine church ★

Ancient sources tell us that there was a settlement here by the name of *Naus-tathmos*, though it is clear from the topography that there must have been two separate settlements, one on the high ground of the headland and the other around the beach and fresh-water spring to the E (behind the petrol station). On top of the headland is an early Christian church, the ruins of which were observed by 19th-century travellers: it was excavated in 1961.

The church (fig. 215) was entered from a paved courtyard to the E, and from arched doorways in the middle of the N and S sides. It may be noted that the lateral entrances are flanked by the same massive stone 'curtain brackets' that are apparent at Qasr ash-Shahdiyn (p. 127), the qasr at Zawiyat al-Arqub (p. 145) and other sites. (See the discussion on p. 14.) The church was a three-aisled arcaded basilica, rectangular externally, and with an apse and flanking rooms internally at the W end. There were galleries above the side-aisles, reached by staircases on either side, and an upper storey (or maybe even two) at the E end, approached by means of a staircase in the SE corner. The arcades of the nave rested on

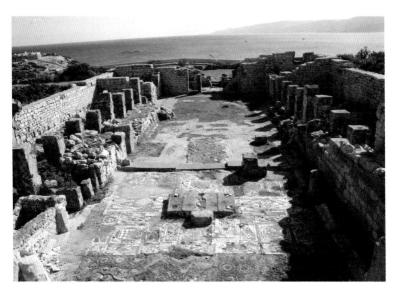

Fig. 215. Ras al-Hilal: the nave of the church, looking eastwards from above the apse.

continuous plinths, and sockets in the sides of the piers suggest that the aisles were further separated from the nave by wooden screens. The nave was paved with mosaic, now very fragmentary but in the same style as those which are so well preserved at Qasr Libya (p. 133). The worshipper entering from the E was faced first by a pattern of fifteen square panels; towards the chancel were larger panels, with figures on either side personifying *Ktisis* and *Kosmesis* ('Foundation' and 'Adornment', now in the museum at Apollonia: p. 283). In the doorway of the room opening off the N aisle at the E end is a simple but charming representation of a chalice with doves drinking from it. The chancel is raised slightly above the level of the nave; it was enclosed by richly carved limestone panels with abstract and floral motifs (one is now on display in the Apollonia Museum, p. 283) and is paved with *opus sectile*. In the centre is the altar-base (a re-used door-slab from an earlier tomb), with sockets for the colonnettes which supported the altar-table. In the SE corner of the chancel enclosure is a stepped block with crosses carved on two sides: this was the *ambon* for scripture readings.

The apse was stuccoed and painted, and fallen fragments of stucco showed that the semi-dome above it had been decorated with a shell-head motif. A regular horizontal line of sockets in the inner face of the apse shows that there was once a wooden *synthronon* here, for the elders of the church. The rooms on either side of the apse constituted (on the S) a baptistery with a circular basin in the floor approached by steps on opposite sides, and (on the N) a chapel with a small hollow platform which probably served as an altar containing a reliquary. The walls of both

rooms were decorated with stucco pilasters framing simple painted designs. In the space between the chancel and the nave arcade on the N side is a plain tomb which was found to contain two skeletons: this was not part of the original design. There are two further tombs in the floor of the N aisle.

Various features show that, subsequent to the original construction, serious measures were taken to strengthen and shore up the building. These may have been necessitated by earthquake damage, but this cannot be said for certain: the excavator considered that aspects of the site and of the original construction may have led to instability in any case. For whatever reason, the outer walls were strengthened on three sides by the addition of a wide sloping revetment, founded more deeply than the original walls. At first, the N and S entrances were retained, but later these were blocked and the revetment made continuous. The nave arcades were also strengthened by inserted walling, and additional arches were inserted into both the entrance vestibule and the NW angle-chapel.

Probably later still were a limeplaster floor laid over the floor of the chancel and nave, two shallow graves in the S aisle and some crude walls in the N aisle.

The original date of construction of the church is disputed. The mosaics were clearly made by the same craftsmen as those dated AD 538/9 at Qasr Libya (p. 133), so the church cannot be much later than that – but they may not have been original and it has been suggested that the building could have been first constructed in the second half of the fifth century. When the church was excavated, numerous graffiti carved into the stucco on the walls, in both Greek and Arabic, were apparent, but they were even then almost impossible to read. The Arabic texts (now displayed in the museum at Apollonia: see p. 284) show that occupation continued after the Arab conquest; one gives a date of AD 722 and another appears to refer to the writer's dwelling place as 'in the monastery of al-Mah...' The site has hitherto yielded nothing to indicate monastic use.

SAFSAF الصفصاف

Coordinates: N 32° 46.91', E 21° 56.55'
Directions: From the Cyrene cross-roads, take the road southward for 600 m and then, at a cross-roads, turn L. Follow this road for a further 6.5 km in an easterly direction; it will take you along the southern boundary-wall of the airport at al-Abraq, and you will see on the open ground between the road and the wall the long vault of the ancient cistern.

Roman cistern ★

The most prominent, and remarkable, ancient feature here, now hemmed in between the airport boundary-wall and the scattered modern settlement to the S, is a huge Roman cistern. It takes the unusual form of a single barrel-vaulted chamber 300 m long (fig. 216). Apart from a break in the centre, the vault of dry stone masonry is largely intact, with skylights along the crown at regular intervals. Most of the blocks show masons' marks in Greek letters. It is possible to venture into the cistern, from where you can see that there were also regularly spaced inlets along the sides at the level of the springing of the vault. The cistern is substantially silted up, and at the time of writing is sadly encumbered by very recent rubbish, but its floor may be assumed to have been several

metres lower, as in the great cisterns of Ptolemais (p. 85). Its capacity has been estimated at about 600,000 gallons or 2,700 cubic metres. Its date is Roman, perhaps Hadrianic.

At the eastern end may be seen settling tanks; on the inside of the N wall at this point is a carved inscription in Arabic which mentions the name of Yusif Pasha, the last Karamanli ruler in Tripoli. This is likely to have been inscribed at the time of his military expedition to Cyrenaica in 1811–12, which was chronicled by his Italian physician Agostino Cervelli; the expedition was based at Safsaf at one point.

The distance from Cyrene is about 8 km, and the fall from Safsaf to the cisterns at the entrance to the city (p. 153) is about 40 m (implying a gradient of 1:200, which is entirely reasonable). Stretches of an aqueduct running beside the ancient road and linking the two have recently been identified.

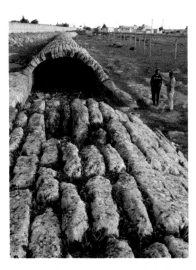

Fig. 216. The Roman cistern at Safsaf.

Ancient village

Behind the houses on the S side of the road, and particularly to the S of the walled football-ground, are extensive traces of an ancient settlement. There are large areas of bare limestone with quarries/cisterns cut into the surface. A substantial rectangular building in large ashlar masonry (at N 32° 46.64′ E 21° 56.46′) is known as **Qasr Safsaf**. It has internal detail which suggests the pressing of grapes or oil, and it is presumably a farm. Ruts in the rock surface nearby indicate a road, which is lined with tombs. Most of these take the form of sarcophagi with flat lids, but there is at least one circular tomb enclosing a rectangular sarcophagus. Some sarcophagi are raised on plinths; others are simply placed in rows on the flattened rock-surface. About 100 m to the ENE of Qasr Safsaf is a group of **monumental funerary enclosures** which seem to be a local peculiarity. These are rectangular, with an enclosing wall of orthostats with drafted edges set on a moulded plinth. Several sarcophagi may occupy the interior. A report of 1915 describes also a temple-tomb at Safsaf which was subsequently damaged by 'unavoidable' artillery fire during a military operation!

SNIBAT AL-AWILAH   صنيبات العويله

Coordinates: N 32° 50.78′, E 22° 9.61′
Directions: The minor modern road which connects the main E–W road on top of the Jabal at Lamludah (p. 298) with the coast at Ras al-Hilal follows, more or less, the line of an ancient route; where the two diverge, the ancient roadway is clear from cuttings in the bare rock. Near the edge of the lower escarpment are some fine examples of Hellenistic tombs, which have been partially restored. Travelling northwards from Lamluda, the first group of these is at the coordinates given.

Hellenistic tombs ★

Travelling northwards from Lamludah, where the road drops down from the uppermost level of the jabal, one passes (on the left-hand side, at N 32° 49.29′ E 22° 9.82′) a small ancient building, **Qasr ar-Rqayq**, standing on a small eminence overlooking the lower plateau. At a distance of 7.8 km from the Lamludah junction, one encounters (on the right-hand side) the first of several monumental tombs. Some take the form of temple-tombs, built in the same style as small temples and set on a plinth of three steps, but without a surrounding colonnade. Because the concept is scaled down in size, the doorway into the funerary chamber is large in proportion, and cuts through the steps of the plinth. The tombs are typically built of fine isodomic masonry and the corners are framed by slightly projecting pilasters. The underside of the roof, inside the chamber, is flat, but the upper side is pitched in imitation of a tiled roof. The style and the rich architectural detail are attributable to the fourth century BC. It is disappointing that their surfaces are now entirely covered in spray-painted graffiti; these will be very difficult to remove when or if there is a will to do so.

Close to one of these tombs in the first group is a slightly later structure which is entirely below ground-level and excavated out of the living rock. A rock-cut stair leads down into a forecourt once lined with a bench, of which a single block remains. This faced the tomb-façade which, like a theatre stage, is raised on two steps and enclosed between slightly flaring side-walls. The façade itself is decorated with five engaged Ionic columns (once with Doric

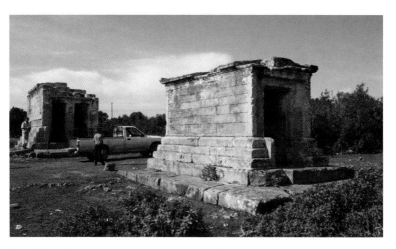

Fig. 217. Hellenistic temple-tombs at Snibat al-Awilah.

capitals!), between which were doors leading into four funerary chambers. The façade is not cut from the living rock but is built up against it in blockwork. This tomb again displays conspicuous wealth; it has been dated to the late third or early second century BC. In this area can be seen the ruts of the ancient road in the rock-surface, and simple rectangular cists cut into the rock for more modest burials.

About 250 m further N, to the W of the modern road, may be seen a tomb in the form of a more-or-less cubic plinth, crowned by a cornice and standing upon a square base of four steps. There is a small opening in one side, sufficient for a cinerary urn. This is considered late Hellenistic or early Roman. (The pock-marks on the walls represent another indignity: use for target-practice at some period!)

Close to this point, the ancient road diverges slightly to the R of the modern one; after another 200 m (at N 32° 51.02' E 22° 9.71') may be found two more fine Hellenistic temple-tombs which preserve exquisite architectural detail

(fig. 217). The larger of these has two doors leading into two chambers side-by-side, and each chamber has two tiers internally. Note the niche for a portrait-head cut into the central pier between the doors: this is an addition, presumably of Roman date.

Alongside the ancient road here there are also a number of simple cist-graves, mere rectangular cuttings in the rock. The presence of this extended necropolis, with its very wealthy tombs, implies the nearby presence of a settlement of some size already in the Greek period; but nothing of note is visible.

ZAWIYAT AL-IZZIYAT   زاوية لعزيات

Coordinates: N 32° 15.11', E 22° 39.82'
Directions: The village lies on the N side of the road between Makhayli and at-Tamimi, approximately 37 km to the E of the former.

Medieval castle

In this village, just to the N of the modern road and close to the mosque, a qasr (fig. 218) has been consolidated by the Department of Antiquities. The

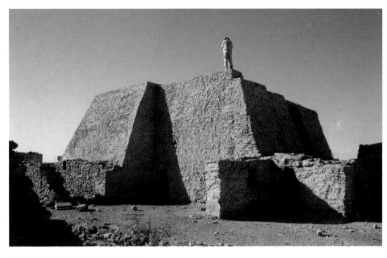

Fig. 218. Zawiyat al-Izziyat: the qasr.

coordinates are for the gate in the wall that encloses it. This is a square defensive building of coursed but uncut stones. The walls are mostly battered and thicker at the base, though it is possible that the sloping revetment is a secondary addition to walls which were originally vertical. If this is the case, there is probably no great interval of time between the two, since they are of identical construction. The principal doorway is on the N side. This leads into a square room with a corbelled (false) dome; off this opens a second domed room. On the L, a barrel-vaulted corridor (with a door to the exterior) leads to a third domed room. On the opposite side of the first room a stone staircase, starting 1.5 m above the floor, leads to the roof.

The building is surrounded by a rock-cut moat/quarry on three sides; on the fourth, a stone-walled courtyard-house (possibly of no great antiquity) almost abuts against it. Remains of modern sanitary ware indicate that it has not long been abandoned. There are many other neighbouring buildings of similarly rough masonry, and several large walled enclosures with large stones in the foundation courses and on the corners. These may have been animal pens or even caravanserais (as at Madinat Bu Hindi, p. 301). The over-all character of the settlement seems to be early medieval rather than Roman. As at Madinat Bu Hindi, the settlement is on the edge of a fan of cultivable alluvium, which in this case lies to the S of the modern road.

9   DARNAH AND SITES TO THE EAST

For this zone, see the map in figure 4. From Darnah eastwards, the land is dry and stony, with little potential for cultivation away from the coast. Darnah itself may have had some importance in late antiquity, if it succeeded *Paraetonium* (Marsa Matruh in Egypt) as the capital of the province of *Libya Inferior* (or *Libya sicca* – Dry Libya) before the seventh century AD (see below). It had a sheltered anchorage and a good perennial water supply in the hills behind the settlement. The Gulf of Bumba was also the scene of initial Greek settlement in the seventh century BC, before the move to Cyrene (see p. 2). The well-protected harbour at Tubruq was important to mariners, and the site (*Antipyrgos*) is named in mariners' guides as early as the fourth century BC. However, while the land-link between Cyrenaica and Egypt will always have witnessed important movements of peoples, this has left little mark on the landscape in terms of the built environment and there is little to draw to the attention of the cultural tourist.

The oasis of Jaghbub, away to the S of Tubruq and close to the Egyptian border, has likewise been important since prehistoric times as a refuge on the challenging caravan route between the Nile and the Maghrib; but in terms of visible archaeology or historic monuments it is a very long way to go in return for comparatively little. Siwa to the E (in Egypt) and Awjilah/Jalu to the W are far more rewarding in that regard.

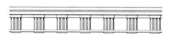

DARNAH (DERNA)   درنة

Darnah is likely to have been chosen as a site for settlement because of its moderately sheltered anchorage and because of the plentiful supply of fresh water which gushes out from the waterfall in the Wadi Darnah, 6 km inland. The earliest mention of *Darnis* is in the second century AD. In AD 411 it is mentioned by Synesius of Cyrene, in regard to an ecclesiastical dispute over Hydrax/Ain Marah (p. 287); the names of five bishops of Darnis are known, covering the period from 366 to the later sixth century. The early seventh-century geographer George of Cyprus described it as the capital of the province of *Libya Inferior*. The capital was *Paraetonium* (Marsa Matruh in Egypt) at an earlier date and the accuracy of George's account, which is not confirmed by any other source, has been questioned. A late antique defensive wall has, however, been traced. After the Islamic conquest, there is a long gap in the literary record until the settlement was 'refounded' by Sephardic Jewish refugees from Spain (al-Andalus) in 1492, following the Christian reconquest of that country.

During the Ottoman period, Darnah was ruled variously from Istanbul (through a governor in Benghazi) or from Tripoli (under the Karamanli dynasty, 1711–1835). In 1805, during a dispute between the Americans and Yusif Karamanli of Tripoli, Darnah was briefly held by an American force which had hoped to replace Yusif with his elder brother Ahmad, who had been in exile in Egypt. The tactic failed and

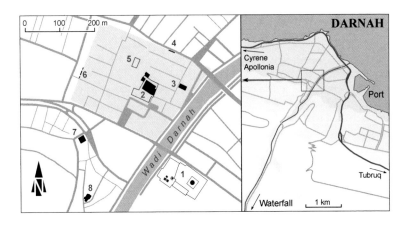

Fig. 219. Plan of Darnah: the historic centre.

1 Masjid as-Sahaba	5 Piazza Rossa	*The shaded area represents*
2 Jami' al-Atiq	6 Defensive wall	*the approximate extent of*
3 Mission church	7 Jami' Rashid	*the Roman town.*
4 Defensive wall	8 Masjid al-Jaraba	

the Americans withdrew under the terms of the ensuing peace agreement.

In 1911, the port of Darnah was one of the primary points of entry of the Italian invasion of Libya, and in the 1930s the town was developed as a fashionable resort, being known as 'The Pearl of Cyrenaica'. Like every other town in Libya (and despite consistent opposition to Muammar Qadhafi throughout his reign), Darnah has undergone considerable expansion and development in recent years. There are more historic monuments to see than in Tubruq, but they can easily be encompassed in a short walk. Their positions are shown in figure 219, and numbered locations refer to this plan.

Perambulation

The Roman and Byzantine settlement was on the W bank of the Wadi Darnah, which now cuts the town in two, but a convenient starting point is the modern **Masjid as-Sahaba (1)**, close by on

the east bank at N 32° 45.73' E 22° 38.52', next to a pleasant shady square and a modern market building. This gleaming mosque with twin minarets is dedicated to Zuhayr ibn Qays al-Balawi and his followers. Zuhayr had been sent from Egypt to avenge the death, in 683, of the veteran Arab general Uqba ibn-Nafi at the hands of Berbers in what is now Algeria. However, following a successful campaign (resulting in the defeat and death of the Mauretanian king Kusayla), on his return in 688 Zuhayr encountered a Byzantine force which had reoccupied Darnah. He and seventy of his warriors died in the fighting which followed. The graves of Zuhayr and his companions (some of them beneath domed mausolea) are in the cemetery on the W side of the mosque: these may be easily seen from the footbridge which crosses the main road just opposite.

If you cross the bridge over the wadi at this point, a turn to the R and then first L will bring you to the front

326

of the oldest mosque in Darnah, the Jami' al-Kibir or **Jami' al-Atiq** ★ **(2)**. (As in Benghazi, these terms signify respectively the Great Mosque or Old Mosque.) This has recently been rebuilt and looks very smart, though it is evident here (as in Benghazi) that the appreciation of historic monuments as part of a cultural heritage to be valued still has some way to go in Libya. There is a marked tendency to 'brighten them up' and modernize them, throwing the historic character out in the process. The mosque was built in 1656 by the Ottoman governor Muhammad Ibn Mahmud Bey, restored in 1772 by Mahmud Karamanli and almost entirely rebuilt in 2001–5. The original plan has been retained, with 42 small domes covering the prayer hall, and these are still supported by a variety of ancient columns with capitals which range in date from the second century AD to the 17th (fig. 220). The columns are all highly polished, which is presumably recent, for the curious profiles of some of them

suggest that they have previously been long exposed to the erosive effects of the weather (or the sea). At the rear of the prayer hall is an elaborately carved old wooden minbar – superior, in the writer's opinion, to the new one which now stands to the R of the mihrab!

At the NW corner of the Jami' al-Atiq is the ablutions building. Opposite that, against the minaret, is an enclosure containing several modest graves. These are apparently the graves of workmen who died during the construction of the mosque. Between these two buildings is one of the entrances to the small covered souk of Darnah.

The Jami' al-Atiq stands in the heart of the ancient settlement of Darnis. The E wall of the late Roman defences has been traced at various points running close to the Wadi Darnah, N of the bridge next to the cemetery of Sidi Zuhayr. In this part of the town there are still dignified houses of the Ottoman period, with moulded doorways and window-frames. In the alley (formerly

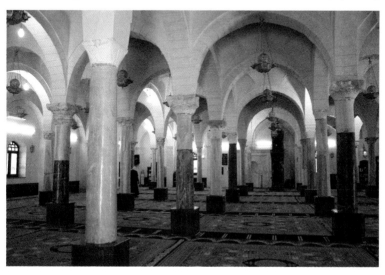

Fig. 220. Darnah: interior of the Jami' al-Atiq.

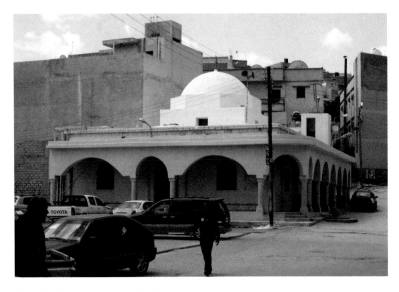

Fig. 221. Darnah: mosque of Rashid Pasha.

via San Francesco) which runs parallel to the wadi, but one block to the W, is the façade of the **Franciscan mission church (3)** established in 1903. If you turn L at the next major intersection to the N (corresponding to the next bridge over the wadi), you will be following the N side of the ancient defences. After about 60 m, you will see that the lower part of the wall on your left is demarcated by a frame of concrete, once painted red. Within this frame is a stretch of **ancient walling (4)**. It appears to be composed largely of reused large blocks, of a size which suggests that it is part of the defences. It is thought to belong to the fourth century AD.

From further along the same street (once via Emilia) you may enter the covered souk and return southwards towards the Jami' al-Atiq. Adjoining the souk on its W side is the charming **Piazza Rossa (5)** with buildings surrounding a central fountain adorned with bronze horses' heads. This was built by the Italians in 1923. If you set off westwards from the front of the Jami' al-Atiq, you will come to what is presently an open space where (in 2012) a stretch of the **western defensive wall (6)** has been exposed. Another section of this has previously been seen to the N, but it is likely that all of it will soon be either destroyed or hidden again.

To the S of the ancient nucleus lie two further mosques of interest. The first of these is the **Jami' Rashid (7)**, on the corner of a spacious road-junction. This was built in 1882 by Rashid Pasha, governor of Cyrenaica (who is buried in the Jami' Osman in Benghazi: p. 45). The mosque is square, with a central dome (fig. 221); it has simple arcaded porticoes facing the two street-frontages. Internally, the dome is supported on four low, square piers of polished limestone. In front of the mosque, on the NW side, is a small public fountain fed by the Darnah aqueduct (see below).

The **Masjid al-Jaraba (8)** is a small irregular building on a street-corner about 150 m to the S of the Jami' Rashid. The building is now sadly derelict, but its timber roof (now gone) was supported by two arches resting on a single antique column with a late Roman Corinthian capital. The name of the mosque reflects the arrival in Darnah of a sizeable community from Djerba in Tunisia, in the second half of the sixteenth century.

The water supply

Darnah is famous within Libya for its perennial waterfall, where fresh water cascades into the narrow cleft of the Wadi Darnah some 7 km from the sea. A modern road runs up the wadi and past the waterfall. The water is now captured and piped from immediately below the waterfall, but in Roman times a shorter aqueduct provided a controlled supply from a catchment point about 2 km from the sea. The channel, partly tunnelled through the soft limestone (tufa) of the wadi wall, has been identified at various points; it divided in order to serve requirements on both sides of the wadi.

In the Ottoman period, a new aqueduct at a higher level was constructed, with conduits running along both sides of the wadi which served arteries beneath the streets. This continued to function until 1973. In parts of the old town, arches over the aqueduct and entry points into it can still be seen.

JAGHBUB الجغبوب
Extended oasis settlement

The desert oasis of Jaghbub covers an extended, irregular area of approximately 45 × 30 km. It lies some 270 km S of Tubruq, but only 100 km to the NW of the oasis of Siwa, which was the home of the oracle of Zeus Ammon in Classical times. Jaghbub will certainly have been culturally close to Siwa in antiquity, as it has been more recently. It has a Berber, rather than an Arab, population. The oasis will always have been an important watering-point on the inland route from the Nile, via the oases of the Western Desert (Kharga, Dakhla, Farafra, Siwa) to Awjilah and so to the Syrtic Gulf and points further west.

The material remains of antiquity are now represented chiefly by tombs. A limited survey in 1955 around Ain Malfah, some 25 km to the E of Jaghbub village and on the Egyptian frontier, recorded many rock-cut tombs which typically contained mummies, ostrich eggs, basketry and occasional pottery. The tombs generally took the form of a simple rectangular chamber, with rectangular recesses for the burials on either side (and sometimes also in the rear wall) at a high level. The pottery indicated that many of the tombs belonged to the Graeco-Roman period, and that the basketry was of this age also. Some of the pottery was identified as Nabatean. A recent radiocarbon date from the area yielded a figure in the early Roman period. A mummy from Jaghbub (recovered in unreported circumstances) is on display in the National Museum in Tripoli Castle and has been dated between the second and third centuries AD.

The character of the burials appears to be very similar to those recorded in the oasis of Siwa. However, unlike Siwa, no substantial habitations or temples have been identified at Jaghbub. In various parts of the oasis (also, for instance, 10 km to the S of Jaghbub village) there are still many rock-tombs, some of which have lain undisturbed since antiquity. They are of various dates (where this can be determined); in one instance a (now fallen) lintel belongs to the Hellenistic period and shows strong Egyptian influence in its mouldings. Cisterns on the higher ground in the same areas suggest the locations of former settlements.

Jaghbub acquired particular importance in 1856, when it was chosen by the Grand Sanusi as the headquarters of his recently founded brotherhood – a location far from state control but with a stake in important caravan routes. He himself was buried there in 1859, but in 1895 the widening grasp of Ottoman authority on the coast caused the brotherhood to move its base to Kufrah, even further to the S. The Sanusi zawiya, which became a noted university, together with the tomb of the Grand Sanusi, were demolished when the order was suppressed in Libya by Colonel Qadhafi in the 1970s.

The long desert journey from the coast to Jaghbub is characterized by the sight, along the latter part of the route, of the extraordinary barbed-wire boundary-fence constructed in 1931 by the Italian General Graziani. This succeeded in preventing the Libyan resistance (or 'insurgents', depending on your point-of-view) from obtaining arms and supplies from Egypt, and contributed to their final defeat. It stretched for over 300 km along the Egyptian border, from the coast to the edge of the Calanshu Sand Sea S of Jaghbub.

TUBRUQ (TOBRUK, ANTIPYRGOS) طبرق

Because of its well-protected natural harbour, the site of Tubruq has always been important to mariners. Its ancient name was *Antipyrgos* and it is mentioned in mariners' manuals of the fourth century BC and the first century AD. Some evidence has been found of a pre-Roman settlement on the S side of the bay. However, the bleak landscape in its vicinity

has never encouraged significant development. The writer Procopius recorded that this was one of the fortress-cities founded in the sixth century AD by Justinian in the Marmaric region, and the walls of this period represent the only signs of antiquity now visible. In the mid 20th century a Roman mosaic and a huge Roman cistern were reported, but of these all trace is now lost.

While the settlement is likely never to have been wholly abandoned, it was never developed in the Ottoman period, and began to be expanded again only by the Italians. It played an important role as a port during the Second World War and consequently suffered greatly, in the same way as Benghazi.

In the 1950s, it was possible to make out fragments of all four sides of the Justinianic fortress, including traces of towers flanking the E Gate. Now, only a battered stretch of the S wall is visible, along the waterfront on the N side of the bay towards its inner end. The wall has a facing (mostly lost) of small ashlar blocks enclosing a core of concrete rubble. In the middle of the surviving stretch, at N 32° 4.79' E 23° 58.36', are the foundations of a projecting rectangular tower. The tower was accessed from inside the defences by means of an arched doorway, which still survives. At the W end of this wall (which must have terminated in a corner-tower) there is an extension running inland at an oblique angle, in smaller blocks and with a sloping outer face. This is of uncertain date.

ZAWIYAT AL-MURASSAS زاوية المرصص

Coordinates: N 32° 7.75', E 23° 40.13'
Directions: At a distance of 27 km W of the centre of Tubruq (and just 2.5 km W of the turning to the Knightsbridge War Cem-

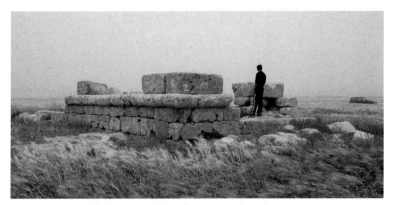

Fig. 222. Zawiyat al-Murassas: podium of Roman temple-tomb.

etery) on the main coast road, turn north-wards at N 32° 6.25' E 23° 41.62' onto a minor road heading NW. The settlement of Zawiyat al-Murassas is at a distance of 3.7 km along this road (ignoring a fork to the R after 2.2 km).

Ancient settlement

At this isolated site, some 5 km from the sea and in a flat coastal plain which sustains arable farming, there is a scatter of modern farm buildings around a zawiya. Immediately facing the zawiya, across the road, may be made out the remains of a rectangular Roman building, constructed of large coursed (but not particularly regular) ashlar blocks. No internal detail is visible, as the structure is now largely enveloped by modern buildings.

Close to the edge of the walled cemetery (which lies to the N of the zawiya) has been found a polychrome Roman mosaic, showing that whoever lived here in the Roman period was not entirely destitute. A similar impression is given by a substantial **temple-tomb** which has been dated to the third century AD. This may be found about a kilometre to the N of the zawiya, at N 32° 8.35' E 23° 39.99'. In order to reach it, return to the fork in the road leading to the zawiya and take the other turning: after 2.6 km, this road passes about 200 m to the E of the monument and it is possible to walk across to it. The tomb (fig. 222) is built of large limestone ashlars and has a podium capped by a projecting course with a simple convex moulding. Above this once rose a squarish tomb-chamber with steps (now missing) in front. The tomb faced slightly E of N.

GLOSSARY

Actian dating/era: A system of dating, widely used in Roman Cyrenaica, which counted years from the defeat of Mark Antony by Octavian/Augustus at the Battle of Actium in 31 BC.

Adyton: The innermost room of a temple, sometimes present at the inner end of the *cella* or *naos*, reserved for the cult statue.

Aedicula: A niche or recess with an architectural frame, such as a pediment supported on a pair of columns.

Aegis: A magical protective cape worn only by the gods Zeus or Athena; characterized by a Gorgon's head in the centre and by tassels around the edge in the form of snakes.

Aeolic (capital): A style of early Greek architecture, named from the part of NW Turkey of which it was typical (Aeolis); similar to Ionic capitals in the use of volutes which, however, are arranged 'botanically' as if springing from the column-shaft beneath.

Agora: The civic centre and marketplace of a Greek city.

AH: Dates in the Muslim calendar (*Hijrah*), which are in lunar years, starting from the flight of the prophet Muhammad from Mecca to Medina in AD 622.

Akroterion: A decorative sculptural element on the roof of a Greek temple, along the ridge or at the corners.

Ambo(n): A pulpit in a church, with the distinction that, in the early Church, this was used for readings from the epistle and gospel rather than for preaching, and that it was provided with two flights of steps, one towards the altar and the other towards the nave.

Amphitheatre: A place of entertainment (usually oval), with tiered seating all around a central arena (like a football ground), for watching gladiatorial combats and wild-beast fights. NOT to be confused with a theatre!

Antae (pl.): Stub-walls projecting forward from the façade of a building, often with the columns of a porch between them.

The Antonine Itinerary: A list of routes of the Roman Empire, probably compiled in the reign of Caracalla (211–217). It gives lists of roads, the settlements along them and the distances between them.

Apodyterium: Part of a Roman bath-building: the changing-room.

Apotropaic: An adjective used to describe objects or carvings intended to avert evil, such as an amulet worn around the neck or a carved phallus at a street-corner.

Architrave: The horizontal lintel which spans a doorway or the space between columns in a colonnade.

Arcosolium: A form of tomb, usually rock-cut, which was widely used in the Roman period. A rectangular recess, of a size to hold a coffin (or in the form of a coffin) roofed with a barrel-vault.

Arcuate (lintel): A single block which is carved as an arch but which (not being composed of multiple elements) is structurally no different from a flat lintel. Typical of the colonnades of Tripolitanian temple-tombs (e.g. at Ghirza).

Arula: A small altar or offering-table, either portable or (often) carved in the form of a shelf or platform on a natural rock-surface.

Ashlar: Masonry cut in regular rectangular blocks and laid in horizontal courses; a block of such masonry.

Atrium: The central hall of a Roman house of Etruscan type.

Attic: The box- or plinth-like uppermost element of a Roman building or triumphal arch, above all other architectural ornament.

Breccia: A geological term used to describe a rock which is formed of large irregular fragments of one or more rock-types, cemented together in a matrix of a finer-grained material, often resulting in a veined appearance.

Byzantine: A cultural and chronological term used to describe the culture of the Roman World during the period when it was ruled from Constantinople (the former Greek city of *Byzantium*) rather than from Rome. In this guidebook, it is used to signify the span between the formal division of the Roman Empire in AD 395 and the conquest of Cyrenaica by the Arabs in 645. It should be noted that the term is a modern construct: the people we describe as 'Byzantine' never thought of themselves as such, but as 'Roman'.

Caduceus: A winged sceptre entwined with snakes, the exclusive attribute of two gods, Hermes/Mercury and Asklepios/Aesculapius. (The association with Asklepios, the god of healing, is responsible for its use in modern times to identify a pharmacy.)

Cal(i)darium: Part of a Roman bath-building: a hot, humid room with hot plunge-bath(s).

Cardo and **Decumanus:** Terms freely employed by modern archaeologists (on the authority of ancient surveyors) to name the streets of Roman towns. The **cardo** (pl. *cardines*) should run N–S and the **decumanus** E–W; the principal street in either direction would be the **cardo/decumanus maximus**.

Cavea: The auditorium of a theatre or amphitheatre.

Cella: Of a Roman temple, the central chamber, housing the cult statue. (See also **naos**.)

Centaur: A mythical being composed of the upper part of a man with the body and legs of a horse.

Chi-rho monogram: A Christian symbol composed of the first two letters of 'Christos' in Greek (XP), often accompanied by the letters alpha and omega (symbolizing Christ as the Beginning and the End).

Ciborium: A regular architectural feature of early churches, in the form of a canopy supported on four columns which enclosed the altar.

Cipollino: A type of marble, quarried in antiquity at Carystos on the Greek island of Euboea and widely used in Roman buildings. It has alternating stripes of green and white colour and has a high content of mica, which sparkles in the light.

Cippus: A short pillar, square or round and usually inscribed (similar to a statue-base, but with no implication that it supported a statue).

Circus: A track with spectator seating for the presentation of chariot-races. Identical to a hippodrome.

Cist: A coffin-like grave, lined with stone slabs; also a small stone chest, for the burial of ashes.

Cithara: A seven-stringed lyre.

Clerestory: That part of the nave of a colonnaded basilica (sacred or secular) which rises above the aisles and is pierced by windows (often the main source of light for the interior of the building).

Colonia: Initially a term for a new settlement of Roman military veterans. This came to symbolize full assimilation to the administrative structure of Rome itself, a status much sought after by pre-existing communities and *municipia* (q.v.).

Comes: A widely-used title under the late Roman Empire, whence the English title 'Count'. The *Comes Africae* held military command over the forces stationed in the former province of Africa.

Corinthian: An order of architecture for Greek and Roman public buildings, in which the capitals of the columns are formed like the base of an acanthus plant, with three tiers of leaves. The columns usually have narrow vertical flutes and the entablature above is decorated with a frieze based on a continuous acanthus scroll.

Cornice: A horizontal projecting moulding which crowns a roof or a lower storey of a classical building.

Cryptoporticus: A partially underground portico, designed to provide protection from the heat of summer.

Damnatio memoriae: The erasure of a name from public inscriptions and documents, as if the individual (or body, since it was applied in AD 238 to the *Legio III Augusta*) had never existed.

Decumanus: See **Cardo**.

Decurio: A member of a Roman town-council (a position of prestige, held for life, but one in which one was expected to use part of one's private wealth for the public good).

Dolium (pl. dolia): A Latin term for a large storage jar, such as would normally be a permanent fixture in a store-room. The Greek term is **pithos**.

Doric: An order of architecture in Greek (and occasionally Roman) buildings identified by the absence of bases beneath the columns and by very plain capitals in the form of squat inverted cones. The columns have wide vertical flutes and the frieze above takes the form of alternating metopes and triglyphs (q.v.).

Dromos: A passageway leading into a (rock-cut) tomb.

Duumvir: One of the two supreme magistrates in the administration of a Roman town (corresponding to the two consuls at Rome itself).

Dux: A military title under the late Roman Empire, subordinate to the *Comes Africae*. The title is the origin of the English 'Duke'.

Emblema (-ata): A small mosaic panel, usually not more than about 60 cm. square, with a picture in fine mosaic (*opus vermiculatum*). This would have been assembled in a workshop as a complete panel, which a less skilled craftsman could then place in the centre of a floor with simpler (and coarser) decoration around it.

Engaged (column): See under **Pilaster**.

Entablature: The totality of the architectural elements which properly surmount a colonnade, composed therefore of an architrave, a decorative frieze and a projecting cornice.

Ephebic organization. This was part of the structure of many Hellenistic city-states, persisting into the Roman period. It was an organization for young men of 15–20 years of age (**epheboi**; to be imagined as a cross between the Boy Scout Movement and National Service) which trained them in military and civic virtues, prior to their admission to full citizenship. The organization was closely associated with the gymnasium, and typically gave rise to numerous informal inscriptions/graffiti on surrounding walls recording their friendships and achievements.

Exedra: A semicircular or rectangular recess ('for sitting out in').

False door: A decorative device on many tombs: the appearance of a wooden double-door, carved in stone on the face of the monument, while the genuine entrance to the burial chamber is located elsewhere.

Forum: The civic centre and market-place of a Roman city.

Frieze: A horizontal band above the architrave (q.v.) in a colonnade, usually decorated in relief with either some sort of vegetal scroll or with figure scenes.

Frigidarium: Part of a Roman bath-building: the cold room, usually with a cold plunge-bath.

Genius: A spirit (of a place); also, decoratively, a winged figure used in classical art in much the same way as angels and cupids are in later periods.

Himation: A rectangular outer garment worn in antiquity as a cloak.

Hippocamp: A mythical sea-creature with the head and forelegs of a horse, and the tail of a fish.

Hellenistic: Conventionally, the period between the death of Alexander the Great (323 BC) and the Battle of Actium (31 BC) which confirmed Augustus as the first Roman emperor. Most of the Mediterranean world shared a similar culture at this time, and the term may be used in both a cultural and a chronological sense.

Herm: A rectangular pillar surmounted by a male bust (originally Hermes) and with genitalia indicated on the front. Often used decoratively, but also as a boundary marker.

Hestiatorion: A dining hall associated with a religious cult.

Hexastyle: See **Tetrastyle**.

Hinshir: Farm (Arabic).

Hippodrome: A track with spectator seating for the presentation of chariot-races. Identical to a circus.

Hypocaust: An under-floor Roman heating system, used particularly in bath-buildings and (in colder climates) for general room-heating. The floor of the room is raised on small piers (*pilae*), and the exhaust gases from an external furnace are conducted beneath the floor and up flues set behind the wall-surface.

Impost block: A moulded or decorated block at the top of a pier and beneath the springing of an arch, similar to the capital of a column.

Impluvium: An ornamental water-basin in the centre of a reception-room in a Roman house, designed to catch the rain-water from an opening in the roof above.

In antis: Of columns, when placed between projecting stub-walls; typically at the front of a temple, where the flanking walls of the *cella* extend forward as two wings (*antae*).

Inhumation: The burial of an intact corpse. This term is used by archaeologists to distinguish the practice from that of cremation, which may involve either the digging of a grave in which the corpse is burnt before it is filled in, or the burial of the ashes (gathered from a pyre elsewhere) in an urn.

Insula (-ae): Conventionally used by modern scholars to indicate a city block bounded by streets.

Ionic: An order of architecture for Greek and Roman public buildings, in which the capitals of the columns are decorated like a scroll which is rolled up (or rather, downwards) on either side of a 'cushion'. The columns usually have narrow vertical flutes and the entablature above is decorated with a frieze based on a continuous acanthus scroll.

Isodomic (masonry): coursed block-work in which all courses are the same height.

Jami': Mosque ('Assembly'), also university. The title is usually given to the principal mosque of a locality. (See also **Masjid**.)

Kore: A sculpture of a standing female figure, clothed and typically with the feet together. Introduced into Greek art in the Archaic period, the pose is initially stiff and formal; it becomes more realistic and relaxed with time.

Kouros: A sculpture of a naked standing male figure with the arms hanging straight by the sides and with one foot slightly in front of the other. This is the typical pose of formal Egyptian statues, adopted by the Greeks (and Phoenicians) and gradually made less stiff and more realistic.

Laconicum or **sudatorium:** Part of a Roman bath-building: a particularly hot room without plunge-baths, intended to generate a dry heat for sweating.

Late Roman: A rather loose chronological term, to describe the Roman period after the crises of the mid-third century AD: partly (but not invariably) synonymous with 'Byzantine'.

Lesche: A Greek term for a room or building which served as a social meeting-place.

Libation: A liquid offering, to a god or to the spirits of the dead.

Loculus: Niche or recess.

Legion: The largest single infantry unit in the Roman army, nominally about 5,000 strong.

Madrasa: A school for Islamic studies.

Maghrib: A term used in Arab sources for north African territories to the W of Egypt (and more particularly W of the Syrtic Gulf).

Martyrion: A church or chapel housing the relics of a venerated holy man or saint (dedicated to their veneration).

Maenad: A female devotee of the god Dionysos, always represented in an ecstatic dance and holding a thyrsos, a kind of staff with a finial in the form of a pine-cone entwined with ivy-leaves.

Masjid: Mosque ('House of prayer'); usually a lesser mosque. (See also **Jami'**.)

Metope: Part of the frieze above a Doric colonnade: a more-or-less square panel with relief decoration (typically either a rosette or a human figure).

Mihrab: A niche, usually semicircular, in the *qibla* wall of a mosque, indicating the direction of Mecca. An additional *mihrab* is often provided externally in a courtyard wall so that those outside the mosque may also know the direction of the Holy City.

Minbar: In a mosque, the pulpit from which the Friday sermon is delivered.

Mithraeum: A temple for the worship of the oriental god Mithras.

Monolith: A term for an architectural element (such as a column or pier) which takes the form of a single block of stone.

Municipium: A town in the Roman Empire enjoying local autonomy under a municipal charter, whose citizens had the status of Roman citizens.

Naos: The building within the colonnade of a Greek temple, often subdivided into a *pronaos* (porch), *naos* (principal chamber, like the *cella* of a Roman temple) and either an *adyton* (inner chamber for the cult statue) or *opisthodomos* (blind rear porch).

Narthex: Vestibule or outer room at the entrance to a church.

Natatio: Swimming pool.

Nereids: Sea-maidens, daughters of Nereus, the Old Man of the Sea.

Nilotic scene: A frequent theme of Hellenistic and Roman decorative art, both in mosaics and in wall-painting. Scenes are portrayed of life in the marshes of the Nile Delta, with fishermen in boats amongst the reeds, ducks and other water-birds, crocodiles and other forms of wildlife.

Nymphaeum: A monumental public fountain (originally dedicated to the Nymphs).

Opisthodomos: See **Naos**.

Opus africanum: A building technique, particularly characteristic of North Africa in the classical period. The main framework of a wall is composed of tall vertical blocks with spaces between them which are infilled with small rubble masonry.

Opus sectile: A decorative treatment, mostly of floors, in which a pattern is composed of shaped tiles of different coloured marbles.

Opus tessellatum: Coarse mosaic paving.

Opus vermiculatum: Extremely fine mosaic decoration, consisting of up to 60 stones per sq. cm., usually reserved for small *emblemata* (q.v.).

Orchestra: The semicircular space in a theatre between the spectator seating (*cavea*) and the stage. Originally used in Greek theatres as a performance space for dancers, in Roman times it was occupied by the (portable and comfortable) seats of the wealthier citizens.

Orthostat: An upright stone block (see *opus africanum*).

Ossuary: A container for human bones (particularly sacred relics).

Ottoman: Culturally/chronologically related to the period 1551–1911, when Tripolitania and Cyrenaica were provinces of the (Turkish) Ottoman empire.

Palaestra: An exercise-ground.

Palmette: A decorative motif in painting or architecture, in the form of a stylized and symmetrical palm-frond.

Pentelic (marble): A warm white, almost honey-coloured marble from the quarries of Mt Pentelikon near Athens.

Peristasis: The colonnade surrounding a Greek temple.

Peristyle: A courtyard or garden surrounded by a colonnaded portico.

Peutinger Table, The: A 12th- or 13th-century copy of a map of the later second century AD, covering the world known to the Romans. It shows named locations (with a variety of conventional symbols), the roads joining them and the distances between them.

Phoenician: A cultural term for the inhabitants of Phoenicia in the Middle East (approximating to the Lebanon of today). Extended to the Phoenicians who settled at Carthage and elsewhere in the western Mediterranean and sometimes used interchangeably with 'Punic' (q.v.).

Pila: A small pier up to 50 cm high and usually composed of square or circular bricks, used to support the suspended floor of a heated room in a Roman bath-building.

Pilaster: A flat-faced, barely projecting, representation of a column on the face or end of a wall. To be distinguished from an engaged column, which is fully rounded but against the wall and linked to it above and below; and an engaged semi-column, half of which projects from the face of the wall.

Pithos: A Greek term for a large storage jar: see **Dolium**.

Podium: The platform upon which a temple or monument stands to raise it above its surroundings.

Praeses: 'President', a widely-used title under the late Roman Empire, sometimes applied to the civil governor of a province.

Proconnesian (marble): A grey and white veined marble quarried at Proconnesos, an island in the Sea of Marmara near Istanbul.

Proconsul: The civil governor of a province in the early years of the Roman Empire, notionally appointed by the Senate of Rome.

Pronaos: See **Naos**.

Propylaeum: A monumental entrance (to a precinct rather than to a building).

Prostyle: Of temple architecture, having columns across the façade only.

Protome: A representation in art of the forepart only of an animal.

Punic: An adjective used to describe the culture of the Phoenicians who settled in the western Mediterranean, primarily at Carthage. Hence used in Tripolitania of the pre-Roman culture of the region.

Glossary

Qasr (pl. qsur): Castle (Arabic); often applied to any ancient monument.

Qibla: The wall in a mosque which faces in the direction of Mecca.

Quadrifrons: See **Tetrapylon.**

Quadriga: A four-horse chariot.

Relieving arch: an arch deliberately constructed in a solid wall in order to transmit the weight from above to either side of it.

Rostra: A platform from which speakers may address the people in the open air. The term literally means 'bows', and is derived from the platform in the Roman Forum, which was decorated with the bows of ships captured in a naval battle.

Satyr: A mythical attendant of the god Dionysus, of human form but with pointed ears and a horse's tail; lustful and always represented with an erect phallus.

Scaenafrons: The elaborately decorated façade of the stage-building of a Roman theatre.

Silenus: A balding, drunken old man, sometimes with pointed ears, supposedly the tutor of the god Dionysos.

Sima: The crowning element of a cornice, or parapet.

Spandrel: The concave triangular space contained between the curve of an arch and its surrounding rectangular frame.

Stele (-ai): A vertical stone marker (similar to a tombstone).

Stoa (-ai): The Greek term for a portico.

String-course: A non-functional horizontal band of masonry in a wall, projecting slightly, to demarcate different storeys of a building.

Stylobate: The linear foundation for a colonnade.

Sudatorium: see **Laconicum.**

Synthronon: Semi-circular seating around the central apse of a church, providing seating for the higher clergy.

Syrian arch: An architectural device much favoured in the mid-Roman period. A wide opening is framed by a pair of columns between pilasters, such that the central passage is substantially wider than the lateral ones; the lateral passages are spanned by flat architraves, while the wider central space is spanned by a semi-circular arch.

Taberna: A shop.

Tabula ansata: A frame for an inscription or the like which is rectangular with projecting dove-tails ('handles') at either side.

Temenos: A sacred enclosure or precinct.

Tepidarium: Part of a Roman bath-building: the warm room which provided a transition between the hot and cold rooms.

Tessera: The small stone cube of which mosaics are composed.

Tetrapylon or **Quadrifrons:** An arch (over a cross-roads) which faces four ways.

Tetrastyle: Of a temple, with four columns across the façade. (Thus 'hexastyle' = six columns across).

Theatre: A place of entertainment with a raised rectangular stage and a tiered semi-circular auditorium (or *cavea*), for the presentation of plays.

Tholos: A circular pavilion or monument.

Toga: The formal white woollen cloak worn by a Roman citizen.

Tondo: A circular decorative feature, such as a roundel or medallion.

Tribunal: A raised dais from which judges presided over judicial proceedings (in a civil basilica), or from which a commanding officer might address his troops (in a military fort).

Triclinium: The dining-room of a Roman house. The word means a room with three couches, and typically a decorated (mosaic) floor will reflect this arrangement, with the principal decoration in the area immediately inside the door and simpler patterns around the three sides, which would largely have been covered by furniture.

Triconchos: An architectural design feature which is common in the Classical architecture of Cyrenaica: apses enclosing three sides of a square or rectangular space.

Triglyph: An element of a frieze above a Doric colonnade, composed of three vertical ribs (thought to have originated as a representation in stone of the ends of the roof-beams).

Triton: A merman, fish-shaped from the waist down.

Tumulus: A circular burial mound.

Tuscan: An order of architecture, not unlike Doric, but characterized by unfluted column-shafts with very simple, moulded but otherwise undecorated, capitals and bases.

Tympanon: The triangular space in a gable-end or above a doorway decorated with similar mouldings.

Unguentarium: A small flask for perfumes or unguents. In the Hellenistic period these are of clay and are fusiform (like a bobbin, with a long neck and a tall foot); in the first century AD this shape is replaced by a piriform type (still with a long neck, but with a pear-shaped body and a flat base), and then in the later first century by a similar shape in glass.

Vitruvius: A Roman writer of the first century BC, whose ten books on architecture and engineering have survived since antiquity. Vitruvius gave detailed specifications for architectural proportions, together with instructions on all manner of practical matters pertinent to the construction industry. We know that he was not up-to-date with the latest practices at the time when he wrote, and it is a seductive delusion to suppose that his precepts were universally read or followed by his contemporaries!

Vomitorium: A vaulted, radial access passage in a theatre or amphitheatre, leading to the seating from outside.

Voussoir: A wedge-shaped block used to construct an arch or vault.

Zawiya: The Muslim equivalent of a monastery or college.

Zeus Ammon: The god worshipped at the oracle in the oasis of Siwa in Egypt, often represented as a man with ram's horns.

CHRONOLOGICAL TABLE

In the table below, ellipsis (…) is used to indicate that an event occurred at some time between the dates indicated.

BC

631	Traditional date for foundation of Cyrene by Greek settlers from Thera
625	Foundation of Tauchira
Late 7th cent.	Foundation of settlement, later to become Ptolemais; foundation of Euesperides
570	Battle of Irasa: the Greeks of Cyrene repulse the Egyptians who have come to the aid of dispossessed Libyans
560+	Traditional date for foundation of Barca
c. 515	Attempt by Greeks under Dorieus to settle at the mouth of the Wadi Caam; driven off by the Carthaginians
322	Cyrenaica becomes subject to the Ptolemaic kings of Egypt; the port of Barca re-founded as Ptolemais?
283–260	Cyrenaica independent under Magas
246	Cyrenaica reunited with Egypt through the marriage of Berenice (daughter of Magas) to Ptolemy III Euergetes; Euhesperides abandoned in favour of Berenice
96	Cyrenaica bequeathed to the Roman people; granted autonomy
74	Cyrene established as a Roman province under the administration of a quaestor
48	Roman Civil War between Pompey the Great and Julius Caesar; Cyrene hosts supporters of Pompey
46	Pompeians defeated at Thapsus; Caesar imposes on Cyrene a fine of 1,500 lbs of Silphium
31	Roman Civil War ended when Octavian defeats Mark Antony and Cleopatra at Actium off the W coast of Greece. Egypt becomes a Roman province; Cyrene combined with Crete as a single province, with its capital at *Gortyn*
27	Octavian takes the title *Augustus*

AD

115–117	Jewish Revolt
117 onwards	Restoration of Cyrenaican cities; foundation of Hadrianopolis
262	Earthquake in Cyrenaica?
293…305	Revision of administrative system of the empire: Cyrenaica is split from Crete to form two new provinces. Ptolemais becomes the capital of *Libya Superior* or *Pentapolis*; Paraetonium (Marsa Matruh) that of *Libya Inferior* or *Libya Sicca*

Chronological table

365	Devastating earthquake and tsunami in the eastern Mediterranean, possibly one of a chain of such events
410	Synesius becomes bishop of Ptolemais
413	Death of Synesius
Mid or late 5th cent.	Apollonia/Sozousa becomes capital of *Libya Superior*
616–628	Egypt under Sasanian (Persian) rule: Cyrenaica possibly under threat
642–645	Conquest of Cyrenaica and Tripolitania by the Arabs under Amr Ibn al-Aasi. Advent of Islam
670	Foundation of Arab capital at Qayrawan (Tunisia). Cyrenaica henceforth loosely under the domination of governors (*emirs*) at Qayrawan or (after 915) at Mahdia
698	Fall of Carthage to the Arabs
800	Aghlabid dynasty established at Qayrawan
909	Overthrow of the Aghlabid rulers by the Fatimids
969	Conquest of Egypt by the Fatimids and subsequent move to Cairo, leaving Zirid governors in Tunisia
1051	Invasion of Libya by the Bani Hilal and Bani Sulaym; end of remaining urban settlements
1551	Establishment of Ottoman rule in Tripoli
1638	Ottoman government takes practical steps to extend rule over Cyrenaica; castle built at Benghazi
1843	Sanusi Brotherhood establishes a presence in Libya at al-Bayda
1911	Italian invasion of Libya

CULTURALLY DEFINED PERIODS

This is a 'thumbnail guide' to terms used in this guide to place monuments or events within broad and approximately defined chronological limits. They apply specifically to the history of Cyrenaica, and may have slightly different meanings elsewhere. (For further detail, see the **Glossary**.)

Archaic (Greek)	Seventh to sixth centuries BC
Classical	Fifth century to 323 BC
Hellenistic	323 to 31 BC
Roman	31 BC to late third century AD
Late Roman	Late third century to 395
Byzantine	395 to 645
Islamic	645 onwards
Medieval	Eighth to fourteenth centuries
Ottoman	1551–1911

RULERS OF CYRENE

631–600 BC	Battos I
c. 600–583	Arkesilaos I
c. 583–560	Battos II
560–550	Arkesilaos II
550–530	Battos III
530–515	Arkesilaos III/Pheretima
515–470	Battos IV
470–c. 440	Arkesilaos IV
c. 440–322	(Republic)
322–283	Ptolemy I Soter of Egypt; Ophellas governor until 300, then Magas
283–246	Ptolemy II Philadelphus king in Egypt; Magas rules Cyrene as independent king 283–260, then reconciled with Ptolemy, dies in 258 or 250
246–222	Ptolemy III Euergetes of Egypt
222–204	Ptolemy IV Philopator of Egypt
204–180	Ptolemy V Epiphanes of Egypt
180–163	Ptolemy VI Philometor of Egypt
163–116	Ptolemy VIII Physcon (of Egypt from 145 after the death of Philometor)
116–96	Ptolemy Apion

SELECTIVE TABLE OF ROMAN EMPERORS

Julio-Claudians

31 BC–AD 14	Augustus
AD 14–37	Tiberius
37–41	Gaius (Caligula)
41–54	Claudius
54–68	Nero
68–69	Galba, Otho, Vitellius

Flavians

69–79	Vespasian
79–81	Titus
81–96	Domitian
96–98	Nerva
98–117	Trajan
117–138	Hadrian

Antonines

138–161	Antoninus Pius
161–180	Marcus Aurelius
161–169	Lucius Verus
180–192	Commodus
192–193	Pertinax
193	Didius Julianus

Severans

193–211	Septimius Severus
211–217	Caracalla
218–222	Elagabalus
222–235	Severus Alexander
235–238	Maximinus Thrax
238	Gordian I
238	Gordian II
238–244	Gordian III
244–249	Philip the Arab
249–251	Decius
251–253	Trebonianus Gallus
253–260	Valerian
253–268	Gallienus
268–270	Claudius II Gothicus
270–275	Aurelian
275–276	Tacitus
276–282	Probus
282–285	Carus, Numerianus, Carinus
284–305	Diocletian
285–305	Maximianus Herculius
293–306	Constantius I Chlorus

Chronological table

293–311	Galerius
305–313	Maximinus Daia
306–312	Maxentius

The approximate period 293–313, during which there were notionally two senior and two junior rulers in either half of the empire is conventionally referred to as the Tetrarchy (Rule of Four).

306–337	Constantine I
308–324	Licinius
337–340	Constantine II
337–350	Constans I
337–361	Constantius II
361–363	Julian (the Apostate)
363–364	Jovian
364–375	Valentinian I
364–378	Valens
367–383	Gratian

375–392	Valentinian II
378–395	Theodosius I the Great

Eastern (Byzantine) Empire

395–408	Arcadius
408–450	Theodosius II
450–457	Marcian
457–474	Leo I
474	Leo II
474–491	Zeno
491–518	Anastasius
518–527	Justin
527–565	**Justinian I**
565–578	Justin II
578–582	Tiberius II (I) Constantine
582–602	Maurice
602–610	Phocas
610–641	Heraclius
641–668	Constans II

FURTHER READING

Guidebooks/picture books

My starting-points were two, both long out of print but still valuable and occasionally available on Amazon:

C. G. C. Hyslop and S. Applebaum, *Cyrene and Ancient Cyrenaica* (Tripolitania 1945: Government Press);

R. Goodchild, *Cyrene and Apollonia, an Historical Guide* (Libya: Dept. of Antiquities, various dates but probably last updated about 1966).

Goodchild also wrote a longer account in German, published posthumously: *Kyrene und Apollonia* (Zürich 1971: Raggi). Because of his premature death and the lack of final reports on his various excavations, this is an important source.

R. Polidori, A. Di Vita, G. Di Vita-Evrard, L. Bacchielli, *Libya: the Lost Cities of the Roman Empire* (Cologne 1999: Könemann) is a lavish picture book of which approximately a quarter is devoted to Cyrenaica (Cyrene, Apollonia and Ptolemais). It has an authoritative text by archaeologists with direct experience of the region.

T. Mickocki, Ptolemais: *Archaeological Tourist Guide* (Warsaw 2006: Warsaw University) is an excellent illustrated guide to the site, and particularly to the recent work carried out by the Polish team.

For readers of Italian, *Cirene*, edited by N. Bonacasa and S. Ensoli (Milan 2000: Electa) is a very thorough review of the work carried out on that site by the Italians over many years.

Journals

There are three scholarly journals dedicated specifically to archaeological research in Libya.

Libya Antiqua is the official (if intermittent) organ of the Libyan Department of Antiquities.

Libyan Studies is the journal of the Society for Libyan Studies, 31–34 Gordon Square, London WC1H 0PY (http://www.societyforlibyanstudies.org/).

The *Quaderni di Archeologia della Libia* are published by L'Erma di Bretschneider, Via Cassiodoro, 19 – P.O.Box 6192 – 00193 Rome (http://www.lerma.it/).

Earlier work carried out by the Italians in the colonial period (1911–43) was initially reported in *Notiziario Archeologico* (Rome 1915–27: Ministero delle Colonie) and *Africa Italiana* (Bergamo 1927–1941: Istituto Italiano d'Arti Grafiche).

Monographs

There is an extensive series of *Monografie di Archeologia Libica*, published by L'Erma di Bretschneider, which represent the major reports of Italian research in Libya, published from 1948 onwards. Of particular importance for present purposes have been:

S. Stucchi, *Architettura cirenaica* (= MAL 9, Rome 1975);

E. Alföldi-Rosenbaum and J. B. Ward-Perkins, *Justinianic Mosaic Pavements in Cyrenaican Churches* (= MAL 14, Rome 1980).

Other works in English relevant to this volume are:

C. H. Kraeling, Ptolemais, City of the Libyan Pentapolis (Chicago 1962: University of Chicago Press);

R. G. Goodchild et al., *Apollonia, the port of Cyrene : excavations by the University* of Michigan, 1965-1967 (Libya Antiqua Supplement 4,Tripoli 1976);

J. A. Lloyd et al., Excavations at Sidi Khrebish, Benghazi (Berenice), vol. 1 (Libya Antiqua Supplement 5.1, Tripoli 1977);

G. Barker, J. Lloyd and J. Reynolds, Cyrenaica in Antiquity (Oxford 1985: British Archaeological Reports, International Series 236).

R. J. A. Talbert (Ed.), Barrington Atlas of the Greek and Roman World (Princeton and Oxford 2000), especially map 38 (compiled by David Mattingly).

The Society for Libyan Studies has published or distributes numerous monographs on British research in Libya. These are generally listed in Libyan Studies and on the Society's website. The following are of particular relevance to Cyrenaica:

J. Reynolds (Ed.), Libyan Studies. Select papers of the late R. G. Goodchild (London 1976);

J. B. Ward-Perkins and R. G. Goodchild, Christian Monuments of Cyrenaica, edited by Joyce Reynolds (London 2003).

The wider background

P. MacKendrick, The North African Stones Speak (London 1980: Croom Helm);

B. Rogerson, A Traveller's History of North Africa (Moreton-in-Marsh 1998: Windrush Press)

J. Wright, A History of Libya (London 2010: Hurst & Co.);

P. Wright, Snakes, Sands and Silphium: Travels in Classical Libya (London 2011: Silphium Press);

J. Wright, Travellers in Turkish Libya, 1550–1911 (London 2011: Silphium Press).

INDEX

Where an entry is followed by more than one reference, that in **bold type** points to the principal description of the topic.

The index is intended additionally to serve as a concordance to place-names, where spellings in previous use are sufficiently different from those used here for the correspondence not to be obvious.

Index

Index

Index

Index

Key to monuments at Cyrene

1 Caravanserai
2 Caesareum and basilica
3 Street of Battos
4 East *propylaeum* of public zone
5 House of the Doric Peristyle
6 Theatre 3
7 Altar beneath Theatre 3
8 *Hestiatorion*?
9 Temple of the Dioscuri
10 Shrine of the Meander Mosaic
11 Temple of Cybele
12 Temple of Aphrodite
13 Stoa of Hermes and Herakles
14 Late defensive tower
15 Theatre 2
16 Twin temples
17 House of Jason Magnus
18 Hall of the Orthostats
19 Temple of Hermes
20 House of Hesychios
21 Temple of the Muses
22 Temple of Asklepios
23 Archeion
24 Prytaneion
25 Temple of Zeus (Agora)
26 Nomophylakeion
27 Hall of the Benches
28 Hellenistic peristyle house
29 West *propylaeum* of public zone
30 Temple of Apollo Archegetes
31 Assembly Building
32 Sanctuary of Demeter and Kore
33 West Stoa
34 Augusteum
35 North Stoa
36 Monument to the Gods
37 'House XI'
38 East Stoa
39 Tomb of Battos
40 Naval monument
41 Monumental Altars
42 House by the Propylaeum
43 Acropolis Gate
44 Sanctuary of Isis and Serapis
45 House of the Mosaic of Dionysos
46 House of Domina Spata
47 Temple A
48 Temple of Commodus
49 Temple of the Nymph Kurana
50 Public building
51 Temples F, I, G
52 Public building
53 Fountain
54 Central Church
55 Central Baths
56 House of the Semi-Circular Couch
57 Mid-Roman defences
58 Market Theatre (theatre 4)
59 Severan *Propylaeum*
60 Building with Windswept Capitals
61 Arch of Marcus Aurelius and Lucius Verus
62 North Gate
63 Pedestal and milestone
64 Greek *Propylaeum*
65 Temple of Aphrodite
66 Byzantine Baths
67 *Strategheion*
68 Roman *Propylaeum*
69 Doric Fountain
70 Temple of Athena
71 Temple of Hades
72 Shrine of Serapis
73 Shrine of the Dioscuri
74 Altar of Artemis
75 Baths of Trajan
76 Altar of Apollo
77 Temple of Apollo
78 Shrine and Exedra of the Palm of Leto
79 Temple of Artemis
80 Lesche
81 Temple of Hekate
82 Myrtle Bower
83 Unidentified temple
84 West Temple 2
85 West Temple 1
86 Doric Treasury/Temple of Zeus Ombrios
87 Wall of Nikodamos
88 Unidentified shrine
89 Greek Theatre
90 Temple (of the Petal Mosaic)
91 Roman house
92 'Grotto of the Priests'
93 Temple of Isis
94 Fountain of Philothales/Shrine of Apollo Kitharoidos
95 Temple of Apollo Nymphegetes
96 Exedra of Apollo Karneios
97 Temple of Jason Magnus
98 'Agora of the Gods'
99 Springs of Apollo and Kura
100 Fountain of Hermesandros
101 Bench of Elaiitas
102 Byzantine lime kilns
103 Aqua Augusta
104 Stepped portico
105 Baths of Paris
106 Temple of Zeus (NE Quarter)
107 East Temple and other buildings around the Sanctuary of Zeus
108 Hippodrome
109 Temple of Eluet Gassam
110 East Church
111 Qasr Shaghiyah
112 Funerary church
113 Demeter Sanctuary: *propylaeum*
114 Temple of Demeter
115 Theatre 5
116 Enclosed Sanctuary of Demeter and Kore
117 South temple precinct